• Al-Arish

AROUND CAIRO
See pp154–165

SINAI AND THE RED SEA COAST
See pp212–229

SINAI AND
THE RED SEA
COAST

• Sharm el-Sheikh

• Hurghada

_uxor

• Aswan

CAIRO AREA BY AREA

CENTRAL CAIRO
See pp68–85

ISLAMIC CAIRO
See pp86–111

RHODA ISLAND AND OLD CAIRO
See pp112–125

GIZA AND HELIOPOLIS
See pp126–139

0 kilometres   140

0 miles   75

EYEWITNESS TRAVEL GUIDES

EGYPT

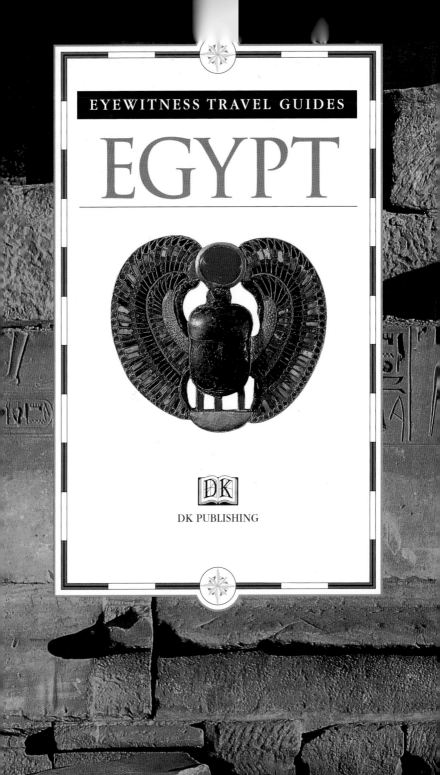

EYEWITNESS TRAVEL GUIDES

EGYPT

DK PUBLISHING

LONDON, NEW YORK,
MELBOURNE, MUNICH AND DELHI
www.dk.com

PROJECT ART EDITOR Jo Doran
PROJECT EDITORS Hugh Thompson, Claire Folkard
EDITORS Liz Atherton, Irene Lyford,
Ferdie McDonald, Marianne Petrou, Martin Redfern
DESIGNERS Emma Rose, Rebecca Milner, Ian Midson,
Sue Megginson, Anthony Limerick
PICTURE RESEARCHERS Monica Allende, Cynthia Frazer,
Katherine Mesquita
MAP CO-ORDINATORS David Pugh, Casper Morris
DTP DESIGNER Maite Lantaron

MAIN CONTRIBUTORS
Jane Dunford, Dr Joann Fletcher,
Andrew Humphreys, Kyle Pakka

MAPS
ERA-Maptec Ltd

PHOTOGRAPHERS
Max Alexander, Jon Spaull, Peter Wilson

ILLUSTRATORS
Gary Cross, Richard Draper, Claire Littlejohn,
Maltings Partnership, Chris Orr & Associates,
John Woodcock

Reproduced by Colourscan, Singapore
Printed and bound by South China Printing Co., Ltd, China

First American Edition, 2001

Reprinted with revisions 2002, 2003

04 05 10 9 8 7 6 5 4

Published in the United States by
DK Publishing, Inc., 375 Hudson Street,
New York, New York 10014

ISSN 1542-1554
ISBN 0-7894-9718-2

THROUGHOUT THIS BOOK, FLOORS ARE REFERRED TO IN ACCORDANCE WITH EUROPEAN
USAGE, I.E., THE "FIRST FLOOR" IS THE FLOOR ABOVE GROUND LEVEL

**The information in this
Eyewitness Travel Guide is checked regularly.**
Every effort has been made to ensure that this book is as up-to-date as
possible at the time of going to press. Some details, however, such as
telephone numbers, opening hours, prices, gallery hanging
arrangements and travel information are liable to change. The
publishers cannot accept responsibility for any consequences arising
from the use of this book, nor for any material on third party websites,
and cannot guarantee that any website address in this book will be a
suitable source of travel information. We value the views and
suggestions of our readers very highly. Please write to:
Publisher, DK Eyewitness Travel Guides, Dorling Kindersley,
80 Strand, London WC2R 0RL, Great Britain.

Fertile fields watered by the Nile at Luxor

CONTENTS

View from the Cairo Tower looking
at the Arab Television Building

◁ A local guide keeps out of the heat of the sun at Luxor Temple in the Nile Valley

Camel trekking in the desert

SURVIVAL GUIDE

CAIRO AREA BY AREA

Fruit stall at Dakhla Oasis showing
the wide variety of produce grown

Colossal foot at the Ramesseum

Ancient Egyptian frieze of lotus
blooms, symbolic of rebirth

EGYPT AREA BY AREA

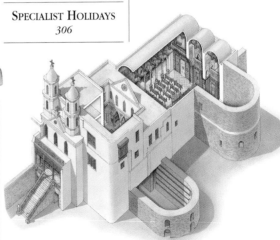

The Hanging Church in Coptic Cairo

How to Use this Guide

THIS GUIDE helps you to get the most from your visit to Egypt by providing detailed practical information and expert recommendations. *Introducing Egypt* maps the country and sets it in its historical and cultural context. The Cairo section and the five area chapters describe important sights using maps, photographs and illustrations. Features cover topics from food and wildlife to hieroglyphics and mythology. Restaurants and hotel recommendations can be found in *Travellers' Needs*, while the *Survival Guide* has tips on everything from making a telephone call to using local transportation, as well as information on money and other practical matters.

CAIRO AREA BY AREA

The city is divided into three areas, each with its own chapter. A fourth chapter covers the peripheral areas of Giza and Heliopolis. All sights are numbered and plotted on each chapter's area map. Information on each sight is easy to locate as the entries follow the numbering used on the map.

A locator map shows where you are in relation to other areas in the city centre.

All pages relating to Cairo have red thumb tabs.

Sights at a Glance lists the chapter's sights by category: Streets and Squares, Holy Places, Museums, Historic Buildings and Mosques.

1 Area Map
For easy reference, sights are numbered and located on a map. The central sights are also marked on the Street Finder *maps on pages 138–49.*

2 Street-by-Street Map
This gives a bird's-eye view of the key area in each chapter.

Stars indicate the sights that no visitor should miss.

Walking routes, in red, take in the area's most interesting streets.

3 Detailed information
City sights are described individually. Addresses and opening hours are given, as well as information on admission charges, guided tours, photography, wheelchair access and public transport.

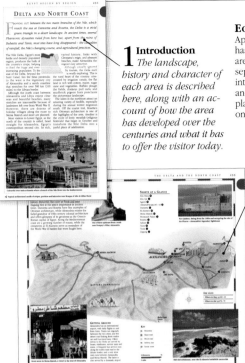

EGYPT AREA BY AREA

Apart from Cairo, the country has been divided into five areas, each of which has a separate chapter. The most interesting cities, towns, ancient and religious sites, and other places of interest are located on a *Pictorial Map*.

1 Introduction
The landscape, history and character of each area is described here, along with an account of how the area has developed over the centuries and what it has to offer the visitor today.

2 Pictorial Map
This shows the road network and gives an illustrated overview of each area. Interesting places to visit are numbered, and there are useful tips on getting to and around the region by car and public transport.

Each area of Egypt can be quickly identified by its colour-coded thumb tabs (*see inside front cover*).

3 Detailed information
All the important towns and other places to visit are described individually. They are listed in order and follow the numbering on the Pictorial Map. Within each town or city there is detailed information on important buildings and other sights.

For all major sights, a *Visitors' Checklist* provides the practical information you will need to plan your visit.

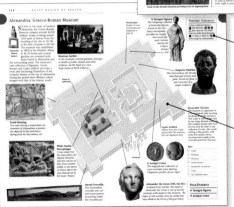

4 Egypt's Top Sights
These are given two or more pages. Historic buildings are reconstructed, or dissected to reveal their interiors. Other interesting sights are shown in bird's-eye view, with important features highlighted.

INTRODUCING EGYPT

Putting Egypt on the Map

Sitting on the northeast corner of Africa, with coastlines along the Mediterranean and Red seas, Egypt borders Libya to the west, Israel to the east and Sudan to the south. Over 90 per cent of the country is desert and most of the 68 million population live along the Nile Valley and in the Nile Delta, with a small percentage living in the oases that dot the barren interior.

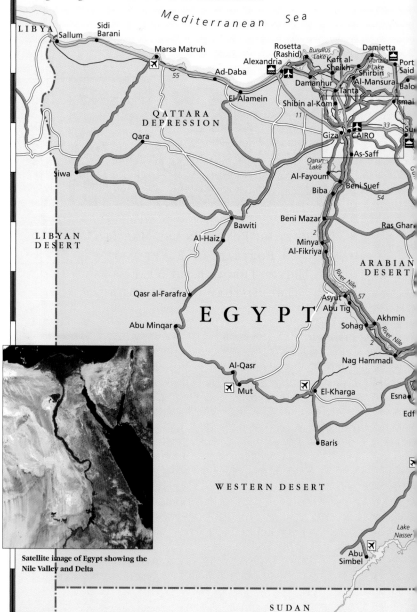

Mediterranean Sea

LIBYA
Sallum
Sidi Barani
Marsa Matruh
Ad-Daba
55
El-Alamein
QATTARA DEPRESSION
Qara
Siwa
LIBYAN DESERT
Bawiti
Al-Haiz
Qasr al-Farafra
Abu Minqar
Al-Qasr
Mut
Baris
WESTERN DESERT

Rosetta (Rashid)
Burullus Lake
Alexandria
Kafr al-Sheikh
Damanhur
Shibin al-Kom
Tanta
Giza
CAIRO
As-Saff
Qarun Lake
Al-Fayoum
Biba
Beni Suef
54
Beni Mazar
2
Minya
Al-Fikriya
Asyut
57
Abu Tig
Sohag
Akhmin
Nag Hammadi
El-Kharga
Esna
Edf
Baris

Damietta
Manzila Lake
Shirbin
Al-Mansura
Port Said
Balo
Ismai
Su
33
11

EGYPT

River Nile

ARABIAN DESERT
Ras Ghar

Lake Nasser
Abu Simbel

SUDAN

Satellite image of Egypt showing the Nile Valley and Delta

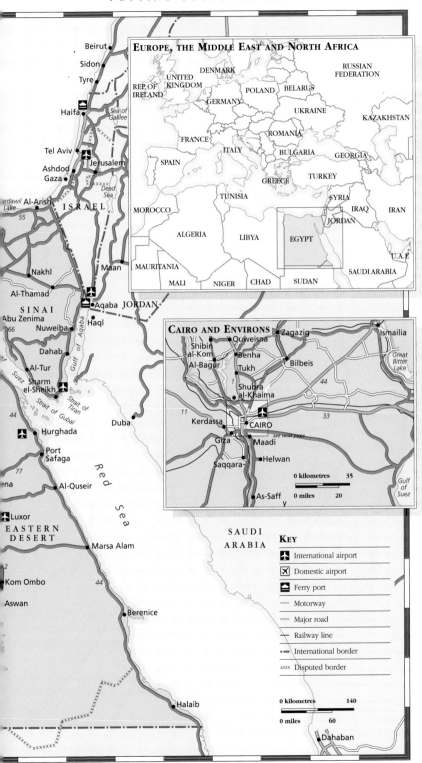

EUROPE, THE MIDDLE EAST AND NORTH AFRICA

Beirut
Sidon
Tyre
Haifa
Sea of Galilee
Tel Aviv
Ashdod
Jerusalem
Gaza
Dead Sea
ISRAEL
Al-Arish
ardawil Lake
55
Nakhl
Maan
Al-Thamad
SINAI
Abu Zenima
66
Nuweiba
Haql
Dahab
Al-Tur
Suez
Sharm el-Sheikh
44
Strait of Tiran
Strait of Gubal
Duba
Hurghada
Port Safaga
77
na
Al-Quseir
Red Sea
Luxor
EASTERN DESERT
Marsa Alam
2
Kom Ombo
44
Aswan
Berenice
Halaib

UNITED KINGDOM
REP OF IRELAND
DENMARK
POLAND
BELARUS
RUSSIAN FEDERATION
GERMANY
UKRAINE
KAZAKHSTAN
FRANCE
ITALY
ROMANIA
BULGARIA
GEORGIA
SPAIN
GREECE
TURKEY
TUNISIA
SYRIA
IRAQ
IRAN
JORDAN
MOROCCO
U.A.E
ALGERIA
LIBYA
EGYPT
SAUDI ARABIA
MAURITANIA
MALI
NIGER
CHAD
SUDAN

Aqaba JORDAN

CAIRO AND ENVIRONS
Quweisna
Zagazig
Ismailia
Shibin al-Kom
Benha
Al-Bagur
Great Bitter Lake
Tukh
Bilbeis
1
Shubra al-Khaima
44
Kerdassa
11
33
CAIRO
see next page
Giza
Maadi
Saqqara
Helwan
0 kilometres 35
As-Saff
0 miles 20
y
Gulf of Suez

SAUDI ARABIA

KEY
✈ International airport
✕ Domestic airport
⛴ Ferry port
Motorway
Major road
Railway line
International border
xxxx Disputed border

0 kilometres 140
0 miles 60

Dahaban

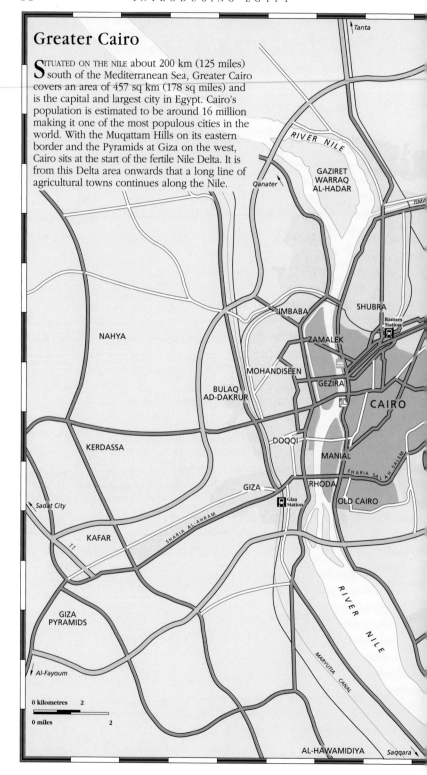

Greater Cairo

Situated on the Nile about 200 km (125 miles) south of the Mediterranean Sea, Greater Cairo covers an area of 457 sq km (178 sq miles) and is the capital and largest city in Egypt. Cairo's population is estimated to be around 16 million making it one of the most populous cities in the world. With the Muqattam Hills on its eastern border and the Pyramids at Giza on the west, Cairo sits at the start of the fertile Nile Delta. It is from this Delta area onwards that a long line of agricultural towns continues along the Nile.

Tanta

RIVER NILE

GAZIRET
WARRAQ
AL-HADAR

Qanater

ISMA

IMBABA

SHUBRA

Ramses
Station

ZAMALEK

NAHYA

MOHANDISEEN

GEZIRA

BULAQ
AD-DAKRUR

CAIRO

DOQQI

KERDASSA

MANIAL

SHARIA SALAH SALEM

GIZA

RHODA

Giza
Station

OLD CAIRO

Sadat City

KAFAR

SHARIA AL-AHRAM

11

RIVER NILE

GIZA
PYRAMIDS

Al-Fayoum

MARYUTIA CANAL

0 kilometres   2

0 miles   2

AL-HAWAMIDIYA   Saqqara

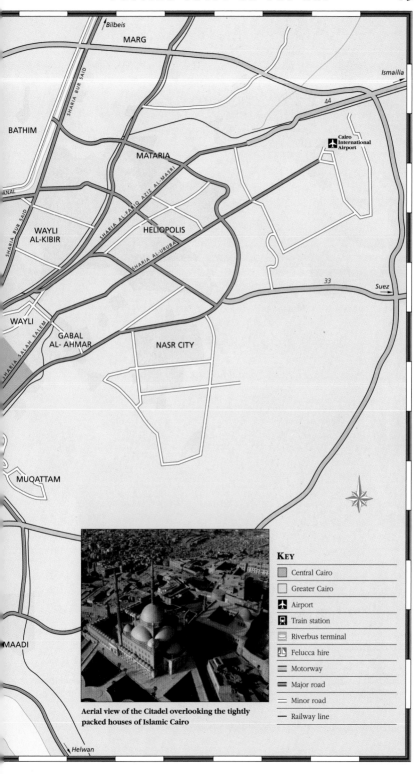

Bilbeis

MARG

Ismailia

44

**Cairo
International
Airport**

BATHIM

MATARIA

SHARIA BUR SAID

CANAL

SHARIA BUR SAID

WAYLI
AL-KIBIR

HELIOPOLIS

SHARIA AL-FARIQ AZIZ AL-MASRI

SHARIA AL-URUBA

33

Suez

WAYLI

GABAL
AL-AHMAR

NASR CITY

SHARIA SALAH SALEM

MUQATTAM

MAADI

**Aerial view of the Citadel overlooking the tightly
packed houses of Islamic Cairo**

KEY

Central Cairo

Greater Cairo

Airport

Train station

Riverbus terminal

Felucca hire

Motorway

Major road

Minor road

Railway line

Helwan

A PORTRAIT OF EGYPT

*S*ETTLING ALONG THE FERTILE BANKS OF THE NILE, *the ancient Egyptians established a magnificent and enduring civilization whose achievements have captured the imagination of the world ever since. Although looking to the future, modern Egypt cannot ignore its glorious past, but the resulting contrasts make it a uniquely fascinating place to visit.*

The world's fascination with this country centres on the civilization of ancient Egypt that flourished from around 3000 BC to 30 BC, ruled by approximately 30 dynasties. The river Nile was the powerful force that enabled the ancient Egyptian kingdom to develop. The river's annual cycle of inundation watered the land and replenished the fertile topsoil. This resulted in an agricultural abundance that allowed them to concentrate on developing the knowledge and culture that formed their unique and sophisticated civilization. Over the succeeding millennia, waves of foreign conquerors passed through the country – Persians, Greeks, Romans, crusaders, Arabs and Turks – leaving traces behind in their descendants. Today most Egyptians are classified as being of Eastern Hamitic descent. The once nomadic Bedouin and Berber tribes of the desert are of Arab descent and the third major racial grouping (less than 200,000) is the Nubian community in the south.

Pectoral of Tutankhamun (1336–1327 BC)

DAILY LIFE

Even today, the river Nile remains the lifeblood of Egypt, with around 96 per cent of the population forced by the harsh environment to live in the Nile Delta or Nile Valley.

The fertile Nile Delta, one of the most intensely cultivated areas of the world

◁ **Traders negotiating at one of Egypt's lively and fascinating camel markets**

Solitary felucca sailing serenely down the tranquil waters of the Nile

The ancient cycle of flooding ended with the completion of the High Dam at Aswan in 1971, forcing the Egyptian *fellaheen* (farmers) to resort to artificial fertilizers. However, it is easy to imagine that life today along the river's edge remains just as it has for thousands of years.

The typical Egyptian rural settlement is a village of between 500 and 10,000 people set amid intensely cultivated fields. Houses are often no more than one or two storeys high and each village also has a mosque or church, and perhaps a colourful pigeoncote, a few shops and an official government building. Most of the inhabitants of

Men chatting in a Cairo coffee house, a popular male Egyptian pastime

smaller villages work in agriculture and the landscape is usually dotted with farmers, wearing the traditional *galabiyya* (long smock), working the green fields or tending their precious animals – buffalo, sheep and goats.

The urban population has been expanding rapidly since the 1980s. Increasing pressure on agricultural land and the growth of city-based service industries have led to large numbers of Egyptians moving from the country to urban areas. The buildings in towns and cities are predominantly two-storey houses or higher apartment blocks with flat roofs and balconies, often built close together. The high population density in cities also leads to problems of traffic congestion. Nowhere is this more evident than in Cairo, where there is a constant cacophony of car engines and horns.

Throughout Egypt the family has remained the most significant unit of a patriarchal society. Traditionally, an individual's social identity was closely linked to his or her status in the network of relations. Today families are far more likely to disperse and the ideal of an extended family that lives together is less frequent. However, strong ties with in-laws, grandparents, nieces and nephews and the rest of the family still create a strong social fabric that binds the whole community together.

RELIGION AND CULTURE

Underpinning all levels of Egyptian society is a powerful religious faith. Islam is constitutionally established as the official religion and around 90 per cent of the population are Sunni Muslim *(see p91)*, the rest being Christian, mainly of the Coptic church *(see p122)*. However, say to an Egyptian of either faith "I'll see you tomorrow" and the answer will be the same – "Inshallah", which means "if God is willing". For the casual tourist, the many casinos, bars, nightclubs and beach resorts can disguise the fact that Egyptians uphold a fairly conservative mix of traditional and religious values, particularly outside the main cities. Gambling or drinking alcohol in public is frowned upon and Egyptian men rarely wear shorts, except maybe at the beach.

Women, too, are almost always well-covered. In the 1970s, as women gained greater independence and access to education, they swelled the

The *begab* or headscarf, increasingly worn by Egyptian women

numbers of the non-agricultural workforce and many Muslim women chose to discard their *begab* (headscarf). With the wide appeal of Islamist conservatives in the 1990s, women started dressing more modestly and, even in Cairo, increasing numbers are once again covering their heads and wearing loose-fitting clothes. However, the numbers of women in employment have remained at a high level.

Egyptians, governed by outsiders for thousands of years, have only been truly independent since 1952 when Gamal Abdel Nasser removed the last foreign royal and forged a truly Egyptian identity for his people. Despite a climate of political turmoil, this period of Egypt's history was a time of cultural vitality, when Umm Kolthum, the diva of the Arab world, gave concerts for the masses and Naguib

Umm Kolthum, "Mother of Egypt"

Modern Cairo with the Pyramids of Giza just visible through the evening haze

Negotiating the streets around Midan Ataba in Cairo on a daily bread round

Egypt's cinema had its heyday in the 1940s and 50s when its studios made films for the whole Arab world. Apart from a few independent films which gain a wider exposure during international film festivals, little of merit emerges these days.

POLITICS AND ECONOMICS

Nasser, President of Egypt 1956–70

After the abolition of the monarchy in 1952, Nasser went on to dissolve all political parties and introduce a new constitution in 1956, declaring the Republic of Egypt. Led by Nasser, the National Union, later the Arab Socialist Union (ASU), became the sole party. In 1971 a new constitution declared Egypt to be "a democratic, socialist state". But it was not until 1977 that the formation of other political parties was allowed. Three years later the ASU was abolished. The current ruling party, the National Democratic Party (NDP) led by Hosni Mubarak, is a direct descendant of Nasser's ASU. Egypt's

Mahfouz penned his most famous novels. Awarded a Nobel Prize in 1988, Mahfouz single-handedly rejuvenated the Egyptian literary scene. However, few other Egyptian writers have managed to emulate his success. Today, as a result of Egypt's population boom and greater exposure to western music, there is a ready market for home-grown modern pop music. Nevertheless Umm Kolthum's soulful music is as all-pervasive as ever, constantly played in shops and taxis throughout Egypt.

Highrise blocks of modern Cairo overlooking the Nile

"dominant party system" allows a large ruling party to straddle the centre of the ideological spectrum, surrounded by small pressure parties. This has limited the possibility for radical reform, but allowed the government to proceed in a slow and cautious manner.

Over the past ten years, the national debt has been reduced, but it is still twice the size of the national budget.

Ancient tombs lying in the path of a motorway

Agriculture is the most important industry. Employing a large amount of the workforce, it feeds much of the country and provides valuable exports, especially the cotton crop. The High Dam project increased arable land by hundreds of thousands of acres and provided a much needed boost to the power supply. However, in the same period, just as much land was swallowed up by industrial and urban development, constantly building over Egypt's celebrated past. Although slowing down, population growth undermines all efforts to foster the economy. Other important sources of income are oil, gas, mining, and of course, the tourist industry. The brutal murder of 58 tourists in 1997 *(see p172)* rocked the country, causing the number of visitors to plummet. While the tourist figures are only now getting back to their former levels, the government is fully aware of the instability and problems that would be caused by further unrest.

A visitor at a Red Sea resort, enjoying Egypt's beautiful beaches and all-year round sun

EGYPT TODAY

Given the importance of tradition and religion to Egyptian daily life, it is perhaps surprising that Western technology and lifestyles have steadily gained influence over the past decade. International fast-food franchises are now found all over the country. However, the "benefits" of this most recent cultural invasion are available only to the select few, due to the seemingly unbridgeable gap between the rich and poor. To make matters worse, television programmes and films from the West have had a huge impact on Egyptian perceptions, raising expectations and creating resentment among the less well-off. This situation is not always helped by the sight of tourists enjoying luxuries beyond the reach of many Egyptians. Even so, the fascinating mix of ancient monuments, modern culture and the natural hospitality of its people ensure that Egypt's popularity continues to grow.

Discovering Ancient Egypt

Greek historian Herodotus

T HE MAGNIFICENCE and longevity of the ancient Egyptian civilization has always held a timeless fascination. As early as 1400 BC, King Tuthmosis IV undertook excavations at Giza, and the Greek historian Herodotus left a detailed account of his tour of Egypt in 450 BC. However, modern Egyptology really started with the study of the country commissioned in 1798 by Napoleon. Since then the subject has developed rapidly. In the last 20 years, computers and electron microscopes have begun to replace the pickaxe and shovel.

Napoleon's scholars amassed the material for the authoritative work Description de l'Egypte *during the French occupation (1798–1802).*

Jean-François Champollion (1790–1832), was a French linguist whose brilliant work in deciphering the hieroglyphic script was the single most important event in the development of Egyptology.

Hieroglyphs were used as early as 3200 BC and are the oldest known writing system. Used primarily in religious contexts, their last datable use was in AD 394 at the Temple of Philae when the script numbered over 6,000 characters.

HOWARD CARTER (1873–1939)

Carter trained as an artist and joined the Archaeological Survey of Egypt in 1891. In 1922, he achieved fame when he found King Tutankhamun's tomb, virtually untouched, in the Valley of the Kings.

The treasures Carter found on opening the tomb were abundant. Most items are on display in the Egyptian Museum (see pp74–7).

Howard Carter had to carefully remove many layers of solidified perfumes and resins covering Tutankhamun's innermost coffin. The body was protected by several layers of coffins, the last one of solid gold.

RELOCATION OF ANCIENT TEMPLES

The construction of the Aswan High Dam and Lake Nasser (1960–71) threatened many temples and rock tombs along the Nile with total submersion. Concern over the loss of such archaeological treasures led UNESCO to promote an international relief campaign. Three stages of operations were necessary: a survey of the area, the excavation of sites, and the final movement of as many endangered monuments as was possible. Twenty monuments from Egyptian Nubia and four from the Sudan were carefully dismantled, then reassembled at safe distances from their original sites. The two largest operations involved the Great Temple at Abu Simbel *(see pp210–11)* and the temple complex at Philae *(see p208)*.

Trajan's Kiosk (also known as the Pharaoh's Bedstead) before relocation at Philae

UNDERWATER DISCOVERIES

In 1996, a team led by the French marine archaeologist, Franck Goddio, began to explore the submerged Royal City of Alexandria, where Egypt's last pharaoh, Cleopatra, held court. The finds so far include statues, sphinxes and ceramics.

Tutankhamun's death mask, shown here at the British Museum with Queen Elizabeth II in 1972, was the top exhibit in a display of Carter's finds that toured the major museums of the world rekindling interest in Egypt's rich history.

ARCHAEOLOGY AND TECHNOLOGY

Egyptology is a relatively young science, but huge advances have been made since Champollion's work opened the door on ancient Egyptian history. Today, Egyptologists are greatly assisted by new technologies, both in the laboratory and in the field – and even under water.

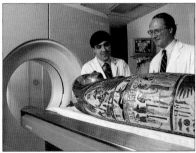

Restoration and preservation work on ancient artifacts involves skilled and painstaking processes, which have to be conducted in a strictly controlled environment.

Modern technologies, such as CAT scanning, radio-carbon dating, DNA and trace element analysis, endoscopy and electron microscopy have all contributed to more accurate dating and a deeper understanding of archaeological finds.

Hieroglyphics

DATING FROM AROUND 3200 BC, ancient Egyptian hieroglyphics are the world's oldest known writing system. The word "hieroglyph" means "sacred carved letter" and refers to the beautiful pictorial script used by ancient Egyptians to express their religious beliefs and engraved onto nearly every available surface of their monuments. Although pictorial, hieroglyphs convey extremely complex semantic information; they could be read from left to right, right to left or top to bottom. However, when writing on papyrus, the hieroglyphic system was too slow and impractical for everyday use and over the centuries more easily written scripts were developed with the last datable hieroglyphic inscription being at Hadrian's Gate at Philae in AD 394.

Hieroglyph for motion or "to go"

Thoth, the ibis-headed god of wisdom and patron deity of scribes, is here portrayed holding his sceptre of power or was.

Egyptian scribes, in a virtually illiterate population, were part of society's elite. It took many years to learn the art of hieroglyphics but the rewards could be high – King Horemheb started off his career as a scribe.

THE ROSETTA STONE – CRACKING THE CODE

Until 1822, the ability to read hieroglyphic inscriptions had been lost. It was a black granite stele, discovered in 1799 in Rosetta by Napoleon's army, that held the key. It contained a text in three scripts: hieroglyphic, demotic and Greek. The two main contestants in the race to decipher the symbols were Thomas Young, a British physician and Jean-François Champollion, a gifted French linguist. By 1819, Young was ahead of the Frenchman, translating the demotic text as well as identifying the cartouches of Ptolemy and Cleopatra. However, Champollion was also able to decipher these names and others, compiling an extensive list of symbols. Using this list, he realised that there were separate types of hieroglyphs with different functions and therefore discovered the basis of the writing system used in hieroglyphic texts.

The Rosetta Stone, inscribed by the priests of Ptolemy V (196 BC)

Ptolemaic scribes raised the number of hieroglyphic symbols from 700 to 6000, in an attempt to keep their knowledge exclusive.

THE IMPORTANCE OF NAMES

Ancient Egyptians believed that names were as vital to one's existence as the soul. Names held great power and speaking the name of the dead could bring them to life. Therefore, funerary texts often included spells to cause the name of the deceased to be remembered in the afterlife and so ensure eternal life.

The oval cartouche forms a protective wall or enclosure.

Hieroglyphs give the name, "Ramses, beloved of Amun".

Egyptian kings protected their names within cartouches and increased their chances of eternal life by the sheer number of epithets they possessed.

This detail of the King List found at Abydos gives some of Ramses II's names, including "the king of Upper and Lower Egypt, Usermaatre Setepenre, son of Ra, and Ramses, beloved of Amun".

HIEROGLYPHIC TEXT

Hieroglyphs were a decorative art and ritual pictures, combined with texts, played a vital part in religious ceremonies. Funerary texts were designed to protect the dead and help guide their passage to the underworld. This detail from the funeral texts of the scribe Nebked (c.1400 BC), shows the deceased (his writing kit tucked into his belt) worshipping the god Osiris with his wife and mother.

Hieratic script was a faster way of writing. Dating from c.2600 BC, it was used for everyday communications until c.600 BC when it was superseded by the even faster demotic or "popular" script.

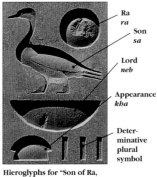

TRANSLATING HIEROGLYPHS

Put simply, there are three main types of hieroglyphs. "Phonograms" convey the sounds of the syllables, for example the ancient Egyptian for "son" was spoken *sa* and this is denoted by the duck. "Ideograms" portray the actual object or action, such as a sun on the horizon to indicate "appearance". The final type is "determinatives" which indicate, confirm or modify the meaning of the word to which they are attached, for example, three bars denote a plural. To further complicate matters, many symbols can be either ideograms, phonograms or determinatives. The basket symbol, *neb*, can be a phonogram for "Lord" or simply represent a "basket". Symbols of humans and animals always face the start of the text, indicating the direction the text runs.

Ra
ra

Son
sa

Lord
neb

Appearance
kha

Determinative plural symbol

Hieroglyphs for "Son of Ra, Lord of Appearances"

Temples and Religious Life

F OR THE ANCIENT EGYPTIANS, the universe was composed of dualities – fertile and barren, life and death, order and chaos – held in a state of equilibrium by the goddess Maat. To maintain this balance, they built enormous temples dedicated to the gods. At the centre of every settlement and devoted to a particular god or set of gods, the "cult" temple served as a storehouse of divine power, maintained by the priesthood for the benefit of all. The temple was also an economic and political centre employing large numbers of the local community and serving as a town hall, medical centre and college.

Statue of a priest praying

***Goddess Maat**, the personification of cosmic order and harmony, set the rules by which all kings must govern. Her power regulated the stars, the seasons and humans' relationship with the gods.*

Funerary priest in a leopard skin, performing sacred rituals

A DAY IN THE LIFE OF A TEMPLE PRIEST

Egyptian priests were literally "servants of the god or goddess", responsible for performing the daily rituals that regulated the workings of the universe. The king, although the intermediary between the mortal and the divine, delegated his duties to the high priest of the temple. This priest was then responsible for the most important of the temple rituals – the honouring of the god within its shrine. Twice daily the "cult" statue was bathed and clothed before receiving offerings of food and drink. Incense was burnt and holy water from the sacred lake scattered to show the purity of the offerings. After the essence of the food had been consumed by the gods, the priests were able to eat the actual offerings.

CULT TEMPLE RECONSTRUCTION
As well as housing the deity, the temple complex symbolized the universe. Its architecture represented the fundamental elements of water, sunlight, stars, forests and, inside the depths of the temple, darkness.

Covered colonnade

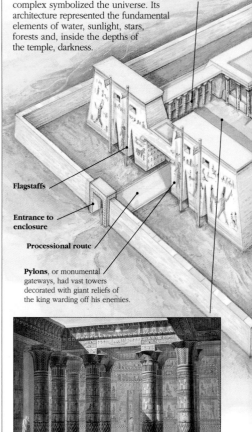

Flagstaffs

Entrance to enclosure

Processional route

Pylons, or monumental gateways, had vast towers decorated with giant reliefs of the king warding off his enemies.

***The central court**, as depicted in this 19th-century reconstruction of the court at Philae (see p208), was a colonnaded courtyard brightly decorated with reliefs showing the king making offerings to the temple's deities.*

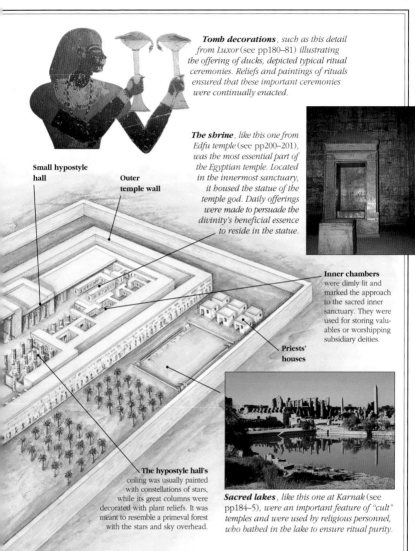

Tomb decorations, *such as this detail from Luxor* (see pp180–81) *illustrating the offering of ducks, depicted typical ritual ceremonies. Reliefs and paintings of rituals ensured that these important ceremonies were continually enacted.*

The shrine, *like this one from Edfu temple* (see pp200–201), *was the most essential part of the Egyptian temple. Located in the innermost sanctuary, it housed the statue of the temple god. Daily offerings were made to persuade the divinity's beneficial essence to reside in the statue.*

Small hypostyle hall

Outer temple wall

Inner chambers were dimly lit and marked the approach to the sacred inner sanctuary. They were used for storing valuables or worshipping subsidiary deities.

Priests' houses

The hypostyle hall's ceiling was usually painted with constellations of stars, while its great columns were decorated with plant reliefs. It was meant to resemble a primeval forest with the stars and sky overhead.

Sacred lakes, *like this one at Karnak* (see pp184–5), *were an important feature of "cult" temples and were used by religious personnel, who bathed in the lake to ensure ritual purity.*

MORTUARY TEMPLES

In addition to the local "cult" temples, each king built a mortuary temple to serve as a place where, following his death, offerings could be made for his soul. The temples were originally attached to the royal tombs of the Old and Middle Kingdoms but by around 1500 BC they had developed into vast, elaborate complexes built at separate locations to the tombs which were now hidden away in secluded desert valleys. The great temples on the West Bank at Luxor *(see pp180–81)* are fine examples of New Kingdom mortuary temples. The magnificent Temple of Queen Hatshepsut *(see pp192–3)* at Deir al-Bahri has one of the most original mortuary temple designs.

The Ramesseum in Thebes *(see pp196–7),* **the mortuary temple of Ramses II**

Mythology

ANCIENT EGYPTIAN RELIGION was a highly complex belief system involving a great number of deities originally based on aspects of the natural world. As these evolved into more cohesive "personalities", each locality developed myths relating to their own particular deities. These myths were many and varied, with even the story of creation having at least three different versions, based on the belief that life first emerged from the waters of chaos as a mound of earth. A number of places claimed to be the original site of this primeval mound and that the first life was created by the gods associated with that particular place, be they the 9 gods of Heliopolis, the 8 gods of Hermopolis or the one god of Memphis.

Household god Bes

Amun, whose name means "the hidden one", became a national deity when Thebes ruled Egypt, in an attempt to unify the country.

CREATION MYTH

This detail from a popular creation myth shows the Egyptian gods in relation to the world. In the beginning there was nothing but the sea of chaos, Nun. Then Atum thought himself into being, sneezing to create Shu and then Tefnut. He caused the seas to recede and called forth all the plants and animals. Shu and Tefnut gave birth to two children: Geb, the earth, and Nut, the sky, who in turn gave birth to the stars.

Nephthys pours the waters of fruitfulness over the earth, where men hoe the land.

Nut, mother of all, swallows the sun each night, giving birth to it again in the morning.

Geb, god of the earth; his bent leg represents the mountains.

OSIRIS, ISIS AND HORUS

One of the most universal Egyptian myths is that of Osiris and Isis. The story has it that Osiris was a king who taught the Egyptians how to live, worship and grow corn. He was murdered by his jealous brother Seth, who cut up the body, scattering it over Egypt. Osiris's beloved wife Isis and her sister Nephthys collected up all the pieces and, with the help of the gods Anubis and Thoth, they put him back together as the first mummy. Isis used her magic to revive him and at the same time conceived a son, Horus, who would avenge his father. Osiris, brought back to life, went down to the underworld to be the lord and judge of the dead.

Statuette of Osiris *(centre)* with his son Horus and loyal wife Isis

Osiris in a typical pose

THE SUN

Fundamental to the Egyptians, the sun was regarded as the source of all life, conquering the forces of darkness each night before emerging victorious at dawn to repeat the eternal cycle. Worshipped under a variety of names and guises, the sun was most often represented by the falcon-headed god Ra, as well as Atum, Khepri, Harakhty and the Aten sun-disk. The sun god's representative on earth, the king was hailed as the "Son of Ra". When Amun was elevated to supreme deity, for political reasons, his status was validated by linking him with Ra's supremacy to create Amun-Ra, the "King of the Gods".

Khepri was represented as a dung beetle or scarab. Identified with the sun god Ra, he was said to roll the sun across the sky like a ball of dung.

Ra-Harakhty was the combination of two gods: the sky god Horus, whose right eye was the sun and left eye the moon, and the all-powerful sun god Ra.

Ra, creator of the universe, wears the sun on his brow.

Maat keeps the world in balance.

Shu, jealous of Geb and Nut, stands keeping them apart.

MAJOR GODS

- **Amun**: powerful local Theban deity.
- **Anubis**: jackal-headed god of embalmers.
- **Atum**: creator aspect of the sun god.
- **Bes**: household god of women in childbirth.
- **Geb**: god of the earth.
- **Hathor**: goddess of love, pleasure and beauty.
- **Horus**: falcon-headed god closely identified with each pharaoh.
- **Isis**: goddess of magic.
- **Khepri**: a sun god as a scarab beetle.
- **Maat**: goddess of truth and universal balance.
- **Nekhbet**: vulture goddess of Upper Egypt.
- **Nephthys**: with Isis, protector of the dead.
- **Nut**: goddess of the sky.
- **Osiris**: god of the underworld.
- **Ptah**: creator god and patron of craftsmen.
- **Ra**: pre-eminent form of the sun god.
- **Sekhmet**: lioness goddess of destruction.
- **Seth**: god of chaos.
- **Shu**: god of the air.
- **Tefnut**: goddess of moisture.
- **Thoth**: the ibis-headed god of wisdom.
- **Wadjet**: cobra goddess of Lower Egypt.

Tomb painting showing the worship of the Benu bird

THE BENU BIRD

The Benu bird flew across the waters of Nun at the dawn of creation and saw land first break the water's surface. The Benu bird was identified with the sun and the primeval mound was symbolized by the Benben stone at Heliopolis, thought to be where the sun's first rays touched land. It was the prototype for obelisks whose tips were gold plated – to catch the first rays of the sun.

Obelisk, symbol of first land

Burial Traditions

Wedjat "eye of Horus" amulet

T HE ANCIENT EGYPTIANS believed in an eternal afterlife and they developed a complex funerary cult aimed at maintaining their life after death. This involved preserving the body of the dead person through a process of mummification so that their soul would live on in their embalmed corpse. The deceased were then supplied with everything they might need in the afterlife before being launched into eternity via a set of elaborate funeral rituals.

Anubis, the jackal-headed god of embalming, is shown putting the finishing touches to a mummy in this 19th-Dynasty tomb relief.

MUMMIFICATION TECHNIQUES

The earliest mummies from prehistoric times were probably accidental. True mummification began in the Fourth Dynasty with the development of artificial embalming techniques. Special priests first removed the internal organs of the deceased, leaving only the heart, to be weighed in the afterlife. Then the corpse was dried out with natron and finally wrapped in linen.

Natural mummification occurred when dead bodies were placed in simple sand graves. The sand absorbed the body's moisture, drying out the corpse and preserving soft tissue.

Canopic jars stored the embalmed internal organs of the deceased. The intestines, stomach, liver and lungs had separate jars, which were buried alongside the coffin in the tomb.

Natron, a naturally occurring mixture of sodium salts, was packed in and around the body to dry it out artificially. This took 40 days.

Ramses III, one of the best preserved of the royal mummies, was discovered in 1881 at Deir al-Bahri. The mummy is now on display in the Egyptian Museum (see pp74–7).

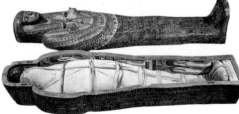

The mummified body was stuffed with linen and sawdust before being wrapped in tight linen bandages. Finally the wrapped mummy was placed in its painted wooden coffin.

ANIMAL MUMMIES

The ancient Egyptians believed that all living things contained the divine essence and were, therefore, worthy of respect. In sharing the attributes of the gods they symbolized, animals were venerated as the gods' representatives on earth and mummified after their death. By the Late Period (664–332 BC), animals of all kinds were being mummified and buried in catacombs, from literally millions of ibises and cats to bulls and lions, shrews, snakes and crocodiles.

Ibis mummy

Cat mummy

MUMMY MASKS

A mask was fitted over the head of the mummy to help the dead person's spirit to recognize its body. From the glittering gold masks of pharaohs such as Tutankhamun to the more common painted masks made of *cartonnage* (a sort of papier-mâché), mummy masks were idealized portraits of the deceased.

A mummy mask showed the face framed by a stylized wig and wide collar.

Roman portrait masks, painted on flat wooden panels, were laid over the face of the mummy. The portraits were often painted during the lifetime of the deceased and were more realistic than earlier masks (see p165).

ACCESSORIES

In addition to significant worldly possessions, the mummy was usually buried with funerary items, including amulets, a set of shabti figures, and a model boat to transport the mummy to Abydos.

Amulets *were worn by Egyptians in life and in death to protect the body from evil and to bring good luck.*

Shabti figures *were models of workers placed in the tomb to carry out manual work on behalf of the deceased in the afterlife.*

A model funerary boat *symbolized the mummy's journey to Abydos, home of Osiris, god of the dead (see p26).*

FUNERARY RITES AND CEREMONIES

At the funeral, relatives left offerings of food and priests performed special funerary rites. These ceremonies and rituals were meant to protect the deceased, ensure a successful journey into the afterlife and sustain them on their way. As further protection, ritual images and texts were placed with the body or used to decorate the tomb.

The Book of the Dead *was a guide through the underworld. The deceased is portrayed here crossing the Lake of Offerings with his gifts.*

The Opening of the Mouth *ritual was performed to the body prior to burial in the belief that this would reactivate the senses, so the deceased would function in the afterlife.*

The Weighing of the Heart *was the final stage in the journey to the afterlife. A jury of gods presided over the ceremony to decide whether the deceased deserved eternal life. The jackal god Anubis weighed the heart against the feather of truth. If the heart was too heavy, it was given to the monster Ammut, who devoured it; only if it balances will the dead live forever.*

Daily Life in Ancient Egypt

Tomb model of man ploughing with oxen

IN THE HIERARCHICAL SOCIETY of ancient Egypt, the importance of the family was fundamental. Early marriages were encouraged, with the hope of producing children to continue the family line and, importantly, to organize a proper burial. Marriage seems to have required no religious or civil ceremony, but simply involved one partner moving into the home of the other. Youngsters enjoyed a brief period of childhood before taking on adult responsibilities. Education was mainly vocational, with boys often being apprenticed to their fathers.

This family group comprises husband and wife (centre), their son (right) and older male (left).

EGYPTIAN HOUSING

Egyptian houses were built of sun-baked mudbricks and so have not survived well. From the evidence that has been preserved it seems that houses were typically square with a central living room, bedrooms and storerooms and sometimes stairs leading to the roof or to an upper floor. Some even had primitive bathroom suites.

Egyptian houses had basic air-conditioning, provided by small windows and roof vents as shown in this painting from the tomb of 18th-Dynasty scribe Nakht.

The roof vent is designed to catch the cool north breezes.

Soul houses, such as this terracotta example, were included in tombs to house the soul of the deceased. The models demonstrate many features of ancient Egyptian housing and even mirror houses in rural Egypt today.

Small, high windows let in light and breezes, but not the sun.

Cooking would take place outside or in outbuildings.

More complex housing, such as this model townhouse, reflected the higher status of the owner.

WORKERS' VILLAGE AT DEIR AL-MEDINA

In a secluded valley on the west bank of the Nile opposite Luxor are the excavated foundations of a village that was inhabited by the craftsmen and labourers who constructed the tombs in the Valley of the Kings. In this early example of urban planning, the houses, arranged in rows, all opened off one central street and were enclosed within an outer wall. A typical house in Deir al-Medina had between 4 and 6 rooms plus a cellar or two for storage. Around the village are the chapels and tombs of the government-employed workers.

The village at Deir al-Medina, founded in the 16th century BC for those working in the Valley of the Kings

Women often worked and looked after the children. In this 26th-Dynasty tomb relief, a mother with her child sorts fruit in an orchard.

WOMEN IN SOCIETY

Although their status generally derived from that of their fathers or husbands, women in ancient Egypt enjoyed a relatively high profile. Equal to men before the law, they could own or rent property, engage in business, receive an equal share of inheritances and, in some cases, even rule as pharaoh. Divorce and remarriage were available to them, and if a man divorced his wife, she was entitled to maintenance. Women were expected to manage the household and family, and the poorer ones had to work alongside the men too.

Two women are depicted in this 30th-Dynasty relief using a tourniquet press to extract the essential oils of lilies for perfume.

Three noble-women are seen in this 18th-Dynasty detail, sharing their pleasure in the perfume of lotus blossoms and mandrake fruit.

WORKING LIFE IN ANCIENT EGYPT

Most of the farmland was owned by the king, the temples and rich individuals. This was farmed by the bulk of the population, who worked either directly for the owner or as a tenant farmer paying large amounts of rent and tax. Slightly better off were the skilled craftsmen, many of whom worked for the pharaoh, the temples or rich nobles. Their crafts included carpentry, jewellery and stone-working. Near the top of the hierarchy was an elite of professionals who ran the country – the scribes *(see p22)*, the priests *(see p24)* and top-ranking officials.

Nile-style farming is depicted in this painting from the 19th-Dynasty tomb of Sennedjem and Iyneferti. Although portraying the idealized afterlife, it shows the methods used to reap grain, plough and harvest flax.

The Nile may have provided fish and fertile soil, but it had its share of risks as well as its rewards. As depicted in this Old Kingdom tomb relief scene, herdsmen had to be mindful of the danger posed to livestock from crocodiles.

Dairy produce, as depicted in this tomb relief, played an important part in the diet. Other livestock reared by ancient Egyptian farmers included sheep, goats and even pigs.

Skilled craftsmen were usually employed in large workshops or in special communities such as Deir al-Medina.

Peasant farmers also supplied most of the labour for large building projects. This was a requirement for everybody except officials. In this tomb painting a team of unskilled workers are making mudbricks.

Islamic Egypt

Islam was founded by Mohammed, a merchant who was born in around AD 570 in Mecca. At the age of 40 he began to receive revelations of the word of Allah (God) and these were transcribed as the Quran. Mohammed's preachings were not well received in Mecca and, in AD 622, he and his followers fled to Medina. This flight *(hejira)* constitutes year zero in the Islamic calendar. Before he died in AD 632, Mohammed returned to conquer Mecca. The armies of Islam swept through the Byzantine provinces of the eastern Mediterranean, arriving in Egypt in AD 640.

The crescent moon, a familiar symbol of Islam, has resonances with the lunar calendar, which orders Muslim religious life.

The Quran, the holy book of Islam, is regarded as the direct word of Allah. Muslims believe that it can only be understood if read in Arabic. It is divided into 114 chapters, or suras, which cover many topics, including matters relating to the family, marriage, and legal and ethical concerns.

This house is decorated with pilgrimage scenes, which include a depiction of the great mosque in Mecca. The picture indicates that the house-owner has made the pilgrimage to Mecca.

Muslims praying outside the Mosque of Sayyidna al-Hussein

THE FIVE PILLARS OF FAITH

Islam rests on the "five pillars of faith". The first of these, the *Shahada*, is a simple declaration that "there is no God but Allah and Mohammed is his Prophet". The second is the set of daily prayers that are supposed to be performed five times a day, facing in the direction of Mecca. The third is fasting during the daylight hours of the holy month of Ramadan. The fourth is the giving of alms. The fifth is *Haj*: at least once in their lifetime all Muslims must, if they are able, make the pilgrimage to Mecca, the birthplace of Mohammed.

VISITING A MOSQUE

Apart from at prayer times and during the Friday congregation, most mosques in Egypt are open to visitors. As well as paying a small entrance fee, it is customary to give a tip to the guardian and to the person who looks after your shoes or provides a scarf to cover your head during your visit. Mosques are open 24 hours, but only open to visitors from 9am–7pm. They close earlier in winter and during the month of Ramadan *(see also p312).*

Arcaded courtyard of the Mosque of al-Azhar, Cairo

Muslim festivals are relatively infrequent, with just four major dates in the calendar (see p41). *The most important of these are* Eid al-Adha, *marking the time of the pilgrimage* (Haj), *and* Eid al-Fitr, *which is held at the end of Ramadan. Islamic celebrations tend to be communal affairs and usually take the form of great feasts, often held outdoors.*

THE CALL TO PRAYER

At times linked to the moon's phases, a *muezzin* traditionally makes the call to prayer from the balcony of a mosque's minaret. Today, the call is most likely to come from a recorded tape broadcast through loudspeakers.

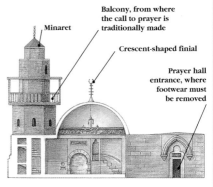

Minaret

Balcony, from where the call to prayer is traditionally made

Crescent-shaped finial

Prayer hall entrance, where footwear must be removed

Mosques have been built in a variety of styles but they all share some common features. Chief of these is the mihrab, *the niche that indicates the direction of Mecca. Most mosques also have a* minbar, *from which the* imam *delivers his Friday sermon.*

Islamic Architecture

Roof detail on a *madrassa*

THE TERM ISLAMIC ARCHITECTURE refers not only to mosques but also to a wide range of interesting buildings. The styles used were developed primarily under the early Islamic dynasties (the Tulunids, Fatimids and Ayyubids) and reached the height of creativity during the Mamluk era *(see p57)*. Craftsmen from all over the Near East were brought to Egypt to build palaces and mausoleums for rich and vainglorious sultans. They also created public institutions such as hospitals, schools and street fountains, many of which are still in use. The last great period of Islamic architecture in Egypt was under the Ottoman Turks *(see p58)*. Although reserving their best work for the imperial city of Istanbul, the Ottoman legacy includes some impressive structures.

Typical mosque-style building with domes and minarets *(see p93)*

DOMESTIC ARCHITECTURE

Private houses (called *beit* in Arabic) owed their design to both climatic and social conditions. Certain features, such as small windows covered with wooden screens, large airy rooms, shady arcades and fountains, kept the rooms cool. Typically these houses would be partitioned into separate male and female zones, known as the *salamlek* and *haramlek* respectively.

Mashrabiyya screens allowed the women of the house to look out without being seen.

Rooftop wind catchers channelled cool breezes into the rooms below.

The grandest private houses could rise as high as three or four storeys. They used recurring features such as ablaq *(striped layers of stone), arcades and fountains.*

The House of Amasyali is one of numerous examples of the exquisite Ottoman merchants' houses that have survived in the town of Rosetta (see p233).

Indoor fountains were built into the homes of the wealthy to keep the room temperature down.

Wooden ceilings were often carved with beautifully intricate geometric patterns and then painted in rich colours.

A qaa or reception room typically formed the sumptuous centrepiece of the wealthy merchants' houses.

SABIL-KUTTAB (FOUNTAIN AND SCHOOL)

Sabils (public fountains) are a typical element of Islamic architecture – some no more than a tap and a trough, some grand like the Sabil-Kuttab of Abdel Katkhuda. The *kuttab* was an open loggia or gallery where teachings of the Quran took place.

Tiles painted *with scenes from Mecca were used to decorate some* sabil-kuttabs *in keeping with the religious nature of these buildings.*

Sabil-Kuttab of Abdel Katkhuda *(see p98)*

MADRASSA (LAW SCHOOL)

A *madrassa* is a Quranic school, where law and theology are taught. Usually a mosque and *madrassa* are one and the same building. Sunni Islam, the variant of Islam followed in Egypt, has four schools of law (Hanafi, Malaki, Shafii and Hanbali), and so typically a *madrassa* will have four separate teaching areas, one for each. These often take the form of *iwans*, which are large arched spaces arranged around a central courtyard.

Fountains existed for the ablutions that had to be carried out before prayer.

Madrassa of Sultan Barquq *(see p97)*

WIKALA (HOTEL)

Also known as a caravanserai, the *wikala* is the precursor of the modern inn. It provided hospitality to the travelling merchant caravans that brought such great wealth to medieval Egypt. Animals were kept on the ground floor, along with goods placed in storage, while upstairs were the lodgings. At night, the whole building was sealed behind a sole gate for security purposes.

The rooms for the travellers overlooked the tiled central courtyard of the *wikala.*

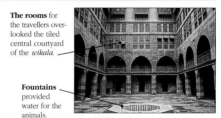

Fountains provided water for the animals.

The Wikala of al-Ghouri *(see p92)*

MAUSOLEUM (TOMB)

Some of the most splendid pieces of architecture in Egypt are mausoleums. Just like the pharaohs before them with their pyramids and immense mortuary temples, medieval sultans sought to glorify themselves in death. This they did by spending lavish amounts on enormous funerary complexes that often incorporated mosques and *madrassas* beside a domed tomb chamber. Inside, the bodies of the dead were laid above ground in a cenotaph marked by a pillar-like headstone. During Ottoman times, soldiers' headstones were frequently decorated with a carved turban.

Elaborate wrought-iron decoration was used to adorn the tomb.

The crescent moon symbol of Islam was an essential component of any Islamic mortuary structure.

Four marble columns supported the roof of the cenotaph.

Pillars, or stelae, stood at either end of the cenotaph, sometimes indicating the rank and gender of the deceased person.

Decorative lattice panelling was a frequent feature.

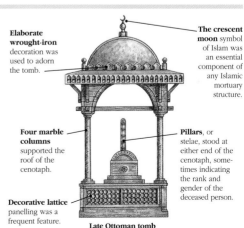

Late Ottoman tomb

The Landscape and Wildlife of Egypt

Although Egypt comprises over 90 per cent desert, it is not a totally barren landscape. A number of plants and animals have developed strategies to cope with extreme temperatures and long periods of drought. Humans, however, are less adaptable and while a tiny percentage lives in desert oases *(see p257)*, 96 per cent live close to water in the green Delta or along the Nile Valley. However, despite plentiful water and rich soil, this land struggles to provide enough food for the rapidly growing population. Around Egypt's coastline the seas teem with marine life and the colourful coral reefs of the Red Sea *(see p223)* are probably the one of the richest natural environments on the planet.

Desert travel, reliant on camels and date palms

DESERTS

The popular image of deserts is of endless seas of sand. However, the rocky interior of Sinai also counts as a desert – strictly defined as an area with less than 25 cm (10 inches) of rainfall a year. Strong winds are also characteristic of the desert, eroding the rocks into bizarre shapes and creating sand which accumulates as slowly moving sand dunes.

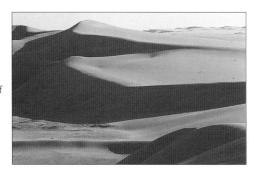

Agriculture in the desert oases is vital to the economy of the country, providing large quantities of sugar cane, dates, figs and other fruit and vegetables.

Scorpions are perfectly adapted to the desert environment: they rarely need to drink, as they obtain their fluids from a diet of insects.

Fennec foxes sleep during the day, only leaving their burrows in the cool dusk. Exceptional hearing enables them to catch insects and small mammals in the dark.

Date palms thrive in the rocky desert environment. Growing "with their head in fire and feet in water", they are a sure sign of a hidden water source.

Sinai's red massif rises in places to over 2,000 m (6,700 ft). Criss-crossed with wadis (dry river beds), the area is brought to life by sporadic flooding.

NILE VALLEY AND DELTA

The Nile creates a habitable tract of land never more than 20 km (13 miles) wide from Lake Nasser to the Delta. In the past, floods replenished the soil with rich silt deposits which enabled the land to support a wide range of flora and fauna. The Aswan Dam *(see p207)* ended the floods, making farmers reliant on chemical fertilizers. Today, the Delta is one of the most intensely farmed areas.

Farmland is irrigated by a complicated system of canals and dykes. The resulting wet croplands provide the ideal environment for cattle egrets, which hunt for frogs, insects and small rodents.

Acacia is easily identified along the banks of the Nile by its eye-catching balls of yellow flowers.

Papyrus, widely used in ancient times, was all but extinct by the 19th century. It is only grown in a few select areas.

The Purple Gallinule is a colourful duck-sized water bird found the length of the Nile. Its long, slender toes enable it to walk on lily pads.

The Spitting Cobra, a symbol of Lower Egypt in Pharaonic times, hunts its prey at night in crop fields. It is not usually a danger to humans, but it might attack if threatened, spitting venom accurately at its attacker's eyes.

COASTAL REGIONS

Egypt's northern coastline is on the Mediterranean Sea where fishing is a key industry. While Egypt's Red Sea and Sinai coastlines also maintain fishing communities, they are far more important as a resource for the tourist industry. These coastlines support several large strips of coral reef *(see p223)* which attract divers from all over the world.

A fragile environment, the reefs are under serious threat from overdevelopment of the coastline.

Coral reefs provide a colourful environment for an equally spectacular array of marine life.

MANGROVE SWAMPS

The mangrove swamps of the Sinai Peninsula perform an important function protecting the shoreline against erosion and filtering pollutants from the water. The mudflats they create provide a vital environment for crabs and wading birds. Mangroves are able to live in salt water by excreting excess salt via their leaves.

Mangrove swamps fringing the Sinai coastline

EGYPT THROUGH THE YEAR

THE EGYPTIAN CALENDAR is crowded with Muslim, Christian, national and local festivals. The dates of these events can be difficult to predict as they are often calculated in different ways. The Islamic calendar is based on twelve 29- or 30-day lunar months, while Egypt's Christian Coptic church uses the Julian calendar and the solar Coptic calendar. Extra confusion is caused by the frequently changing dates of non-religious events or festivals.

Making sweets in the market

Visitors should confirm the date of the event locally. Whatever the calendar, these are mostly joyous events and a great way to experience Egyptian culture at close hand as both Muslims and Copts often enjoy celebrating *moulids* or festivals together. A wide range of esoteric sports events is staged throughout the year which range from the interesting to the bizarre, from camel racing to long-distance swimming in the Nile at Cairo.

SPRING

SPRINGTIME IS A PLEASANT time to visit Egypt. The main visitor attractions such as the Pyramids at Giza, Luxor and Aswan are not too crowded and the temperature has yet to reach the scorching highs of summer. One weather phenomenon that can cause problems is the *khamseen*, a hot, dry wind that blows up from the Sahara Desert in the south. This can turn the air orange with dust and drive everyone indoors.

The main spring festivals are the beginning of the Islamic New Year in March and the Christian festival of Easter. On the Monday after Easter Sunday, all Egyptians celebrate Sham an-Nessim or the "sniffing the breeze". They go on picnics or hold events outdoors to take in the fresh spring air.

MARCH

Flower Show at the Orman Gardens, Sharia Giza, Giza.
Feast of the Annunciation *(Mar 23)*. This Coptic feast celebrates the announcement to the Holy Virgin that she was to give birth to Jesus.
Easter is the most important date on the Coptic calendar. The Coptic Pope celebrates Easter Mass at St Mark's Cathedral in Cairo.
Sham an-Nessim, celebrated by both Copts and Muslims, is a day when families enjoy outdoor pursuits and reputed to date from Pharaonic times.

APRIL

International Camel Race Competition. The bumpiest race in the world takes place around Sharm el-Sheikh.
Sinai Liberation Day *(Apr 25)*, celebrates Israel's withdrawal from Sinai in 1982.

Coptic Christians celebrating Palm Sunday, a week before Easter

MAY

Labour Day *(May 1)* is a public holiday when most businesses will be closed.
Moulid of St Damyanah *(May 15–20)*, a Coptic festival celebrating one of their important saints.
National Fishing Competition, Sharm el-Sheikh. These events take place regularly at Red Sea resorts.
Nile Swimming Race, Zamalek, Cairo. Amazingly an international field swims the murky waters of the Nile in the popular Egyptian sport of long-distance swimming.
Ragabiyya is a local festival in Tanta, Egypt's fifth-largest city. The festival lasts for three days in celebration of the Sufi saint, Sayyid Ahmad al-Badawi, and is held when the Nile rises in late spring.

Families celebrating the arrival of spring on Sham an-Nessim

MUSLIM FESTIVALS

Celebrated with great feasts, family gatherings, music and street processions, Muslim festivals are joyous occasions. The largest of the festivals are Eid al-Fitr, which takes place at the end of Ramadan, the month of ritual fasting, and Eid al-Adha, which marks the time of the pilgrimage to Mecca. Other Muslim festivals include the Moulid an-Nabi which celebrates the birth of the Prophet Mohammed, Ras as-Sana, the Islamic New Year, and various saints' name days known as *moulids*.

Cookies for Eid al-Fitr are traditionally baked in preparation for the three-day feast that marks the end of Ramadan. Food plays an important part of Muslim festivals and preparing it is often a social affair.

Sufi dancers are a feature at moulids. Wearing brightly coloured outfits, they chant and sway for hours in an effort to achieve unity with God. The dancers may also be led on a procession through the town.

ISLAMIC CALENDAR

The Islamic calendar has twelve months, each with 29 or 30 days. Purely lunar based, the Islamic year is around 11 days shorter than that of the Western calendar. Because Islam relies on actual sightings of the crescent moon at a given place, it is difficult to give dates in advance. Local Islamic centres will be able to provide the dates for the current year.

Eid al-Adha
This marks the time of the *Haj*, or pilgrimage to Mecca.

Ras as-Sana
The Islamic equivalent of New Year's Day and quite a low-key affair.

Moulid an-Nabi
Birth of the Prophet and one of the major holidays of the year. The streets burst into colour and noise with the celebrations.

Ramadan
The ninth month of the Muslim calendar when most Muslims observe a degree of fasting and abstinence. The *iftar*, or breaking of the fast, occurs every evening when the sun sets.

Eid al-Fitr
The end of Ramadan and the signal for a joyous, three-day feast.

Eid al-Fitr is a happy celebration marking the end of Ramadan. During the festivities, which usually last for three days, new clothes are worn and gifts are exchanged.

Religious holidays provide the perfect opportunity for family gatherings. Muslim celebrations often centre around the enjoyment and sharing of food and picnics are therefore a popular choice.

Donkey trekking in the heat of summer, Valley of the Kings, Luxor

Summer

FROM JUNE to August the temperature in Egypt climbs to unbearable levels in Upper Egypt, although the sites are often less crowded and hotel accommodation is plentiful. Many Egyptians choose to holiday on the North Coast where the temperature is slightly cooler. The Red Sea coastal resorts, although also very hot, have beautiful, clear water in which visitors can keep themselves cool. In the summer heat and smog, Cairo can get very uncomfortable and there are fewer interesting festivals.

June

Al-Ahram International Squash Competition, Giza, attracts large audiences and an international field. It takes place in floodlit, glass courts against the spectacular backdrop of the Pyramids.
Evacuation Day *(Jun 18)* celebrates the departure of the British Forces from the Canal Zone in 1956 and the start of the Egyptian Republic.

July

Revolution Day *(Jul 23)* commemorates the 1952 coup which toppled the puppet monarchy *(see p62).*

Shopping and Tourism Festival, Cairo *(Jul–Aug).*

August

International Folk Festival, Ismailia, attracts folk groups from all over the world.
International Song Festival, Cairo, often features an interesting range of artists.

Autumn

AUTUMN BRINGS cooler weather to Egypt and a proliferation of events and festivals. While some of these are obvious attempts to boost tourist revenues, the best can be truly magical events that are well worth making the effort to go to. However, it is worth noting that the time of year some of these events take place is liable to change at the whim of the Egyptian authorities.

September

Nile Festival Day or Wafaa an-Nil, Cairo. This is a series of processions, parades and sporting competitions which take place on the Nile.

Coptic Festivals

Christmas, Epiphany, Easter and the Annunciation are the main Christian festivals of the year and all are celebrated by Copts, with Easter being the most important. Saints' days also feature strongly and, as with Islamic feasts, they are usually celebrated with a lively moulid. The main saints' days include the Moulid of St Damyanah, the Feast of the Apostles Peter and Paul and various moulids of the Virgin and St George which take place throughout August. The spring festival of Sham an-Nessim is celebrated by both Muslims and Copts with family picnics of painted eggs and salted fish.

Pope Shenouda III, *the patriarch of the Coptic Christian church, presides over important religious ceremonies and events.*

Coptic Calendar

While some Coptic festivals correspond to the Julian calendar, others rely on the solar Coptic one. This calendar has 13 months, 12 of 30 days each and an intercalary month at the end of the year of 5 or 6 days, depending whether it is a leap year or not.

Easter
This is the most important date in the Coptic calendar. However, it can differ by up to a month from the date of the Orthodox church's festival.

Coptic festivals are primarily religious affairs with celebrations centred around church services for the young and old.

A colourful pageant at the Arabian Horse Festival, Az-Zahraa

International Cinema Festival, Alexandria. The Egyptians pride themselves on their cinema. This festival features more home produced films than the very popular Cairo festival in December.

OCTOBER

Aida Opera, Giza. This spectacular Egyptian-themed extravaganza was written by Verdi for the opening of the Suez Canal. Performed in front of the pyramids, this is a very popular production.
Alexandria Mediterranean Biennale (for artists) brings Mediterranean artists together for an exchange of cultural and artistic ideas.

National Day (Armed Forces Day) *(Oct 6)* is a day of parades, fly-bys and non-stop patriotic songs and films.
The Battle of El-Alamein Commemoration, with services conducted by former Allied and Axis countries, remembers those that died in the campaigns in North Africa during World War II.
Ramses Festival, Abu Simbel *(Oct 22)*. On this day, and again in February, the sun reaches 55 m (185 ft) into the inner chamber of the Temple of Ramses and illuminates the statues inside.
Moulid of Sayyid Ahmed al-Badawi, Tanta. Egypt's largest festival, up to two million revellers attend this

week-long celebration at the end of the cotton harvest.
National Liberation Day *(Oct 23)* and the **Suez Victory Day** *(Oct 24)* are public holidays celebrating Egypt's martial past.
Pharaoh's Rally (International Egypt Rally), is a gruelling 12-day, 6,400-km (4,000-mile) motor vehicle race through the Egyptian deserts. Major car manufacturers and competitors come from all over the world to participate in this event.

NOVEMBER

Arabian Horse Festival, Az-Zahraa. Proud of its Arabian horses, Egypt holds two festivals for displaying these beautiful animals. The other is held at Sharkeya in the Delta during May.
International Fishing Competition, Sharm el-Sheikh. These competitions are staged at several of the Red Sea resorts and attract international competitors.
Luxor National Festival *(Nov 4)* is combined with a commemoration of the discovery of the Tomb of Tutankhamun in 1922.
World Bowling Championship, Cairo. Ten-pin bowls, which claims its origins in ancient Egypt, is rapidly growing in popularity in the modern country.

One of the cultural highlights of the Egyptian calendar, Verdi's spectacular opera, Aida

WINTER

WINTER BRINGS some slight relief from the heat and, in Cairo and Alexandria and along the North Coast, even the odd shower of rain. The days are still sunny and warm but the nights can be quite cold, especially in desert areas. It also brings the start of the tourist season and a large influx of foreign visitors seeking winter sun and a glimpse into the fascinating, civilization of ancient Egypt. Cruise tours and hotels in Upper Egypt tend to get busy during this period and prices increase accordingly.

The organized chaos of the International Book Fair, Cairo

DECEMBER

The International Nile Regatta is organized by the Egyptian Rowing Federation, this event attracts teams of young and more experienced rowers from all over the world. The Regatta takes place in Luxor and Cairo.

The International Cinema Festival, Cairo, is an often chaotic festival which brings the very best of world cinema to Egypt. However, the event's popularity is partly due to the fact that it is the only time of the year that Egyptians get to see uncensored films. While films notorious for sex or nudity are well-attended and lively affairs, there are a lot of other good films to see.

JANUARY

International Sailing Championship, Port Safaga. This event is best viewed from the shore, watching the colourful sails gliding across the usually calm sea.

New Year's Day (*1 Jan*) is a public holiday.

Coptic Christmas (*7 Jan*). On this day, Copts throughout Egypt dress up in their Sunday best, visit their relatives and feast together. It is not an official public holiday, but many Egyptian Copts take this day off.

International Egyptian Marathon, Luxor. As many as 2,000 competitors brave the heat to take part in this run around Luxor. As well as the marathon there is also a

Windsurfing on the Red Sea

"Pharaonic Race". This 100-km (62-mile) run started in 1977 supposedly after an archaeologist found an inscription describing a similar length race run by royal soldiers in the 7th century BC.

International Windsurfing Competition, Hurghada. The Red Sea provides ideal conditions for such watersport competitions and similar events are held around the year.

Epiphany (*19 Jan*), a Coptic celebration of the revelation of Jesus's divinity after his baptism by John.

The Paris-Dakar-Cairo Rally is one of the most famous rallies in the world. A brave field of competitors traverse Africa from West to East finishing the 11,000-km (7,000 mile) race in front of the Pyramids at Giza, in clouds of fumes and dust.

Cairo International Book Fair, Nasr City. Ostensibly for the book trade, this event also attracts regular book lovers and Cairenes simply looking for a day out among the fast food stalls. During the event a bus service departs for Nasr City from Midan Tahrir.

FEBRUARY

Abu Simbel Festival (*22 Feb*). This festival celebrates one of the two days in the year (the other is in October) when the sun's rays penetrate the sanctuary of Ramses's Great Temple at Abu Simbel.

A competitor in the motorcycle class of the Paris-Dakar-Cairo Rally

The Climate of Egypt

Snorkelling in the Red Sea

EGYPT'S WEATHER is predominantly hot, sunny and very dry. The only rain that falls regularly is on the North Coast during winter, but this is under 100 mm (4 inches) a year. There are two seasons – May to October , the hot season, and November to April, the cool season. In general, it is warm all the year round, although the deserts can get cold during winter nights. The most striking meteorological phenomenon is the *khamseen*, a dry wind during April and May that causes sandstorms.

THE DELTA AND THE NORTH COAST

°C			
		30	28
	23	23	20	18
	15			11

	10	12	9	7
☂	3 mm	- mm	5 mm	48 mm
month	Apr	Jul	Oct	Jan

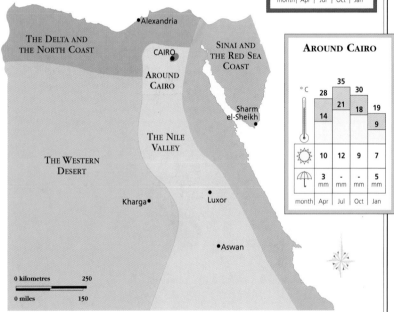

Alexandria

THE DELTA AND THE NORTH COAST

CAIRO

AROUND CAIRO

SINAI AND THE RED SEA COAST

Sharm el-Sheikh

THE NILE VALLEY

THE WESTERN DESERT

Kharga

Luxor

Aswan

0 kilometres 250

0 miles 150

AROUND CAIRO

°C		35		
	28		30	
		21	18	19
	14			9

	10	12	9	7
☂	3 mm	- mm	- mm	5 mm
month	Apr	Jul	Oct	Jan

THE WESTERN DESERT

		42		
	37		37	
°C	20	23	21	21
				5

	11	12	11	10
☂	- mm	- mm	- mm	- mm
month	Apr	Jul	Oct	Jan

THE NILE VALLEY

		40		
	34		35	
°C	18	25	19	24
				8

	9	10	8	7
☂	- mm	- mm	- mm	- mm
month	Apr	Jul	Oct	Jan

SINAI AND THE RED SEA COAST

°C		32	30	
	26	25	23	21
	16			10

	11	12	11	10
☂	- mm	- mm	- mm	- mm
month	Apr	Jul	Oct	Jan

ΚΡΟΚΟΔΙΛΟΠΑΡΔΑΛΙϹ

THE HISTORY OF EGYPT

EGYPT'S HISTORY *has been crucially influenced by its environment. When lack of rain forced the early nomadic inhabitants to migrate towards the Nile Valley, the fertile floodplain gave birth to a nation that produced some of the most important achievements in human history and established a culture that would remain largely unchanged for over 3000 years.*

Although the beginning of Egyptian history is generally given as 3100 BC, human activity in the Predynastic Period can be traced back many thousands of years before this date. The Sahara Desert used to be a green and fertile savannah, home to a nomadic population who hunted the wildlife they portrayed in rock drawings (petroglyphs). Archaeologists have also discovered that cattle-herders in Nabta Playa in the Western Desert built stone-circle calendars dating from 8000 BC.

King Narmer's Palette c.3100 BC

The way of life of these early peoples remained much the same for around 4000 years, but as the climate became increasingly arid, the population left the growing areas of desert (*deshret* or red land) for the banks of the river Nile where the annual flooding sustained a region of great fertility (*kemet* or black land). The excavation of their settlements has revealed the rapid development of a sophisticated culture of mud-brick houses and workshops, together with primitive temple structures.

The need to organize these settlements led to the invention of the world's first form of writing – hieroglyphs. Excavations at Abydos have shown that this script was in use from around 3250 BC, several centuries before the earliest writing in Mesopotamia. Further expansion meant settlements inevitably came into conflict with each other. The country polarized into two opposing kingdoms of north (Lower Egypt) and south (Upper Egypt). Around 3100 BC, the two were unified for the first time into a single state. This event was commemorated on the cosmetic slate palette of King Narmer (sometimes known as Menes), found at Hierakonpolis. The palette is possibly the most important historical document from the whole of Egyptian history, recording the creation of the world's first nation state. The dramatic pose as he is about to smash the skull of his defeated foe became the standard way to portray Egypt's kings throughout the next 3,000 years.

TIMELINE

10,000 BC	5000 BC	4500 BC	4000 BC	3500 BC	3000 BC

8000 BC Early human settlement of Nabta Playa in Western Desert builds huge sculptures and a stone-circle calendar

Pots from 4000 – 3000 BC

3400 BC Egypt's oldest temple built at Hierakonpolis

3250 BC Invention of hieroglyphs – world's first script

10,000 BC Nomadic population of Sahara draw petroglyphs of the animals they hunt

Earliest known human sculpture

c. 4000 BC Earliest known human figure sculpted in Africa, at Neolithic settlement in western Delta

3100 BC Political unification of Egypt by King Narmer. Memphis becomes the capital city

◁ **Graeco-Roman mosaic showing the flooding of the Nile, Egypt's temples and its fabled wildlife**

THE OLD KINGDOM (3100–2180 BC)

The power base of the Old Kingdom was established at Memphis, the first capital of a united Egypt. This was strategically located where Upper Egypt meets Lower Egypt at the apex of the Delta close to modern Cairo. Whereas the earliest kings chose Abydos as

Statue of King Khafre protected by the falcon god Horus

their funeral site to reflect their southern origins, later rulers preferred to be buried close to their new capital in its necropolis, Saqqara. The site of Egypt's earliest pyramid (c.2650 BC), Saqqara is also home to many stone *mastaba* (bench-shaped) tombs built for members of the royal court and beautifully decorated. The king was seen as the living incarnation of the god Horus and his court sought to be buried close to his divine power.

King Narmer's successors managed to suppress any outside threat to Egypt's stability whilst organizing the country into 42 provinces or *nomes*. These were administered by means of a highly efficient bureaucracy of

officials. The great wealth created through a carefully organized system of taxation – based on the collection and redistribution of Egypt's abundant grain supplies – was also used to fund ambitious building schemes. This culminated in the massive pyramid complexes of the Old Kingdom god-kings such as Djoser, Sneferu, Khufu and Khafre. The organization required for such huge projects helped to unify the nation, while the vast numbers of skilled craftsmen involved meant that art and technology developed at a rapid pace.

Of all the pyramid-building pharaohs, Sneferu was the greatest, building three such structures, including the first true pyramid at Dahshur. It was only with techniques perfected by Sneferu that his son Khufu was able to construct the largest of all Egypt's pyramids at Giza in 2589 BC.

Eventually centuries of pyramid-building, together with a series of poor harvests, severely depleted the economy. This led to a decline in royal power, which was reflected in the small size of the later pyramids built at Abusir and Saqqara. The incredibly long reign of Pepi II (2278–2184 BC), only added to the problem and with the pharaoh seen as a feeble old man, royal authority was further undermined. After an incredible

The Pyramids at Giza, magnificent symbols of the divine power of the early Egyptian kings

TIMELINE

	2665 BC The world's oldest stone monument, the step Pyramid of King Djoser, built at Saqqara		**2613–2589 BC** Reign of King Sneferu, builder of 3 pyramids at Dashur and Meidum	
2900 BC	**2800 BC**	**2700 BC**	**2600 BC**	**2500 BC**
Figurine from a unified Egypt fashioned in c.2900 BC	**2686 BC** Oldest surviving mudbrick building built by King Khasekhemwy at Hierakonpolis	**2589 BC** The Great Pyramid of Khufu (Cheops) built at Giza	**2558 BC** Pyramid of Khafre (Chephren) built at Giza. Its complex includes the oldest surviving temple in Egypt	

94 years on the throne Pepi II was succeeded by Egypt's first female pharaoh Nitocris, but despite being remembered as "the bravest and most beautiful" of her time, it was too late to reverse the decline in royal fortunes.

FIRST INTERMEDIATE PERIOD, MIDDLE KINGDOM AND SECOND INTERMEDIATE PERIOD (2180–1550 BC)

As royal power declined, officials began to relocate to their home provinces. No longer reliant on the king, they created their own small kingdoms maintained with private armies. As the country gradually fragmented, central authority finally broke down into anarchy and the First Intermediate Period began c.2180 BC.

The lack of overall authority is clearly expressed in provincial and rather "idiosyncratic" art styles typical of local trends. The breakdown of social order is also reflected in the literature – "All is ruin…men kill their brothers…blood is everywhere".

The remnants of royal power relocated to Herakleopolis, at the entrance to the Fayoum Oasis, and attempted to rule through the forging of alliances with the southern regions. However, any temporary unity was shattered when Thebes formed an independent monarchy. Civil war and fierce fighting between neighbouring tribes tore the whole country apart.

After a long and bitter struggle the powerful Theban warlord Montuhotep II conquered the north to reunite the country under the 11th Dynasty. His reign took Egypt from the chaos of the First Intermediate Period into the stability of the Middle Kingdom (c.2055 BC). Thebes now grew into a major metropolis, home to skilled craftsmen who created new art styles at a rate not seen since the Age of the Pyramids. The old trade routes and mines were reopened and expansionist policies prevailed. Although the office of pharaoh would never again reach the absolute divinity of earlier times, the Theban monarchy restored royal power as growth in revenue led to a resumption of building projects. The greatest new structure was Montuhotep's imposing funerary complex built at Deir al-Bahri which, 500 years later, would serve as the prototype for Hatshepsut's temple.

Statue of Montuhotep II, Theban founder of the 11th Dynasty

Model of the private army of the Governor of Asyut (c.2000 BC)

2278 BC Pepi II ascends throne and rules for 94 years	2184 BC Reign of Nitocris begins, Egypt's first female ruler	2180 BC First Intermediate Period – decentralization of authority and civil war		2004 BC Montuhotep II buried at Deir al-Bahri
2400 BC	2300 BC	2200 BC	2100 BC	2000 BC
Life-size copper statue of King Pepi I 2321-2287 BC	2160 BC Kings of the 9–10th dynasties based at Herakleopolis		2125 BC Warlords of Thebes form independent 11th ruling dynasty	2055 BC Montuhotep II of Thebes defeats Herakleopolis and reunites Egypt ruling from Thebes. The local god Amun becomes important

Teams of workers dragging a huge stone statue, from the Middle Kingdom tomb of Djehutyhotep (c.1850 BC)

The kings of the 12th Dynasty, which lasted from c.1985–1795 BC, moved the royal residence back to the traditional capital, Memphis, in order to be closer to the centre of the country. They continued with ambitious building projects, and the art and literature of this time is regarded as the "classic" period of Egyptian culture. Pharaohs such as Senusret III and Amenemhat III constructed impressive pyramids at Saqqara, Dahshur, Lahun and Hawara, where they were buried alongside their relatives with beautiful jewellery made of gold, amethyst, carnelian and lapis lazuli.

Successful military campaigns expanded Egypt's borders, whilst at home the crown centralized its authority by removing power from provincial governors and replacing these governors with a vast bureaucracy of loyal officials. Many of these officials were migrants from nearby Palestine

Sphinx bearing the face of Amenemhat III

who had settled peacefully in northern Egypt and had been gradually absorbed into Egyptian society over a period of about 150 years. By infiltrating the government they took advantage of the instability caused by a series of short-lived rulers during the 13th and 14th Dynasties. In 1650 BC, these settlers, referred to as the Hyksos (Rulers of Foreign Lands), finally assumed control.

This marks the beginning of the Second Intermediate Period, when Egypt was once again divided geographically. Based in their northern capital Avaris, the Hyksos formed an alliance with Nubia to help them to control southern Egypt, where the native Egyptian opposition to foreign rule had organized itself in Thebes. The country was once again subject to intermittent civil war until the Theban warlord Seqenenre Taa II and his sons Kamose and Ahmose finally drove the Hyksos out of Egypt to reunite the Two Lands.

TIMELINE

1965 BC Assassination of Amenemhat I and accession of his son Senusret I

Statue of Senusret III

1795–1725 BC Unstable 13th Dynasty of 70 kings

1750–1650 BC Minor rulers of the 14th Dynasty

1900 BC
1800 BC
1700 BC

1874–1855 BC Reign of Senusret III

1855 BC Senusret III and his family buried at Dahshur

1799–1795 BC Reign of Egypt's second female ruler Sobekneferu

Middle Kingdom Horus head pendant

THE NEW KINGDOM
(1550–1070 BC)

With the reunification of north and south, the New Kingdom began. This is Egypt's "Golden Age", when a series of unrelenting warrior pharaohs turned the country into the most powerful empire in the ancient world. The expulsion of the Hyksos was followed by vigorous military campaigns as far north as the river Euphrates and as far south as Nubia. The enormous wealth amassed from foreign tribute was channelled into massive building projects in and around Thebes, with successive monarchs trying to outdo their predecessors. The magnificent temple of Karnak – the cult centre of the local Theban deity Amun – was embellished by successive pharaohs, as Amun was linked with the sun-god Ra to create Amun-Ra, "King of the Gods". Meanwhile, pharaohs built huge funerary temples for themselves on the west bank of the Nile, and were buried in spectacular rock-cut tombs in the Valley of the Kings, designed to ensure their eternal afterlife.

As the first king of the New Kingdom, Ahmose continued his family's military successes and established a pattern for his successors. His son Amenhotep I followed in his father's footsteps by pacifying Nubia. He also founded a village for royal tomb builders at Deir al-Medina,

Statue of Hatshepsut as a bearded pharaoh

where both he and his mother and co-ruler Ahmose-Nofretari were worshipped long after their deaths.

Then began the succession of the Tuthmosis pharaohs: men born to minor wives of the king who strengthened their claims to the throne by marrying into the female royal line. Tuthmosis II was succeeded by his wife and half-sister Hatshepsut, the most familiar of Egypt's female pharaohs, who is often portrayed in statues as a bearded pharaoh. Her successor, Tuthmosis III, the so-called "Napoleon of Ancient Egypt", expanded the Egyptian Empire into Asia Minor and as far as the Euphrates. His son Amenhotep II, a great warrior like his father and an accomplished athlete, consolidated Egypt's control over the vassal states of Asia Minor. Their foreign conquests created the wealth used so wisely by the greatest of all the pharaohs, Amenhotep III. Known as "the Magnificent", his peaceful 38-year reign marks the height of Egypt's cultural and artistic achievement.

Tuthmosis III making offerings to Amun-Ra, the national deity during the New Kingdom

The Egyptian Pharaohs

THE ANCIENT EGYPTIANS dated events to the particular year in the reign of a king or pharaoh (regnal dating). It was a Ptolemaic scholar, Manetho, who later sorted the kings into dynasties, a system still used today along with ancient king lists, astronomical records and modern archaeological dating methods. The resulting chronology is, however, neither fixed nor complete and liable to change.

EARLY DYNASTIC PERIOD

3100–2890 BC		2890–2686 BC	
IST DYNASTY		**2ND DYNASTY**	
Narmer	3100	Hetepsekhemwy	2890
Aha	3100	Raneb	2865
Djer	3000	Nynetjer	
Djet	2980	Weneg	
Den	2950	Sened	
Anedjib	2925	Peribsen	2700
Semerkhet	2900	Khasekhemwy	2686
Qaa	2890		

aka Amenhotep IV (see p171) † aka Amenophis
* denotes female pharaoh ‡ aka Sesostris

FIRST INTERMEDIATE PERIOD

MIDDLE KINGDOM

2181–2125 BC	2160–2055 BC	2055–1985 BC	1985–1795 BC
7TH & 8TH DYNASTIES	**9TH & 10TH DYNASTIES** Herakleopolitan	**11TH DYNASTY** All Egypt	**12TH DYNASTY**
During this unstable period of ancient Egyptian history there were numerous ephemeral kings. The weakening of centralized power led to the establishment of local dynasties.	Kheti Merykare Ity	Montuhotep II 2055–2004 Montuhotep III 2004–1992 Montuhotep IV 1992–1985	Amenemhat I 1985–1955 Senuset I ‡ 1965–1920 Amenemhat II 1922–1878 Senuset II ‡ 1880–1874 Senuset III ‡ 1874–1855 Amenemhat III 1855–1808 Amenemhat IV 1808–1799 Sobekneferu* 1799–1795
	11TH DYNASTY (Thebes Only)		Overlaps in dates indicate periods of co-regency
	Intef I 2125–2112 Intef II 2112–2063 Intef III 2063–2055	"Block" statue from the 12th Dynasty	

NEW KINGDOM

	1550–1295 BC	1295–1186 BC	1186–1069 BC
	18TH DYNASTY	**19TH DYNASTY**	**20TH DYNASTY**
	Ahmose 1550–1525	Ramses I 1295–1294	Sethnakhte 1186–1184
	Amenhotep I † 1525–1504	Seti I 1294–1279	Ramses III 1184–1153
	Tuthmosis I 1504–1492	Ramses II 1279–1213	Ramses IV 1153–1147
	Tuthmosis II 1492–1479	Merneptah 1213–1203	Ramses V 1147–1143
	Tuthmosis III 1479–1425	Amenmessu 1203–1200	Ramses VI 1143–1136
	Hatshepsut* 1473–1458	Seti II 1200–1194	Ramses VII 1136–1129
	Amenhotep II † 1427–1400	Siptah 1194–1188	Ramses VIII 1129–1126
	Tuthmosis IV 1400–1390	Tawosret* 1188–1186	Ramses IX 1126–1108
	Amenhotep III † 1390–1352		Ramses X 1108–1099
	Akhenaten # 1352–1336		Ramses XI 1099–1069
	Nefertiti		
Bracelet of Queen Ahotep, mother of Ahmose, first king of the 18th Dynasty	Smenkhkare* 1338–1336 Tutankhamun 1336–1327 Ay 1327–1323 Horemheb 1323–1295		Head of Ramses III, who built the great mortuary Temple at Medinat Habu

LATE PERIOD

672–525 BC	525–359 BC	404–c.380 BC	380–343 BC
26TH DYNASTY (Saite)	**27TH DYNASTY** (Persian Period 1)	**28TH DYNASTY** Amyrtaios 404–399	**30TH DYNASTY** Nectanebo I 380–362 Teos 362–360 Nectanebo II 360–343
Necho I 672–664	Cambyses 525–522	**29TH DYNASTY**	
Psamtek I 664–610	Darius I 522–486	Nepherites I 399–393	
Necho II 610–595	Xerxes I 486–465	Hakor 393–380	
Psamtek II 595–589	Artaxerxes I 465–424	Nepherites II c.380	
Apries 589–570	Darius II 424–405		
Ahmose II 570–526	Artaxerxes II 405–359		
Psamtek III 526–525			

One of the stone sphinxes from Luxor Temple, carved with the face of Nectanebo I

OLD KINGDOM

2686–2613	2613–2498 BC	2494–2345 BC	2345–2181 BC
3RD DYNASTY	**4TH DYNASTY**	**5TH DYNASTY**	**6TH DYNASTY**
Sanakht 2686–2667	Sneferu 2613–2589	Userkaf 2494–2487	Teti 2345–2323
Djoser 2667–2648	Khufu 2589–2566	Sahure 2487–2475	Userkare 2323–2321
Sekhemkhet 2648–2640	Djedefre 2566–2558	Neferirkare 2475–2455	Pepi I 2321–2287
Khaba 2640–2637	Khafre 2558–2532	Shepseskare 2455–2448	Merenre 2287–2278
Huni 2637–2613	Menkaure 2532–2503	Raneferef 2448–2445	Pepi II 2278–2184
	Shepseskaf 2503–2498	Nyuserre 2445–2421	Nitocris* 2184–2181
		Menkauhor 2421–2414	
		Djedkare 2414–2375	
		Unas 2375–2345	

The Pyramids at Giza, built in the 4th Dynasty

SECOND INTERMEDIATE PERIOD

	1795–1650 BC	1650–1550 BC	1650–1550 BC
	13TH DYNASTY	**15TH DYNASTY**	**17TH DYNASTY**
	1795–c.1725	**(Hyksos)**	In addition, several kings ruled from Thebes including the following:
	14TH DYNASTY	Salitis	
	1750–1650	Khyan c.1600	Intef
	Minor rulers probably contemporaneous with the previous dynasty.	Apepi c.1555	Ta I
		Khamudi	Seqenenre Taa II c.1560
		16TH DYNASTY	Kamose 1555–1550
		1650–1550	
		Minor Hyksos rulers contemporary with the 15th Dynasty.	

Limestone relief of Senusret I from the Temple at Karnak

THIRD INTERMEDIATE PERIOD | LATE PERIOD

1069–945 BC	945–715 BC	818–715 BC	747–656 BC
21ST DYNASTY	**22ND DYNASTY**	**23RD DYNASTY**	**25TH DYNASTY**
Smendes 1069–1043	Sheshonq I 945–924	Several continuous lines of rulers at Herakleopolis Magna, Hermopolis Magna, Leontopolis and Tanis including the following:	Piy 747–716
Amenemnisu 1043–1039	Osorkon I 924–889		Shabaqo 716–702
Psusennes I 1039–991	Sheshonq II c.890		Shabitqo 702–690
Amenemope 993–984	Takelot I 889–874		Taharqo 690–664
Osorkon the Elder 984–978	Osorkon II 874–850	Pedubastis I 818–793	Tanutamani 664–656
Siamun 978–959	Takelot II 850–825	Sheshonq IV c.780	
Psusennes II 959–945	Sheshonq III 825–773	Osorkon III 777–749	
	Pimay 773–767		
	Sheshonq V 767–730	**24TH DYNASTY**	
	Osorkon IV 730–715	Bakenrenef 727–715	

Silver coffin of Psusennes I from Tanis

PTOLEMAIC PERIOD

343–332 BC	332–305 BC	305–80 BC	80–30 BC
PERSIAN PERIOD 2	**MACEDONIAN DYNASTY**	**PTOLEMAIC DYNASTY**	**PTOLEMAIC DYNASTY (CONT.)**
Artaxerxes III		Ptolemy I 305–285	Ptolemy XI 80
Ochus 343–333	Alexander the Great 332–323	Ptolemy II 285–246	Ptolemy XII 80–51
Arses 338–336	Philip Arrhidaeus 323–317	Ptolemy III 246–221	Cleopatra VII* 51–30
Darius III	Alexander IV 317–305	Ptolemy IV 221–205	Ptolemy XIII 51–47
Codoman 336–332		Ptolemy V 205–180	Ptolemy XIV 47–44
		Ptolemy VI 180–145	Ptolemy XV 44–30
		Ptolemy VII 145	
		Ptolemy VIII 170–116	
		Ptolemy IX 116–107	Egypt becomes part of the Roman Empire in 30 BC (see pp56–7)
		Ptolemy X 107–88	
		Ptolemy IX 88–80	

Alexander the Great in Egyptian headgear

With the death of Amenhotep III in 1352 BC, the succession passed to his son Akhenaten *(see p171)*. His mismanagement of the political situation, relocation of the capital to Akhetaten (modern Tell al-Amarna) and attempts to overturn the traditional religious hierarchy destabilized Egypt and brought the country close to ruin. Akhenaten's successor, probably his wife

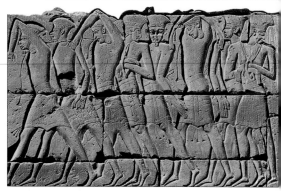

Philistines, one of the "Peoples of the Sea", being taken prisoner by Egyptians, from Ramses III's mortuary temple at Medinat Habu

Nefertiti, restored order by returning the seat of power to Thebes and re-establishing the traditional religion. The reign of Akhenaten's son Tutankhamun was largely devoted to restoring internal stability before trying to reverse Egypt's fortunes abroad. But it took the military prowess of Horemheb, who had worked his way up from scribe to general and finally

king, to restore the country to its former greatness. The last king of the 18th Dynasty, he soon began recovering Egypt's empire. This military policy was continued by the rulers of the 19th Dynasty, which began in 1295 BC. Under Seti I, Egypt regained much of her prestige abroad, whilst at home the monarchy's reputation was consolidated and enhanced by

Bust of Queen Nefertiti, 18th Dynasty

great new building projects such as Karnak's hypostyle hall *(see pp184–5)* and Seti's temple at Abydos. Seti was succeeded by his son Ramses II – also known as Ramses the Great – whose 66-year reign saw royal construction on a massive scale. Huge monuments, including the awesome Great Temple of Abu Simbel *(see pp210–11)*, were erected in a deliberate effort by Ramses to impress his subjects and preserve his reputation for posterity.

Ramses was succeeded by his son Merneptah, and four more pharaohs in less than 20 years. In c.1186 BC, Sethnakhte inaugurated the 20th Dynasty; nine kings followed, all named Ramses. The greatest of these was Ramses III, who successfully defended Egypt's northern borders against repeated invasions by Libyans and settlers from the Mediterranean region – the so-called "Peoples of the Sea". But his weak successors could not sustain his victories, and foreign infiltration grew rapidly. With internal disorder and social unrest, even the royal tombs were ransacked. The New Kingdom finally collapsed in 1070 BC.

TIMELINE

1279–1213 BC Reign of Ramses II	**c.1274 BC** Ramses II claims victory over the Hittites at the Battle of Qadesh	**1070 BC** Fall of New Kingdom. Egypt divided between north and south	**747–656 BC** Nubians conquer Egypt and rule as 25th Dynasty

1300 BC	1150 BC	1000 BC	850 BC

1352–1336 BC Reign of Akhenaten. Relocation of capital to Akhetaten	*Collar of Tutankhamun*	**1070 BC** Kings rule from Tanis in the Delta, with Theban priests in control of the south	**945–924 BC** Sheshonq I, thought to be "Shishak" from the Old Testament, invades Israel

THIRD INTERMEDIATE PERIOD, LATE PERIOD AND PTOLEMAIC PERIOD (1070–30 BC)

The New Kingdom gave way to four centuries of disunity and foreign infiltration, known as the Third Intermediate Period. Egypt was again divided between north and south: the south remained under the control of the semi-royal high priests of Thebes, while the monarchy was located in the north and ruled from Tanis in the eastern Delta.

Egypt was further fragmented by the Libyan invasion of the western Delta, but in 747 BC the country was united by the Nubians, who managed to hold onto power for over a century, ruling as the 25th Dynasty.

Alexander the Great

The Late Period began with the Assyrian invasion of Egypt in 669 BC. The Assyrians meant to rule the country through their vassal king Nekau then Psamtek of the western Delta city Sais, but Psamtek outmanoeuvred his former masters and the 26th "Saite" Dynasty saw a brief flowering of native Egyptian culture.

Hopes of a permanent revival were, however, cut short by the Persians' invasion in 525 BC. Two hundred years of Persian domination was only interrupted by the short-lived 30th Dynasty – the last native Egyptian rulers. Finally the Macedonian king Alexander the Great "liberated" Egypt from the Persians and founded his new capital Alexandria on the Mediterranean coast, followed by the Ptolemaic Period.

On Alexander's death in 323 BC, his most trusted general assumed power, and over the next three centuries (305–30 BC) 14 of Ptolemy's successors and namesakes ruled from their capital Alexandria. The Ptolemies were accepted by the native Egyptians because they ruled as traditional pharaohs and built temples, such as Edfu, Dendara and Philae, in deliberate imitation of ancient Egyptian design. They also embellished Alexandria, which became the most important city of the ancient world. The last of the Ptolemies, Cleopatra VII, inherited the throne in 51 BC. Her 21-year reign briefly restored Egyptian greatness in the face of the expansionist ambitions of Rome. Her suicide marks the notional end of ancient Egypt, as the country finally became a Roman province.

Ptolemy V, wearing traditional Pharaonic clothing, making offerings to the sacred Buchis bull

Cleopatra VII (69 BC – 30 BC)

Cleopatra's cartouche

PERHAPS THE MOST FAMILIAR of ancient Egyptian figures, the real Cleopatra is hidden beneath centuries of misinformation. Most of the detail about her is supplied by Roman sources who waged a propaganda war against her. To them she was the ruler of a decadent eastern culture who seduced two of Rome's generals in order to sieze the Roman Empire. In fact, Cleopatra was an educated Macedonian Greek, who had one child with Julius Caesar and three during her 11 years with Mark Antony. These two men used Egypt's wealth for their imperial ambitions as much as she used their military might to assure her position.

Ptolemy I (305–285 BC) *ruled Egypt after his close friend Alexander the Great died, founding a dynasty that lasted nearly 300 years.*

ORIENTALIST PAINTING OF CLEOPATRA
Part inspired by reliefs on temple walls, part by a confusion of the exotic and the erotic, this painting by Alexandre Cabanel (1823-89) misrepresents Cleopatra in seductive Pharaonic attire.

This Classical bust *is probably a more realistic representation of Cleopatra. She was portrayed in Pharaonic dress on the walls of temples such as Dendera (see p175) to reinforce her position in the eyes of her subjects as the rightful heir to the great pharaohs.*

This Ptolemaic papyrus *bears Cleopatra's signature. Although fluent in seven languages, including Egyptian, she used Greek for official documents.*

EGYPT AND ROMAN EXPANSION

Rome's expansion from the 4th to the 1st century BC was fuelled in part by the need for ever-increasing quantities of grain. Grain's importance to the ancient economies is somewhat analogous to the value of oil to modern economies. Thanks to its efficient Greek administration, Egypt's vast grain harvests made it incredibly wealthy and a threat to Rome, if the country fell into the wrong hands. Therefore the Romans knew they had either to ensure Egypt's ruler was sympathetic towards them, or annex the country. At first, Egypt avoided being absorbed by Rome through a skilful combination of bribery and diplomacy – on different occasions, Julius Caesar and Mark Antony were paid large sums of money to restore the throne of Egypt to Cleopatra's father, Ptolemy XII. When Cleopatra and her brother were installed on the throne in 51 BC, Rome expected simply to add Egypt to their empire·

EXTENT OF THE EMPIRES

▮ *Rome 300 BC*

▮ *Rome 51 BC*

▯ *Ptolemaic Kingdom 51 BC*

CLEOPATRA AND ROME

In 51 BC, Cleopatra and Ptolemy XIII, her brother, were named co-rulers of Egypt. When they fought for sole control, Rome sent Julius Caesar to settle the dispute. He put Cleopatra on the throne and formed a close relationship with her. Three years after Caesar's murder, Mark Antony paid a visit to Cleopatra seeking funding for his expeditions. They became lovers and when Antony handed Roman territories over to Egypt in 34 BC, Rome, at Octavian's urging, declared war on Cleopatra.

Julius Caesar, after moving Cleopatra to Rome, was killed by Republicans who feared that, under her evil influence, he wanted to return Rome to monarchy.

Mark Antony was derided by Rome for his lack of self control towards Cleopatra. Forced to marry the sister of Octavian, he later returned to his Egyptian lover.

Octavian, with the prize of the Roman Empire at stake, decided to fight Antony at sea near Actium, off the coast of Greece.

At the Battle of Actium (31 BC) the two fleets quickly clashed, opening up a gap in Octavian's formation. Seeing her chance, Cleopatra headed for Egypt closely followed by Antony. His men, thinking him a deserter, defected to Octavian. A year later Octavian's army routed Antony's troops and marched on Alexandria.

The African asp is a cobra, which, as the uraeus snake, protected the pharaoh in this world and the next. It is possible, therefore, that Cleopatra did in fact choose to die by snake bite.

THE ENDURING APPEAL OF CLEOPATRA

The appeal of Cleopatra's story is magnified by her tragic death: defeated by Octavian and believing reports that Cleopatra was dead, Antony committed suicide; Cleopatra realising all was lost then took her own life. As told by Roman writers, this tale of sex, power, greed and ultimately tragedy proved irresistible for artists from the Renaissance, Shakespeare and Hollywood.

Shakespeare's play was based on Plutarch's Lives (c.AD 75), the Roman account most sympathetic to Cleopatra.

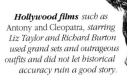

Hollywood films such as Antony and Cleopatra, starring Liz Taylor and Richard Burton used grand sets and outrageous outfits and did not let historical accuracy ruin a good story.

Eye makeup was one detail Hollywood did not get wrong, except that it was worn by both sexes. Ancient Egyptians used ground minerals mixed with water and stored in tubes.

FROM CHRIST TO MOHAMMED

Egypt was now a province of mighty Rome, whose emperors established themselves as the successors of the pharaohs. As Christianity spread throughout the Roman Empire, its Egyptian adherents, known as Copts, came into conflict with the Roman authorities. Even when Christianity was adopted as the official religion of the Eastern half of the now divided Roman Empire in 323 AD, there were differences in theology, and the Copts were mercilessly persecuted.

The Eastern Romans, later known as Byzantines, remained largely unchallenged in power until in the 7th century they were confronted by a new force sweeping up from Arabia. Following the teachings of the Prophet Mohammed, the army of Islam defeated the Byzantines in battle and entered Egypt. Ignoring Alexandria, the Arab army, led by the general Amr Ibn al-Aas, marched on the fortress of Babylon-in-Egypt near to the old capital of Memphis. After a brief siege it surrendered and Amr settled his men just to the north, where he founded a new city known as Fustat.

Egypt became a province of an already vast Islamic empire ruled first from Damascus (the Umayyad dynasty), then from Baghdad (the Abbasids). Ahmed Ibn Tulun, an administrator sent from Baghdad, decided to declare the territory independent. His mosque still stands but his dynasty did not outlive him long; his son was assassinated and rule from Baghdad reimposed.

Salah ad-Din al-Ayyubi (1138–93), the scourge of the European Crusaders

In AD 969 Egypt was seized by the Fatimids from Tunisia. They built a new city north of Fustat, encircled by fortified walls and containing palaces, great mosques and plazas. They called their new city Al-Qahira, "The Victorious", a name later corrupted by European tongues to "Cairo". Their reign in Egypt lasted for barely more than 200 years, until it was brought to an end in 1171 by the arrival of a Syrian warrior-general, Salah ad-Din al-Ayyubi, known in English as Saladin. In Cairo, Salah ad-Din expanded the city walls and added a fortress that survives as today's Citadel (*see pp104–7*). A hero of the Arab world, who recaptured Jerusalem from the European Crusaders, Salah ad-Din's role in Egyptian history is, however, overshadowed by the dynasty that succeeded him, a warrior caste called the Mamluks.

Detail of a manuscript showing Mamluk cavalrymen in training (1348)

TIMELINE

Roman mummy portrait from 4th century AD

30 BC–395 AD Roman Period		451 Egypt's Coptic church splits from Eastern Christianity at the Council of Chalcedon	527 St Catherine's Monastery founded in Sinai	
AD 1	**150**	**300**	**450**	**600**	**75**

394 End of ancient Egypt as Roman Empire accepts Christianity as official religion and closes all temples

640 Islamic army under Amr Ibn al-Aas invades and conquers Egypt

19th-century lithograph of Sultan Baybars I (c.1265) executing Christians who refuse to convert to Islam

SLAVES AND SOLDIERS

The word "Mamluk" means "one who is owned," and reflects their origins as slaves brought to Egypt to be palace guards. Their service was rewarded by land and eventual freedom. By the middle of the 13th century the Mamluks were the most powerful force in the land, and were able to claim Egypt for themselves.

The Mamluks retained the slave system, and whoever had the largest slave army installed himself as sultan at the top. There was no hereditary lineage, instead it was succession by the strongest. Once in power, there remained constant challenges, and only the exceptionally able and ruthless survived.

The Mamluks prided themselves on their martial skills and were known particularly for their masterful horsemanship. From their base in Cairo they fought victorious campaigns throughout Palestine and Syria, completing the job begun by Salah ad-Din by finally evicting the Crusaders from the Holy Land in 1291. They governed Jerusalem and Damascus, and carved out an empire that extended north as far as eastern Turkey. With these territories came control of East-West trade. The taxes raised on spices, perfumes, silks and

dyes made Cairo one of the richest cities in the world. This wealth remains evident in the legacy of superb architecture left behind from this time, built with fine marble panelling, intricate ivory-inlaid woodwork, and carved stone ornamentation.

Mamluk monopolies forced Europe to seek alternative routes to the East, and when, in 1498, Vasco da Gama rounded the Cape of Good Hope, the fortunes of Egypt were dealt a crippling blow. Worse still, the Ottoman Turks from their capital of Constantinople were eroding the Mamluks' empire from the north. Sultan Qansuh al-Ghouri (1501–16) rode out to meet this new threat. His Mamluk army was defeated, and the following year the Ottoman Turks entered Cairo to take control of Egypt.

Magnificent interior of the Mosque of Qaitbey (1475), built with money raised by taxes

876–9 Construction of the Mosque of Ibn Tulun	969 Fatimids found the city of Al-Qahira, forerunner of modern Cairo	1171 Salah ad-Din becomes ruler of Egypt	1250 Mamluks accede to power	1468–96 Reign of Qaitbey, enthusiastic patron of architecture	1516 Al-Ghouri's Mamluk army defeated by Ottomans, who take control of Egypt

Mamluk jacket (c.13th century)

Mamluk tile from the 15th century

900	1050	1200	1350	1500

The defeat of the Mamluks by Napoleon's army during the 1798 Battle of the Pyramids

OTTOMAN RULE

Under Ottoman rule, Egypt ceased to be the centre of the Mediterranean world and Cairo became just one of numerous provincial capitals ruled from Constantinople. The Turkish sultan Selim "the Grim", so called for his habit of executing his advisers, ruled Egypt and the Mamluks lived on as lords or *beys* still wielding considerable power.

The Ottoman empire reached its peak during the reign of Suleiman the Magnificent, but his death in 1566 heralded a long era of decline for the empire. A succession of weak Ottoman sultans enabled the Mamluks to re-emerge in the mid-17th century as the most powerful force in Egyptian politics. However, internal rivalry and bloody feuding prevented them

Sultan Selim I (1467–1520), also known as Selim "the Grim"

from exploiting power to the full. At the same time, economic decline and recurrent outbreaks of plague further weakened the country.

EUROPE "DISCOVERS" EGYPT

In 1798 Egypt was invaded by a French army under the command of Napoleon Bonaparte. With France and Britain at war, Napoleon saw the occupation of Egypt as a way of threatening British rule in India. The French defeated the Mamluks at the Battle of the Pyramids but this success was short lived. Napoleon's fleet was destroyed at Abu Qir *(see p246)* by the British Navy, led by Admiral Nelson. A declaration of war by the Ottoman sultan followed, and by 1801 the French expedition had come to an end. Their legacy is

TIMELINE

1520–66 Reign of Suleiman the Magnificent

1528 Egypt's first Ottoman mosque (Suleiman Pasha) built at the Citadel

Suleiman the Magnificent

1566 Death of Suleiman the Magnificent

1623 First overt rebellions in Egypt against rule from Constantinople

1650 Mamluks re-emerge as a powerful force

1550   1600   1650

the *Description de l'Egypte*, an exhaustive scientific study of the country which encouraged many other writers and artists to visit Egypt.

MOHAMMED ALI AND HIS HEIRS

In the resulting power vacuum, the Mamluks, Ottoman troops and a contingent of Albanian mercenaries locked horns in a struggle for power which was won, in 1805, by Mohammed Ali, commander of the Albanians. To consolidate his

Mohammed Ali in negotiations with the British, following his threat to overthrow the Ottoman sultan

position he eliminated the threat of the Mamluks by inviting the leading *amirs* to a banquet and having them massacred on the way home. He then began to transform Egypt into an industrialized nation. Bringing agriculture under state control, he built textile plants, shipyards and munitions factories to supply his new Western-style army. After a series of military victories in Greece, Arabia and the Sudan, Mohammed Ali threatened the Ottoman sultan, but was forced to back down after the British intervened and he died in 1849.

The 1811 massacre of the leading Mamluk *amirs* ordered by Viceroy Mohammed Ali

Two successors followed before Khedive Ismail acceded to power. He was determined to transform Egypt into a modern nation and introduced the first national postal service, extending railroad networks throughout the country. His greatest achievement was to preside over the opening of the

19th-century advertisement showing Europeans at Giza

Suez Canal in 1869 *(see pp60–61)*. Such projects were funded by loans from European banking houses at exorbitant rates of interest. As the national debt rose, Ismail was forced to sell the majority of Suez Canal shares to the British and the French.

In 1882, Egyptian army officers led by Colonel Ahmed Orabi staged popular uprisings in an attempt to establish a more independent regime. The breakdown in local order led the British to send in the warships, shelling Alexandria and landing an army of occupation which routed Orabi's forces at Tell al-Kebir.

1719 Plague decimates the population of Egypt

1798 Egypt invaded by Napoleon

1805 Mohammed Ali wins control of Egypt

1882 British troops occupy Egypt

1700 — 1750 — 1800 — 1850

1707 Mamluk power struggle reaches new heights in Cairo

Napoleon Bonaparte

1822 Translation of hieroglyphs by French scholar Champollion

1869 Khedive Ismail opens the Suez Canal

Khedive Ismail

The Construction of the Suez Canal

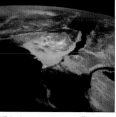

AS EARLY AS THE 7th century BC, the ancient Egyptians had connected the Nile and Red Sea with an east-west canal. A north-south canal, slicing through the Isthmus of Suez to connect the Mediterranean with the Red Sea was first considered in the Middle Ages by Venetian merchants. At the end of the 18th century, Napoleon's engineers took up the idea but dropped it when they mistakenly calculated that one sea was 10 m (33 ft) higher than the other. The canal project was taken up by Ferdinand de Lesseps, the French consul to Egypt, who received the go-ahead during the reign of Khedive Said. Construction began on 25 April 1859.

Statue of Ferdinand de Lesseps

This impressive satellite picture shows how the Suez Canal separates Africa (Egypt) from Asia (Sinai).

THE CANAL ROUTE

This 19th-century painting by Albert Rieger shows how the Suez Canal utilizes lakes as passing places for shipping – Lake Manzila at its northern end, Lake Timsah, and the Bitter Lakes at the mid-point of the canal. This route is 163 km (101 miles) in length.

Rosetta branch of the Nile

Cairo

The Bitter Lakes provided a natural passing point for shipping.

Ferdinand de Lesseps *(1805–94) was a French diplomat descended from a long line of civil servants. It took him 20 years to receive approval for his canal plans.*

Suez remains the most important of Egypt's ports.

Construction *of the canal began in a manner that recalled the great building projects of ancient Egypt. Hampered by a lack of drinking water, huge numbers of labourers worked in awful conditions, aided only by camels with baskets.*

DIGGING THE SUEZ CANAL

At the outset, the building of the canal was largely carried out by hand, but acquiring the 20,000 workers needed each month proved extremely difficult. In addition, fatalities were high, running at about 200 per year, and work was periodically halted by waves of infectious diseases, such as cholera. After five years of construction, the Egyptian government discontinued its supply of unhappily drafted peasant labour and work continued with the use of mechanical diggers and a smaller number of labourers. It took ten years to plough through the 96 km (60 miles) of lake and 64 km (40 miles) of land, but finally, in March 1869, the waters of the Mediterranean flowed into the basins of the Bitter Lakes finally bringing into existence a new sea route between Europe and Asia.

The Cairo Marriott Hotel, built along the lines of Spain's Alhambra as a palace for Empress Eugénie of France, was one of the extravagant projects designed for the opening of the canal.

BUILDING BOOM

The construction of the Suez Canal inspired a building boom in Cairo where grand new buildings, such as the Khedival Apartments on Sharia Emad al-Din, were constructed to house the various dignitaries invited for the opening celebrations. An opera house was erected for their entertainment and a palace (now the Marriott Hotel) built for the guest of honour Empress Eugénie, wife of Napoleon III of France. A tree-lined road, still in use today, was also laid for the Empress's visit to the Pyramids. The canal also resulted in the founding of three new towns – Port Said, Ismailia and Suez.

Ismailia was the headquarters of the Suez Canal Company.

Lake Timsah

Lake Manzila

Port Said is the Mediterranean gateway to the canal.

Inaugural celebrations for the canal began on 17 November 1869. Khedive Ismail, escorting the French Empress Eugénie and Austro-Hungarian Emperor Franz Josef in this painting by Mahmoud Said, offered weeks of lavish hospitality to visiting dignitaries.

AIDA

ICED I V. E. CHILLEAUX

MUSICA DI

G. VERDI

EDIZIONI RICORDI

The opera Aida was written by Giuseppe Verdi for the canal opening. However, it was not completed in time and another Verdi opera, Rigoletto, was performed in its place.

THE SUEZ CRISIS

The cost of building the canal and financing the accompanying lavish celebrations bankrupted Egypt. Ismail was forced to sell his shares and full ownership passed to the French and British who kept control over the canal for the next 80 years. When, in the wake of Egyptian independence, President Nasser nationalized the canal in 1956, Britain and France, in collusion with Israel, invaded the canal zone in an attempt to take it back by force. In the face of widespread international condemnation they were forced to retreat, leaving the canal in Egyptian hands.

President Gamal Abdel Nasser (1918–70)

British troops at Port Said during the 1956 invasion

Early 20th-century photograph of members of the British elite at Shepheard's Hotel in Cairo

the king, Britain still controlled Egypt's legal system, communications, foreign policy and the Suez Canal. During World War II, Egypt was vital to British war aims. At El-Alamein the Eighth Army under Montgomery repulsed Rommel's Afrika Korps, changing the course of the war in North Africa.

BRITISH OCCUPATION

When Egypt's soaring national debt rendered the country unable to repay British loans, Britain invaded. The occupation, motivated by the need to protect British interests in the Suez Canal, was intended as a temporary policing measure. Although the *khedives*, the heirs of Mohammed Ali, remained on the throne, all real power was held by the British.

With the outbreak of World War I in 1914, Britain took an even firmer hold on Egyptian affairs. The demands of the British war effort fell hard on the country's peasants and popular discontent spread. At the end of the war, Egyptian demands for autonomy, led by nationalist leader Saad Zaghloul, were curtly dismissed, causing the 1919 rebellion. The violence of the rebellion forced Britain to proclaim the end of its protectorate and recognize Egypt as an independent state with a hereditary monarch, King Fuad I, sixth son of Khedive Ismail. Despite

Nasser receives a hero's welcome after the successful coup of 1952

1952 REVOLUTION

At the conclusion of the war, the British withdrew most of their soldiers from the country, but new forces in Egyptian politics were demanding nothing less than full independence. The disaster of the 1948 War, in which the Egyptian army was defeated by the newly-formed state of Israel, contributed to the mood for independence. Fuad's son, King Farouk, who was rumoured to have made a fortune by selling faulty equipment to Egyptian troops, was blamed for the disaster. In 1952 Egyptian anger resulted in "Black Saturday", when European businesses in central Cairo were torched by rampaging mobs. Six months of rioting and political instability followed until, on 23 July, a group calling itself the Free Officers, led by Gamal Abdel Nasser, seized power in a bloodless coup. The following year the monarchy was deposed and King Farouk exiled. In June 1956 Egypt was proclaimed a republic and Nasser became the country's first elected president as well as the first native Egyptian to hold power in his own country since the

TIMELINE

Howard Carter exiting the tomb of Tutankhamun

1919 Nationwide anti-British riots

1922 King Fuad I is made king by the British

1922 Howard Carter discovers tomb of Tutankhamun

1935 King Farouk succeeds his father, King Fuad I

1942 Battle of El-Alamein, a turning point in Allied fortunes in WWII

1952 Free Officers seize power, paving the way for an independent republic

| 1900 | 1920 | 1940 |

time of the pharaohs. Nasser's ideology of socialism, allied with Arab nationalism, made him a hero to the masses. During the Suez Crisis of 1956 he took on the combined forces of Britain, France and Israel, who invaded following Nasser's announcement of his intention to nationalize the Suez Canal. The invaders were forced to withdraw after intervention by the United Nations and America.

This golden era for Nasser was brought to an abrupt end in 1967, with the shattering defeat of Egypt in the Six Day War with Israel. Nasser died a broken man three years later.

US President Bill Clinton and President Mubarak of Egypt during Middle East peace talks in 2000

SADAT AND MUBARAK

Nasser's successor was his vice-president, Anwar Sadat. Sadat turned his back on his predecessor's socialist policies and encouraged private and foreign investment. On 6 October 1973, he launched a surprise attack on Israeli lines along the Suez. This early military success, though quickly reversed, paved the way for peace talks that culminated in the signing of the Camp David peace treaty in 1979.

Sadat was assassinated in 1981 by Islamic extremists and was succeeded by his vice-president, Hosni Mubarak. Mubarak inherited an ailing economy caused by overpopulation and lack of arable land. Economic recovery was slow and for much of Mubarak's reign Egypt was ostracized by the other Arab nations because of its peace with Israel. In 1992 Boutros Boutros-Ghali became the first African and Arab Secretary-General of the United Nations, a position he held until 1996.

During the 1990s, Egypt was rocked by Islamist-inspired violence, including fatal attacks on tourists. Visitor numbers plummeted, seriously damaging the economy. Today, however, unrest is largely confined to Middle Egypt. The country still maintains a cool peace with Israel and plays a key role as a peace broker in the Middle East crisis.

Lasers and fireworks illuminate the Giza Pyramids on Millennium night

1956 Newly elected as president, Nasser provokes Suez Crisis

Anwar Sadat (1918–81)

1981 Sadat is assassinated and succeeded by Hosni Mubarak

2000 International coverage of Millennium celebrations at the Pyramids

| 1960 | 1980 | 2000 |

1967 Defeat by Israel in the Six Day War

1970 Nasser dies and is succeeded by Anwar Sadat

1988 Egyptian novelist Naguib Mahfouz wins Nobel Prize for Literature

Naguib Mahfouz

CAIRO
AREA BY AREA

Cairo at a Glance

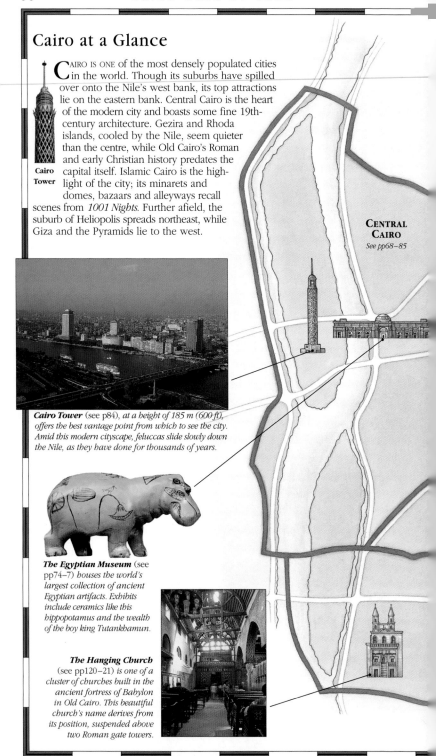

CAIRO IS ONE of the most densely populated cities in the world. Though its suburbs have spilled over onto the Nile's west bank, its top attractions lie on the eastern bank. Central Cairo is the heart of the modern city and boasts some fine 19th-century architecture. Gezira and Rhoda islands, cooled by the Nile, seem quieter than the centre, while Old Cairo's Roman and early Christian history predates the capital itself. Islamic Cairo is the highlight of the city; its minarets and domes, bazaars and alleyways recall scenes from *1001 Nights*. Further afield, the suburb of Heliopolis spreads northeast, while Giza and the Pyramids lie to the west.

Cairo Tower

CENTRAL CAIRO
See pp68–85

Cairo Tower (see p84), *at a height of 185 m (600 ft), offers the best vantage point from which to see the city. Amid this modern cityscape, feluccas slide slowly down the Nile, as they have done for thousands of years.*

The Egyptian Museum (see pp74–7) *houses the world's largest collection of ancient Egyptian artifacts. Exhibits include ceramics like this hippopotamus and the wealth of the boy king Tutankhamun.*

The Hanging Church (see pp120–21) *is one of a cluster of churches built in the ancient fortress of Babylon in Old Cairo. This beautiful church's name derives from its position, suspended above two Roman gate towers.*

◁ **Surrounded by the domes of Fatimid Cairo, the minaret of the Madrassa and Mausoleum of Sultan Qalawun**

Khan al-Khalili (see pp88–90) is an Aladdin's cave of spices, perfumes, jewellery and souvenirs. The bazaar spills over into the nearby areas which, dotted with some superb Mamluk architecture, have buzzed with similar commercial activity since the Middle Ages.

The Mosque of al-Azhar (see p91), at the heart of the Fatimid capital of "Al-Qahira" (Cairo), has been a centre for Islamic scholarship and teaching for more than a thousand years.

ISLAMIC CAIRO
See pp86–111

| 0 metres | 900 |
| 0 yards | 900 |

The Citadel (see pp104–5) was built by Salah ad-Din in the 12th century and crowned with the Mosque of Mohammed Ali 700 years later. This stone fortress dominates Cairo's eastern horizon.

RHODA ISLAND AND OLD CAIRO
See pp112–125

The Mosque of Ibn Tulun (see pp110–11) is said to be Cairo's oldest mosque. Its size and simple geometric shapes give it an air of tranquillity which contrasts nicely with the eclectic collection of the nearby Gayer-Anderson Museum.

CENTRAL CAIRO

WHEN ISMAIL (see p63) acceded to power in 1863, Cairo was an almost medieval city with a street plan little changed in 500 years. But the khedive, educated in France, set about transforming his capital into a modern, fashionable city that could compare with Paris. Rather than try to impose order on the existing city, he

Sculpture outside Opera Complex

chose to drain the marshy flood plains between it and the Nile and start again. His creation is the heart of Central Cairo. Fine 19th-century European architecture – albeit battered and worn – is the backdrop to thoroughly Middle Eastern streetlife, with the placid Nile offering a refuge from the noise and crush of people and cars.

SIGHTS AT A GLANCE

Areas, Streets & Squares
Corniche el-Nil **13**
Garden City **12**
Midan Opera and
    Midan Ataba **7**
Midan Ramses **6**
Midan Tahrir **2**
Sharia Qasr el-Nil **5**
Sharia Talaat Harb **4**
Zamalek **19**

Museums & Historic Buildings
Abdeen Palace Museum **9**
American University in Cairo **3**
Beit as-Sennari **10**
Cairo Tower **17**
Egyptian Museum pp74–7 **1**
Mahmoud Khalil Museum **15**
Manial Palace **14**

Mausoleum of Saad
    Zaghloul **11**
Museum of Islamic Art **8**
Opera House Complex **16**

Walks
River Promenade **18**

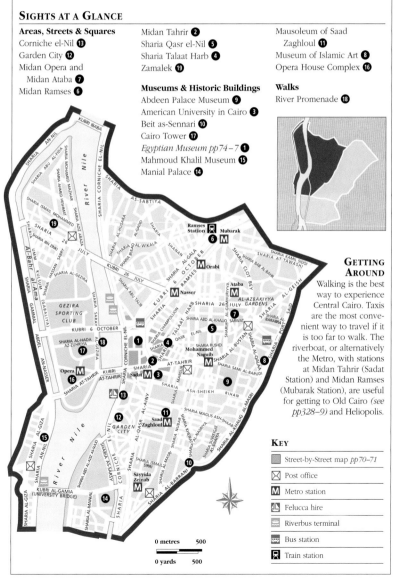

GETTING AROUND

Walking is the best way to experience Central Cairo. Taxis are the most convenient way to travel if it is too far to walk. The riverboat, or alternatively the Metro, with stations at Midan Tahrir (Sadat Station) and Midan Ramses (Mubarak Station), are useful for getting to Old Cairo (see pp328–9) and Heliopolis.

KEY

▨	Street-by-Street map *pp70–71*
⊠	Post office
Ⓜ	Metro station
⚓	Felucca hire
🛥	Riverbus terminal
🚌	Bus station
🚉	Train station

0 metres   500
0 yards   500

◁ **The faded grandeur of a typical apartment balcony near Midan Ataba (see p78)**

Street-by-Street: Around Midan Tahrir

O VERRUN BY TRAFFIC and far from pretty, Midan Tahrir is the hub of Central Cairo. All routes lead here and within just a few days most visitors become very familiar with its Brutalist landmarks: the Nile Hilton Hotel, the Arab League Building and the Mogamma, home to 18,000 bureaucrats. Brighter spots include the dusky pink Egyptian Museum and the elegant curve of façades between Sharia Qasr el-Nil and Sharia Talaat Harb – the location of airline offices, travel agents, souvenir shops and cafés.

Ramses Station

Bus Station

SHARIA RAMSES

SHARIA CHAMPOLLION

KUBRI 6 OCTOBER

Central Cairo
Cairo's bustling modern centre is flanked to the west by the tranquil waters of the Nile.

Zamalek

CORNICHE EL-NIL

★ **Egyptian Museum**
The museum has the greatest collection of Pharaonic treasures in the world and is one of Cairo's most popular sights ❶

The Nile Hilton Hotel *(see p72)* was built in 1959 and was the first modern hotel to be erected in Egypt.

| 0 metres | 130 |
| 0 yards | 130 |

Gezira

Corniche el-Nil
This boat-lined boulevard is wide and shady and the city's favourite place for an evening stroll ❸

KEY

— — — Suggested route

STAR SIGHTS

★ **Egyptian Museum**

Groppi's café (see p72)

LOCATOR MAP
See Street Finder Map 5

Sharia Qasr el-Nil
The shops along Qasr el-Nil are filled with glitzy paraphernalia. The street is situated in the heart of the financial district where some fine architecture can still be seen **5**

Felfela restaurant (see p283)

Sharia Talaat Harb
Central Cairo's main street is a bustling, thoroughfare filled with colourful hoardings, shops and cafés **4**

Midan Tahrir
The cafés located on the south and east sides of Midan Tahrir are ideal spots to break during sightseeing or to simply sit and people-watch **2**

Mogamma Building

Omar Makram Mosque

Semiramis Intercontinental Hotel (see p265)

The Arab League Building, meeting place for Arab world leaders.

American University in Cairo
Housed in a Neo-Islamic style building, the American University is a prestigious educational establishment attended by wealthy young Egyptians and foreigners **3**

Two Cairenes, dressed in traditional garments called *galabiyyas*, in Midan Tahrir

Egyptian Museum ❶

See pp74–7.

Midan Tahrir ❷

Map 5 B4. Ⓜ *Sadat.*

MIDAN TAHRIR was not always the dauntingly urban square that it is today. Until the 19th century, the area was a swampy plain, flooded each summer by the Nile. When Khedive Ismail (1863–79) came to power, however, he had the land drained as part of his grand scheme to transform Cairo by building a European-style city of tree-lined boulevards and grand public squares.

The Qasr el-Nil (Palace of the Nile) was built beside the river, fronted by an extensive plaza named Midan Ismailia (Ismail's Square). However, Ismail's glory was short-lived: his ambitious scheme drained not only the swamps, but also the state coffers, as Egyptian debt to European lenders spiralled out of control.

In 1882, the British stepped in to take control *(see p59)*, requisitioning Qasr el-Nil as their headquarters, and later as the barracks for their army of occupation. Overcrowded with Allied soldiers during World War II, the building gained a reputation for the remarkable tenacity of its bedbugs. The barracks were evacuated at the end of the war and the palace was demolished. In 1959, the Nile Hilton Hotel was built on the site – the first modern international hotel to be built in Egypt. The

1952 revolution saw all traces of the old regime wiped away, including the name of Ismail, and the largest square in the city was reincarnated as Midan Tahrir (Liberation Square).

Midan Tahrir is the closest Cairo gets to having a centre, and several major airlines have their offices here, along with tourist agencies, the Omar Makram Mosque which serves as a venue for state funerals, and the enormous monolithic structure of the Mogamma Building. Housing around 18,000 civil servants, this is where foreign tourists have to go if they need to extend their visas.

American University in Cairo ❸

Qasr al-Aini, Midan Tahrir. **Map** 5 B4.
Ⓜ *Sadat.* ◯ *8:30am–5pm Sun–Thur, 10:30am–5pm Sat.*

ALTHOUGH overshadowed by an ugly concrete wing, the core building of what is now the American University in Cairo (AUC) is built in an attractive Neo-Islamic style. Originally erected as a palatial residence for an Egyptian aristocrat, it next housed a cigarette factory before being taken over by the Cairo University and then the AUC. Attending the private AUC is Egypt's equivalent of an Ivy-

Flags fly above the Neo-Islamic façade of the American University

League education and beyond the means of most Egyptians. Visitors are admitted, on proof of identity, to the excellent bookstore and art exhibitions in the Sony Gallery.

Shar Hashamaim Synagogue, near Sharia Talaat Harb

Sharia Talaat Harb ❹

Map 5 C3. Ⓜ *Sadat.*

RUNNING FROM Midan Tahrir to Midan Orabi, Sharia Talaat Harb is quintessential modern Cairo. Its pavements are permanently crowded and the road is jammed with horn-honking traffic. As you walk along, music blares from cars on one side and shops on the other, while the air is heavy with car fumes mingled with the smells of cooking and incense. Rising above this pandemonium is some grand architecture, especially around Midan Talaat Harb, where Parisian-style buildings dwarf the statue of Talaat Harb, founder of the National Bank.

On the square is **Groppi's**, a tearoom that once supplied confectionery to the royalty of Great Britain; the only clues to its more glamorous past are the delightful, spangly mosaics around the entrance. More memories of a golden era now past are evoked by the Art Deco lines of the

PARIS BY THE NILE

Inspired by Baron Haussmann's plans for the modernization of Paris in the mid-19th century, Khedive Ismail turned to foreign architects to realize his dream of a modern Cairo. Drawing on Renaissance, Baroque and even Gothic styles, their buildings were adorned with wrought-iron grilles, plaster mouldings, carved foliage, cherubs and angels, plus some local flavouring in the form of scarabs and sphinxes. Later buildings began to take more account of Egypt's heritage, incorporating Islamic motifs such as striped stonework and crenellations. Downtown streets, including Qasr el-Nil and the intersecting Mohammed Farid and Emad ad-Din, still contain a wealth of these beautiful buildings.

Kubri Qasr el-Nil (Qasr el-Nil Bridge), part of the European-style Cairo planned by Khedive Ismail

---

Metro Cinema, which opened in 1939 with *Gone With the Wind*. It now screens low-budget action movies – fun to attend for the experience of Egyptian cinema-going, where the bad guys are dispatched to a round of applause.

Little mention is made, in the current climate of Arab-Israeli tension, of Egypt's own Jewish community. However, in Sharia Adly (which joins Sharia Talaat Harb beside the Metro Cinema) the Babylonian-style Shar Hashamaim Synagogue is evidence of their historical presence. It can only be viewed from the outside.

Talaat Harb terminates in another elegant square, named after the nationalist politician Ahmed Orabi who sought political reform in 1881. Off to the east is pedestrianized Sharia Alfy, full of small bars and restaurants, including the excellent Alfy Bey *(see p282)*.

Sharia Qasr el-Nil ⑤

Map 5.C3. **M** *Sadat.*

A FRENETICALLY BUSY shopping street running in front of the Nile Hilton Hotel in Midan Tahrir to Midan Opera, Qasr el-Nil is taken up almost exclusively with shop windows that display the brightest and gaudiest of goods. The streets on either side of Sharia Qasr el-Nil traditionally constituted Cairo's financial district. At the junction with Sharia ash-Sharif is the National Bank of Egypt building. Here, too, is the Bourse, or stock exchange, which is enjoying a new lease of life since the government undertook a programme of privatization in the late 1990s.

Statue of Mustafa Kamel overlooking his square

The boom in trading was reflected in a renovation programme that covered a huge 60,000-sq m (645,000-sq ft) section of downtown Cairo. The area around the Bourse has been pedestrianized and many of the roads are now paved. These walkways are also furnished with 19th-century-style lamp posts, along with flower beds, greenery and palm trees. Some of the buildings in this area have also been renovated, including the lovely Trieste Insurance Building on the corner with Sharia Sherif. This was designed by the Italian architect Antonio Lascaic (1856–1946), who was responsible for many of central Cairo's most beautiful Belle Epoque buildings.

Sharia Qasr el-Nil crosses over Midan Mustafa Kamel, named after the founder of the Egyptian Nationalist Party, formed in 1907. Kamel was an early opponent of British occupation and his statue looks out over the square.

Sharia Qasr el-Nil continues past some jewellers' shops and a few outlets selling street signs (you can have your name put on one) to emerge on Sharia al-Gumhuriyya. This leads into Midan Opera *(see p78)*, which was once one of Cairo's grandest squares, but is now occupied by a vast car park and the derelict Continental-Savoy hotel.

Small fruit stall set up in an alleyway off Sharia Talaat Harb

Egyptian Museum ●

Gold bracelet from Tanis

Founded by a frenchman, Auguste Mariette (1821–81), Egypt's first national museum of Pharaonic antiquities opened in 1863. It quickly outgrew two homes before settling in the present purpose-built premises in 1902. More than 120,000 items are on display, with another 150,000 reputedly stored in the basement. Pride of the collection are the artifacts recovered from Tutankhamun's tomb but there are excellent pieces from every period of ancient Egyptian history, from the Narmer Palette, dating from around 3100 BC, through to the haunting Graeco-Roman Fayoum Portraits of the 2nd century AD.

Gallery Guide
The museum has two floors. Artifacts on the ground floor are organized in a roughly chronological order, running clockwise from the entrance and atrium, while the first-floor collection is arranged by themes. The central hall houses large monumental statuary.

Royal Tombs of Tanis

Middle Kingdom Models

Yuya and Thuyu collection

Animal mummies

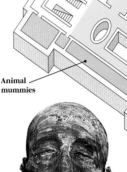

Prince Rahotep and Nofret
These life-like limestone statues (c.2620 BC) were found in their mastaba *(tomb-chapel) near the Meidum Pyramid (see p164).*

★ **Royal Mummy Room**
In respectful silence, the mummies lie in state, arranged chronologically around the room in an anti-clockwise order.

First floor

Ground floor

Triad of Menkaure

Entrance

★ **Statue of Ka-Aper**
This skilfully carved statue's eyes have rims made of copper, whites of opaque quartz and corneas of clear rock crystal, drilled and filled with black paste.

Star Exhibits

★ **Tutankhamun Galleries**

★ **Royal Mummy Room**

★ **Amarna Room**

★ **Statue of Ka-Aper**

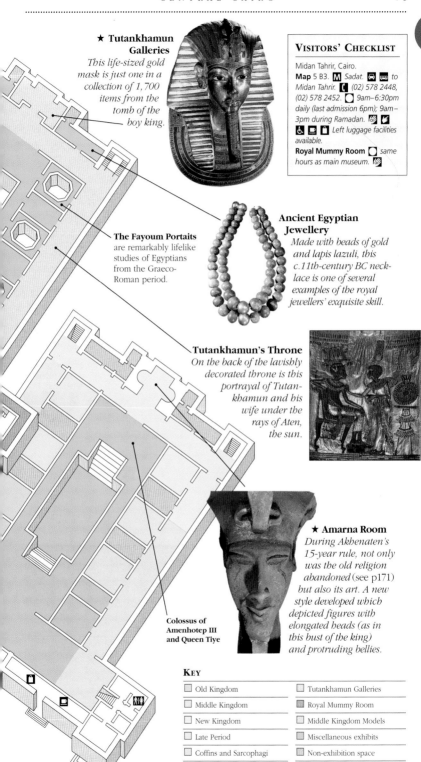

★ **Tutankhamun Galleries**
This life-sized gold mask is just one in a collection of 1,700 items from the tomb of the boy king.

VISITORS' CHECKLIST

Midan Tahrir, Cairo.
Map 5 B3. Ⓜ *Sadat.* 🚌 🚐 *to Midan Tahrir.* 📞 *(02) 578 2448, (02) 578 2452.* 🕐 *9am–6:30pm daily (last admission 6pm); 9am–3pm during Ramadan.* ♿ 📷 🔇 💺 📖 📦 *Left luggage facilities available.*
Royal Mummy Room 🕐 *same hours as main museum.* 🔇

The Fayoum Portaits
are remarkably lifelike studies of Egyptians from the Graeco-Roman period.

Ancient Egyptian Jewellery
Made with beads of gold and lapis lazuli, this c.11th-century BC necklace is one of several examples of the royal jewellers' exquisite skill.

Tutankhamun's Throne
On the back of the lavishly decorated throne is this portrayal of Tutan-khamun and his wife under the rays of Aten, the sun.

★ **Amarna Room**
During Akhenaten's 15-year rule, not only was the old religion abandoned (see p171) but also its art. A new style developed which depicted figures with elongated heads (as in this bust of the king) and protruding bellies.

Colossus of Amenhotep III and Queen Tiye

KEY

☐ Old Kingdom	☐ Tutankhamun Galleries
☐ Middle Kingdom	☐ Royal Mummy Room
☐ New Kingdom	☐ Middle Kingdom Models
☐ Late Period	☐ Miscellaneous exhibits
☐ Coffins and Sarcophagi	☐ Non-exhibition space

Exploring the Egyptian Museum

Tuya's golden funeral mask

W HILE NOT PARTICULARLY large, the museum is densely packed with artifacts and anybody with more than a passing interest in ancient Egypt will need more than one visit to take everything in. When the museum is busy, long queues can form outside the room holding Tutankhamun's funeral mask. To view the mask at some leisure, it is best to visit the museum just as it opens or late in the afternoon and make straight for the Tutankhamun Galleries, visiting the rest of the museum afterwards. Independent guides tout for business at the entrance to the museum and, as the labelling inside is sparse, it may be worthwhile hiring one.

Wall frieze, known as the Meidum Geese, painted on plaster (c.2620 BC)

OLD KINGDOM

A LL THE MUSEUM'S great pieces of monumental statuary are housed on the ground floor. These start in the museum's atrium with King Djoser's empty-eyed statue carved in limestone nearly 5,000 years ago. It was discovered at Saqqara *(see pp158–160)* in his *serdab*, a small sealed room beside his Step Pyramid. Other Old Kingdom highlights on the ground floor include a statue of Khafre, builder of the middle pyramid at Giza, in Room 42. He is seated on his throne with the wings of the falcon god Horus wrapped protectively around his head, symbolizing the divine sanction of the king's rule (the term *pharaoh* was rarely used before 1500 BC). Also in Room 42, the figure of Ka-Aper, a 5th-Dynasty official, puts his left foot forward in a stylized pose that suggests movement and, along with his gleaming eyes, brings the statue to life. Further examples of the vitality of the ancient artists are exhibited in Room 32 in the lifelike, seated

statues of Prince Rahotep and Princess Nofret, whose real hairline can be seen poking out from under her wig, and in the carefully observed Meidum Geese panels, which were discovered at Fayoum *(see p158)*. Room 37 contains a touchingly personal collection of alabaster ornaments and bedroom furniture, including a golden four-poster bed, an armchair and a jewellery box all of which belonged to Hetepheres, the mother of

Khufu, builder of the Great Pyramid. The room also contains an alabaster canopic chest that was used to store the internal organs of the deceased. The chest was found in Hetepheres's tomb at Giza, with the remains of its contents still visible.

NEW KINGDOM

A NCIENT EGYPT's New Kingdom represented an artistic golden age, but many of the best pieces are housed at the Luxor Museum *(see p183)*. However, Room 3 contains fine artifacts from Amarna, the short-lived capital of the 'heretic king' Akhenaten *(see p171)*. Here, the sleek muscular forms of traditional Pharaonic art are replaced by swollen bellies, heavy thighs and almost cartoon-like elongated faces. This is particularly evident on a set of reliefs showing the king and his young family worshipping the sun god, Aten, whose solar rays end in strange hook-like hands.

Head of Queen Nefertiti (c.1340 BC)

One of the notable exceptions to this style is an unfinished, sculpted head of Nefertiti, Akhenaten's wife, which displays a stunning and wholly human beauty.

18th-Dynasty relief of Amenhotep III riding over bound Nubian captives

Tutankhamun's carved throne inlaid with gold and ebony

TUTANKHAMUN GALLERIES

COMMENCING WITH the two life-size statues of the young king that stood guard at the entrance to his tomb, the Tutankhamun Galleries fill the upper floor's east and north wings. There are some 1,700 items on display, ranging from board games and hunting implements to couches and beds and, of course, the fabulous death mask. A great glass cabinet is filled with some of Tutankhamun's *shabtis*. These were small effigies of the deceased that were buried with the body to carry out any tasks that the deceased might be asked to do in the afterlife. In all, 413 *shabtis* were found in the tomb; one for each day of the year, plus foremen. Nearby is the dazzling royal "lion" throne, named after the golden lion heads and legs on each side. Aside from the craftsmanship, this throne is of great interest in that it reveals influences of the "Amarna period" when the Aten cult still thrived *(see p171)*. The Aten sun-disk and rays resemble reliefs from Amarna, and the pharaoh's name from this period, Tutankhaten, is inscribed on the back of the throne.

In the north wing is the alabaster canopic chest holding four jars with Tutankhamun-head stoppers. This stands in front of Room 3, which holds Tutankhamun's solid gold death mask and the two inner coffins, one of gilded wood set with semi-precious gems, the other cast of solid gold. The young king's body lies in its tomb in the Valley of the Kings on the west bank of the Nile.

MIDDLE KINGDOM MODELS

THE DAILY LIFE of the less-exalted ancient Egyptian is well illustrated in several rooms in the west wing, which hold finely detailed 11th-Dynasty models of domestic scenes. These include a weaver's workshop, a house with a garden and pool and a set of seated scribes recording their master's cattle. The models provide a wealth of detailed information about Egyptian life, as well as reflecting an interest in factual artistic representation. These models were found in a tomb at Deir al-Bahri on the west bank at Thebes *(see pp192–3)*.

ROYAL MUMMY ROOM

THERE IS A SEPARATE fee to see the mummies, which is payable at the ticket desk at the top of the southeast stairs. This allows the experience of coming face to face with some legendary kings such as Tuthmosis II, Seti I and the mighty Ramses II. The good condition of the bodies belies the fact that they all died more than 3,000 years ago. The beak-nosed face of Ramses II barely resembles his sleek bust downstairs in the New Kingdom galleries.

Model servant girl (c.2010 BC)

One of Tutankh-amun's gilded fans

MISCELLANEOUS EXHIBITS

IN ADDITION to the human mummies, the museum holds a fascinating collection of neatly parcelled animals in Rooms 53 and 54. The ancient Egyptians revered certain animals, for example the ibis and baboon were sacred to the god Thoth, the crocodile sacred to Sobek, and cats sacred to Bastet. In the regions where these cults thrived, great numbers of these mummified creatures have been unearthed at sanctuaries associated with such gods. Most recently, tombs full of thousands of mummified birds were discovered at Saqqara.

Across the hall, in Room 43, are 18th-Dynasty funerary artifacts from the tomb of Yuya and Tuya, the great grandparents of Tutankhamun who were buried on the west bank at Thebes. Discovered in 1905, the tomb is overshadowed by Tutankhamun and his treasures, the beautiful sarcophagi and other lustrous items here undeservedly ignored by most visitors.

Better known are the Graeco-Roman funerary paintings known as Fayoum Portraits, after the oasis where many of them were discovered *(see pp164–5)*; Room 14 contains a collection of these haunting faces, along with some of the mummies to which they were attached.

Two relatively new galleries devoted to the Royal Tombs of Tanis and Ancient Egyptian Jewellery contain some of the museum's finest small pieces. Tanis was a major city in the Delta during the 21st and 22nd Dynasties *(see p233)*. In 1939 archaeologists found a series of intact royal tombs that contained a marvellous haul of death masks, coffins and intricate jewellery. One of the items, the coffin of Psusennes I is interesting not just for its striking hawk's head but also for the fact that it is made of solid silver. Rare in Egypt, silver had to be imported, making it a highly prized commodity.

Midan Ramses ❻

Map 2 D3. Ⓜ *Mubarak.*

MARKING THE northernmost extent of central Cairo, Midan Ramses is the gateway to the city. In ancient times, when the river followed a different course, a port here served the Pharaonic city of Heliopolis. When Salah ad-Din (Saladin), ruler of Egypt, refortified Cairo in the 12th century, he built a great gate here, the Bab al-Hadid, or Iron Gate, which remained standing until 1847, when it was demolished to make way for the new railway station.

Mahattat Ramses (Ramses Station) is still Cairo's main rail terminus and the place to catch trains for all destinations, such as Alexandria, Aswan and Luxor. The **Egyptian National Railway Museum**, housed at the eastern end of the station, has a fascinating collection of engines, ornate carriages and numerous models and plans.

Standing in the centre of the square, but dwarfed by a massive six-lane flyover, the colossus of Ramses II is a replica of one found in the 1950s at Memphis. Until as recently as the late 1990s, the original colossus stood here, but the authorities finally acknowledged that the intense pollution must be damaging the ancient statue. The 9-m (30-ft) high colossus has now been returned to where it was found, for display in a new, open-air museum at Memphis.

🏛 **Egyptian National Railway Museum**
Midan Ramses. **Map** 2 D3.
Ⓜ *Mubarak.* 🄲 *(02) 576 3793.*
◯ *8am–2pm Tue–Sun.* 📷

Replica pink, granite colossus of Ramses II in Midan Ramses

Former Tiring department store designed by Oscar Horowitz in 1911, Midan Ataba

Midan Opera and Midan Ataba ❼

Map 6 D2 & E2. Ⓜ *Ataba.*

IN JUST FIVE MONTHS in 1868, labour gangs constructed a completely new opera house for the inaugural celebrations marking the opening of the Suez Canal. To mark the occasion, the Italian composer Giuseppe Verdi had been commissioned to write a new opera, *Aida,* but he was unable to finish it in time, so the new Cairo Opera House opened instead with a performance of Verdi's *Rigoletto.*

Modelled on Milan's La Scala and built entirely of wood, the Opera House was the loveliest landmark in central Cairo – until it was burnt to the ground in 1971. A less lovely multistorey car park was built on the site, but the square is still known as Midan Opera. In the middle of the paved plaza is a statue of Ibrahim Pasha (1789–1848), general and viceroy of Egypt, who successfully campaigned in Syria in 1832–3.

Just beyond Midan Opera is Midan Ataba, which forms a dividing point between so-called "European" Cairo to the west and the old medieval city, known as Islamic Cairo, to the east. From this point, the streets get narrower, the buildings smaller and more decrepit. The square itself is a knot of snarled traffic, but in the surrounding streets are various markets. To the northwest is an extensive area of secondhand bookstalls; there is a clothing market to the northeast, electronics to the southeast and, in the southwest, a few stalls sell cards and stationery. The latter run, appropriately enough, in front of the central post office, an old building with an attractive courtyard and an annexe where the **National Postal Museum** is housed. Egypt was one of the first countries in the world to issue stamps (1866) and although the museum is small, there is a lot crammed into the space, including models of carriages and delivery bikes, old mail boxes and a vast collection of stamps.

Also on Midan Ataba is the **Cairo Puppet Theatre** which puts on regular colourful puppet shows for children and adults.

Ibrahim Pasha's statue, Midan Opera

🏛 **National Postal Museum**
Midan Ataba. Ⓜ *Ataba.*
◯ *9am–1pm Sat–Thu.*

📺 **Cairo Puppet Theatre**
Midan Ataba. Ⓜ *Ataba.* 🄲 *(02) 591 0954.* ◯ *Oct–May: show at 11am Tue–Sun, also 6:30pm Thu & Fri.*

Clothes stall in front of mosque in Midan Ataba

Museum of Islamic Art ❽

Sharia Port Said. **Map** 6 E3. **M** Mohammed Naguib. **C** (02) 390 9930. **O** 8:30am–4pm daily (9am–3pm Ramadan). **●** 11:30am–1pm Fri.

OFTEN OVERLOOKED by the crowds that throng the Egyptian Museum, this little-visited place contains some beautiful pieces of medieval decorative art salvaged from the houses, mosques and palaces of Islamic Cairo at the instigation of Khedive Tawfiq. Most striking of all are the large *mashrabiyya* screens, which are constructed of thousands of individual pieces of wood. Still seen today in many old buildings, such screens shaded rooms from the sun, at the same time admitting cooling breezes. They were also important as they allowed the women of the house to look out without themselves being seen.

The museum houses other examples of creative wood-working taken from mosques around the city, including huge ivory-inlaid doors, carved friezes and a fine 14th-century *minbar* (pulpit).

Three ornamental fountains provide the best examples of another speciality of Egyptian craftsmen – inlaid stone and marblework. These pieces, dating from the Mamluk and Ottoman periods, would have decorated the reception halls

Cannon yard of the Abdeen Palace Museum

of rich merchants' houses. Look out, also, for enamelled glass lamps displayed in one of the rooms; these beautiful objects, many of which are decorated with stylized Arabic lettering, would have been suspended by chains from the ceilings of mosques. Other exhibits include Persian and Turkish ceramics, illuminated manuscripts and books, and a number of carpets and rugs.

Abdeen Palace Museum ❾

Sharia al-Gamaa. **Map** 6 D4. **M** Mohammed Naguib. **C** (02) 391 0042. **O** 10am–2pm Sat–Thu (10am–1pm Ramadan).

ABDEEN IS a former royal palace, part of which is now open to the public as a museum that embraces several collections. These include displays of weaponry,

presidential gifts, royal acquisitions and silver plate.

From the time of Salah ad-Din in the 12th century, Egypt was ruled from the safety of the Citadel (*see pp104–7*), but tradition was broken 700 years later by Khedive Ismail, who ordered a new European-style residence to be built on the edge of his new city. Designed by the French architect Rousseau, the 500-roomed palace was begun in 1863 and took over ten years to complete. Over the years, it was constantly remodelled and expanded, with the addition, in the 1930s, of a Byzantine throne room.

Following the overthrow of King Farouk in 1952, the Abdeen Palace was vacated, but later put to its present use as a venue for receiving visiting heads of state.

In the late 1980s, President Mubarak ordered that the Palace be restored. The work took longer than anticipated because the palace was hit by the earthquake that shook Egypt in 1992. The museum was eventually inaugurated by the president in 1998.

Entered via neat gardens at the rear of the palace, the museum occupies a complex of unadorned halls; the more extravagantly decorated state rooms remain off-limits to the public. A lot of space is given over to the collection of guns, swords and daggers, many of which were gifts to Egypt's various khedives, kings and presidents. There are also displays of medals and other decorations, as well as a room of awards and gifts presented to President Mubarak. A silver-ware section contains a display of silver, crystal and *objets d'art* belonging to the family of Pasha Mohammed Ali.

Centrally located in the museum is the fountain court-yard, where the fountain is surrounded by the busts of Mohammed Ali, Khedive Ismail and King Fuad I.

Entrance to Abdeen Palace, museum and gardens

Beit as-Sennari 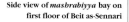❿

Harat Monge, off Sharia Khayrat.
Map 4 D2. ☎ *(02) 391 5565.* Ⓜ *Saad Zaghloul.* ◯ *9:30am–3pm Sat–Wed.*

NAPOLEON INVADED Egypt in 1798, bringing with him an army of scientists, scholars and artists to establish a French cultural base in the country. Over the next few years, they carried out the first European study of Egypt and published their findings in the *Description de l'Egypte (see p20).*

This *beit* (house), which was built in 1794 for Ibrahim Katkhuda as-Sennari, an occultist from Sudan, was requisitioned by Napoleon and housed many of his artists during the occupation. It has some fine wooden *mashrabiyya* screens, an attractive court-yard and a well-preserved complex of rooms. After extensive renov-ation, the house has reopened as the Institute for Applied Arts, with displays of glass-ware, textiles, and pottery and other work by local artists.

Side view of *mashrabiyya* bay on first floor of Beit as-Sennari

Mausoleum of Saad Zaghloul ⓫

Sharia Mansour. **Map** 5 B5. Ⓜ *Saad Zaghloul.*

SAAD ZAGHLOUL (1853–1927) spent most of his life trying to get the British out of Egypt. He became a national spokes-man for self-rule and held the post of prime minister for a time. Zaghloul was highly respected, even by the foreign governors he opposed, and shortly after his death this vast mausoleum was erected in his honour. Built of granite, the mausoleum's design echoes that of a Pharaonic temple, with an outward-curving cornice and entrance flanked by two great lotus pillars.

Elegant, curving façade of a building in Garden City flanked by tree-lined pavements

It is also possible to visit Zaghloul's house, **Beit al-Umma** (House of the Nation), which is just a short distance west. Most of the rooms have been preserved with Zaghloul's original furnishings and belongings still in place.

🏛 **Beit al-Umma**
Sharia Darih Zaghloul. Ⓜ *Sadat.* ◯ *daily.* 🎫

Garden City ⓬

Map 5 A5. Ⓜ *Sadat.*

GARDEN CITY, one of the most attractive and tranquil of Cairo's quarters, was created by the British in the early years of the 20th century as a leafy green suburb, where officers and administrators could pretend they were still living in rural England, far from the dusty, dry streets of Cairo. The roads were designed to curve and wind like country lanes but, instead of England's oaks and beeches, leafy coverage was provided by native palms, rubber and mango trees.

As well as housing the British, the villas of this exclusive suburb were home to Egypt's most prominent doctors, lawyers, bankers and politicians.

Today, Garden City suffers from an onslaught of concrete high-rise buildings, but it remains a very desirable address: the British, American and several other embassies are located here. Garden City still offers a welcome respite from the hustle of Cairo, and a walk through the area reveals a wonderfully eclectic array of architecture, including the building known as **Grey Pillars** – the British Army's headquarters in Egypt during World War II. This can still be seen on Sharia as-Suraya.

Corniche el-Nil ⓭

Map 5 A4. Ⓜ *Sadat.*

ALTHOUGH IT is one of the city's busiest highways, the Corniche el-Nil is also where Cairo comes to relax. In a city chronically short of public green spaces, this is as

View across the Nile from the Corniche north of Rhoda Island

◁ **Sharia Ramses and Kubri 6 October winding their way into the heart of Downtown Cairo**

close as it gets to a park. Each evening, the wide pavements of the Corniche are packed with promenading families, roaming college kids, and young lovers, all enjoying the pleasant water-borne breezes and the sense of open space that the river provides.

An even better way to enjoy the river is on a *felucca*, one of the small triangular-sailed boats used on the Nile since antiquity. The boats (which can be hired by the hour) and their captains gather at various landing stages, including one opposite the Semiramis Hotel and another at Dokdok, opposite the northern tip of Rhoda Island. Lazily scudding about the river while the sun drops towards the skyline makes for a calming end to a hectic day of sightseeing.

Regnault's painting of a fleeing Mamluk, in the Manial Palace

Manial Palace ⑭

Sharia al-Saray, Rhoda. **Map** 3 B2.
█ (02) 531 5587. Ⓜ *Sayyida Zeinab*. ◯ 8:30am–4pm daily.

L OCATED ON the northern tip of the island of Rhoda, the Manial Palace is a former royal residence, now open to the public. It was built for Prince Mohammed Ali Tawfiq, a descendant of Egypt's famed ruler Mohammed Ali, and the uncle of King Farouk. The palace was constructed between 1899 and 1929 and is a curious ensemble of five separate buildings, executed in a variety of Islamic styles.

Façade of Cairo's Mahmoud Khalil Museum

Beside the mock-Medieval gateway is a Moorish tower attached to the Turkish-tiled Mosque of Mohammed Ali. Nearby, the building called the Hunting Museum has a somewhat grim display of over 300 mounted gazelle heads strung along its narrow gallery.

The eccentrically contrived design extends to the interiors. The Main Residence is a series of rooms decorated in a mixture of styles. The Syrian room has an elaborately painted wooden ceiling, an Ottoman room is furnished with turquoise ceramics from Anatolia, while the Egyptian corner has windows featuring *mashrabiyya* screens. Also included among the valuable displays is a painting of a Mamluk and his mount leaping over the Citadel walls. The painting, by Henri Regnault (1843–71), hangs in the Blue Salon, and depicts an alleged incident that took place during Mohammed Ali's suppression of the Mamluks' 1826 revolt.

Behind the residence, through the banyans, palms and Indian rubber trees, is the Throne Hall, complete with red carpet, sunburst ceiling and portraits of the prince's illustrious forebears. While Prince Mohammed Ali Tawfiq never attained the throne of Egypt, he was able to hold his own court of aristocratic friends here at Manial Palace.

Detail of Mohammed Ali Mosque, Manial Palace

Mahmoud Khalil Museum ⑮

1 Sharia Kafour, off Sharia Giza.
Map 1 A4. █ (02) 336 2358, (02) 336 2359. Ⓜ *Doqqi*.
◯ 10am–5:30pm Tue–Sun.

I T MAY COME as a surprise to learn that Cairo has a fine collection of Impressionist paintings. They were amassed by Mohammed Mahmoud Khalil (1876–1953), a devout Francophile and patron of the arts, and an important figure on the political scene during the 1930s and 40s. Khalil bequeathed his art collection to the state, along with the house – a beautiful late-19th-century Parisian-style mansion overlooking the Nile.

Khalil's paintings were removed when the house was taken over as the official residence during Sadat's term as Egyptian president (1970–81). In the early 1990s, after the assassination of Sadat, however, the house was refurbished and returned to the public domain.

The paintings are now on show in cool, temperature-controlled rooms and include three floors of works by Corot, Degas, Ingres, Millet, Monet, Pissarro, Renoir, Sisley and Toulouse-Lautrec. Pride of place goes to Gauguin's *La Vie et la Mort* and Van Gogh's *Genêts et Coquelicots*.

Sculpture in the grounds of the Opera House Complex

Opera House Complex ⑯

Sharia at-Tahrir, Gezira. **Map** 1 A5.
Ⓜ Gezira. Ⓒ (02) 739 8144.

A GIFT TO EGYPT from Japan, the Opera House Complex was opened in 1988, replacing the original Opera House, which burned down in 1971 (*see p78*). At the heart of the complex is the **New Cairo Opera House**, where a busy programme of classical music and dance, including visits from international performers such as the Bolshoi Ballet, is staged (*see pp300–01*).

Situated across the lawn, the **Museum of Egyptian Modern Art** displays the work of Egyptian artists since 1908. One who deserves far greater recognition than he is currently given is Mahmoud Said (1897–1964) (*see p240*), whose use of warm, glowing colours and subject matter of dignified, proud *fellaheen* (peasants) is reminiscent of the Mexican artist Diego Rivera (1897–1964). Several of Said's paintings are displayed in the

museum. There are two more art galleries within the grounds: the Nile Gallery and the Hanager Gallery, which both host changing exhibitions of contemporary work.

🏛 **Museum of Egyptian Modern Art**
Opera House Complex, Gezira.
Ⓜ Gezira. Ⓒ (02) 736 6665.
◯ 10am–1pm, 5–9pm daily. 📷

Cairo Tower ⑰

Sharia Hadayek el Zuhreya. **Map** 1 B5.
Ⓜ Gezira. Ⓒ (02) 735 7187.
◯ 8am–midnight daily. 📷

THE SOUTHERN half of Gezira (the Arabic word for "island") is almost completely flat, making it the ideal site for the 185-m (610-ft) Cairo Tower, which affords excellent views of the city. Built in the late 1950s, the tower takes the form of a latticework tube that fans out slightly at the top, supposedly in imitation of the lotus blossom. From the top, it is possible to make out the easternmost extent of Cairo, where the dark grey buildings run up against the cliff face of the Muqattam Hills. Looking to the west, the Pyramids mark the limits of the city and the start of the desert while, directly below, the Nile flows serenely north to the Mediterranean, slicing Cairo in two.

The best time to come up here is at sunset, when millions of lights twinkle into life, accompanied by the haunting evening call to prayer.

River Promenade ⑱

Gezira. **Map** 1 B5. Ⓜ Gezira.

NEWLY CREATED in the late 1990s, Gezira's river promenade is a wide paved avenue down by the Nile, with fine views of the central city skyline opposite. The promenade starts at the foot of the elegant Qasr el-Nil Bridge, which was designed and built by Dorman Long & Co., the British architects responsible for Australia's Sydney Harbour Bridge. The promenade will eventually extend to Zamalek, in the northern part of the island.

Between the promenade and the main road is the small, neat **Andalusian Garden**, with lawns, benches and an obelisk from Heliopolis. A small admission charge keeps out the crowds. On the street beside the garden, *hantours* (also called *caleches*) wait for hire. A quick spin in one of these horse-drawn black carriages is a fine way to see the

Horse-drawn carriage (hantour) for hire on the River Promenade

island – but expect to pay inflated prices for the pleasure.

Moored off the promenade is a string of former Nile cruisers, most of which have now been converted into upmarket floating restaurants and bars (*see pp282–4*).

Zamalek ⑲

Gezira. **Map** 1 A3. 🚌

OCCUPYING THE northern half of Gezira, Zamalek is a well-to-do residential district. The main thoroughfare Sharia 26 July, which runs diagonally through the area, is the best place to come for European-style comforts. Simonds makes the only decent cappuccino in town and Maison Thomas does the best pizza in Egypt. European newspapers and magazines are sold at local news stands.

View from Rhoda Island of New Cairo Opera House and Cairo Tower

Entrance to Cairo Marriott Hotel, formerly the Gezira Palace

Zamalek's most prominent landmark is the twin orange towers of the Cairo Marriott. This modern and luxurious hotel *(see p265)* was built around the palace created for Empress Eugénie of France when she attended the opening of the Suez Canal in 1869. It has an attractive garden terrace, open to non-residents, which is an excellent spot for lunch or a beer.

Tucked away behind the Cairo Marriott is a small 19th-century, Islamic-style villa, now home to the **Gezira Arts Centre**. It houses a collection of decorated ceramic jugs, plates, lamps, bowls and tiles. Nearby, the **Akhenaten Centre of Arts** is housed in a larger, luxurious, European-style villa. This state-run gallery complex organizes regularly changing exhibitions of the work of contemporary local artists. To the north of

the island, the quiet, orderly streets are a treasure trove of splendid villas and mansion blocks in a variety of styles, from Gothic to Baroque to Arts and Crafts. Many of the finest properties here are embassies, but the **Greater Cairo Library** is open to visitors. This is now Egypt's main resource for information about its capital and contains many interesting books, maps, documents and surveys relating to the history of the city.

🏛 **Gezira Arts Centre**
1 Sharia Sheikh al-Marsafi. 🅒 (02) 737 3298. 🕐 10am–1:30pm & 6–10pm (5–9pm winter) Sat–Thu. 🎫

🏛 **Akhenaten Centre of Arts**
1 Sharia Mahaad al-Swissri. 🅒 (02) 735 8211. 🕐 10am–1:30pm & 6–10pm (5:30–9pm winter) Sat–Thu.

🏛 **Greater Cairo Library**
15 Sharia Mohammed Mazhar. 🅒 (02) 736 2280. 🕐 9am–5pm Sat–Thu.

HOUSEBOATS

On the narrow stretch of water separating Zamalek from the Nile's western bank sits a small flotilla of tatty, two-storey wooden houseboats. They are all that remains of the floating neighbourhood that once lined the river from the city's southern edge to the north. The community flourished in the early 20th century when, supplied with gas, electricity, fresh water and telephones, the boats provided homes or served as cafés, casinos and nightclubs. In 1943, on a houseboat owned by belly-dancer Hekmat Fahmy, a German spy, John Eppler, was arrested. The episode formed the basis of Ken Follett's thriller *The Key to Rebecca*. All the boats are now private residences and are not open to visitors.

One of the houseboats moored near 15th May Bridge

Looking south from 15th May Bridge towards high-rise buildings lining the waterfront in west Zamalek

ISLAMIC CAIRO

OLLOWING THEIR conquest of Egypt in 641 AD, the Muslims built their city, Al-Fustat, on what is now the southern border of modern Cairo. Successive dynasties established their own capital, each one further to the northeast of the old, until Salah ad-Din built the impressive Citadel (*Al-Qalaa*) on a rocky spur and settled the capital's location. During the Mamluk era

Sacks of spices in Khan al-Khalili

which lasted from 1250 to 1517, a wealth of mosques, mausoleums and islamic buildings were added. Today, Islamic Cairo's maze of narrow, congested streets teems with life, challenging the senses with its unique blend of sights, sounds and smells, and vivid glimpses of the past. Most of the mosques are open to non-Muslims, and charge a small entrance fee.

SIGHTS AT A GLANCE

Mosques and Historic Buildings
Al-Ghouri Complex **7**
Bein al-Qasreen **8**
Beit as-Suhaymi **12**
Beit Zeinab Khatoun and Beit al-Harawi **5**
The Citadel pp104–7 **21**
Dervish Theatre **24**
Mosque of al-Aqmar **11**
Mosque of al-Azhar **4**
Mosque of al-Hakim **14**
Mosque of ar-Rifai **23**
Mosque of as-Salih Talai **19**
Mosque of Ibn Tulun pp110–11 **26**
Mosque of Sayyidna al-Hussein **3**
Mosque of Sultan Hassan **22**
Northern Cemetery **16**
Qasr Beshtak **9**
Sabil-Kuttab of Abdel Katkhuda **10**
Sabil-Kuttab of Qaitbey **25**
Sharia al-Muizz li-Din Allah **13**
Wikala of al-Ghouri **6**

Bazaars and Markets
Carpet Bazaar **17**
Khan al-Khalili **1**
Sharia Muski **2**
Tentmakers' Market **20**

Walls and Gates
Bab Zuweila **18**
Northern Walls and Gates **15**

KEY

	Street-by-Street map *See pp88–9*
	Street-by-Street map *See pp94–5*

GETTING AROUND
The best way to explore this area is on foot, spending at least a couple of days wandering the densely-packed, historic streets and buildings. Start at a point easily accessible from Downtown Cairo, such as Khan al-Khalili or the Citadel, and explore the sights at a comfortable pace.

0 metres		800
0 yards		800

◁ **Dominating the skyline of Islamic Cairo, the silver domes of the Mosque of Mohammed Ali in the Citadel**

Street-by-Street: Around Khan al-Khalili

Aᴺʸ ᴇxᴘʟᴏʀᴀᴛɪᴏɴ of Islamic Cairo begins at the medieval bazaar of Khan al-Khalili, the commercial heart of the quarter. The original Khan area lay between Al-Muizz li-Din Allah and Midan Hussein but today it encompasses a wider area made up of several markets selling everything from souvenirs to spices. Traders line the streets all the way to the old city gates, a mile to the north and south, but the bazaar's narrow alleyways are at their densest and most beguiling in the original Khan area. The quarter's many old mosques, houses and palaces offer an escape from the incessant sales pitches.

Stall on Al-Muizz li-Din Allah

Mosque of al-Ashraf Barsbey
Built in 1423, this mosque boasts a beautifully-carved wooden pulpit, inlaid with ivory.

Al-Muizz li-Din Allah
This congested thoroughfare was for centuries the main route through the medieval city of Cairo.

SHARIA AL-MUIZZ LI-DIN ALLAH

SHARIA AL-MUSKI

SHARIA AL-AZHAR

Al-Ghouri Complex
The mausoleum and madrassa complex of Al-Ghouri is housed in twin striped buildings and boasts a unique, red-chequered minaret ❼

Egyptian Pancake House *(see p285)*

Mosque of Abu Dahab

Egyptian Pancake House *(see p285)*

KEY

– – – Suggested route

★ Wikala of al-Ghouri
This wikala or caravanserai is Cairo's best preserved example of a medieval merchants' hostel. It is now an arts and crafts centre, its courtyard occasionally serving as a theatre ❻

Sᴛᴀʀ Sɪɢʜᴛs

★ Mosque of al-Azhar

★ Khan al-Khalili

★ Wikala of al-Ghouri

★ Khan al-Khalili

Filled with glittering paraphernalia, this bazaar is Cairo at its most magical. The lanes of the original Khan area are lined with shops selling everything from waterpipes and handicrafts to silks and spices ❶

Medieval gates

SIKKET AL-BADESTAN

LOCATOR MAP
See Street Finder Map 2

0 metres	50
0 yards	50

Mosque of Sayyidna al-Hussein

The holiest site in Cairo, this mosque is said to contain the head of Hussein, grandson of the Prophet Mohammed. Built in 1870 on the site of a 12th-century mosque, it is off-limits to non-Muslims ❸

Gates

MIDAN HUSSEIN

Fishawi's coffee house *(see p90)*

Sharia Muski

This busy market street is where Cairenes come for serious bargains on everything from wedding dresses to plastic furniture and children's toys ❷

SHARIA AL-AZHAR

★ Mosque of al-Azhar

Founded in AD 970, this mosque and centre for Islamic study is one of the oldest in the city. It displays a mix of architectural styles including this 18th-century Gate of the Barbers ❹

One of two medieval, carved stone gates in Khan al-Khalili

Khan al-Khalili ❶

Map 2 F5. 🚌 or taxi to Midan al-Hussein. ◯ daily (most shops closed Sundays).

Built in 1382 by Garkas al-Khalili, Master of Horses to Sultan Barquq, Khan al-Khalili is one of the biggest bazaars in the Middle East. This is the oriental bazaar of fable, where gold, silver, brass and copper goods glitter enticingly in the cave-like interiors, and sacks overflowing with exotic spices fill the air with their pungent scents. Its maze of narrow, canvas-covered alleyways is crammed with shops selling a huge variety of goods. Here, too, traditional Egyptian crafts, such as dyeing, carving and sewing, are practised as they have been for centuries.

Khan al-Khalili is, of course, also a major tourist attraction. Hordes of tourists arrive here, by the coachload, to haggle and stock up on the kitsch trinkets and souvenirs that are sold in nearly every shop in the main part of the bazaar.

The bazaar grew up around several *khans* (also known as *wikalas*), which served as both warehouses and lodgings for travelling merchant caravans. Most have been swallowed up by later structures, but a few remain. On a side street off Sharia Muski, stairs lead to the upper level of the **Wikala**

of Silahdar (1837), where the former living quarters can be made out, ranged around the central courtyard. Two carved stone gates in the Badestan area, added during the reign of Sultan al-Ghouri (1501–16), are the oldest surviving part of Khan al-Khalili.

Apart from exploring and haggling, the bazaar's other great attraction is **Fishawi's**, located in an alley one block in from Midan al-Hussein. Open day and night for the past 200 years, it is possibly Cairo's oldest coffee house and is crammed with small copper-topped tables, while huge antique mirrors line the walls. Here, patrons puff on *sheeshas* (waterpipes) and sip mint tea round the clock.

For further information on shopping in Egypt and Cairo see What to Buy (*pp296–7*).

Apple vendor in the bustling street market of Sharia Muski

Sharia Muski ❷

Runs between Midan Ataba and Midan al-Hussein. **Map** 6 F3.

In a city that is bursting at the seams, Sharia Muski is possibly the single most crowded street of all. Before

Sharia al-Azhar was bulldozed through the area in the mid-20th century, Muski was the main route between Khan al-Khalili and downtown Cairo. The street is crammed with budget-end clothing emporia and bargain-basement market stalls that are piled high with synthetic goods: clothing that is guaranteed to bobble and fade; wedding outfits, plastic toys and garden furniture. At the Khan al-Khalili end of the street, clothing gives way to perfume and "antiques" but, just before Midan al-Hussein, there is one last glorious burst of glitzy glamour in the form of outfitters selling lavishly decorated belly-dancing outfits.

The sounds that fill Sharia Muski are as much part of the experience as the goods on display. The sales patter of the stall-keepers, the warning cries of barrow-men as they push through the crowds, drink vendors selling liquorice water, all contribute to the lively character of the street.

Mosque of Sayyidna al-Hussein ❸

Midan al-Hussein. **Map** 2 F5. ● to non-Muslims.

This is the most important mosque in all Egypt, so sacred that only Muslims are allowed to enter. Hundreds come here to pray each day, and as many as 10,000 on Fridays. Replacing an earlier 12th-century mosque, it was built in 1870 and is reputed to shelter one of the holiest relics of Islam – the head of

Brass and leather goods for sale in Khan al-Khalili

Domes and minarets of Mosque of al-Azhar seen from Zeinab Khatoun

Al-Hussein, grandson of the Prophet Mohammed. After the Prophet's death in AD 632, control of the caliphate was assumed by the Umayyad clan. The Prophet's son-in-law Ali, claiming to be the natural successor, took up arms and was killed. His son, Al-Hussein, led a revolt but died in AD 680 at the battle of Kerbala, Iraq, where the rest of his body is said to lie. Islam is still divided into followers of Al-Hussein (Shiites) and Sunnis, who hold the Umayyads to be the true successors to Mohammed.

During the annual ten-day Moulid of Al-Hussein and other feast days, thousands throng Midan al-Hussein to enjoy the fair and join in the festivities.

Mosque of al-Azhar 4

Sharia al-Azhar. **Map** 2 F5. ◯ daily. ● for noon prayers Fri. 🖼

JUST SOUTHWEST of Midan al-Hussein is one of Cairo's most venerable institutions. Al-Azhar was founded in AD 970 as the main mosque and centre of learning for the city that had just been built by the new Fatimid rulers from North Africa. Though the Fatimids were swept from power some 200 years later, their mosque and university remained central to religious and political life in Egypt.

Today, the Sheikh of al-Azhar is the highest religious authority in the land and the university the most revered centre of learning in the Sunni Islamic world. Although now housed in several modern campuses around the country, including a separate faculty for women, the university continues to provide free education and board for Muslim students from all over the world. They come to study the Quran and Islamic law along with other traditional subjects such as grammar, logic and rhetoric.

Since a reorganization of Al-Azhar in 1961, new faculties have been formed for the study of medicine, agriculture, engineering and commerce.

Little remains of the original structure of the mosque, which now exhibits a mix of styles from different periods. The double-arched **Gate of the Barbers**, where students traditionally had their heads shaved, dates from the mid-18th century. Visitors now enter through this gate, which leads into an enclosure flanked by two *madrassas* (places of study). Both *madrassas* date to the early part of the 14th century; the one on the left is usually open and is worth visiting to see the beautifully ornate *mihrab* (niche indicating the direction of Mecca).

In the centre of the mosque is the main *sahn* (courtyard), which dates as far back as Fatimid times. Although classes are no longer held here, small circles of students still come to sit in the peace and shade of its arcades to memorize their Quranic texts, much as they have done for centuries.

Before entering the mosque, women must cover their heads; no admission will be granted to anyone with bare legs.

Beit Zeinab Khatoun and Beit al-Harawi 5

Harat al-Azhar. **Map** 2 F5. ◯ daily. 🖼

RUNNING BETWEEN the south wall of Al-Azhar Mosque and a long, low, medieval *wikala*, a narrow alley leads to a small garden square. Projecting into the square on its northern side is Beit Zeinab Khatoun, an Ottoman-era house (*beit*) originally built in 1486 and restored in the 1990s. On the southern side of the square is Beit al-Harawi, built in 1731 as the home of a rich Cairo merchant and also recently restored.

Both houses are beautiful examples of the sophisticated domestic architecture that once filled the city. Beit al-Harawi, in particular, contains some fine *mashrabiyya* (carved wooden screens) and elegant painted ceilings. Built around central courtyards, both houses are designed to stay as cool as possible with their airy rooms, shaded stone floors and interior fountains.

The houses are open to visitors during the day and, since being restored, also operate as cultural centres, where regular performances of music and theatre are staged (*see pp298–301*).

Wooden *mashrabiyya* screen covering the window of Beit Zeinab Khatoun

Tapestry of women carrying water, an example of the craft items on sale in the Wikala of al-Ghouri

Wikala of al-Ghouri ⑥

Sharia al-Azhar. **Map** 2 F5. 🅒 *(02) 511 0472.* ⬜ *9am–3pm daily.* 📷

ALSO KNOWN AS *khans* or caravanserais, *wikalas* were hostels used by merchants arriving in caravans from North Africa, Arabia and the east. As well as accommodation, they provided stables, storage space and a place where merchants could trade. *Wikalas* were typically rectangular in shape with a central courtyard and a main gate that could be locked at night. On the ground floor were the storage rooms and stables while the merchants slept in private rooms on the upper floor. During the Mamluk era, Cairo's golden age, some of the city's *wikalas* were up to four or five storeys high. Unfortunately, none of these has survived. The finest remaining example is the Wikala of al-Ghouri,

Central courtyard of the three-storey Wikala of al-Ghouri

which dates from the early 17th century and is three storeys high. It boasts beautiful *mashrabiyya* (carved wooden screens) on the upper floors and a once graceful fountain in the courtyard. Although parts of the building are closed for restoration, it now serves as an arts and crafts centre. Its rooms have been converted into artists' studios, a shop and a small exhibition of Bedouin crafts, while its courtyard is used as a concert hall and theatre.

Al-Ghouri Complex ⑦

Sharia al-Muizz li-Din Allah. **Map** 2 F5. 🅒 *(02) 511 0472.* ⬜ *9am–midnight daily.* 🌑 *11:30am–1:30pm Fri.*

ONE OF THE finest buildings in Cairo, the Al-Ghouri Complex is made up of twin,

Carpenter at work in the Wikala of al-Ghouri

boldly-striped black-and-white buildings situated opposite each other across a narrow market street. Dating from 1505, the structure was built by Qansuh al-Ghouri, the last of the powerful Mamluk sultans, who ruled between 1501–16 and died at the hands of the Ottoman Turks. The sultan's body was never recovered from the battlefield and his mausoleum, the building on the east side of the complex, was used for his short-lived successor, Tumanbey. Several attempts to construct a dome over the tomb chamber failed, hence the tomb's unusual flat, wooden roof. Part of the mausoleum now serves as a cultural centre and theatre where Whirling Dervishes perform every Wednesday and Saturday evening. Opposite the mausoleum, on the west side of the complex, is the Al-Ghouri Mosque and Madrassa offering fine views from its rooftop. Of note is the mosque's unique square minaret which is topped by five bulbs. In the 18th century these twin buildings were linked by a wooden roof, creating a covered area that housed the city's silk market.

WHIRLING DERVISHES

Cairo's Whirling Dervishes are members of the Mawlaiyya sect of Sufis, followers of a semi-mystical branch of Islam. Sufis were originally associated with poverty and self-denial and wore rough woollen clothes next to their skin – the name Sufi originates from *suf*, the Arabic for wool. Sufis aspire, through meditation, recitation, dance and music, to attain union with God. The Whirling Dervishes, so called because of their ritual spinning dance, offer a rare glimpse of this otherwise underground phenomenon. The group performs twice-weekly at the Al-Ghouri Complex. Questions of authenticity aside, the show is a marvellous spectacle. Dancers in brightly coloured outfits turn like spinning tops while a line of musicians create a hypnotic pulse, tossing their heads jerkily from side to side. Performances are popular so it is necessary to arrive well before the 8pm start time to be sure of a seat. See p298 for more details.

Whirling Dervishes performing their mesmerising dance ritual

Minarets and Domes

ONE OF THE GREATEST achievements of Cairo's medieval artisans was the decorative carving of stone surfaces, seen at its best on the city's myriad minarets and domes. The craft flourished under the Mamluk dynasty (1250–1517) during which time minarets evolved from short, stubby towers, with little decorative detail, to slender, elegant spires boasting carved balustrades and stalactites. The stone domes of the city's mausoleums are also a characteristic of Mamluk architecture, beginning their development in the early 14th century and reaching their zenith in the latter part of the 15th century. Originally small and plain, domes rapidly progressed to vast structures adorned, in the first instance, with a simple rib pattern followed by zigzags and finally explosions of star patterns and floral arabesques. The flourishing of this art form was brought to an abrupt end by the Ottoman invasion.

Crescent moon symbol

MINARETS

These elegant towers, attached to Cairo's mosques, fall broadly into three categories: the square-based towers of the Fatimid period, the lavish three-tiered spires of the late-Mamluk era and the pencil minarets of the Ottoman Turks.

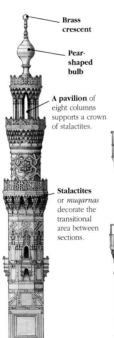

Brass crescent

Pear-shaped bulb

A pavilion of eight columns supports a crown of stalactites.

Stalactites or *muqarnas* decorate the transitional area between sections.

This three-tiered spire, adorning the Mosque of Qaitbey (see p102), displays the elaborate decorative stonework typical of late Mamluk minarets.

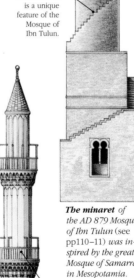

Pepperpot caps adorn these early, square-based minarets.

This external staircase is a unique feature of the Mosque of Ibn Tulun.

The minaret of the AD 879 Mosque of Ibn Tulun (see pp110–11) was inspired by the great Mosque of Samarra in Mesopotamia.

Simple wooden railings and modest stalactite decoration were favoured by the Ottomans.

This simple minaret of the 1528 Mosque of Suleiman Pasha (see p107) has typical Ottoman styling such as a pointed cap and little decorative detail.

STONE DOMES

Developed by the Mamluks, decorating domes became an increasingly sophisticated art form.

The dome of Madrassa Sultaniya (c.1370) in the City of the Dead (see p103) has a rib design.

This cupola, in the City of the Dead, illustrates the progression to a more elaborate zigzag pattern.

The dome of the Mosque of Qaitbey (1474) combines geometric and floral designs in its decoration.

Street-by-Street: Fatimid Cairo

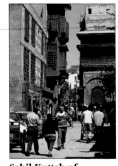

FOUNDED BY THE CONQUERING Fatimid dynasty in AD 969 as "Al-Qahira" (the Victorious), Islamic Cairo became the imperial capital of Egypt. Although they created an extensive royal quarter of grand palaces and mosques hidden by towering walls, little remains of the Fatimids' architectural achievements. Later dynasties recycled the earlier monuments, constructing their own displays of grandeur, such as the Mamluk complexes on al-Muizz li-Din Allah and fine Ottoman residences. Today, the narrow streets of this small quarter serve as a living museum of medieval architecture.

A horse-drawn cart

Sabil-Kuttab of Abdel Katkhuda
In the centre of what was once Cairo's main street is one of many sabil-kuttabs (structures with fountains) in Islamic Cairo ❿

Madrassa of Sultan Barquq
(see p97)

★ Bein al-Qasreen
Once the site of two Fatimid palaces, Bein al-Qasreen is now dominated by the minarets of three grand Mamluk complexes ❽

The Madrassa and Mausoleum of Sultan Qalawun is an example of the ambition of Mamluk architecture. As well as the madrassa and mausoleum it also houses an ancient hospital *(see p96)*.

Madrassa and Mausoleum of Sultan an-Nasr Mohammed *(see p96)*

BEIN AL-QASREEN

SHARIA BEIT AL-QADI

MIDAN BEIT AL-QADI

Khan al-Khalili

Glass Goods
Locally made "Muski" glassware can be found in the alleys off Sharia al-Muizz li-Din Allah.

Qasr Beshtak
This 14th-century palace affords fine views over Islamic Cairo from its upper storeys ❾

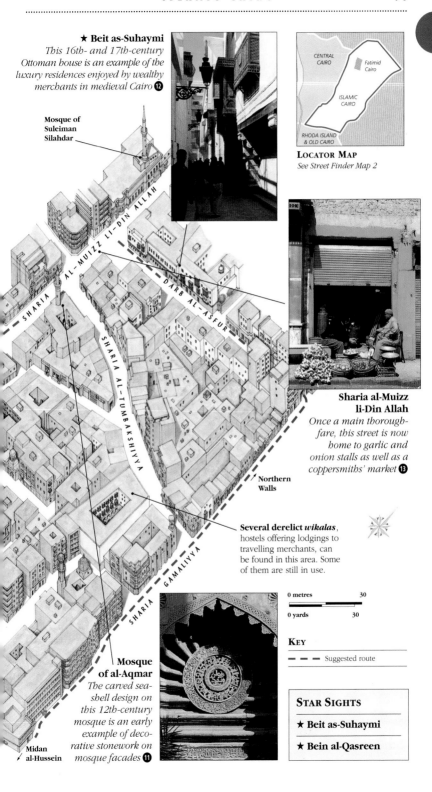

★ Beit as-Suhaymi
This 16th- and 17th-century Ottoman house is an example of the luxury residences enjoyed by wealthy merchants in medieval Cairo **12**

Mosque of Suleiman Silahdar

SHARIA

AL-MUIZZ LI-DIN ALLAH

DARB AL-ASFUR

SHARIA AL-TUMBAKSHIYYA

SHARIA GAMALIYYA

Northern Walls

LOCATOR MAP
See Street Finder Map 2

CENTRAL CAIRO

Fatimid Cairo

ISLAMIC CAIRO

RHODA ISLAND & OLD CAIRO

Sharia al-Muizz li-Din Allah
Once a main thorough-fare, this street is now home to garlic and onion stalls as well as a coppersmiths' market **13**

Several derelict *wikalas*,
hostels offering lodgings to travelling merchants, can be found in this area. Some of them are still in use.

0 metres		30
0 yards		30

KEY

━ ━ ━ Suggested route

Mosque of al-Aqmar
The carved sea-shell design on this 12th-century mosque is an early example of deco-rative stonework on mosque facades **11**

Midan al-Hussein

STAR SIGHTS

★ **Beit as-Suhaymi**

★ **Bein al-Qasreen**

Detail of inscription and motifs in the Mausoleum of Sultan Qalawun

Bein al-Qasreen ❽

Sharia al-Muizz li-Din Allah. **Map** 2 F4.

BEIN AL-QASREEN, which translates as "between the two palaces," is the local name for the stretch of Sharia al-Muizz li-Din Allah that runs immediately to the north of Khan al-Khalili. The name is a testament to the tenacity of history in Cairo, because the two palaces to which it refers ceased to exist more than 600 years ago. Facing each other across a busy public square, the two palaces formed the splendid centrepiece of Al-Qahira (the Victorious), the original Fatimid city, which was founded in AD 969.

Subsequent dynasties replaced them with buildings of their own, but the area was always reserved for only the grandest of building projects.

Today, Bein al-Qasreen is lined on the western side by a sequence of spectacular façades, belonging primarily to three early Mamluk religious complexes. The most southerly is the **Madrassa and Mausoleum of Sultan Qalawun**, which also happens to be the oldest of the three, having been completed in 1279. Three hundred Crusader prisoners took part in its construction, which was completed in

only 13 months. The Christian involvement may account for its almost Gothic façade. Inside, a long, dark corridor separates the *madrassa*, on the left, from the mausoleum, on the right. The latter is one of the most spectacular and stunning interiors in Cairo. Inspired by Jerusalem's Dome of the Rock, it has an octagonal arrangement of columns, two pairs of which are massive granite pillars that originated in some Pharaonic structure. The walls are covered in vivid geometric mosaics tracing the name "Mohammed" in florid strokes. Lavish amounts of gold gleam as they are picked out by the coloured rays of sun-light filtering through countless stained-glass windows.

View across the rooftops to the balconies on the minaret of the Madrassa of Sultan Barquq

Despite the sumptuous interior decor, the complex as a whole still has a slightly decrepit air, which nevertheless adds to its charm. Built as part of the complex, set back from the street, is a *maristan* or hospital which treated the sick for free and amazingly, over 700 years later, still operates as a clinic.

Continuing north, adjoining the Qalawun complex is the lower, less expansive façade of the **Madrassa and Mausoleum of Sultan an-Nasr Mohammed**. It was erected between 1299 and 1304 by a sultan who, despite being deposed twice, fought back to regain the throne on both occasions and reigned for a total of 42 years. During this time, he endowed Cairo with over 200 buildings, the best known of which is his mosque at the Citadel *(see pp104–7)*.

NAGUIB MAHFOUZ

The West was introduced to the work of writer Naguib Mahfouz in 1988 when he was awarded the Nobel Prize for Literature. Born in 1911, he grew up in the back streets of Islamic Cairo, and his work has been greatly influenced ever since by the neighbourhoods and people of his youth. His best-known work is *The Cairo Trilogy*, a vast work spanning the generations of one family. Each title in the trilogy takes its name from a particular locale: the first, *Bein al-Qasreen*, was translated as *Palace Walk*. The award of the Nobel Prize rekindled opposition to Mahfouz's earlier novel *Children of the Alley,* which caused uproar when serialized in *Al-Ahram* in 1959. In 1994 the author was attacked near his home, receiving injuries that affected his physical ability to write.

1966 novel by Naguib Mahfouz

Dome and minaret in Bein al-Qasreen

Sultan an-Nasr's monument in Bein al-Qasreen is in a bad state of repair and may not be open to the public. It is possible, however, to admire from the outside the detailed North African-style stucco-work covering the minaret and the Gothic black and white doorway. The latter was removed from a church in Acre (now Akko, Israel) and re-erected in Cairo to mark the final defeat of the Crusaders by the Mamluks in the Holy Land in 1291.

The northernmost building in Bein al-Qasreen is the **Madrassa of Sultan Barquq**, built around 1384–6. While a *madrassa* does not appear to be noticeably different to a mosque on the outside, it is actually a school for teaching Islamic law. Barquq's complex, has four doors, each intricately decorated with bronze, leading off the main courtyard to four separate sets of classrooms and student cells – one for each of the schools of Islamic law. The mausoleum, just off the prayer hall, resembles an ornate jewellery box, with marbled walls under a lovely gilded dome. It is not Barquq but rather his daughter who lies here: the sultan is buried in the Northern Cemetery *(see pp102–3)*. Sometimes visitors are permitted to go up the minaret and on to the roof for a splendid panoramic view across Cairo.

🇨 **Madrassa and Mausoleum of Sultan Qalawun**
Map 2 F4. 🔘 *daily.*
🔘 *11:30am–1:30pm Fri.* 🖼
🇨 **Madrassa and Mausoleum of Sultan an-Nasr Mohammed**
Map 2 F4. 🔘 *daily.*
🔘 *11:30am–1:30pm Fri.* 🖼
🇨 **Madrassa of Sultan Barquq**
Map 2 F4. 🔘 *daily.* 🔘 *11:30am–1:30pm Fri.* 🖼

Qasr Beshtak ❾

Sharia al-Muizz li-Din Allah.
Map 2 F4. 🔘 *daily.* 🔘 *11:30am–1:30pm Fri.* 🖼

Q ASR BESHTAK or Beshtak Palace is easy to miss: from the outside it presents just a plain, two-storey façade, decorated with a few small *mashrabiyya* windows. However, a narrow alleyway on the left leads to a courtyard with steps leading up to an impressive reception hall, complete with a marble floor and inlaid panelling.

Beshtak was a powerful emir in the 14th century, a notorious rake who married the sultan's daughter and accrued great wealth and influence. His palace, which was built in 1334, was the sumptuous venue for fabulous balls.

During the Mamluk era, however, great wealth and influence was a dangerously double-edged sword, and so it was almost inevitable that a jealous rival succeeded in having Emir Beshtak arrested and executed, at the same time seizing all his possessions.

From what is now the roof of the palace (but which used to be just the second storey of five), there is an excellent panoramic view of Islamic Cairo, looking down Sharia

***Mashrabiyya* screens on the façade of Qasr Beshtak**

al-Muizz li-Din Allah and over the rooftops to the impressive collection of minarets and domes around the Citadel.

The second-floor chamber *(qaa)*, with its *mashrabiyya*-screened galleries, stained-glass windows and gilt and painted wood panelling is a fine example of a private chamber of the period.

The entrance ticket for the Qasr Beshtak also includes admission to the Sabil-Kuttab of Abdel Katkhuda *(see p98)*.

RECYCLING HISTORY

Since Pharaonic times, the rocky Muqattam Hills to the east of Cairo have been quarried for stone. However, it was often found to be more convenient to use materials from closer to hand – in particular, from other buildings. Throughout history, Cairo has been shaken by earthquakes that have reduced great swathes of the city to rubble. Just as frequently, succeeding dynasties have not been above dismantling the existing monuments and reusing the materials for new ones. The Mausoleum of Qalawun, for example, is supported on red granite pillars of Pharaonic origin, while the Mosque of an-Nasr Mohammed at the Citadel *(see pp104–7)* has a

Pharaonic carving on Cairo's Northern Walls

courtyard arcade that is made up of oddments of Roman and Coptic columns and capitals. Most striking of all, though, are the blocks embedded in the interior corridors and rooms of the Northern Walls, which are carved with ancient Egyptian gazelles, hippos and figures – clear evidence of the fact that the stone for these fortifications was scavenged from the ruins of the ancient city of Memphis.

Sabil-Kuttab of Abdel Katkhuda ❿

Sharia al-Muizz li-Din Allah.
Map 2 F4. ☐ *daily.* ● *11:30am–1:30pm Fri.* 🖼

ISLAMIC CAIRO is dotted with odd-shaped buildings with large windows covered by lacy grilles and what looks like a water trough where the windowsill would be. The *sabil*, or fountain, was kept full of fresh water and copper cups were attached to the grille so that thirsty passers-by could help themselves to a drink. Wealthy warlords and nobles would often build a *sabil* to curry favour with both the city populace and their god above.

On an upper floor above the *sabil* was often a small terrace open to the breezes on three sides, which was set aside for the teaching of the Quran and known as a *kuttab*. Thus a *sabil-kuttab* provided two things commended by the Prophet Mohammed – water for the thirsty and spiritual enlightenment for the ignorant.

Built in 1744, this structure has been carefully renovated. Faïence tiles depicting Mecca adorn the lower floor, while the upper floor is decorated with carved wooden pillars and beams. The exterior of the building has some fine "joggling" – panels of different coloured blocks of marble fitted together like a jigsaw. The entrance fee should be included in that of the Qasr Beshtak, whose guardian also holds the key.

Carved stone stalactites between ribbed arches on Mosque al-Aqmar

Mosque of al-Aqmar ⓫

Sharia al-Muizz li-Din Allah.
Map 2 F4. ☐ *daily.* ● *for noon prayers Fri.*

THE NAME OF the Mosque of al-Aqmar (the Moonlit Mosque) was supposedly inspired by the luminous quality of its grey stone. These days, coated in centuries of Cairo grime, the mosque does anything but shine. Nevertheless it is considered to be an architectural gem.

The mosque was built in 1125 by one of the last Fatimid caliphs, and is the oldest stone-built mosque in Egypt (earlier buildings were made of brick faced with plaster). The layout of the mosque is interesting as it uses an outer wall of varying thickness to realign the interior, reconciling the conflicting geometry imposed by the street plan and the direction of Mecca. The façade also displays the earliest use of decorative features that were later to become popular under the Mamluks, such as the sculpted stone "stalactites" (*muqarnas*) and carved ribbing in the hooded arch.

Beit as-Suhaymi ⓬

19 Darb al-Asfar, off Sharia al-Muizz li-Din Allah. **Map** 2 F4. ☐ *daily.* ● *for noon prayers Fri.* 🖼

THE MOST ELEGANT remaining residence in Islamic Cairo, Beit as-Suhaymi is really two houses, one built in 1648 and the other in 1796, joined to create a structure of almost palatial proportions. Its traditional design means entry is gained through a right-angled passage (which ensured complete privacy) into a central courtyard. Originally this would have had been filled with copious greenery ranged around a central fountain.

The rooms on the ground floor comprise the *salamlek*, an area reserved for men; those on the upper floor form part of the *haramlek*, for women and the family. Here, the effect of the stained glass and wonderful painted ceilings combined with the dappled light from the *mashrabiyya*-covered windows is entrancing. These large wooden screens overlook the courtyard, filtering sunlight and cool breezes into the rooms, as well as allowing the women to observe the goings-on below without themselves being seen.

Some of the newly restored decoration is sumptuous, particularly in the ground floor *qaa* or reception room, which features intricate paintwork and a polychrome marble fountain set into the floor.

Sharia al-Muizz li-Din Allah ⓭

Map 2 F5.

AL-MUIZZ LI-DIN ALLAH was the Fatimid caliph who conquered Cairo in AD 969. This street was the former main thoroughfare of medieval times, entering the city through the southern gate of Bab Zuweila and exiting out of Bab al-Futuh to the north. Over the centuries, buildings have encroached on its width and it is no longer very grand, but it is still vital and busy. Lined with stalls, at

"Joggling" on southern facing arch of Sabil-Kuttab of Abdel Katkhuda

Onion and garlic stalls setting up along Sharia al-Muizz li-Din Allah

Khan al-Khalili it is home to the coppersmiths' market and an assortment of workshops. Further along are shops selling a miscellany of coffee-house equipment such as tin-topped tables and *sheeshas*, before finishing with the garlic and onion stalls near Bab al-Futuh.

Sheesha pipe manufacturer on Sharia al-Muizz li-Din Allah

Mosque of al-Hakim ⓮

Sharia al-Muizz li-Din Allah. **Map** 2 F4. ☐ *daily.* ◐ *for noon prayers Fri.* 🎫

A L-HAKIM, the third Fatimid caliph (997–1021), was one of the most notorious rulers in Egyptian history. He ruled from the age of eleven and had his tutor murdered when he was fifteen. Infamous for his bizarre laws and arbitrary acts of violence, he proceeded to burn areas of Cairo, when people objected to the substitution of his name for Allah at Friday prayers. He was also a virulent misogynist and banned the manufacture of women's shoes in order to keep them indoors.

The mosque that bears his name was actually started by his father, but completed by Hakim in 1013. Since that time it has been variously used as a prison for captured Crusaders, as a stable by Salah ad-Din, a warehouse by Napoleon and a boys' school. After existing for centuries in a ruined state, the mosque underwent a somewhat heavy-handed restoration during the 1980s. Now it gleams with polished marble and glitzy golden chandeliers. The minarets are the only original features

of the mosque. They are unique in style, with stubby little pepper-pot tops supported on massive bases, reminiscent of the pylons of Pharaonic temples.

Northern Walls and Gates ⓯

Sharia al-Galal. **Map** 2 F4. ☐ *daily.* ◐ *11:30am–1:30pm Fri.* 🎫

T HE MEDIEVAL CITY of Cairo was completely walled around with at least ten huge gateways, but only a short northern section of the ramparts and two gates now remains, as well as one other gate to the south, Bab Zuweila (*see p103*). The two northern gates, the square-towered Bab an-Nasr (Gate of Victory) and the rounded Bab al-Futuh (Gate of Conquests), were built in 1087 and later strengthened by Salah ad-Din. It is possible to explore the interiors of the gates and walk along the top of the walls by climbing the stairs just inside the neighbouring Mosque of al-Hakim and crossing the roof.

Steps in the gate towers lead into a vaulted corridor running the whole length of the wall, through which mounted guards could ride. The passage is lit by daylight filtering through arrow slits. These were widened to accommodate cannons in 1789 when, a year into his failed conquest of Egypt, Napoleon garrisoned troops within the walls. Evidence of their stay remains in the names the French gave to the towers, which they painted over the doorways.

Immediately north of the walls is Bab an-Nasr cemetery containing the tomb of Jean-Louis Burckhardt (1784–1817). He was the first European in modern times to visit ancient Petra and also to rediscover the two amazing temples at Abu Simbel (*see pp210–11*).

Unique style of minaret at the Mosque of al-Hakim

Intricate Mamluk designs on the Mosque of Qaitbey's minaret, Northern Cemetery

Northern Cemetery ⑯

East of Sharia Salah Salem.
🚌 🚐 *102, 103 from Midan Tahrir.*

ON THE EDGE of the city, across the six-lane Salah Salem highway, the Northern Cemetery (al-Qarafah) is not just a place of burial, it is home to the living too. While several magnificent funerary complexes dominate the area, a lot of the more modest, low-rise tombs double as family homes.

By the end of the 14th century, Cairo's population may have numbered 500,000, making it the largest urban centre in the world. Land was at a premium, so the Mamluk sultans looked beyond the city walls for the building space to match their egos. The great mausoleums they built here rank as some of their finest achievements. Best of these is the **Mosque of Qaitbey**, completed in 1474. A beautifully proportioned structure, with a simple but dazzling sunlight-infused interior, it is topped by the most elegant of minarets and intricate carved stone domes. The Qaitbey mosque features on the Egyptian one pound note.

Further south, down the sandy main street, a stone wall encloses **Complex of Sultan Ashraf Barsbey**. Much of this has been lost over the centuries but the central mosque remains, topped by a beautiful dome carved with interlocking stars. If the door is unlocked, it is worth

looking at the fine marble floor and the ivory-inlaid *minbar*.

Further north lies the fortress-like bulk of the **Mausoleum of Ibn Barquq**. This was built by the son of the Barquq whose complex sits on Bein al-Qasreen *(see p96)*. The building is quite unique in being perfectly symmetrical with two domes and two minarets. It served as a *khanqah*, a monastery for Islamic mystics called Sufis *(see p92)*, and has rows of small cells ranged around the courtyard. Beneath the twin domes are tomb chambers, one for the women, one for the men, with bright, painted ceilings. It is possible to get up onto the roof and climb the minarets.

The best route to the cemetery is to walk east for ten minutes along Sharia al-Azhar from the Khan al-Khalili area.

🄲 **Mosque of Qaitbey**
Sharia Sultan Qaitbey.
◐ daily. ● *for noon prayers Fri.*

🄲 **Complex of Sultan Ashraf Barsbey**
Sharia Sultan Qaitbey. **Map:** 4 D2.
◐ daily. ● *for noon prayers Fri.*

🄲 **Mausoleum of Ibn Barquq**
Sharia Sultan Qaitbey. **Map:** 4 D2.
◐ daily. ● *for noon prayers Fri.* 🖼

Carpet Bazaar ⑰

Sharia al-Muizz li-Din Allah. **Map** 6 F3.

KHAN AL-KHALILI'S markets continue south of Sharia al-Azhar, where tourist trinkets give way to items that the locals might want to buy. The alleyways east of the Al-Ghouri Complex *(see p92)* are home to the Carpet Bazaar. Here, rugs of coarse wool or camel hair are sold, either striped in varying shades of beige and brown, or featuring colourful, stylized images of birds, camels and country scenes.

Back on Sharia al-Muizz li-Din Allah, just south of the Al-Ghouri Complex, are two *tarboush* workshops, making the hat better known in the

Northern Cemetery, including dome of Sultan Ashraf Barsbey Mosque

◁ **View through the morning mist over Islamic Cairo**

West as a fez. Once common street wear, they are now a parody of their former elegant self, sported only by a few waiters and restaurant staff.

Courtyard of Mosque of Sultan al-Muayyad, by Bab Zuweila

Bab Zuweila ⓲

Sharia Ahmed Mahir. **Map:** 6 F4.
⬚ daily. ⬚ 11:30am–1:30pm Fri. ▣

Bab Zuweila is the sole remaining southern gate of the city walls of Fatimid Cairo. It was first constructed in the latter years of the 11th century. In Mamluk times, it was from the platform of Bab Zuweila that the sultan would watch the departure of the annual pilgrimage caravan to Mecca. This was also the site of gory public executions, and the heads of criminals were displayed along the top of the walls here. This bloody habit persisted until the 19th century; after the massacre at

the Citadel in 1811 *(see p106)*, the heads of all the slain Mamluks were also exhibited here, mounted on spikes.

The towering minarets that soar over the gate were added when the adjacent **Mosque of Sultan al-Muayyad** was built in 1415. It is possible to climb the minarets, entering through a small wooden door in the mosque's prayer hall, for one of the best views of the city.

ⒸMosque of Sultan al-Muayyad

Sharia Ahmed Mahir. **Map:** 6 F4.
⬚ daily. ⬚ for noon prayers Fri.

Mosque of as-Salih Talai ⓳

Sharia Ahmed Mahir. **Map:** 6 F4.
⬚ daily. ⬛ for noon prayers Fri.

The last of the Fatimid mosques of Cairo, the Mosque of as-Salih Talai was built in 1160. It is of particular interest because it was also the first mosque to be built on an upper storey, resting on top of a layer of shop units; the intention was that the rent from the shops would pay for the upkeep of the mosque. However, over the centuries, through the gradual accumulation of compacted rubbish and dirt, the street level has risen by some 3 m (10 ft), so the mosque is now at ground level and the shops are in the basement.

The façade has five pointed arches, while the interior reveals columns with florid capitals taken from pre-Islamic sites. The prayer hall walls are decorated with superb stained-glass windows.

Tentmakers' Market ⓴

Sharia al-Khaimiyya. **Map:** 6 F4.

Leaving the Fatimid city via Bab Zuweila, the old main street runs south, passing through a venerable covered market known in Arabic as Sharia al-Khaimiyya, or the Street of the Tentmakers. Cairo's only remaining covered market, it was built in 1650 by Radwan Bey, who was in charge of the annual pilgrimage to Mecca. It is here that at one time a huddle of small workshops produced the brightly coloured printed fabrics that adorned the caravans bound for Mecca. Similar decorative material is now used in the large pavilions, frequently seen around Cairo, that are erected for weddings and funerals and the opening of new **Appliqué motif from** businesses. Huge **the Tentmakers' Market** rolls of the mainly blue or orange cloth are sold at the small, open-fronted kiosks that line the dimly lit street. These places also stitch brightly coloured appliqué work more suited to the tourist.

Living with the Dead

Death has always been a significant part of Egyptian life. Even when the country abandoned Pharaonic beliefs, becoming first Coptic and then Islamic, practices such as visiting the dead were maintained. Most family tombs included a room where visitors could eat and rest and even stay overnight. Inevitably, the city's homeless took to occupying these tombs, some as early as the 14th century. Today, the Northern (and Southern) Cemeteries contain a mixture of tombs and homes, as well as tombs that are homes, where the living and the dead coexist side by side.

Children playing amongst the tombs in the Northern Cemetery, sometimes known as the "City of the Dead"

The Citadel ㉑

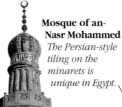

HOME TO EGYPT'S RULERS for almost 700 years, the Citadel (Al-Qalaa) is today one of the most popular tourist sites in Cairo. Originally founded in 1176 by the famed Muslim commander Salah ad-Din (also known as Saladin), its mosques, museums and battlements reflect a diverse heritage. Divided into three sections, the Citadel's main tourist area is in the Southern Enclosure, where the Mosque of an-Nasr Mohammed (the Citadel's only surviving Mamluk structure) is dwarfed by the 19th-century Mosque of Mohammed Ali. The upper terraces of the Citadel offer spectacular views over the city.

Mosque of an-Nasr Mohammed
The Persian-style tiling on the minarets is unique in Egypt.

Police Museum
Entered via a mock-Gothic gateway, the museum traces the gory history of Egyptian crime and punishment.

Bab al-Azab (1754) was built in the Ottoman period as the new main gate.

Lower Enclosure

★ **Mohammed Ali Mosque**
Built in a wholly Turkish style between 1830 and 1848, this mosque has nevertheless become a symbol of Cairo.

Qasr al-Gawhara, also called the Jewel Palace, is now a museum depicting the court life of Mohammed Ali.

Southern Enclosure

★ **Views over Cairo**
Superb views of the city's minarets and domes are afforded from the Citadel's fortifications. In the foreground here is the Mosque of Sultan Hassan.

THE HIPPODROME

Now a large roundabout known as Midan Salah ad-Din, the area to the west of the Citadel walls was once the Hippodrome, an important site in medieval Cairo. Created by An-Nasr Mohammed as a cavalry training ground, this was where the Mamluks – renowned for their feats of horsemanship – practised complex military manoeuvres. Equestrian games were also frequently held here, including horse-racing and polo.

19th-century engraving of Bab al-Azab and the Hippodrome area

VISITORS' CHECKLIST

Sharia Salah Salem. **Map** 4 F2. summer: 8am–6pm daily; winter: 8am–5pm daily (museums close at 4:30pm). religious holidays. (additional charge for Northern Enclosure).

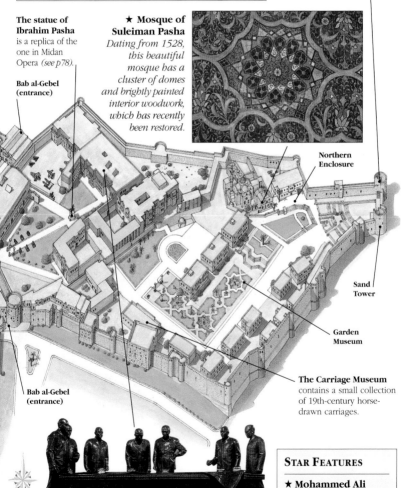

The upper ramparts, entered at ground level, can be explored, offering views across the Citadel.

The statue of Ibrahim Pasha is a replica of the one in Midan Opera (see p78).

Bab al-Gebel (entrance)

★ **Mosque of Suleiman Pasha**
Dating from 1528, this beautiful mosque has a cluster of domes and brightly painted interior woodwork, which has recently been restored.

Northern Enclosure

Sand Tower

Garden Museum

The Carriage Museum contains a small collection of 19th-century horse-drawn carriages.

Bab al-Gebel (entrance)

Military Museum
Once the Harem Palace of Mohammed Ali, the museum has displays of weapons, uniforms and decorations, and a scale model of the Citadel.

STAR FEATURES

★ **Mohammed Ali Mosque**

★ **Mosque of Suleiman Pasha**

★ **Views over Cairo**

Exploring the Citadel

A LTHOUGH ITS MAIN ATTRACTION is the Mohammed Ali Mosque, the Citadel has a great many other features worthy of attention. This fortified complex serves as a museum of Islamic architecture, with numerous fine examples of Mamluk and Ottoman-era mosques and fortifications from the time of Salah ad-Din (1171–91). With four separate museums also enclosed within its walls, a visit to the Citadel can occupy the best part of a day. Visitors should be aware that certain parts of the complex are out of bounds, notably the lower enclosure leading down to the Bab al-Azab gate.

Arcaded courtyard of the Mosque of an-Nasr Mohammed

Detail of a water fountain in the Mosque of Mohammed Ali

🄲 Mosque of Mohammed Ali

Dominating the eastern Cairo skyline, the Mohammed Ali Mosque is a relative newcomer, having been constructed as recently as the mid-19th century. It was erected on the orders of the reformist ruler Mohammed Ali, who is regarded as the founder of modern Egypt. When he came to power in 1805, Egypt was a backwater province of the Ottoman empire. By the time of his death in 1849, however, the country was once again a regional superpower.

Mohammed Ali's imposing mosque was a grand gesture that was meant to echo the great imperial mosques of the Ottoman capital. It is modelled along classic Turkish lines, with a great central dome and two towering, yet slender, minarets. The ornate clock in the courtyard near the entrance to the mosque was a gift from King Louis-Philippe of France, in exchange for the obelisk in the Place de la Concorde in Paris. The clock was damaged

on delivery and has yet to be repaired. Mohammed Ali's body lies in a marble tomb to the right on entering the vast space of the prayer hall.

🄲 Mosque of an-Nasr Mohammed

When Mohammed Ali came to power, the greatest threat to his authority came from the Mamluks, former overlords of Egypt and still a force to be reckoned with. In addition to his infamous massacre of 500 Mamluks at the Citadel in 1811 *(see p59)*, Mohammed Ali ordered all the Mamluk structures in the Citadel to be destroyed. This one mosque survived because it had been put to use as a stable.

Situated just behind the Mosque of Mohammed Ali, this simple structure is all that remains of a massive building programme undertaken by Sultan an-Nasr Mohammed (1294–1340), whose *madrassa* and mausoleum stand on Bein al-Qasreen *(see p96)*.

Built between 1318 and 1335 as a congregational mosque, where everyone gathered to pray, the building has two unique, corkscrew minarets with bulbous finials, covered with faïence tiles in a fashion more Persian than Egyptian.

There are two entrances to the mosque: one is in the form of a three-lobed arch and was used by soldiers, while the other arch was used exclusively by the Sultan.

Although many of the columns within the arcaded courtyard were salvaged from Pharaonic, Roman and Byzantine buildings, they nevertheless all blend together surprisingly well.

The marble panelling that once graced the mosque's courtyard was removed by Sultan Selim I in 1517 and sent to Constantinople.

A view of the Mosque of Mohammed Ali, within the Citadel walls

Police Museum

Built on top of the former Mamluk-era Lion's Tower – so-called because of the statues of big cats at the base of the building – this small museum illustrates the history of Egyptian policing through the ages. Exhibits include uniforms and weapons, a small display on political assassinations and accounts of infamous Egyptian criminals, including Raya and Sakina. Included in the museum is the small row of cells that were in use as recently as 1983. Among their last inhabitants were President Sadat's assassins, held here while awaiting trial in 1981. The museum terrace offers some of the best views over the city.

Statue of a lion at the entrance of the Police Museum

Military Museum

Built by Mohammed Ali in 1827, this was the residence of the Egyptian royal family until 1874, when Khedive Ismail moved into the newly built Abdeen Palace (see p79).

The building served as a military hospital during British occupation in World War II but it became a military museum when control of the Citadel reverted to Egypt in 1946.

Displays include uniforms, weaponry and dioramas of battles. Some of the palatial interiors are impressive, especially the superb *trompe l'oeil* in the main salon.

Mosque of Suleiman Pasha

This mosque was built in 1528 by Suleiman Pasha, who ruled Cairo after the Turks defeated the Mamluks in 1517. It was the first of many Ottoman mosques to be built in Egypt and, though modest in scale, it is one of the most charming. On the underside of the domes is some exquisitely painted decoration inspired by Turkish tiling. There are also some fine examples of traditional

Mihrab **(prayer niche) and** *minbar* **(pulpit) in Mosque of Suleiman Pasha**

inlaid marblework. In the mosque is a small mausoleum with tombs marked by turban-like headstones. These mark the burial places of Ottoman military officers, who were known as Janissaries.

Towers, Gates and Walls

Punctuated by towers and gates, the Citadel walls extend for over 3 km (2 miles). The former main gate, the Bab al-Azab, has been closed for decades and entrance is now through the Bab al-Gebel (Mountain Gate), created in 1786, or the Bab al-Gadid (New Gate). This enormous vaulted portal was built in 1826 by Mohammed Ali.

The oldest parts of the walls are those around the northern enclosure. Fortifications here date back to the Ayyubid era. Salah ad-Din built the original walls and all the small half-round towers (1171–93). These were strengthened in the early 13th century by his successors, who also added most of the larger towers. It is possible to visit the interiors of Salah ad-Din's two eastern-most towers, Burg al-Haddad and Burg al-Ramla.

Other Museums

Al-Gawhara Palace was built by Mohammed Ali in 1814 to house his administration and as a place to receive guests. The former Audience Hall now serves as a museum and is crammed with furniture, portraits and life-sized models of Mohammed Ali and other monarchs and their courtiers. Numerous royal carriages, mainly from the reign of Ismail (1863–79), are on display in the **Carriage Museum**. They include one used at the Suez Canal opening in 1869.

RAYA AND SAKINA – SISTERS IN NOTORIETY

Egypt's most infamous criminals, sisters Raya and Sakina, were tried and hanged in 1921 for the murders of 17 young women. The sisters lived in the poorest quarter of Alexandria where, with the connivance of their husbands, they ran a string of brothels. Their victims were picked up in the market place, lured back to one of their houses and strangled. The motive was money: only girls wearing expensive-looking jewellery were selected. The eventual arrest of Raya and Sakina occurred after a policeman became suspicious of the strong smell of incense emanating from Raya's home. He ordered a search that led to the discovery of the corpses. Since then, the grisly murders have provided lasting inspiration for writers, dramatists and film-makers, and Raya and Sakina have become part of popular Egyptian mythology.

Raya

Sakina

Mosque of Sultan Hassan (*left*) and Mosque of ar-Rifai (*right*) seen from the Citadel

Mosque of Sultan Hassan 🌫

Midan Salah ad-Din. **Map** 4 E2.
🗌 *daily.* ⬤ *for noon prayers Fri.* 🖼

ONE OF THE MOST interesting of the capital's mosques, this is also Cairo's finest example of early Mamluk architecture. The mosque overlooks what were the fields of the Hippodrome (now Midan Salah ad-Din), across from the precipitous walls of the Citadel. The dimensions of this massive structure are truly staggering: 150 m (492 ft) long, with walls 36 m (118 ft) high, the tallest minaret rising to 68 m (223 ft).

The construction of the mosque was funded with money from the estates of people who had died in the Black Death (which struck Cairo in 1348). This policy increased the unpopularity of the sultan, An-Nasr Hassan, who was already renowned for his greed. Building work began in 1356 and five years later, in 1361, one of the minarets collapsed, killing hundreds of people. This turned out to be a bad omen: it was only a matter of time before the downfall of the sultan himself. By the end of 1361, two years before his mosque was completed, Hassan had been murdered. Despite the unhappy history of Hassan's grand monument,

the interior of the mosque is overwhelming. Through a magnificent portal, a dimly lit corridor leads to a high-walled central courtyard. On the four sides of the courtyard are great, recessed arches, known as *iwans*, which were formerly used for teaching. Each *iwan* was devoted to one of the main schools of Sunni Islam.

At the rear of the eastern *iwan*, situated to the right of a particularly beautiful *mihrab* or niche, a bronze door leads to the mausoleum. The largest in Cairo, it was never occupied by the sultan, whose murdered body was not recovered. However, the mausoleum was used for the burial of two of his sons.

Detail of wall and steps from the Mosque of Sultan Hassan

Tickets for the mosque are sold at a kiosk to the right of the main entrance, in a small, unkempt garden that also contains an open-air café.

Mosque of ar-Rifai 🌫

Midan Salah ad-Din. **Map** 4 E2.
🗌 *daily.* ⬤ *for noon prayers Fri.* 🖼

SEPARATED FROM the Mosque of Sultan Hassan by a canyon-like pedestrian street, the similar scale and symmetry of the Mosque of ar-Rifai suggests that it was erected at the same time as its neighbour. In fact, 450 years separate them.

Founded in 1819, the Mosque of ar-Rifai was not completed until 1912. Its patron was Princess Khushyar, mother of the Europhile Khedive Ismail, who intended the mosque as a tomb for her family. It was deliberately built in a pseudo-Mamluk style, with decoration copied from existing period mosques. The result is rather clumsy compared with the Mosque of Sultan Hassan. The over-wrought interior is filled with glitzy tombs of members of the royal family, including the Khedive Ismail and Farouk, the last king of Egypt. Also buried here is the last shah of Iran, who found refuge in Egypt after fleeing Khomeini's Islamic revolution in 1979.

Directly in front of the Mosque of ar-Rifai, facing the Citadel, is the **Mosque of Amir Akhur**. Dating from the late Mamluk period, the building is distinguished by its *ablaq* banding of red and white stone, its imposing dome and double minaret finial. The lower end of its sloping site incorporates a *kuttab* or Quranic school.

⊙ **Mosque of Amir Akhur**
Midan Salah ad-Din. **Map** 4 F2.
○ *daily.* ● *for noon prayers Fri.* 🖼

Dervish Theatre ㉔

Sharia as-Suyufiya. **Map** 4 E2.
○ *daily.* 🖼

Iᴺ ᴛʜᴇ ɢᴀʀᴅᴇɴs behind the Mosque of Hassan Sadaqa (also known as Sunqur Sadi) is a restored 19th-century theatre. Entrance to the theatre is from a small courtyard garden, which is reached via a door on the right of the façade of the mosque, in Sharia as-Suyufiya. Its circular, polished-wood stage is surrounded by a two-storey gallery. The theatre was built by an order of Mevlevi Dervishes, who extended the religious complex on this site to include a hostel (*khanqah*) and a theatre. The Dervishes (*see p92*) are Sufis, who follow a spiritual offshoot of Islam, and who believe that their whirling dance leads to

A view of the interior of the Mosque of Sultan Hassan

oneness with Allah. From the floor of the theatre, you can see down into the tomb of Hassan Sadaqa, for whom the mosque was built.

Part of a complex dating from 1321, the Mosque of Hassan Sadaqa is in poor condition, its foundations threatened by rising ground water. It is, however, distinguished by the fine stuccowork on its minaret and dome, visible from the street. The complex originally included a monastery (*ribat*), which was replaced by the theatre, and a place of study (*madrassa*), which no longer exists.

⊙ **Mosque of Hassan Sadaqa**
Sharia as-Suyufiya. **Map** 4 E2.
○ *daily.* ● *for noon prayers Fri.*

Sabil-Kuttab of Qaitbey ㉕

Sharia as-Saliba. **Map** 4 E2.

Jᴜsᴛ 200 m (650 ft) west of Midan Salah ad-Din, at the western end of Sharia as-Saliba, is the huge, block-like structure of the 15th-century Sabil-Kuttab of Qaitbey. Although in poor condition, this Quranic school is notable for the fine marble-inlay decoration on its western façade. The building itself is closed to the public.

Qaitbey was a ruthless sultan who started life as a slave-boy to the previous sultan. He built some of Cairo's most beautiful monuments, including his spectacular mosque in the Northern Cemetery (*see p102*).

Further west, Sharia as-Saliba passes between the **Mosque of Sheikhu** on the right and the **Khanqah of Sheikhu** on the left. These buildings were built around the middle of the 14th century and are still in use. A *khanqah* is a Sufi hostel, where the sheikh resides, teaching his disciples.

Beyond another small mosque, a dusty street leads up on the left to the entrance to the Mosque of Ibn Tulun (*see pp110-11*). Back on Sharia as-Saliba, a short walk straight ahead takes you to Midan Sayyida Zeinab - a good place to get a taxi back to the centre.

⊙ **Mosque and Khanqah of Sheikhu**
Sharia as-Saliba. **Map** 4 E2.
○ *daily.* ● *for noon prayers Fri.*

Dᴇᴄᴏʀᴀᴛɪᴠᴇ Mᴀᴍʟᴜᴋ Mᴏᴛɪғs

The buildings created between 1250 and 1517, in the time of the Mamluk sultans, represent the pinnacle of Islamic art in Egypt. A fusion of the building traditions of the Near East, they blend Armenian stonework with North African stucco, Byzantine golden mosaics, and Syrian polychrome marble inlays. It is the latter that provide the most striking element. Created by painstakingly cutting small pieces of different coloured stone and fitting them together like a jigsaw puzzle, the intricate ornamentation forms incredibly complex geometric patterns that are completely abstract in character. Repetitive and hypnotic, it has been suggested that the complex decoration aided prayer by heightening the viewers' sensory experience.

Detail of the marble inlay on the Sabil-Kuttab of Qaitbey

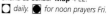

Mosque of Ibn Tulun ㉖

ONE OF THE LARGEST and oldest mosques in the country, Ibn Tulun was built between AD 876 and AD 879 by an Abbasid governor sent from Baghdad to rule Egypt. Called a "Friday Mosque", its open-air courtyard is large enough to hold the whole male congregation of the district for prayers on the holiest day of the week. Built entirely of mudbrick, the mosque is surrounded by an outer courtyard, which was meant to act like a moat and keep the secular city at bay. This, and its curious spiral minaret, make it unique in Egypt. Contrasting with the geometric simplicity of the mosque, the maze of rooms in the nearby Gayer-Anderson Museum is filled with a diverting collection of artifacts.

Decorative motif on arch

★ Mihrab
A niche indicating the direction of Mecca, this mihrab *dates back to the 13th century. Next to it is the* minbar, *or pulpit, one of the finest in Egypt.*

Gayer-Anderson Museum

Lectern
Called a dikka *in Arabic, the wooden platform, in line with the* mihrab, *is used for Quranic recitations and calls to prayer inside the mosque.*

Entrance

Outer Courtyard

Arcades
Running around the courtyard, the arcades (riwaq) *provide shade for worshippers. The largest, on the southeast side, is five columns deep and serves as the mosque's prayer hall. Quranic verses are inscribed along the whole length of the ceiling in the arcade.*

STAR FEATURES

★ **Mihrab**

★ **Spiral Minaret**

★ **Fountain**

GAYER-ANDERSON MUSEUM

This charming museum is the legacy of John Gayer-Anderson, a British officer serving in Cairo. In the 1930s, he lovingly restored two adjacent 16th- or 17th-century houses. Lavishly decorated with *mashrabiyya* screens and marble inlays, they were further ornamented by a vast amount of interesting and often intriguing orientalia. He also added a room, decorated in lacquer and gold, taken from a 17th-century house in Damascus. The cumulative effect of all these items makes the museum one of the most magical places to visit in Cairo.

Reproduction bust of Nefertiti

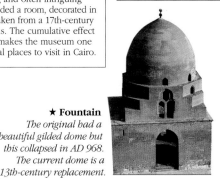

★ **Fountain**
The original had a beautiful gilded dome but this collapsed in AD 968. The current dome is a 13th-century replacement.

Inner courtyard or *sahn*

Pointed arches are inscribed with geometric designs.

The windows have ornately decorated stucco grills, no two of which are the same.

Outside staircase

★ **Spiral Minaret**
Inspired by the tower at the Great Mosque of Samarra in Iraq, Ibn Tulun's minaret is an easy climb, rewarded by excellent views of the city.

Crenellations
The design of these brick-built crenellations is supposed to have been inspired by ranks of standing soldiers.

RHODA ISLAND AND OLD CAIRO

For several centuries following the decline of the old Pharaonic religions and before the arrival of Islam, Egypt was a predominantly Christian country. Alexandria was then the country's capital, while Cairo had yet to be founded. Around the 6th century AD the site of the city consisted of little more than a Roman fortress beside the Nile, guarding a crossing point on the route between the ancient Egyptian cities of Heliopolis and Memphis. When Arab general

Virgin icon in Hanging Church

Amr Ibn al-Aas set up camp in its shadow and built a capital nearby, he was placing the marker for the future foundation of Cairo. Known today as Old Cairo (Misr al-Qadima), this ancient part of the city contains a bastion of Egyptian Christianity, known as Coptic Cairo, and many historic churches. The area also takes in the southern tip of the island of Rhoda, site of the Nilometer which has been used to measure the height of the river Nile since Pharaonic times.

SIGHTS AT A GLANCE

Holy Places
Ben Ezra Synagogue ③
Church of St George ①
Church of St Sergius ⑤
Church of St Barbara ④
Convent of St George ⑥
Hanging Church ⑦
Monastery of St Mercurius ⑩

Mosque of Amr Ibn al-Aas ⑨
Tomb of Suleiman al-Faransawi ⑪

Archaeological Sites
Fustat ⑧

Museums & Historic Buildings
Coptic Museum ②
Nilometer ⑫

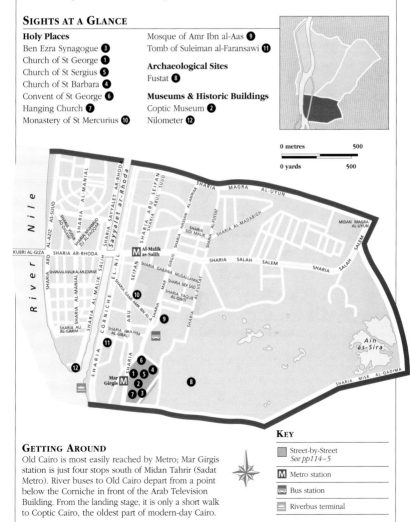

0 metres 500
0 yards 500

GETTING AROUND

Old Cairo is most easily reached by Metro; Mar Girgis station is just four stops south of Midan Tahrir (Sadat Metro). River buses to Old Cairo depart from a point below the Corniche in front of the Arab Television Building. From the landing stage, it is only a short walk to Coptic Cairo, the oldest part of modern-day Cairo.

KEY

◻ Street-by-Street
See pp114–5

Ⓜ Metro station

🚌 Bus station

🚢 Riverbus terminal

◁ **A haven of peace and tranquillity among the high-walled cobbled alleyways of Coptic Cairo**

Street by Street: Coptic Cairo

Coptic Museum window panel

COPTIC CAIRO IS THE modern name for the oldest part of the city. The compound lies within the walls of the 3rd-century AD Roman fortress of Babylon and is a haven of quiet, narrow lanes and ancient holy places. The main entrance, leading to the interesting Coptic Museum and the beautiful Hanging Church, is between two round Roman towers, against which the waters of the Nile once lapped before the river shifted course to the west some centuries ago. A second, stepped entrance to the north leads along a sunken alley to the rest of the churches, the synagogue and the cemeteries.

Convent of St George
While not allowed inside, visitors can re-enact the persecution of Palestinian St George, famed for his dragon slaying, and be wrapped in chains 6

Church of St George
Although Coptic Cairo is a prime destination for tourists, its churches are still frequented by members of the local Christian community who regularly come here to light candles and say prayers 1

Subterranean entrance to compound

Entrance

Mari Girgis Station M

Entrance to Hanging Church

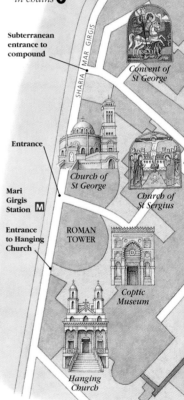

SHARIA MAR GIRGIS

Convent of St George

Church of St George

Church of St Sergius

ROMAN TOWER

Coptic Museum

Hanging Church

ΑΓΓΕΛΟC ΚΥΡΙΟΥ

★ Coptic Museum
Artifacts here trace the origins of Christian art in the Near East. The building itself is beautiful, especially the older, southern wing. There is also a garden and a café (currently under restoration) 2

★ Hanging Church
This most beautiful of Cairo's churches has an ornately decorated interior consisting of three barrel-vaulted, wooden-roofed aisles, ivory inlaid screens and a finely carved marble pulpit 7

KEY

▨	Built-up area
▬	Roman wall
—	Railway line
M	Metro station

Amr Ibn
al-Aas
Mosque

Church of St Barbara
*Dedicated to the saint
who was beaten to
death by her father
for trying to convert
him to Christianity,
St Barbara's is one
of Egypt's largest
and finest churches.
There is a domed
apse behind the altar
with seven steps
decorated in bands
of black, white and
red marble* ❹

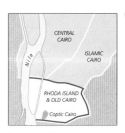

LOCATOR MAP
See Street Finder Map 4

| 0 metres | 50 |
| 0 yards | 50 |

The Nuptial Hall
was part of a church
first founded in AD 681.

**Ben Ezra
Synagogue**
*This is Egypt's
oldest synagogue
and it has been
heavily restored
in recent times.
Ben Ezra is a testa-
ment to the ancient
and significant
presence of Jews
in this region* ❸

*Church of
St Barbara*

**GREEK
ORTHODOX
CEMETERY**

*Ben Ezra
Synagogue*

Church of St Sergius *Since
this, the oldest church in
Coptic Cairo, was built,
ground levels have risen. It
is now entered down some
steps. Legend says that
the Holy Family
sheltered in a
cave below
the altar* ❺

**GREEK
CATHOLIC
CEMETERY**

Cemeteries
*The cemeteries around the
compound belong to the
Coptic, Greek Orthodox
and Greek Catholic com-
munities. They are filled
with impressive statues
and elaborate mauso-
leums, such as this one.*

STAR SIGHTS

★ **Coptic Museum**

★ **Hanging Church**

A 7th-century painting in the Coptic Museum depicting the Virgin Mary and the infant Jesus flanked by saints

Church of St George ❶

Coptic Cairo compound. **Map** 3 B5.
M *Mar Girgis.* ○ *8am–12:45pm & 2:30–3:15pm daily.*

LONG BEFORE the Crusaders carried tales of his legend-ary exploits back to Europe, St George was venerated throughout the Christian Middle East as Mar Girgis. He is said to have been a Roman legionary who defied a decree by the Emperor Diocletian outlawing the worship of Christ and was martyred for his beliefs some time in the 3rd century.

There has been a church dedicated to St George on or near the present site since at least the 10th century, but today's striking round

Worshippers at the entrance to the Church of St George in Old Cairo

structure dates only to the beginning of the 20th century. The circular form of the church echoes the shape of the 1st century AD Roman gate tower on top of which it was built. The remains of the tower are still visible beneath the church on the north side and previous floodwater has been drained.

Coptic Museum ❷

Coptic Cairo compound. **Map** 3 B5.
M *Mar Girgis.* ⬛ *(02) 363 9742.* ○ *9am–5pm daily (9am–3pm Ramadan).* ⬛

LARGELY BUILT in 1947 this charming museum houses the finest collection of Coptic art in the world. The building itself boasts elaborately painted wooden ceilings, elegant *mashrabiyya* windows, and a garden courtyard. The exhibits date back to Egypt's Christian era and both Pharaonic and Islamic influences are evident in the artifacts on display. Early exhibits carry motifs and symbols, such as *ankhs* and Horus-like falcons, that are recognizably ancient Egyptian. Elsewhere, carved capitals from an early Coptic cathedral in Alexandria display a mastery of stone carving that would later come to fruition during the era of the Mamluks. A 6th-century Coptic stone pulpit resembles the stairs and shrine of the pyramid complex at Saqqara (*see pp158–9*), and also prefigures the *minbars*

found in all Cairo mosques. Still more fascinating are the crudely painted depictions of Mary suckling Jesus, which directly echo images found all over Egypt of Isis nursing Horus. Many of the pieces are also Classical in inspiration, a legacy of Alexander's Ptolemaic dynasty and Roman rule.

On the upper floor are the finely woven textiles for which the Copts were once famous. There are also lavishly embroidered silk garments, icons, and what is claimed by some to be the oldest book in the world, the 1,600-year-old Coptic book of the Psalms of David.

Carved stone capital, Coptic Museum

The south wing of the museum will re-open to the public this year. The north wing is closed for restoration.

Ben Ezra Synagogue ❸

Coptic Cairo compound. **Map** 3 B5.
M *Mar Girgis.* ○ *8am–4pm daily.*

JEWISH HISTORY IN EGYPT dates back to the era of the Old Testament and the stories of Moses and the persecution by the pharaohs. After the Roman expulsion of Jews from Jeru-salem in the first century AD, Alexandria became the world's most important centre of Judaism. As recently as the early 20th century the Jewish community in Egypt remained significant and prominent. This changed dramatically with the creation of Israel in 1948. Those Jews that had not already left by choice were forced out of Egypt when the country went to war against the newly formed Jewish state. Monuments to the long history of the Jews in Egypt are few and, of these, Ben Ezra is the oldest. Legends link it with Moses but in fact the synagogue was formerly a church, built in the 8th century. Around 300 years later the church was destroyed and the site and its ruins given to Abraham ben Ezra, a 12th-century rabbi of Jerusalem.

Repairs in the 19th century unearthed hundreds of Hebrew manuscripts from the synagogue's intact *geniza*, or treasury. In Egypt any paper bearing the name of God had to be preserved and this has resulted in a legacy of thousands of documents dating largely from the 11th and 12th centuries. Together, they amount to a minutely detailed chronicle of life in medieval Cairo.

The synagogue underwent extensive renovation in the 1980s and although it is no longer used for worship it is in a pristine state.

Church of St Barbara ❹

Coptic Cairo compound. **Map** 3 B5.
Ⓜ Mar Girgis. ◯ 8am–4pm daily.

THIS CHURCH WAS named after an early Christian martyr who lived in the 3rd century AD. Daughter of a merchant, she was killed by her father for trying to convert him to Christianity. Occupying the site of an earlier church dedicated to St Cyrus and St John, the church of St Barbara was built in the 11th century and is one of the largest and finest in Egypt. It boasts a beautiful 13th-century iconostasis, or sanctuary screen, of wood inlaid with finely carved

Carved 13th-century iconostasis in the Church of St Barbara

ivory. There is also a series of striking icons, dating to around 1750, depicting Jesus, Mary, two archangels and various saints and apostles.

Church of St Sergius ❺

Coptic Cairo compound. **Map** 3 B5.
Ⓜ Mar Girgis. ◯ 8am–4pm daily.

PERHAPS THE MOST famous church in all Egypt, St Sergius owes its reputation to the widely held belief that the Holy Family took shelter in a cave on this spot during their "Flight into Egypt" *(see p123).*

The cave is preserved in the form of a crypt, currently in the process of being cleared of underground water.

Whatever the truth of the Holy stopover, the church is likely to be the oldest existing structure within the fortress, with foundations dating back to the 5th century AD. Rebuilt and reconstructed many times, most of the fabric of the building dates to between the 10th and 12th centuries.

Convent of St George ❻

Coptic Cairo compound. **Map** 3 B5.
Ⓜ Mar Girgis. ◯ 8am–4pm daily.

THIS CONVENT dates back at least as far as the 15th century when it was written about by the Arab chronicler Al-Maqrizi. The convent is still inhabited by nuns but visitors are permitted to enter the high-ceilinged Great Hall where there is a shrine containing a famed icon of St George.

The convent is also known for its unusual chain-wrapping ritual still practised by the nuns. The chains symbolize the persecution of St George.

The shrine dedicated to St George in the Convent of St George

Hanging Church ❼

Icon of St George

DEDICATED TO THE Virgin Mary, this church is popularly called the "Hanging" or "Suspended" Church (*Al-Muallaqa* in Arabic) because it was built on top of the Water Gate of the old Roman fortress of Babylon. The original structure was built possibly as early as the 4th century AD, but it was destroyed and rebuilt in the 11th century. Expansion and reconstruction has gone on ever since, making it difficult to date precisely any specific part of the church. A marble pulpit and the inlaid ivory screens that hide the three altar areas date from between the 10th and 13th centuries. Despite its venerable nature, the church is still used for regular public services, which are held every Friday and Sunday morning.

Outer Porch
Decorated with glazed tiles in geometrical designs, the porch dates from the 11th century.

Carved Frieze
The church incorporates some fine old decoration, such as this frieze of Christ flanked by angels, but the earliest pieces are now housed in the nearby Coptic Museum (see p116).

Inner courtyard

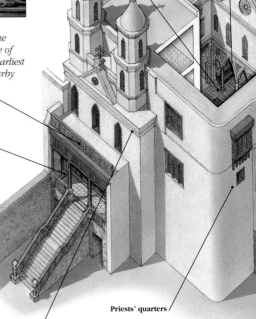

On the porch at the top of the staircase are stalls selling cassettes of Coptic liturgies and videos of papal sermons.

Priests' quarters

★ Façade
Surmounted by its distinctive twin bell towers, the whole front section is a relatively recent addition, dating only from the 19th century.

STAR FEATURES
★ Façade
★ Sanctuary Screen

◁ **Detail from the interior of the dome in the Coptic Museum**

★ Sanctuary Screen

Carved from cedarwood and delicately inlaid with ivory, the central screen that shields the main altar is the finest of its kind in Egypt.

VISITORS' CHECKLIST

Coptic Cairo compound, Sharia Mar Girgis. **Map** 3 B5. **M** Mar Girgis. from Midan Tahrir. from Maspero terminal. **(** (02) 363 9742. **○** 9am–4pm daily. **✝** 8–11am Fri, 7–10am Sun. (Restoration of the church interior is currently taking place.)

Icons of St George, the Virgin and John the Baptist also adorn the walls.

Barrel-vaulted roof supported on columns

Top of the screen adorned with icons

Pulpit

Made of marble and dating from the 11th century, the pulpit rests on 13 columns representing Christ and his disciples.

The Chapel of Takla Haymanot was part of the original 4th-century church. Built in one of the bastions of the Water Gate, it honours the patron saint of Ethiopia.

Roman Towers

The towers belonged to the southwestern bastion of the original Roman fortress and date from around the 1st century AD.

The foundations of the Church can be seen from the courtyard of the Coptic Museum.

Interior of Church

Three barrel-vaulted roofs are supported on columns with Corinthian capitals, indicating that they were recycled from earlier buildings.

Coptic Christianity

THE WORD "COPT" is a corruption of the Arabic *Qibti*, which is derived from the Greek word *Aegyptios*, meaning "Egyptian". According to tradition, St Mark, one of the 12 Apostles, introduced Christianity into Egypt in the first century AD. Alexandria was one of the first five patriarchates – branches of the Christian church headed by patriarchs claiming descent from the Apostles – and by the 4th century, Christianity was the official religion of Egypt. Egyptian Christians split from the orthodox church after the Council of Chalcedon proclaimed, in AD 451, the dual human and divine nature of Christ. Dioscurus, patriarch of Alexandria, refused to accept this definition, believing only in Christ's divinity.

The ankh, *symbol of eternal life in ancient Egypt, is transformed into a Christian cross.*

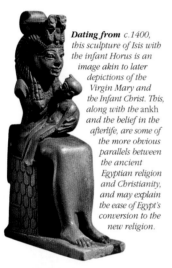

Dating from *c.1400, this sculpture of Isis with the infant Horus is an image akin to later depictions of the Virgin Mary and the Infant Christ. This, along with the ankh and the belief in the afterlife, are some of the more obvious parallels between the ancient Egyptian religion and Christianity, and may explain the ease of Egypt's conversion to the new religion.*

POPE SHENOUDA III

The 117th patriarch of the Coptic church, Pope Shenouda III, and several Coptic priests attend midnight mass at St Mark's Cathedral in Cairo. The Pope was once a monk at Wadi Natrun (see p165), from where the Coptic pope is traditionally chosen.

The Coptic language, *shown here on an early engraving, has its origins in ancient Greek and Egyptian hieroglyphics. Copts claim to be direct descendants of ancient Egyptians. The Coptic language is still used today in religious ceremonies.*

Boutros Boutros-Ghali
(see p63), the former UN Secretary-General, is an internationally-renowned Copt. Always an economically powerful minority, Copts have long provided an educated elite in Egypt, filling many of the country's important posts.

THE HOLY FAMILY IN EGYPT

According to biblical tradition, the Holy Family fled to Egypt to escape Herod's "massacre of the innocents". Coptic tradition links their visit to several sites around the country. At Matariyya, a northeastern suburb of Cairo, is the Virgin's Tree, a gnarled sycamore under which Mary is said to have rested. In Coptic Cairo *(see pp116–7)*, part of the Church of St Sergius is a cave in which the family dwelt, while the town of Asyut *(see p172)* is the southernmost point associated with the route the family took.

The Flight into Egypt **by Jean-Léon Gérôme (1824–1904)**

Monks, *like this one from the Monastery of St Anthony in the Eastern Desert, still wear traditional black robes and a hood with distinctive gold embroidery. Today, monasticism is experiencing a renaissance and attracting many new recruits.*

St Anthony's Monastery (see p228) *represents the beginning of the Christian monastic tradition. It was later followed by Coptic monasteries like Wadi Natrun* (see p165) *and St Catherine's in Sinai* (see pp218–21).

This is a typical Egyptian town in Middle Egypt, dominated by a Coptic church and surrounded by fertile fields. There are approximately 6 million Copts – 10 per cent of Egypt's population – and most live in Middle Egypt. Despite the odd claim and counter-claim, Copts and Muslims live harmoniously side by side.

Fustat

Sharia Ain as-Sirah. **Map** 3 C5.
Ⓜ *Mar Girgis.*

THERE IS LITTLE for the visitor to see at Fustat except hard, sun-baked earth but it represents nevertheless almost 1,400 years of Egyptian history.

When the armies of Islam, led by their general Amr ibn al-Aas, conquered Egypt in AD 640 they chose not to occupy any of the existing cities of Alexandria, Memphis or Karnak. Instead they set up camp immediately north of the Roman fortress of Babylon beside the Nile.

In time the canvas city was replaced by one of mudbrick and stone but was still known as Fustat, meaning "tent". It flourished and became Egypt's first Islamic capital. Under the Fatimid dynasty (969–1171), however, the new rulers built their own city further to the north (*see pp94–5*) and in 1168 put Fustat to the flame rather than risk its capture by the Crusaders. From the 13th to the 16th century, the Mamluks used the area as a rubbish dump and today it is a vast wasteland. Once inhabited by thousands of people who earned a living as potters and rubbish-collectors, now only a few remain on the outskirts. To archaeologists it is a treasure chest waiting to be opened – an ancient city preserved under the garbage of hundreds of years. To date, only the foundations and remnants of the city walls have been revealed.

A pottery on the edge of Fustat, Egypt's first Islamic city

Mosque of Amr ibn al-Aas ❾

Midan Amr ibn al-Aas. **Map** 3 B4.
Ⓜ *Mar Girgis.* ◯ *daily.* ● *to non-Muslims at prayer times.* 🅿

NAMED AFTER the general who conquered Egypt for Islam in AD 640, the original Mosque of Amr ibn al-Aas was the first place of Islamic worship in Egypt and therefore the first mosque on the continent of Africa.

According to contemporary accounts, the mosque was a basic building of mudbrick walls, unpaved floor and a palm-thatch roof supported on palm columns. It had no *mihrab*, courtyard or minaret, but it was large enough to hold Amr's army at prayer. Apart from the site, however, nothing of the original remains in the present mosque, which is a patchwork of countless rebuildings and restorations. It is said that no two of its 200 or so columns are the same. The earliest existing parts date to the 9th century, when the original mosque was rebuilt, almost doubling in size. However, other areas, such as the entrance, were reconstructed as recently as the 1980s.

The mosque has retained an air of simplicity, in keeping with its humble origins and it still fills each day for prayers with a devout congregation. Visitors to the mosque are welcome at other times.

Monastery of St Mercurius ❿

Sharia Abu Seifan. **Map** 3 B4.
Ⓜ *Mar Girgis.* ◯ *9am–5pm daily.* 🅿

TO THE NORTHWEST of the Mosque of Amr ibn al-Aas is a complex consisting of three churches and a convent. Surrounded by a high wall, the compound is entered via a small doorway off the main street. This leads to a narrow, sunken alleyway that connects the various buildings. The monastery complex was reputedly named after a martyred Roman legionary and dates from the early 6th century, but it has been destroyed and rebuilt on at least four occasions.

Relief painting, Church of St Mercurius

The main building in the complex is the **Church of St Mercurius**, which in its current form dates back to 1176. It was destroyed in the blaze when the Fatimid overlord Vizier Shawar ordered Fustat to be razed to the ground.

The church is now a repository of fine early Coptic art with unique wall paintings, an extraordinary collection of icons and a fine wooden altar canopy. A flight of stairs in

Façade and entrance to the Mosque of Amr ibn al-Aas

Ornate ironwork exterior of the Tomb of Suleiman al-Faransawi

the north aisle of the church leads down to a small crypt where, in the 4th century, the ascetic St Barsum the Naked is said to have spent the last 20 years of his life with only a snake for company.

The **Church of the Holy Virgin** and the **Church of St Shenouda** are both open to visitors but the **Convent of St Mercurius**, also part of the complex, is still inhabited by nuns and is off limits.

Tomb of Suleiman al-Faransawi ⓫

Sharia Mohammed al-Saghir.
Map 3 B5. Ⓜ *Mar Girgis.*

A SMALL CAST-IRON TOMB in a residential square, this is one of the most unusual monuments in Cairo, built in the 19th century in honour of an extremely unusual man.

Suleiman "the Frenchman" (originally a soldier named Joseph Sèves) was a veteran of Napoleon's campaigns who came to Egypt to train the armies of the viceroy Mohammed Ali *(see p59).* It is said that the Frenchman, who died in 1860, was so despised by his conscripts that they would shoot at him during target practice. Sèves later converted to Islam, taking the name Suleiman, and was rewarded with the honorary title "Pasha" following Egypt's successful campaigns against Greece and Syria. A statue of Suleiman mounted on his horse used to stand in Downtown Cairo on what was Sharia Suleiman Pasha. During the 1952 Revolution

the statue was consigned to the Citadel and the street renamed in honour of the Egyptian nationalist and banker, Talaat Harb.

Nilometer ⓬

Sharia al-Malik Salih. **Map** 3 B5.
Ⓜ *Mar Girgis.* ⬚ *daily.* 🎟

U NTIL THE CONSTRUCTION of the dams at Aswan, Egyptian life was governed by the annual flooding of the Nile. Most years, its waters rose to swamp the river valley, then retreated, leaving behind richly fertile deposits of alluvial soil. Occasionally, however, the floods failed to cover the whole agricultural area and this resulted in low crop yields and sometimes famine. In order to forecast what kind of harvest a particular year might bring,

the ancient Egyptians constructed a series of Nilometers, one of which is cut into the bedrock of the island of Rhoda. It takes the form of a deep, square pit containing an octagonal column, marked off with graduations. Water was let in through three channels – these are now blocked up but are still visible. At the annual meter-reading ceremony, a sufficiently high level of water would be greeted by festivities, while a shortfall would trigger anxious prayers.

Although there is evidence that a Nilometer has been here since Pharaonic times, in its existing form it dates from the 9th century – hence the elaborate Islamic inscriptions adorning the walls. Set over the Nilometer is a small Ottoman kiosk with a distinctive conical cap, dating from the 19th century. Decorating its wooden ceiling are some impressive painted arabesques.

Adjacent to the Nilometer is the Rococo **Munasterli Palace**, built in the 1850s. In spring 2002 an arts centre with a museum dedicated to the revered Egyptian singer Umm Kolthum opened here. Classical concerts are held during the winter.

Nilometer on Rhoda Island showing the simple calibration used to predict the floods

UMM KOLTHUM: THE VOICE OF EGYPT

For much of the 20th century Umm Kolthum was the greatest living cultural icon not just in Egypt, but in the whole of the Arab world. She began singing with her father at weddings in the villages of the eastern Delta around 1910. Astonished by the strength of her voice, friends and family encouraged her to move to Cairo and establish her career. From the 1930s onwards for almost the next 40 years the whole of the country came to a standstill on one Thursday night each month when her concert would be broadcast live on national radio to audiences of millions. During this time she also recorded over 300 songs and appeared in countless films. When she died in 1975 her funeral was the biggest ever witnessed in Cairo. She remains inescapable today; her music is played constantly in coffeehouses and taxis, her voice providing a powerful soundtrack to any visit to Egypt.

Umm Kolthum, Egypt's favourite singer

GIZA AND HELIOPOLIS

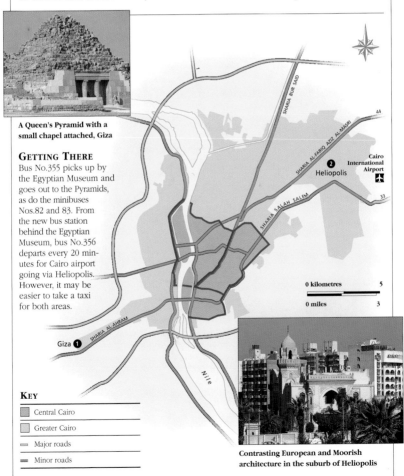

GIZA AND HELIOPOLIS are two Cairo suburbs that are not only geographically opposed, they also epitomize two extremes of Egypt's history. Giza, in the southwest, is famed for its ancient monuments. The Sphinx, usually dated to around 2500 BC and the earliest known monumental sculpture, stands guard over the Pyramids at Giza, and their attendant Queens' pyramids, temples, and tombs. The Pyramids are the only one of the Seven Wonders of the Ancient World to survive. Even the accompanying circus of camel and horse rides, souvenir

Moorish detail from a façade in Heliopolis

and soft drinks vendors, persistent beggars and the nightly Sound and Light show do not diminish their splendour. In the diagonally opposite suburb of Heliopolis, history moves on to the late 19th century and Baron Edouard Empain, the entrepreneur whose vision inspired this garden city in the desert. Built in a mixture of European and Moorish styles, Heliopolis attracted wealthy Egyptians to its leafy grandeur. Although it is no longer separate from Cairo, visitors still come to enjoy its stylish architecture, restaurants and nightlife.

A Queen's Pyramid with a small chapel attached, Giza

GETTING THERE

Bus No.355 picks up by the Egyptian Museum and goes out to the Pyramids, as do the minibuses Nos.82 and 83. From the new bus station behind the Egyptian Museum, bus No.356 departs every 20 minutes for Cairo airport going via Heliopolis. However, it may be easier to take a taxi for both areas.

Heliopolis ❷

Cairo International Airport

Giza ❶

0 kilometres 5
0 miles 3

SHARIA BUR SAID
SHARIA AL-FARIQ AZIZ AL-MASRI
SHARIA SALAH SALEM
SHARIA AL-AHRAM
Nile

KEY

	Central Cairo
	Greater Cairo
—	Major roads
—	Minor roads

Contrasting European and Moorish architecture in the suburb of Heliopolis

◁ **The Sphinx, carved from an outcrop of soft limestone, in front of the Pyramid of Khafre at Giza**

The Giza Plateau ❶

Nearly 5,000 years ago, Giza became the royal burial ground (necropolis) for Memphis, capital of Egypt. In less than 100 years, the ancient Egyptians built the three pyramid complexes to serve as the tombs for their dead kings. After the king's death, his body was brought by boat to the valley temple for preparation before being taken up the causeway and buried under, and in some cases within, the pyramid. The mortuary temples were maintained for many years afterwards with priests making daily offerings to the dead god-king. The king's close family and the royal court were buried in satellite pyramids and stone tombs called *mastaba* nearby, seeking to share in the king's power in death, as they had in life.

Pyramids of Giza
Three successive generations built these monumental structures during the 4th Dynasty of the Old Kingdom (2686–2181 BC).

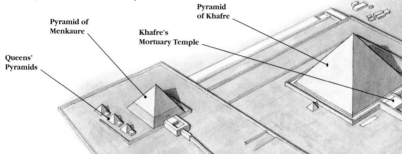

Pyramid of Khafre

Pyramid of Menkaure

Khafre's Mortuary Temple

Queens' Pyramids

Giza Plateau Reconstruction
The funerary complex included the main pyramid, covered in white limestone, various satellite pyramids and a mortuary temple joined by a causeway to a valley temple.

Causeway

Pyramids of Menkaure and Khafre
While Khafre's Pyramid is nearly as grand as that of his father, Khufu, the Pyramid of Menkaure, Khafre's successor, is much smaller, hinting perhaps at a decline in power and commitment or simply a change in priorities.

Tomb of Khentkawes
This was the last major tomb built at Giza. Queen Khentkawes, daughter of Menkaure, probably gave birth to a new dynasty that moved its necropolis to Abu Sir.

Star Sights
★ **The Great Pyramid**
★ **The Sphinx**

MEANING OF THE GIZA PYRAMIDS

Archaeologists agree that pyramids served as monumental structures for the burial of kings. They were topped with gold-covered pyramidions (pyramid-shaped capstones) which caught the first rays of the sun and their shape perhaps symbolized the mythical, primeval mound of creation (*see p26*). However, because the exact purpose of some of the rooms and shafts of the Giza Pyramids is unknown, the fact that some air shafts point towards important constellations, that the southeast corners lie on a near perfect diagonal and that their sides align with true north inspires many to look hard for fanciful explanations. However, such alignments are simply consistent with ancient Egyptian funerary beliefs that the king's soul would rise up to join the "eternal stars".

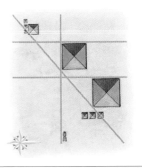

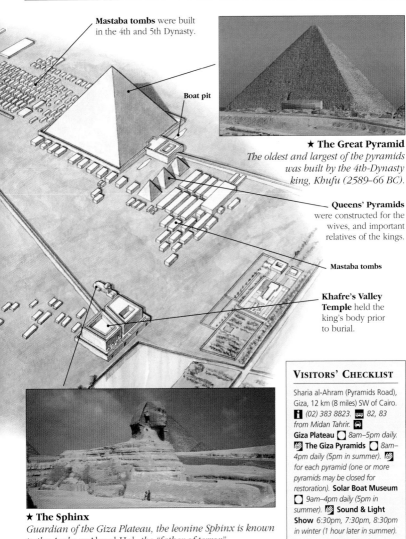

Mastaba tombs were built in the 4th and 5th Dynasty.

Boat pit

★ **The Great Pyramid**
The oldest and largest of the pyramids was built by the 4th-Dynasty king, Khufu (2589–66 BC).

Queens' Pyramids were constructed for the wives, and important relatives of the kings.

Mastaba tombs

Khafre's Valley Temple held the king's body prior to burial.

★ **The Sphinx**
Guardian of the Giza Plateau, the leonine Sphinx is known to the Arabs as Abu al-Hol, *the "father of terror".*

VISITORS' CHECKLIST

Sharia al-Ahram (Pyramids Road), Giza, 12 km (8 miles) SW of Cairo.
(02) 383 8823. 82, 83 from Midan Tahrir.
Giza Plateau 8am–5pm daily.
The Giza Pyramids 8am–4pm daily (5pm in summer). for each pyramid (one or more pyramids may be closed for restoration). **Solar Boat Museum** 9am–4pm daily (5pm in summer). **Sound & Light Show** 6:30pm, 7:30pm, 8:30pm in winter (1 hour later in summer).

The Giza Plateau: The Great Pyramid

THE FACTS OF KHUFU'S PYRAMID, commonly referred to as the Great Pyramid, are staggering. It is estimated to contain over two million blocks of stone weighing on average around 2.5 tonnes, with some stones at the base weighing as much as 15 tonnes. Until the 19th century it was the tallest building in the world. Yet for such a vast structure the precision is amazing – the greatest difference in length between the four 230-m (756-ft) sides is only 4 cm (2 inches). The construction methods and exact purpose of some of the chambers and shafts are unknown, but the fantastic architectural achievement is clear.

Statue of Khufu (Cheops)
Khufu's only surviving statue is this 7.5-cm (3-inch) high ivory figure from Abydos, now kept in the Egyptian Museum.

The Queen's Chamber probably held a statue representing the *ka* or life-force of the king.

The "air shafts" may have been symbolic paths for the king's soul to ascend to the stars.

Queens' Pyramids
These three small pyramids were built for members of the king's family, although the actual identity of the occupants is unknown.

Underlying bedrock

★ **King's Chamber**
Probably emptied 600 years after being built, the chamber, despite holding only a lidless sarcophagus, was often broken into by treasure seekers.

Unfinished underground chamber

STAR FEATURES

★ King's Chamber

★ Great Gallery

★ **Great Gallery**
Soaring nearly 9 m (30 ft) high, this is thought to have been used as a slipway for the huge blocks that sealed the passageway.

◁ **The Pyramids at Giza set in a timeless desert landscape**

RECONSTRUCTION OF THE KING'S CHAMBER

Built to protect the chamber, the stress-relieving rooms also hold the only reference to Khufu in the pyramid – graffiti, from the time of construction, stating the names of the gangs who built the pyramid - one such name being "How powerful is the great White Crown of Khufu".

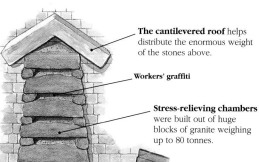

The cantilevered roof helps distribute the enormous weight of the stones above.

Workers' graffiti

Stress-relieving chambers were built out of huge blocks of granite weighing up to 80 tonnes.

King's Chamber

The "air shaft" would have been closed off by the outer casing.

Counter-balanced slabs of granite were lowered to seal the tomb.

This vertical shaft probably served as an escape route for the workers.

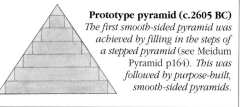

Entrance
The original entrance is now blocked and visitors use a lower opening made by the Caliph Maamun in AD 820.

THE DEVELOPMENT OF PYRAMIDS

It took the ancient Egyptians around 400 years to progress from mudbrick mastaba to smooth-sided pyramid. The last stage, from stepped to "true" or smooth-sided pyramid took only 65 years. In this time each pyramid was a brave venture into the unknown. Rarely in the history of mankind has technology developed at such a rate.

The Red or North Pyramid, at Dahshur (c.2600 BC)

Mastaba
Around 3000 BC the sandy mounds of the graves of the upper echelons of society were formalized into low, box-like mastabas.

Stepped pyramid (c.2665 BC)
A more impressive memorial was made by putting six stone mastabas on top of each other (see King Djoser's Pyramid pp158-9).

Prototype pyramid (c.2605 BC)
The first smooth-sided pyramid was achieved by filling in the steps of a stepped pyramid (see Meidum Pyramid p164). This was followed by purpose-built, smooth-sided pyramids.

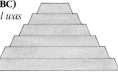

Exploring the Giza Plateau

F OR PRESERVATION PURPOSES, each of the pyramids is
closed for a spell on a rotating basis and the
number of visitors allowed inside is limited. Early
morning is therefore the best time to visit, before the
heat and crowds become unbearable; it is also worth a
trip in the evening for the kitsch but spectacular Sound
and Light Show. It can get hot and airless inside the
pyramids so clambering inside is not recommended for
claustrophobics or the unfit. Horse and camel owners
tout expensive rides between the monuments but the
area is compact enough to get around on foot.

**Egyptian offering camel rides or
simply a photo opportunity**

**The space-age shape of the Solar
Boat Museum**

🏛 Solar Boat Museum

On the south side of the Great
Pyramid sits the pod-shaped,
Solar Boat Museum. This holds
a full-size ancient Egyptian
boat discovered in pieces in
1954, lying in a pit beside the
pyramid. Experts spent 14
years putting its 1200 pieces
together again using only
ancient Egyptian materials of
wooden pegs and grass rope.

It is called a solar boat by
archaeologists because it
resembles the vessels seen in
tomb paintings in which the
sun-god makes his daily trip
across the heavens. It is not
clear whether the boat was
buried for the sun-god or for
the pharaoh's own journey
across the heavens. Marks on
the wood suggest that the
boat had been sailed
before being buried. It
could be that it
served as a
funerary barque,
carrying the
body of
Khufu
from

Memphis to his tomb at Giza.
A second similar boat was
located in a nearby pit but
remains unexcavated.

⋔ Pyramid of Khafre

The base of the Pyramid of
Khafre (also called Khephren),
is just 15 m (50 ft) shorter
than the Great Pyramid, while
in height there is a difference
of only 3 m (10 ft). Today,
however, Khafre's pyramid
appears the larger by virtue of
being built on higher ground,
and because its summit
remains intact. This
summit is the only area
that retains the limestone
casing that originally
covered all three
pyramids. The rest was
taken by the medieval
rulers of Cairo who
used it for their
own monuments.

The interior is
simpler than that
of the Great
Pyramid. It has
two descending passageways
converging and leading to
a single tomb chamber.
Whereas Khufu's tomb
chamber sits high up
inside the structure,
Khafre's is dug
deep into the
bedrock
beneath his
pyramid.
There

**Idu,
guardian of
the burial complexes**

is little to see except the king's
granite sarcophagus. Khafre's
mortuary temple still has parts
of a small sanctuary and a
courtyard, and sections of the
500-m (550-yard) granite-lined
causeway are still visible.

⋔ Pyramid of Menkaure

The last pyramid built on the
Giza Plateau, Menkaure's
pyramid has a base area less
than a quarter of
that of its two neigh-
bours. Some
attribute this to a
reduction in the
power of the king.
However, others
point to a change
in priorities; the
size of the pyramid
has been reduced
but its valley and
mortuary temples
are larger and more
elaborate. This can perhaps
be viewed as the start of a
process that eventually saw
pyramids abandoned, in
favour of secret, rock-cut
tombs with separate large
funerary temples.

In the 12th century one of
Cairo's sultans attempted to
dismantle this pyramid. After
eight months the project was
abandoned, merely having
achieved the vertical scar
visible on the north face.

Inside, a passageway
descends from the entrance
to an antechamber decorated
with a stylized false-door
motif. Beyond that is another
antechamber, from where a
passage leads down to the
tomb chamber carved from

The Sphinx and Pyramid of Khafre viewed from the edge of the plateau

the bedrock. Its barrel-ceiling is carved from a giant granite roof slab. A beautifully decorated sarcophagus was discovered here in the early 19th century but it was lost at sea while being shipped to the British Museum in London.

⋔ The Sphinx

Standing guard at the approach to the Pyramid of Khafre, the Sphinx is the earliest known monumental sculpture of ancient Egypt. Archaeologists date it to around 2500 BC, crediting Khafre as the inspiration. It stands 20 m (66 ft) high with an elongated body, outstretched paws and a royal headdress framing a fleshy face, possibly that of the king himself. It is carved from an outcrop of natural rock, augmented by shaped blocks around the base, added during repeated renovations from the 18th Dynasty onwards.

Although it is often written that the Sphinx's nose was shot off by the Mamluks, Ottomans or Napoleon's French army, it was in fact lost some time before the 15th century. Originally the Sphinx also had a stylized false beard, symbol of royalty, but that too fell off. A piece taken from where it lay on the sand is now held by the British Museum in London.

Directly in front of the statue are the remains of the Sphinx Temple, closed to the public. Access to the area around the Sphinx is gained via the adjacent Valley Temple of Khafre, one of the oldest surviving temples in Egypt. At the time the pyramids were built, during the annual Nile flood, the waters came up to the edge of the Giza Plateau. Khafre's Valley Temple stood on a quay and served as a gateway to the pyramid, connected by a long, mostly covered, causeway. Buried in the sand, this was discovered by Auguste Mariette in 1852 and traces of it can still be seen today. The other two pyramids had similar complexes but their temples are not so well preserved.

The historic Mena House Hotel, at the edge of the Giza Plateau

Around the Giza Plateau

There are also several tombs worth a visit. The mastaba tombs near Khufu's Queens' Pyramids include the 6th-Dynasty **Tombs of Qar and Idu**. Qar was a high ranking official in charge of maintaining the pyramids and their associated ceremonies and his son, Idu, was the royal scribe. These have reliefs and statues of the deceased. The nearby tomb of Khufu's son **Khufu-khaf** has some perfectly preserved reliefs, while the tomb of Khafre's wife **Meresankh III** is intriguing. Its painted reliefs show Meresankh, a priestess dressed in the leopardskin usually associated with male priests, while her mother, the blonde-haired Hetepheres III, wears a dress with pointed shoulder pads.

After the dusty heat of the plateau, it makes a nice end to the day to have a drink at the luxurious **Mena House Hotel** and to contemplate the Pyramids as they take on the colour of the setting sun.

CLIMBING THE GREAT PYRAMID

At one time, a complete visit to the Great Pyramid entailed not only an exploration of the passages within, but a clamber to the top as well. A 1902 guidebook to Egypt describes how it was done: "Assisted by two Bedouins, one holding each hand, and, if desired, by a third (no extra payment) who pushes behind, the traveller begins the ascent of the steps". Once up there, many commemorated their climb by carving their names in stone. A recent archaeological project has been cataloguing each block of the pyramid. The graffiti noted includes the will of someone who climbed to the top and committed suicide and the names of two lovers carved together for all eternity. As early as 1840 writers complained about the excessive amount of graffiti. This is no longer an issue as since the 1980s, climbing the pyramids has been forbidden, although some people still try. This has been done as much to protect the monuments as to prevent injury and even death to climbers.

19th-century photograph of tourists climbing the Great Pyramid

A Walk Through Heliopolis ②

Hindu motif from Baron's Palace

A PRODUCT OF THE visionary ambitions of a wealthy Belgian entrepreneur, Baron Edouard Empain (1852–1929), Heliopolis was built in the first decade of the 20th century. It was designed by a team of European and Egyptian architects as a self-contained garden city in the desert to the northeast of Cairo, linked to the centre by a tram system. Known in Egypt as Masr al-Gedida (New Cairo), Heliopolis has since been swallowed up by the expanding capital, but still retains some of its extraordinary original architecture. A magnet for wealth, this elegant, leafy suburb has good shops, restaurants and nightlife.

On the terrace of the Amphitrion cafeteria, Heliopolis

Around Uruba Palace

The walk begins where the bus from Cairo swings left beside the high walls of the Uruba Palace ①. Formerly the Heliopolis Palace Hotel, one of the grandest hotels in the African continent, this is now the official residence of the Egyptian president. The palace's distinctive, drum-shaped wing once housed a magnificent ballroom.

Diagonally opposite the palace, at the junction of Sharia al-Ahram and Sharia Ibrahim Laqqany, is the venerable Amphitrion ②, a bar/restaurant that is as old as Heliopolis itself. The food is basic, but it is one of the few places in Egypt where it is possible to drink beer while sitting on the pavement terrace, in full view of passers-by on the street.

SIGHTS ON WALK

Amphitrion ②
Baron's Palace ⑦
Basilica ⑥
Le Chantilly ⑨
Normandy Cinema ④
Palmyra ⑤
Sharia Baghdad ⑧
Sharia Ibrahim Laqqany ③
Uruba Palace ①

Colonnaded façades and teardrop turrets in Sharia Ibrahim Laqqany

Turn left from Sharia al-Ahram into Sharia Ibrahim Laqqany ③, which is the most complete remaining example of the original city planning. Baron Empain's architects designed elaborate façades that owe more to Western fantasies inspired by *The 1001 Nights* than to any authentic Islamic architectural traditions. This particular street has a wonderful sweep of arcades with Moorish arches and balconies, punctuated by pretty little towers and turrets.

The Baron, a train enthusiast, was also responsible for what was then a state-of-the-art electric tramway connecting his satellite city to central

TIPS FOR WALKERS

Starting point: Sharia al-Ahram.
Length: 4 km (2.5 miles).
Duration: 1.5 hours.
Getting there: Airport bus No. 356 from new bus station behind the Egyptian Museum or taxi.

Cairo. Trams still rattle up the middle of Sharia al-Ahram, but now they are robust Eastern European models rather than the quaint double-deckers of old.

Turning right from Sharia Ibrahim Laqqany into Sharia Sayyid Abdel Wahid and right again, return to Sharia al-Ahram where, a little further along, on the left, is the Normandy cinema ④. Operating as an

Baron Empain's Byzantine-style Basilica, modelled on Istanbul's Aya Sofya

open-air auditorium during the summer, the cinema regularly screens English-language films.

At the junction of Sharia al-Ahram and Sharia Ibrahim Sawra, almost opposite the Normandy, is the Palmyra ⑤, another of Heliopolis's original terrace cafeterias (in Egypt the term "cafeteria" nearly always denotes a bar rather than a place to eat).

Basilica to Sharia Baghdad
Continuing up Sharia al-Ahram, the distinctive central arch of Empain's Basilica ⑥ can be seen straight ahead, serving as a reminder that Heliopolis was built by and for (Christian) Europeans. Empain and his family are buried in a crypt within the

Basilica, which is designed in a highly stylized Byzantine manner. Unfortunately the church is usually kept locked.

Turning right at Shahid Tayyar Nazih Khalila, a ten-minute walk leads to the most magnificent of follies, known as the Baron's Palace (Qasr al-Baron) ⑦. Built in 1910, this was Baron Empain's Cairo residence and, for reasons unknown, he had it designed to resemble a Hindu temple. The French architect, Alexander Marcel, based his design on a temple at Angkor Wat in Cambodia. Its sandstone exterior is covered with carved animals, Hindu symbols and gods. The building originally had a revolving tower, which allowed the owner to follow the sun throughout the day. Sadly, the palace has been empty for decades and its ornate architecture is now home to a variety of birdlife and a colony of bats.

Return to central Heliopolis along Sharia Abd al-Salaam Zaky, turning left onto Sharia Baghdad ⑧, which, like Sharia Ibrahim Laqqany earlier, contains a wealth of fantasy Oriental architecture. About halfway along, on the left, is Le Chantilly *(see p286)* ⑨, an excellent place to stop for a meal or a beer in the garden.

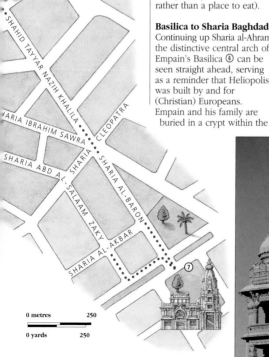

0 metres 250
0 yards 250

KEY
• • • Walk route
🚋 Tram stop
═ Tram route

Carved sandstone façade of the Baron's Palace

CAIRO STREET FINDER

THE MAP BELOW shows the areas of the city covered by the *Street Finder*. The maps include the major sightseeing attractions, railway, bus and Metro stations, as well as other useful locations. Map references are given for Cairo's restaurants *(see pp282–91)*, hotels *(see pp264–75)* and entertainment venues *(see pp298–305)*. Some of Cairo's small streets and alleyways may not be named on the maps.

Sightseeing in Cairo

Some monuments have two names: one in Arabic and often a commonly used English-language form. What we call the Citadel, taxi drivers sometimes know only as *Al-Qalaa*. Refer to the Survival Guide for guidance on taxis *(see p326)*. In this guide and on the following maps, where there is a well-recognized English name, we have used it; otherwise we have used the local Arabic names.

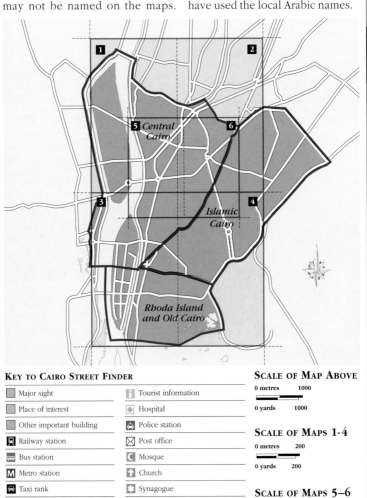

KEY TO CAIRO STREET FINDER

Major sight		Tourist information	
Place of interest		Hospital	
Other important building		Police station	
Railway station		Post office	
Bus station		Mosque	
Metro station		Church	
Taxi rank		Synagogue	
River taxi		One-way street	
Felucca boarding point			

SCALE OF MAP ABOVE

0 metres   1000
0 yards   1000

SCALE OF MAPS 1-4

0 metres   200
0 yards   200

SCALE OF MAPS 5–6

0 metres   200
0 yards   200

◁ **Cairo at night – view from the Cairo Tower looking south down the Nile over the Opera House Complex**

Street Finder Index

Because of different preferences in the transliteration of Arabic into English, our spellings of street and place names may differ from those on street signs – which, of course, also carry Arabic script.

Note that the word "Sharia", pronounced *shareb*, denotes a street. Other Arabic words used here include "Midan" (a square), "Bab" (a gate), "Beit" (a house), "Kubri" (a bridge) and "Qasr" (a palace).

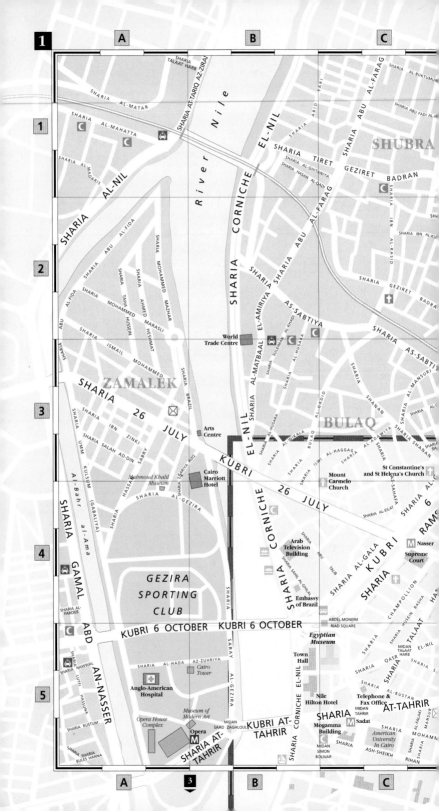

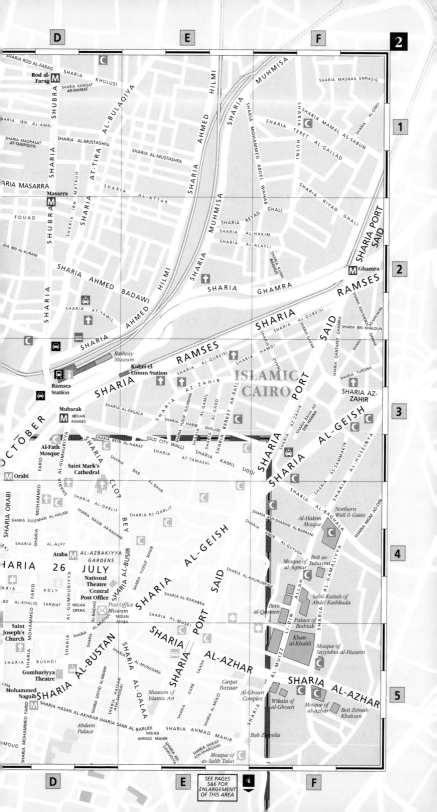

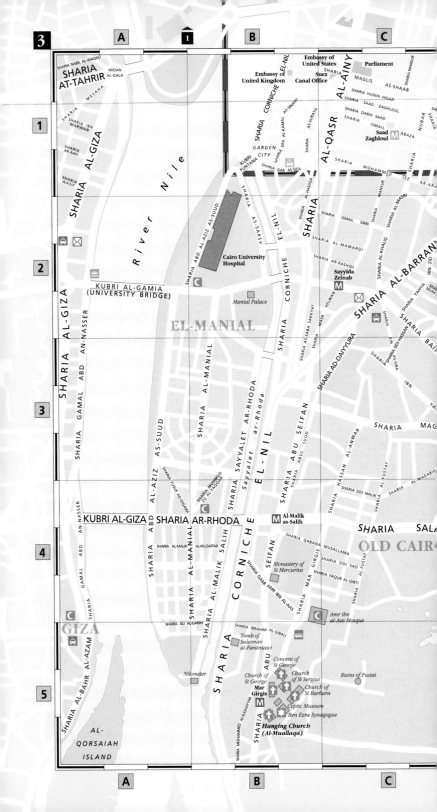

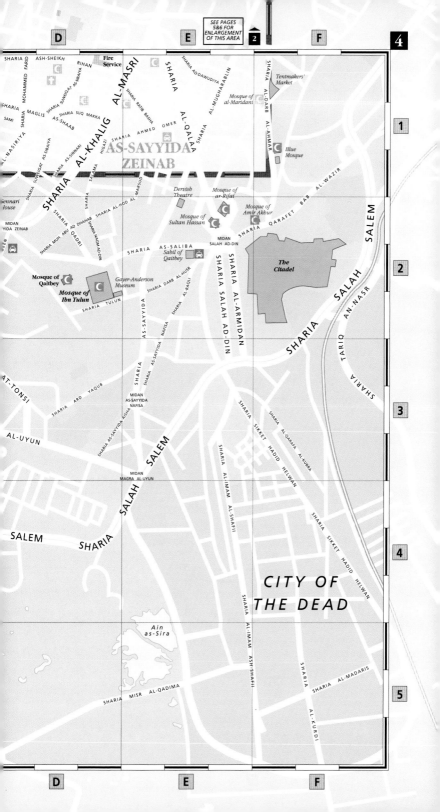

SEE PAGES
5&6 FOR
ENLARGEMENT
OF THIS AREA

D **E** **2** **F** **4**

SHARIA ASH-SHEIKH
SHARIA MOHAMMED FARID
RIHAN
Fire Service

SHARIA AD-DAWUDIYA

Tentmakers' Market

SHARIA SAMI

SHARIA MAGLIS

AS-SHAAB

SHARIA SIMROAT AS-SIBAIYA

SHARIA SUQ MAKKA

SHABA RATIB BASHA

SHARIA AL-MUGHARABLIN

Mosque of al-Maridani

SHARIA AD-DARB AL-AHMAR

1

SHARIA AL-NASIRIYA

SHARIA AS-SIBAIYA

SHARIA AS-SINNARI

AHMED OMER

HIGAZI

SHARIA AL-QALAA

AS-SAYYIDA ZEINAB

Blue Mosque

SHARIA SUWEIQAT AS-SIBAIYA

SHARIA S'AMA

SHARIA AL-HOD AL-MARSUD

Dervish Theatre

Mosque of ar-Rifai

Mosque of Amir Akhur

BAB AL-WAZIR

SALEM

Sennari House

SHARIA MUH. ABU'L QADRI

SHARIA NAGM AD-DIN

SHARIA AL-HOD AL-MARSUD

Mosque of Sultan Hassan

QARAFET

2

MIDAN SAYYIDA ZEINAB

SHARIA AL-BAQLI

MIDAN SALAH AD-DIN

SHARIA SALAH AD-DIN

The Citadel

Mosque of Qaitbey

AS-SALIBA
Sabil of Qaitbey

Gayer-Anderson Museum

SHARIA DARB AL-HUSR

SHARIA SALAH AD-DIN

SHARIA AL-ARMIDAN

SHARIA SALAH AD-DIN

AN-NASR

Mosque of Ibn Tulun

SHARIA TULUN

SHARIA AS-SAYYIDA

SHARIA AS-SAYYIDA NAFISA

SHARIA SALAH AD-DIN

2

AT-TONSI

SHARIA ARD YAQUB

SHARIA AS-SAYYIDA

MIDAN AS-SAYYIDA NAFISA

SHARIA AL-QARAFA AL-KUBRA

SHARIA SIKKET HADID HELWAN

3

AL-UYUN

SHARIA AS-SAYYIDA AISHA NAFISA

MIDAN MAGRA AL-UYUN

SHARIA AL-IMAM AL-SHAFII

SHARIA SIKKET HADID HELWAN

SALEM

SHARIA SALAH SALEM

4

SHARIA SALAH

CITY OF THE DEAD

Ain as-Sira

SHARIA AL-IMAM ASH-SHAFII

SHARIA AL-MADARIS

SHARIA MISR AL-QADIMA

SHARIA AL-KURDI

5

D **E** **F**

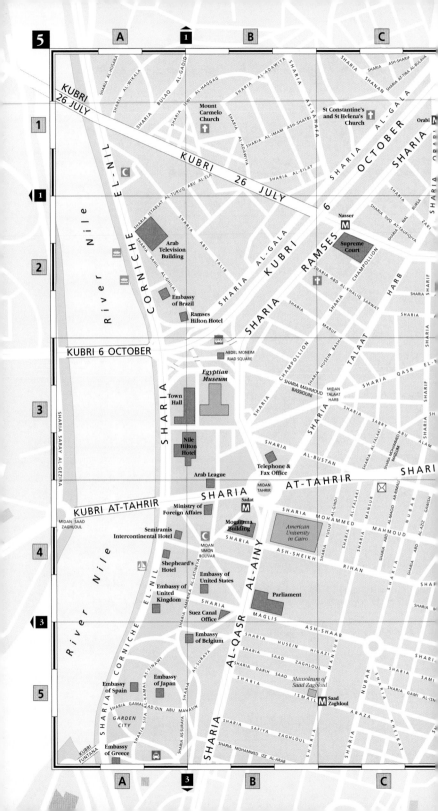

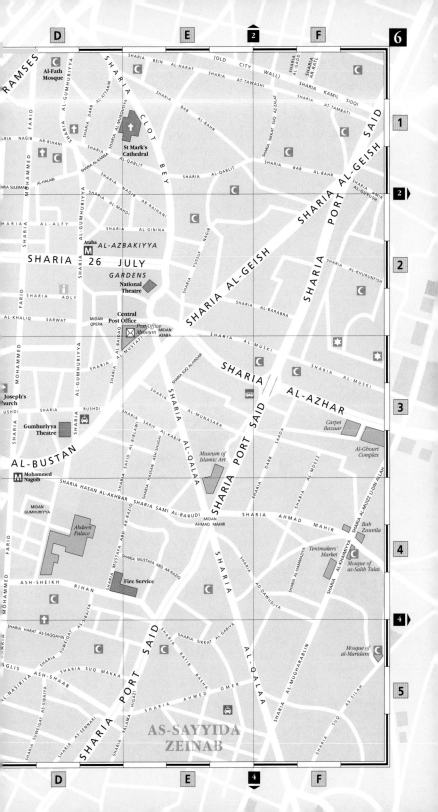

EGYPT
AREA BY AREA

Egypt at a Glance

MOST OF EGYPT'S great Pharaonic monuments
lie along the Nile Valley, but visitors should
not ignore the variety of sights and activities on
offer elsewhere. From the vast desert expanses
to the biblical scenery of the rocky Sinai interior,
Egypt fully engages the senses. For those who
need to be near the sea, the north coast is lined
with Mediterranean-influenced cities
and beaches, while the
resorts and dive centres
on the Red Sea coast
allow access to the
stunning coral reefs.

The Bent pyramid at Dahshur *(see p161)*
in the pyramid fields around Cairo

**THE DELTA AND THE
NORTH COAST**
(pp230–47)

**AROUND
CAIRO**
(pp154–65)

**Statue in the Graeco-Roman
Museum gardens in
Alexandria** *(see pp236–43)*

**THE WESTERN
DESERT**
(pp248–57)

Siwa *(see p256)*, the most isolated of Egypt's oases and a
living antiquity in the midst of the Western Desert

0 kilometres   150

0 miles   100

**Farmer working in the well-watered fields
around Dakhla Oasis** *(see p252)*

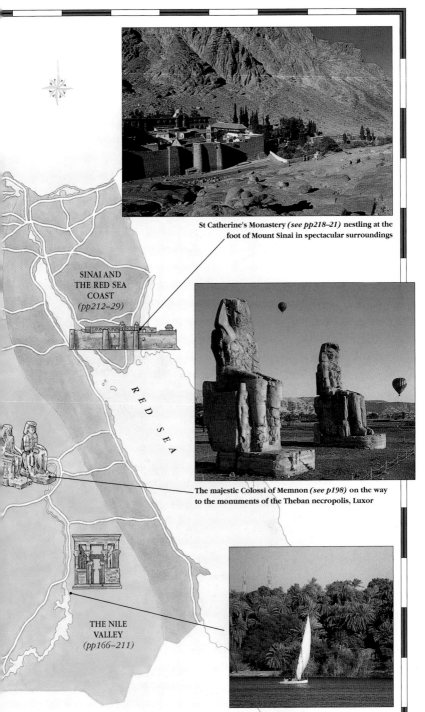

St Catherine's Monastery *(see pp218–21)* nestling at the foot of Mount Sinai in spectacular surroundings

SINAI AND
THE RED SEA
COAST
(pp212–29)

R E D   S E A

The majestic Colossi of Memnon *(see p198)* on the way to the monuments of the Theban necropolis, Luxor

THE NILE
VALLEY
(pp166–211)

One of the many feluccas that glide among the leafy islands at Aswan *(see pp204–7)*

AROUND CAIRO

DESERT EXPANSES AROUND *the modern capital offer escapism in many forms. Cairenes flock to the greenery of Fayoum and Qanater, while visitors can explore millennia of human ingenuity and achievement in the glorious monuments of Egypt's Old Kingdom burial sites and the monastic retreats of early Christians.*

The ruins of Memphis, a religious and commercial centre of vast importance nearly 4,000 years before the birth of Egypt's present capital, are situated on the left bank of the Nile about 30 km (19 miles) south of Cairo. One of the main necropolises of Memphis, Saqqara is rich in fascinating sites: prototype pyramids; tombs with the earliest known examples of Pharaonic decorative writing; the mysterious Serapeum, an underground tomb dedicated to the sacred Apis bulls, and some of the deepest burial chambers in Egypt. Other ancient burial sites nearby include Abusir, where a cluster of pyramids built for the principal 5th-Dynasty pharaohs is located on the edge of the desert, and remote Dahshur, home to several stone and mudbrick pyramids including the intriguing Bent Pyramid. West of the Delta region, between Alexandria and Cairo, are the monasteries of Wadi Natrun. Valued by the ancient Egyptians as a source of *natron*, the salt used during mummification, Wadi Natrun became, in the Roman era, a bolt hole for persecuted Christians, and later a centre of monasticism. Of several monasteries here, Deir as-Suriani, Deir Abu Makar and Deir Anba Bishoi are the most beautiful.

Fayoum is famed for its abundant fruits and vegetables, fragrant flowers and orange blossom. Its vast salt lake hosts a rich population of waterfowl. The area is renowned for its prehistoric remains and has numerous Ptolemaic and Roman archaeological sites. To sail along the Nile from Cairo to the gardens of Qanater is another favourite excursion of city residents.

Boating on the lake at Wadi Rayyan, a popular leisure activity for modern Cairenes

◁ **The Step Pyramid and vast funeral complex of Djoser, a 3rd-Dynasty king, in the desert at Saqqara**

Exploring Around Cairo

WHEN THE HUSTLE of Cairo gets too much, it is easy to slow down the pace a little by visiting one of the many interesting sights outside the capital. Saqqara attracts far fewer visitors and covers a larger area than the Pyramids at Giza and so rarely feels crowded, while the pyramid fields of Abusir and Dahshur are often practically deserted. Pharaonic remains are also dotted throughout Fayoum Oasis, although most make the trip for the lush vegetation. The other option for grassy spaces and trees is to sail down the Nile to Qanater, but this is so popular at the weekends that it is often just as congested as the city everyone is looking to escape. For real peace and quiet the best option, as the early Christians discovered, is to head out into the desert. Wadi Natrun is one of the founding sites of monasticism and the monks, although on holy retreat, are gracious when receiving visitors.

View of the mortuary temple and pyramid of Sahure at Abusir

WADI NATRUN ⑧

Alexandria

11

GEBEL QATRAN

LAKE QARUN

Bahariyya Oasis

FAYOUM OASIS

WADI RAYYAN

Egyptian farmers tending their sheep near Memphis, the first capital of ancient Egypt

GETTING AROUND

Abusir, Saqqara, Memphis and Dahshur all lie on the same road; unfortunately, it is not served by public transport and the only option is to hire your own. Most hotels in Cairo can arrange a taxi or, even better, a car and driver for the day. Birqash camel market is only really accessible by car or taxi, too. Buses for Wadi Natrun go from Cairo's Turgoman bus station, while those for Fayoum depart from beside the Maryutia Canal, east of Midan Giza.

0 kilometres   25

0 miles   15

SIGHTS AT A GLANCE

Abusir ①
Birqash ⑥
Dahshur ④
Fayoum ⑤
Memphis ③
Nile Barrages (Qanater) ⑦
Saqqara pp158–9 ②
Wadi Natrun ⑧

Date palms at Fayoum Oasis, inspiration for Pharaonic columns

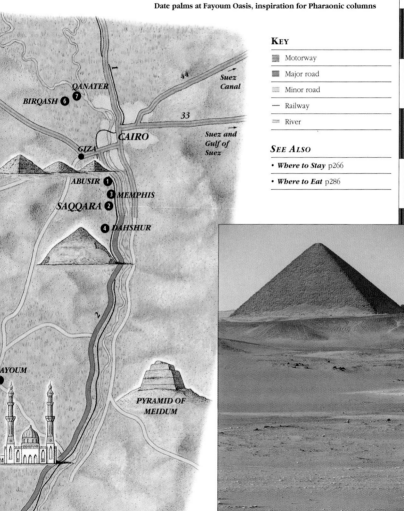

KEY

▦ Motorway
▦ Major road
▦ Minor road
— Railway
═ River

SEE ALSO

• *Where to Stay* p266
• *Where to Eat* p286

The Red Pyramid at Dahshur, so called because of ancient red graffiti found inside

Abusir ❶

Off Hwy 27, 27 km (17 miles) S of
Cairo. 🚌 🚐 *333 from Giza.*
🕐 *8am–sunset daily.* 🎫

THE CLUSTER OF four 5th-
Dynasty pyramids at Abusir
has not aged as well as the
Giza complex *(see pp28–9)*.
Instead, the site's appeal comes
from its location at the edge
of the desert and the fact that
few tourists ever venture here.

Only the northernmost and
best-preserved **Pyramid of
Sahure** can be entered, though
this is not recommended for
claustrophobics. The pyramid
is fronted by a mortuary
temple, which has partially
reconstructed walls with
reliefs of sea voyages and
scenes of the king hunting.
To the left, the **Pyramid of
Nyuserre** is badly dilapidated
but has the most complete
causeway linking its valley
and mortuary temples.
Further south is the **Pyramid
of Neferirkare**. The brother
and successor of Sahure,
Neferirkare died while his
pyramid was still being
constructed, so it was hastily
completed with a facing of
perishable mudbrick. This has
since crumbled away to reveal
a six-stepped stone inner core,
similar to Djoser's pyramid at
Saqqara. Finally, to the
southwest lies the unfinished
Pyramid of Neferefre, still
being excavated by Czech
archaeologists.

Abusir has also been the site
of two major archaeological
finds. In the 19th century, a
famed set of Old Kingdom
papyri, describing schedules of
ceremonies and festivals, was
discovered. Then, in 1998, a
team of Czech archaeologists
found the undisturbed tomb
of a 6th-century BC Egyptian
priest, Iufaa, containing Iufaa's
mummy and hundreds of
artifacts such as amulets and
*shabtis (see
p29)*.

The pyramids of Abusir on the edge of the desert

Saqqara ❷

**A mounted
policeman**

SAQQARA IS ONE OF the richest archaeological
sites in Egypt. Its monuments span 3,000
years, from the earliest ancient Egyptian
funerary structures to Coptic monasteries.
Saqqara developed as the royal necropolis
for the Old Kingdom capital of Memphis,
just to the west. As Memphis grew, so did
this city of the dead until it covered an area
of 7 km (4 miles), north to south. While
Saqqara continued to be used as a burial site for officials
for a time, it was eventually abandoned and, apart from
Djoser's pyramid, lay buried under sand for centuries.
Then, in 1851, Auguste Mariette discovered the Serapeum,
since when regular finds have been made at Saqqara.

Step Pyramid of Djoser at Saqqara, built by the architect Imhotep

⋔ Step Pyramid of Djoser
The centrepiece of the
Saqqara necropolis is the Step
Pyramid of Djoser, the prototype for the pyramids of Giza
and all other pyramids that
followed. This remarkable
structure was built for
3rd-Dynasty King Djoser by
his architect, the high priest
Imhotep, in the 27th century
BC. It marks an unprecedented
leap forward in the history of
world architecture. Until then,
Egyptian royal tombs had
been underground rooms
covered with low, flat, mudbrick *mastabas (see pp130–1)*.
The great innovator Imhotep
chose to use stone rather than
mudbrick, and to build not
just one *mastaba* but six, one
on top of the other, with
each additional layer
smaller than
the one beneath
it. The vast
enclosure sur-
rounding the
step pyramid
marked yet
another major

achievement, as it provided
the template for subsequent
Egyptian art and architecture.
Bounded by a finely cut limestone wall originally 10.5 m
(34 ft) high, this complex
included vast open courts,
pavilions, chapels.

A part of the ancient wall,
complete with
bastions and
recesses, has
been restored
in the south-
east corner,
and this
provides the
entrance to
the enclosure.
A colonnaded
corridor of 40 pillars, ribbed
in imitation of palm stems,
leads into the Great South
Court, where things to look
out for include a restored
section of wall bearing a
frieze of cobras. Some of the
oldest known examples of
tourist graffiti, dating from the
12th century BC, can be seen
preserved under perspex in
buildings east of the pyramid.

**Frieze of cobras,
Saqqara**

On the north side of the pyramid, there is a life-size painted statue of Djoser installed within a *serdab*, a stone box designed to allow the dead king's *ka* (spirit) to interact with the living world. The statue is a replica – the original is in Cairo's Egyptian Museum *(see p76)*.

Pyramid of Unas

Just south of the enclosure walls is the crumbled Pyramid of Unas, the tomb of the last king of the 5th Dynasty. Its chambers are covered with vertical columns of hieroglyphic text, recording hymns, prayers and magical spells, designed to protect the king in the afterlife. These so-called Pyramid Texts are the earliest known examples of decorative writing in a Pharaonic tomb chamber. They later formed the basis

Pyramid Texts in the chambers of the Pyramid of Unas, Saqqara

of the New Kingdom Book of the Dead *(see pp28–9)*. Unfortunately, deterioration caused by too many visitors means that the pyramid is now closed to the public.

More than 200 *mastabas* and tombs line the causeway running east of the pyramid. Many of them are beautifully decorated and open to visitors.

VISITORS' CHECKLIST

Off Hwy 27, 44 km (27 miles) S of Cairo. [icon] or tour from Cairo. [icon] daily. [icon]

Persian Tombs

Some of the deepest underground burial chambers in Egypt, the Persian Tombs, are situated immediately south of the Pyramid of Unas. A winding spiral staircase leads down from a wooden hut to the final resting places of three Persian noblemen. Psamtik, Djenhebu and Pediese were all officials of the 27th Dynasty, which was founded by the Persians in 525 BC. Colourful inscriptions on the walls of the tombs reveal that Psamtik was chief physician of the pharaoh's court and Djenhebu was a famous Persian admiral.

MAP OF SAQQARA

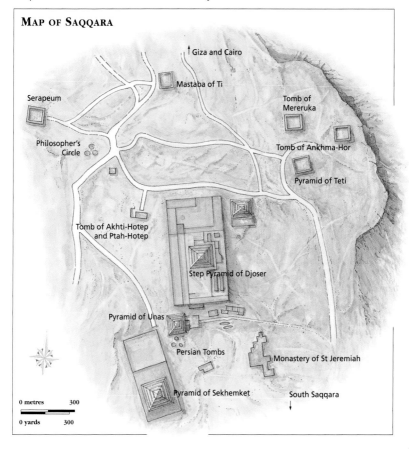

Giza and Cairo

Mastaba of Ti

Serapeum

Tomb of Mereruka

Philosopher's Circle

Tomb of Ankhma-Hor

Pyramid of Teti

Tomb of Akhti-Hotep and Ptah-Hotep

Step Pyramid of Djoser

Pyramid of Unas

Persian Tombs

Monastery of St Jeremiah

0 metres   300
0 yards   300

Pyramid of Sekhemket

South Saqqara

↑ Pyramid of Teti

From the outside, the pyramid of Teti, first king of the 6th Dynasty, looks like nothing more than a mound of rubble. However, it is worth visiting for its burial chamber, which contains the king's well-preserved giant basalt sarcophagus. The ceiling of the chamber is decorated with stars, and the walls are inscribed with sections of Pyramid Texts. Though found in several pyramids on the Saqqara site, this is currently the only place where these ancient funerary writings are accessible to the public.

Statue of Mereruka emerging from a false door in his tomb at Saqqara

↑ Tomb of Mereruka

An extensive complex of 33 chambers, the tomb of Mereruka, Teti's son-in-law, is one of the highlights of Saqqara. The tomb has some magnificent wall paintings, including a marsh scene with Mereruka hunting among birds, fish and hippos, and in another chamber a scene showing tax evaders being punished. The largest hall, which has a stone ring at its centre for tethering sacrificial animals, contains a life-size statue of Mereruka striding forward from a false door.

↑ Tomb of Ankhma-Hor

A short walk from Mereruka's tomb is the tomb of Ankhma-Hor, also referred to as the "Physician's Tomb" because of its fascinating wall reliefs depicting surgical operations.

These include surgery being performed on a man's toe and, apparently, a circumcision, as practised in the 6th Dynasty.

↑ Serapeum

Saqqara's strangest monument is the eerie underground burial chamber of the sacred Apis bulls. The Serapeum consists of a series of long, dark passageways lined with side chambers, which house 25 giant granite sarcophagi. Weighing up to 70 tons each, the sarcophagi once contained the mummified corpses of the Apis bulls. Seen as an incarnation of Ptah, god of Memphis, the Apis bulls were looked after by priests. When they died they were buried with great ceremony in the rock-cut, subterranean galleries of the Serapeum. The catacombs were begun by Amenhotep III (1390–52 BC) and remained in use until 30 BC.

When Auguste Mariette discovered the site in 1851, he found that all the tombs had been broken into and pillaged except for one, which was remarkably still intact. Inside was a sarcophagus containing a mummified bull, now in the Agricultural Museum in Cairo.

↑ Mastaba of Ti

East of the Serapeum, the Mastaba of Ti is the tomb of a court official who served three kings during the 5th Dynasty. Its wall paintings are unrivalled for the wealth of information they provide about everyday life in Old Kingdom Egypt. The far chamber has the best reliefs and also three slits in the wall revealing Ti's statue in its *serdab*. This was a room for the deceased's statue in which his spirit or *ka* resided.

↑ Philosopher's Circle

This grouping of statues, near the Serapeum, was set in place by the Ptolemaic Greeks. The circle of figures includes such illustrious Greek scholars as Plato and Homer. The circle was originally designed as an adjunct to a temple built by the last truly Egyptian pharaoh, Nectanebo, in the 4th century BC. The temple has long since disappeared, leaving the philosophers sitting alone.

Statue in the Philosopher's Circle, built by the Ptolemies at Saqqara

ENVIRONS: Beginning 2 km (1 mile) south of the main complex, **South Saqqara** is a field of smaller, dilapidated pyramids built by pharaohs Pepi I, Pepi II, Djedkare and Merenre. The pyramid of Pepi II in particular contains some fine examples of hieroglyphic text. Nearby, the Mastabat al-Faraun, or "Pharaoh's Bench", is a large monolithic mortuary complex of a 4th-Dynasty king. Hiring a horse, donkey or camel from near the Serapeum is the best way to reach these secluded southern sites.

An agricultural scene from the Mastaba of Ti, Saqqara

Palm groves at Memphis, covering the site of the ancient city

Memphis ❸

Off Hwy 27, 47 km (29 miles) S of Cairo. 🚌 from Cairo.

THE ANCIENT CITY OF Memphis was the capital of Egypt during the Old Kingdom and most of the Pharaonic period. It is thought it was founded in about 3100 BC by King Menes, the ruler responsible for uniting Upper and Lower Egypt. Situated at the head of the Nile Delta, this majestic city controlled important overland and river routes. While Thebes (the site of modern-day Luxor) became the ceremonial centre of Egypt during the New Kingdom, Memphis was still an important administrative and commercial centre until well into the Ptolemaic era. There are countless descriptions of the city in Classical texts from Greek writers and historians such as Plutarch and Strabo. In the 5th century AD, the historian Herodotus described Memphis as a "prosperous city and cosmopolitan centre". The extent and grandeur of the city's necropolis, centred on Saqqara, give some indication of how large and prosperous Memphis must once have been. Sadly, there is little remaining evidence of this former glory. The city has

Giant calcite sphinx at Memphis

almost completely vanished. Its magnificent temples and palaces were torn down and pillaged by foreign invaders from the Romans onwards, and the ruins were then buried under the alluvial mud deposited by the annual flooding of the Nile. Palm groves, cultivated fields and villages now cover the site of this once impressive city.

What little has been discovered at Memphis is gathered together in a small open-air **Museum** in the village of Mit Rahina. The showpiece is a colossal limestone statue of Ramses II, which lies, truncated at the knees, in a viewing pavilion. The statue is similar to the colossus of Ramses II found in Memphis and replicated in Midan Ramses *(see p78)*. In the garden there are more statues of Ramses II and an 18th-Dynasty sphinx, at 80 tons the largest calcite statue ever found. The garden also contains several calcite slabs, on which the sacred Apis bulls were mummified before being buried in nearby Saqqara.

Museum
⭘ daily. 📷

Dahshur ❹

Off Hwy 27, 64 km (40 miles) S of Cairo. 🚌 from Cairo. ⭘ daily. 📷

DAHSHUR is a remote desert pyramid field of great significance in the history of pyramid building. The two Old Kingdom pyramids at the site were constructed by 4th-Dynasty king Sneferu (2613–2589 BC), father of Khufu, the builder of the Great Pyramid *(see pp130-1)*. Chronologically they come after Saqqara and Meidum and before Giza and Abusir. The **Bent Pyramid** is considered to be Egypt's first proper pyramid because until this time pyramids were stepped, like Djoser's at Saqqara. The prevailing theory is that the pyramid is bent because once it began to rise the whole structure became unstable and so it had to be completed at a shallower slope. Unusually for pyramids dating from this period, much of its outer limestone casing is still intact, giving a good impression of what a visually stunning sight it must once have been.

Not happy with his Bent Pyramid, in the thirtieth year of his reign Sneferu began construction of the northern **Red Pyramid**, so called because of its ancient red graffiti. Second in size only to the Great Pyramid, it can be entered via a passage on the north face. At the foot of a long shaft are three chambers, two of which have corbelled ceilings – where the arch is formed by a series of steps.

The two smaller pyramids at Dahshur date from the Middle Kingdom, when there was a revival in pyramid building. They are badly dilapidated and of less interest.

Sneferu's Bent Pyramid at Dahshur with much of its outer limestone casing still visible

Fishermen mending their nets on the shores of Lake Qarun, Fayoum

Fayoum ❺

Off Hwy 27, 100 km (62 miles) SW of Cairo. 👥 *2 million.* 🚌 *from Cairo.* ℹ️ *Governorate Building, Medinat al-Fayoum (084) 342 313.*

JUST AN hour-and-a-half's drive from Cairo, Fayoum is Egypt's largest oasis and a popular escape for the smog-choked inhabitants of the big city. They avoid the ugly, modern town of Medinat al-Fayoum (Fayoum City), the oasis's administrative centre, and head instead for the heart of the area, **Lake Qarun**.

This tranquil lake, which existed in antiquity, was linked to the Nile by a series of canals built by the 12th-Dynasty pharaoh Amenemhat III. The area later became a favoured Pharaonic vacation spot.

The Greeks knew the area as Crocodilopolis, named after the reptiles in the lake, which they worshipped. Remains of crocodile temples can be seen at **Kom Aushim**, once the 3rd-century BC city of Karanis, north of Medinat al-Fayoum on the road to Cairo. Some of the objects found on the site are exhibited at the nearby museum. Although the crocodiles are long gone, Lake Qarun is home to an amazing variety of birds. As well as the indigenous species, there are also many migrants and winter visitors.

The ancient Egyptians were aware of bird life throughout the country, which they recorded here in friezes on tomb walls – most famously the Meidum Geese, now in Cairo's Egyptian Museum (*see pp76–7*).

Birding opportunities also exist at **Wadi Rayyan**, a stunning bit of land reclamation, in which excess water from the oasis has been channelled into the desert to create new lakes amongst the dunes. These lakes are well stocked with fish and are a major nesting ground for birds, as well as a big draw for picnicking daytrippers.

Of the pyramid sites around the Fayoum oasis, two are worth visits – but only by keen pyramidologists. Dating from the 12th Dynasty, the **Pyramid of Hawara** was once part of a vast complex: now, only a pile of rubble remains. On the margins of the oasis, the **Pyramid of Meidum** sits alone in the desert. Marking an important stage in pyramid development, it was originally built as a 4th-Dynasty step pyramid. The steps were later filled in and an outer casing added, but design flaws caused the sides to collapse some time after the alterations were made.

The inner core of the Meidum Pyramid at Fayoum

🏛 **Kom Aushim**
30 km (18 miles) N of Medinat al-Fayoum. 🚗 🅾️ *daily.* 📷

🦅 **Wadi Rayyan**
45 km (28 miles) SW of Medinat al-Fayoum. 🚗 🅾️ *daily.* 📷

🏛 **Pyramid of Hawara**
12 km (7 miles) SE of Medinat al-Fayoum. 🚗 🅾️ *daily.* 📷

🏛 **Pyramid of Meidum**
32 km (20 miles) NE of Medinat al-Fayoum. 🚆 *to Al-Wasta, then taxi.* 🅾️ *daily.* 📷

Birqash Camel Market ❻

Off Mansuriyya Canal Road, 30 km (18 miles) NW of Cairo. 🚗 *from Cairo.* 🅾️ *mornings.* 📷

CONTRARY TO what many might think, the camel is not indigenous to Egypt: it was probably introduced to Egypt by the Persians or the Ptolemies in the 6th century BC. Having since proved themselves indispensable, camels are now brought up to Egypt in their thousands from western Sudan. Most are taken to Birqash, Egypt's largest camel market, which relocated here from its original site in Cairo in 1995. Hundreds of camels are sold every morning, but trade is at its briskest on Fridays. The sound of the animals bawling competes with traders' voices raised in haggling, and the smell is truly appalling.

Camels and traders at the daily Birqash camel market

◁ **Camels, cattle and other livestock on sale at the Birqash camel market**

Nile Barrages (Qanater) 7

16 km (10 miles) N of Cairo. 🏛 56,000.
📷 Corniche el-Nil, in front of Arab
Television Building. 🚌 from Cairo.

THE NILE divides into its eastern Damietta and western Rosetta branches at Qanater, where the main attraction is the Nile Barrages, built to control the flow of water to Lower Egypt. Work on the barrages began in 1834, under Mohammed Ali, and was completed in 1863, when it was discovered that they were ineffectual. The barrages were abandoned until 1883 when a group of British engineers, led by Sir Colin Scott-Moncrieff, finally completed the work.

View across Deir Anba Bishoi monastery at Wadi Natrun

Today the Nile Barrages are surrounded by gardens and are popular with picnickers. Although busy at weekends, Qanater is a pleasant destination for day trips from Cairo, the journey by river bus taking approximately two hours.

Nile Barrages at Qanater, where the two branches of the river fork

Wadi Natrun 8

Off Desert Hwy, 100 km (62 miles)
NW of Cairo. 🚌 from Cairo.

JUST WEST of the Delta region, Wadi Natrun was valued by the ancient Egyptians as a source of the salt deposit natron, a vital ingredient in the mummification process (see p28). Later, during the Roman era, the valley's isolation made it an ideal retreat for early Christians escaping Roman

persecution. Initially these monks and hermits lived in caves, but over the years they built many monasteries, of which only four remain today.

The monasteries are easily reached from Cairo by bus, which terminates at the small village of Bir Hooker. All four are surrounded by high, mud-brick walls and resemble desert fortresses. Within the fortified keep of **Deir Anba Bishoi** (the Monastery of St Bishoi), are a well, kitchens, church and storerooms large enough to hold provisions for a year. The church is believed to contain the body of St Bishoi, perfectly preserved in a sealed tube on the altar. He is also commemorated at the Monastery of the Syrians, **Deir as-Suriani**, whose main church (dedicated to St Mary) is built over a cave where St Bishoi is believed to have received a vision of Christ. A bigger draw are the icons and wall paintings, some of which date back to the 8th century.

A little to the north is **Deir al-Baramus**, where the bodies of two sons of the Roman emperor Valentinus are reputed to be buried in a crypt below one of its five churches. 20 km (12 miles) to the southeast is **Deir Abu Makar**, the most secluded of the monasteries: permission to visit must be arranged in advance. Each monastery has a full complement of monks, who will show visitors around and may provide a simple meal, for which a small donation should be offered.

THE FAYOUM PORTRAITS

Although Fayoum is visited by few tourists, many know the name because of the Fayoum Portraits. Several of the portraits, which have been exhibited throughout the world in recent years, were discovered here. Some of the earliest ever examples of portraiture, these eerily lifelike faces with their wide staring eyes date back to the Graeco-Roman period. What makes the portraits particularly haunting is that these are funerary artifacts, painted on wooden boards during the subject's lifetime then, at death, laid over the face of the mummified corpse. Many portraits are now on display at the Egyptian Museum (see pp74–5).

Portrait of an Egyptian dating from 3rd century AD, found at Fayoum

THE NILE VALLEY

···

GYPT HAS BEEN DESCRIBED *as the "gift of the Nile" because without the river the whole country would be a barren desert. Instead, a narrow and verdant strip of cultivated land cuts through the arid country. In ancient times, a great civilization flourished along the river's banks and the incredible wealth of temples and tombs left behind makes the Nile Valley the greatest open-air museum in the world.*

For Egypt's *fellaheen* (farmers), the Nile is as central to life today as it was to the farmers and fishermen depicted in the Pharaonic tombs dotted along the valley. For thousands of years the annual flooding of the Nile deposited fresh, fertilizing silt on the surrounding land. Once the flood subsided, the peasants built irrigation channels, planted their crops and waited for the harvest. Though the construction of Aswan's High Dam in the 1960s put an end to the annual inundation, many of Egypt's farmers still live in simple, mudbrick villages and cultivate the precious fertile belt using the same age-old methods.

Since the 19th century, visitors have come to the Nile Valley to gaze in awe at the countless treasures that have been excavated along the banks of the river. Most of the ancient monuments here were rediscovered after being buried for centuries under sand and debris. As a result, some have been preserved in amazing condition.

In addition to the magnificent monuments, the Nile itself is part of the region's attraction. The traditional feluccas, with their distinctive white sails, are part of the Nile Valley landscape as they dart between cruise ships gliding up and down the river between Luxor and Aswan.

Tourism remains the region's main industry. Despite the setback caused by a series of attacks on foreign tourists in the 1990s, visitors continue to flock to the Nile Valley to experience the sense of living history found along the banks of this majestic river – the lifeblood of Egypt.

Villager in Luxor *(see pp180–3)*, setting out his vegetable stall with crops grown in the fertile Nile Valley

◁ View of the Aga Khan Mausoleum *(see p206)* from across the other side of the Nile at Aswan

Exploring the Nile Valley

MOST VISITORS TO THE Nile Valley head for the tourist magnet of Luxor, where the magnificent Luxor and Karnak temples and the Theban necropolis are the major attractions. Further south, the beautiful ancient garrison town of Aswan is a relaxing place to stay and a good base for exploring the temples on the banks of Lake Nasser, including the stunning Abu Simbel. The sheer number of ancient monuments in the Nile Valley can be overwhelming and to enjoy the region fully it is a good idea to combine sightseeing with a felucca trip on the Nile or a visit to the colourful souqs of Luxor and Aswan.

MINYA **1**

2 BENI HASAN

HERMOPOLIS **3**

4 TELL AL-AMARNA

ASYUT **5**

SOHAG **6**

ABYDOS

SIGHTS AT A GLANCE

Donkey and cart, a traditional mode of transport for Nile farmers

GETTING AROUND

Luxor and Aswan have airports served by regular flights from Cairo. Trains run frequently between Cairo, Luxor and Aswan, stopping at major towns en route. However, the current political situation means that care should be exercised if visiting sites between Cairo and Luxor *(see p172)*. The road from Cairo to Aswan is good, and buses and service taxis operate between the main cities. Dendara and Abydos are currently best visited on a day trip from Luxor, and Abu Simbel can be reached by air or road from Aswan. There are many cruises on offer between Luxor and Aswan or alternatively, a relaxing two or three-night felucca trip may appeal to the more adventurous *(see pp330–1)*.

W E S T E R N   D E S E R T

ABU SIMBEL 20

The graceful Kiosk of Trajan on the enchanting island of Philae, near Aswan

A selection of exotic spices on sale in Aswan's famous souq, one of the most colourful markets in Egypt

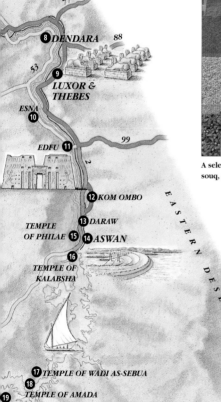

8 DENDARA

77

88

53

9 LUXOR &
THEBES

ESNA
10

EDFU 11

99

2

12 KOM OMBO

13 DARAW

TEMPLE
OF PHILAE 15 14 ASWAN

16

TEMPLE OF
KALABSHA

EASTERN DESERT

17 TEMPLE OF WADI AS-SEBUA

18

19 TEMPLE OF AMADA
QASR IBRIM

KEY

▦	Major road
▦	Minor road
▦	Scenic route
—	Railway line
═	River

SEE ALSO

- **Where to Stay** pp266–9
- **Where to Eat** pp287–9

0 kilometres	100
0 miles	50

Minya ●

Al-Minya governorate, 245 km (152 miles) S of Cairo. 🏙 200,000. 🚉 🚌 ℹ️ *Governorate Building, Corniche el-Nil (086) 360 150.*

SITUATED ON THE west bank of the Nile, the regional capital Minya was a wealthy centre of the cotton industry in the early 20th century. Today it is a semi-industrial city, although it still feels distinctly rural. With its green squares, pretty, tree-lined corniche and run-down Italian villas built by cotton magnates, Minya is a pleasant place to simply wander around. Unfortunately, the surrounding countryside's association with Islamic militants and the relatively high police presence mean that few tourists now venture here. If the security situation improves, Minya is an excellent base for exploring local historical sites such as Beni Hasan. The tourist office is keen to encourage people to come to the town and will help arrange tours to the sites, although the police may insist on escorting visitors.

Beni Hasan ●

Al-Minya governorate, 20 km (12 miles) S of Minya. 🚉 to Abu Qirkis, then ferry. 🔲 *daily.* 📷

CARVED INTO limestone hills on the east bank of the Nile, the rock tombs of Beni Hasan date from the Middle Kingdom (2055 to 1650 BC).

The necropolis belonged to military and regional rulers who, in a clear assertion of their growing independence, chose to be buried in their own *nome* (province) rather than close to the king at Saqqara (*see p158*). With their deeper shafts and more elaborate layout and decoration than earlier *mastabas*, these tombs mark a transition in style between the Old and New Kingdoms.

Only a handful of the 39 tombs are open to the public but the vivid murals on some of the walls reveal much about life in the Middle Kingdom. Among the most beautiful is the **Tomb of Khnumhotep** (No. 3), which contains colourful scenes of daily life and shows Khnumhotep, a 12th-Dynasty regional governor, hunting with a throwstick and fishing with spears. The **Tomb of Amenemhat** (No. 2) is decorated with desert hunting scenes, while wall paintings in the **Tomb of Kheti** (No.17) depict many aspects of rural life, including wine-making. The wrestling scenes in the **Tomb of Baqet** (No.15) are precursors of the battle reliefs found in New Kingdom tombs.

Tall granite columns, which once supported a Coptic basilica, amid the ruins of Hermopolis

Hermopolis ●

Al-Minya governorate, 8 km (5 miles) N of Mallawi. 🚉 to Al-Ashmunein. 🔲 *daily.* 📷

BELIEVED BY ancient Egyptians to be one of the sites of creation, the city of Khmun was the cult centre of Thoth, god of writing and wisdom. The city was later renamed Hermopolis Magna by the Ptolemies, who associated their own god Hermes with Thoth. During the Ptolemaic era the city was a flourishing centre but it now lies in ruins. Standing out among the rather scant remains are 24 huge **columns** from a Christian basilica and four **sandstone baboons** of Amenhotep III from his original Thoth temple.

Sandstone baboon from Amenhotep III's Thoth temple

ENVIRONS: The ancient city's vast necropolis, **Tuna al-Gebel**, lies to the southwest. Thousands of mummified baboons and ibises, animals

The Tomb of Kheti (No.17) in Beni Hasan with detailed scenes of daily life during the Middle Kingdom

sacred to Thoth, once filled the labyrinth of catacombs here. A short walk further south is the "City of the Dead", where streets lined with chapels and tombs lie semi-buried in sand dunes. Most remarkable is the tomb of Petosiris, high priest of Thoth in the 4th century BC, which resembles a small temple and is decorated with detailed reliefs. The Tuna al-Gebel necropolis bordered on Akhetaten *(see below)* and a boundary stele showing Akhenaten and his family is visible north of the tombs.

⋔ Tuna al-Gebel
7 km (4 miles) SW of Hermopolis.
⬤ *daily.* 🗖

Relief showing wine-pressing in the Tomb of Petosiris, Tuna al-Gebel

Tell al-Amarna ④

Al-Minya governorate, 12 km (7 miles) SW of Mallawi. 🚍 to Deir al-Mawas, then ferry. ⬤ *daily.* 🗖

THE REMAINS OF the city of Akhetaten, built by the rebel pharaoh Akhenaten and his wife Queen Nefertiti, lie at a site known today as Tell al-Amarna. The site, which once stretched an impressive 15 km (9 miles) north to south and boasted magnificent temples and palaces, is now almost desolate but the sense of history and romance remains.

The widely dispersed ruins are spread around a desert plain bounded by the Nile to the west and surrounded by cliffs. South of the landing stage at At-Till, a cemetery covers part of what was once the **Great Temple of Aten**. In contrast to traditional Egyptian temples which had darkened sanctuaries *(see pp24–5)*, this temple had a roofless sanctuary, designed to allow the rays of the sun-

god Aten to flood in. To the south, the **Small Temple of Aten** is being restored and the outline of two royal palaces can be made out. Better preserved are the remains of Nefertiti's **Northern Palace**, to the north of At-Till. Here, the remains of some mosaics can still be seen on the floor of summer residence.

The highlights of Tell al-Amarna are the two sets of cliff tombs at either end of the city. Of the **Northern Tombs**, 3 km (2 miles) north of At-Till, one of the finest is the **Tomb of Huya** (No.1), Superintendent of the Royal Harem and Steward to Queen Tiye, Akhenaten's mother. This fascinating tomb is carved with royal banquet scenes, including one that shows the queen wining and dining with her son and his family. In the highly decorated **Tomb of Mery-Re I** (No.4), Akhenaten is shown presenting Mery-Re I with the high priest's golden collar. Reliefs depicting Akhenaten and the Great Temple on the eastern wall of the tomb give an indication of what the city must have looked like during its brief period of glory.

Relief of Nefertiti and her daughter praying to the sun-god Aten, in Cairo's Egyptian Museum

Grouped in clusters, 8 km (5 miles) south of At-Till, the **Southern Tombs** are less accessible but equally rewarding. The **Tomb of Ay** (No.25), Akhenaten's vizier, is considered the finest tomb in Tell al-Amarna. The wall paintings show Ay and his wife receiving ceremonial golden collars from Akhenaten and Nefertiti, watched by a crowd of cheering onlookers. The well-preserved **Tomb of Mahu** (No.9) contains reliefs of Mahu carrying out his duties as Akhenaten's chief of police.

AKHENATEN THE HERETIC

In the 14th century BC, Amenhotep IV turned his back on Thebes and the practice of worshipping several gods to establish a religion based on the worship of just one god, Aten, god of the sun disc. He changed his name from Amenhotep to Akhenaten, meaning servant of Aten, and built a huge city dedicated to Aten at Akhetaten. The city was the capital of Egypt for 14 years but, when Akhenaten died, Thebes was re-established as the capital by Akhenaten's son-in-law and successor Tutankhamun. Akhetaten was destroyed on the order of the priests of Karnak who were determined to eradicate all trace of the heretical pharaoh's new religion.

The rebel pharaoh Akhenaten

Asyut

Asyut governorate, 110 km (68 miles)
S of Minya. 🏙 *280,000.* 🚊 🚌
ℹ️ *Sharia ath-Thawra (088) 310 010.*

I N PHARAONIC TIMES Asyut
was capital of the 13th *nome*
(province) and centre of the
cult of Wepwawet, the jackal-
headed god and avenger of
Osiris. At the crossroads of
caravan routes to the Western
Desert oases and across the
Sahara, the city has a long
history as a centre of trade.
Until the mid-19th century,
slaves who had survived the
torturous "Forty Days Road"
from Darfur in Sudan were
sold here alongside camels in
Egypt's biggest slave market.

Today Asyut is the largest
city in Upper Egypt and has
the third largest university in
the country. Known for its
carpet making,
Asyut remains
the region's
main agricultural
trading centre.
The area is also
associated with
the Virgin Mary.
In August 2000,
the Virgin was
reportedly seen
above St Mark's
Church. For a few months
afterwards there were reports
of lights around the church
towers and many thousands
flocked to see them. The
apparitions have now ceased.

Convent of the Holy Virgin, built into the cliffs at Dirunka, near Asyut

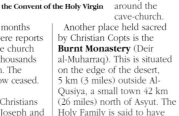

**Icon showing the Holy Family in
the Convent of the Holy Virgin**

ENVIRONS: Coptic Christians
believe that Mary, Joseph and
the baby Jesus sheltered in
caves at Dirunka, 12 km
(7 miles) southwest of Asyut.

They were escaping from King
Herod, who had ordered the
killing of all baby boys under
the age of two in Bethlehem.
A large convent, the **Convent
of the Holy Virgin**, was built
nearby. During
the annual
Moulid of the
Virgin, held
between 7 and
22 August,
around 50,000
pilgrims flock
here to see
icons paraded
around the
cave-church.

Another place held sacred
by Christian Copts is the
Burnt Monastery (Deir
al-Muharraq). This is situated
on the edge of the desert,
5 km (3 miles) outside Al-
Qusiya, a small town 42 km
(26 miles) north of Asyut. The
Holy Family is said to have
lived in a cave here for a
month and it is thought that
the church built over it was

the first in Egypt. What is
now the church's altar stone
once blocked the entrance to
the cave. The annual moulid,
which is held here between
21 and 28 June, attracts
many thousands of visitors.

A further 7 km (4 miles)
west of the monastery are
the **Tombs of Mir**, a burial
ground dating from the Old
and Middle Kingdoms.

♙ **Convent of the Holy
Virgin**
12 km (7 miles) SW of Asyut. 🚌 *from
Asyut.*

♙ **Burnt Monastery**
47 km (29 miles) N of Asyut. 🚗 🚌
to Al-Qusiya, then a local taxi.

Sohag ❻

Sohag governorate, 115 km (71 miles)
S of Asyut. 🏙 *133,000.* 🚊 🚌 ℹ️
Governorate Bldg (093) 604 453.

A N AGRICULTURAL TOWN and
commercial centre, Sohag
has a large Coptic Christian
community and, like many
other cities in Middle Egypt,
is a place of sporadic unrest.
Although the atmosphere is
less tense than in Asyut,
Sohag is not recommended
as a place to stay. However
the Egyptian government
wants to encourage tourists,
and a new 6-hectare (15-acre)
tourist village is being built
on Araman island in the Nile,
opposite the city. A museum
is also planned to house
archaeological finds from the
area. A large animal market is
held in the town each Monday.

SECURITY IN THE REGION

This area has long been associated with religious extremists
who want to turn the country into an Islamic state. Asyut
University was a hotbed for Islamic fundamentalists in the
late 1970s, and the early 1990s saw several attacks on tourists
around Qena, Asyut and Dairut. The Egyptian government
has tightened security, especially since the 1997 massacre
at Luxor, but tension continues and police presence is high.
Although tour groups tend to avoid the region, officially it
is possible to travel freely in this area and visitors rarely
encounter trouble. The most common way to see sites such
as the Temple of Hathor at Dendara (see pp174–5) is on a
day trip from Luxor, usually with a police escort. The situation
is always changing, however, and visitors should contact local
tourist authorities and their embassy for the latest advice.

ENVIRONS: A short drive west of Sohag, the **White Monastery** (Deir al-Abyad) dates from the early 5th century AD. Named for the colour of its masonry, the monastery was built by the Coptic saint Shenouda using chunks of white limestone taken from local Pharaonic temples. The monastery was once home to 2,000 monks. Today little remains within its high fortress walls apart from a church dedicated to its founder. On 14th July every year thousands of pilgrims attend a moulid at the site.

Four kilometres (2.5 miles) north of the White Monastery lies the **Red Monastery** (Deir al-Ahmar). Built in the 6th century AD by Shenouda's disciple Bishoi – a repentant robber who became a saint – the monastery has two churches within its grounds. The main church contains several interesting, though faded, 10th-century wall paintings. The monastery is hidden within a sprawling village so it may be necessary to ask for directions.

On the eastern bank of the Nile, just across the river from Sohag, is **Akhmim**, which can be reached by microbus. The town is known for its hand-woven hangings and carpets. The town's main attraction, an 11-m (36-ft) high statue of Queen Meret Amun – the daughter of Ramses II – was discovered here in 1982.

Icon of Christ in the White Monastery

White Monastery
10 km (6 miles) W of Sohag.
daily. 14th July.
Red Monastery
14 km (9 miles) NW of Sohag.
daily.

The chapel of Osiris in the Cenotaph Temple of Seti I in Abydos

Abydos ❼

Sohag governorate, 46 km (29 miles) SW of Sohag; 10 km (6 miles) W of Al-Balyana. or day trip from Luxor, with convoy.

ABYDOS, THE CULT centre of Osiris, god of the dead, was regarded as the holiest of Egyptian towns in Pharaonic times. All ancient Egyptians tried to make the pilgrimage to the town during their lifetime or hoped to be buried here. Many tombs were painted with scenes of the deceased making the posthumous journey to Abydos. Tradition had it that Osiris – or at least his head – was laid to rest here after he was murdered by his brother Seth and his mutilated body strewn over the country.

Abydos was once a vast walled town with several ancient cemeteries, lakes and temples, including the important Temple of Osiris. Today, almost all that can be seen is the stunning 19th-Dynasty **Cenotaph Temple of Seti I**. Built during Seti I's reign between 1294–1279 BC, it is one of the most intact temples in Egypt. Constructed using white limestone, this secondary mortuary temple possesses some of the finest bas-reliefs of the New Kingdom; many have retained their original colour. After the death of his father, Ramses II (1279–1213 BC) built his own temple to the north of Seti's temple. Although only partially intact, it is noted for its interesting hieroglyphs.

Entrance to the temple is gained via the first hypostyle hall. The temple's highlights include the bas-relief scenes in the second hypostyle hall, which show Seti I with the gods Osiris and Horus. Just beyond, the seven chapels dedicated to a deified Seti I and the gods Ptah, Ra-Harakhty, Amun, Osiris, Isis and Horus are remarkable for their coloured reliefs and delicate decoration. Each chapel contained the statue and barque of the relevant god and would be served daily by the high priests. Behind the temple, Seti had built the Osireion (the tomb of Osiris) from huge blocks of stone. Today it is partly underwater.

Cenotaph Temple of Seti I
daily.

The Red Monastery near Sohag, founded by the Coptic saint Bishoi

Dendara ⑧

Bes, patron god of childbirth

Dendara, where Hathor supposedly gave birth to Horus's child, the god Ihy, was Hathor's cult centre from pre-Dynastic times. Buried under sand until the 19th century, the vast Temple of Hathor remains remarkably intact. The current temple is Graeco-Roman but its design imitates typical Pharaonic temple architecture – a series of large hypostyle halls leading to a dark sanctuary, surrounded by a maze of store rooms, chapels and crypts. Other buildings within the mudbrick walls of the complex include two *mammisi* (birth houses) and a Coptic basilica.

★ **Astronomical Ceiling**
In this detail from the ceiling, the sun-god Ra is shown sailing his sacred barque across the sky.

The roof offers glorious views of the whole Dendara site.

Temple Façade
The pylon-shaped façade shows Roman emperors Tiberius and Claudius making offerings to Horus and Hathor.

TEMPLE OF HATHOR RECONSTRUCTION
The intricate carved reliefs that adorn the temple were originally painted in vivid colours.

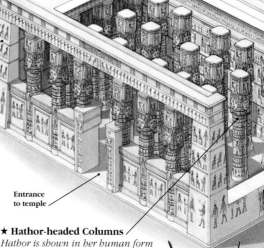

Entrance to temple

★ **Hathor-headed Columns**
Hathor is shown in her human form with cow's ears at the head of the 18 columns in the hypostyle hall.

CULT OF HATHOR

Hathor was the goddess of pleasure and love, and wet nurse and lover of Horus. Every year she was carried on a barque to Edfu *(see p177)* to be reunited with Horus. The Festival of Drunkenness, celebrating the divine union, followed. On New Year's Day, Hathor's statue was carried up the decorated west staircase of the temple to the open-air kiosk on the roof, where it was revitalized by the sun.

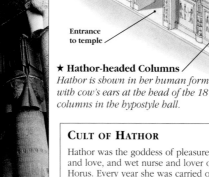

Hathor with the sun disk and cow horns

STAR FEATURES

★ **Astronomical Ceiling**

★ **Hathor-headed Columns**

Cleopatra and Caesarion
A huge relief on the southern exterior wall shows Cleopatra making offerings to Hathor. Caesarion, her son by Julius Caesar, stands in front of her burning incense.

The east staircase
led back down into the temple.

The open-air kiosk
was the focus of the New Year celebrations. It may have had a light wooden cover that was removed to expose the statues to the sun.

The New Year Chapel
is where rituals were performed before Hathor's statue was taken up to the roof. The ceiling shows Nut giving birth to the sun.

Roman Mammisi
This small temple celebrated the divine birth of Hathor's son. The southern wall has some exquisite reliefs on its exterior.

Elaborate bas-reliefs depicting offerings to Hathor

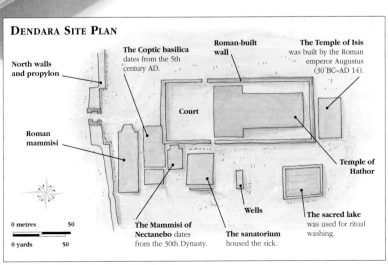

DENDARA SITE PLAN

North walls and propylon

The Coptic basilica
dates from the 5th century AD.

Roman-built wall

The Temple of Isis
was built by the Roman emperor Augustus (30 BC–AD 14).

Court

Roman mammisi

Temple of Hathor

The Mammisi of Nectanebo dates from the 30th Dynasty.

Wells

The sanatorium housed the sick.

The sacred lake
was used for ritual washing.

0 metres   50

0 yards   50

Luxor and Thebes ❾

MODERN LUXOR GREW out of the ruins of Thebes, once the capital of ancient Egypt's New Kingdom (1550–1069 BC). The monumental temples at Luxor and Karnak were famed throughout the ancient world and have attracted tourists since Greek and Roman times. Across the Nile, on the West Bank, lies the Theban Necropolis, perhaps the world's richest archaeological site. To foil thieves, the Theban kings hid their tombs deep in the surrounding hills, away from their mortuary temples on the flood plain. Visiting the Luxor monuments is straight-forward, but due to the number of sights and the distances involved, some planning is needed to get the most out of a visit to the West Bank.

Detail from the Colossi of Memnon

Medinat Habu ❿
Second only to Karnak in size, the Mortuary Temple of Ramses III was modelled on the Ramesseum.

LUXOR AND THEBES

① Luxor Temple *(pp182–3)*
② Luxor Museum *(p183)*
③ Karnak Temple *(pp184–6)*
④ Valley of the Kings *(pp188–90)*
⑤ Tombs of the Nobles *(p191)*
⑥ Hatshepsut Temple *(pp192–3)*
⑦ Valley of the Queens *(pp194–5)*
⑧ The Ramesseum *(pp196–7)*
⑨ Colossi of Memnon *(p198)*
⑩ Medinat Habu *(p198)*
⑪ Deir al-Medina *(pp198–9)*
⑫ Temple of Seti I *(p199)*
⑬ Howard Carter's house *(p199)*
⑭ New Gurna *(p199)*

KEY

🚉 Train station

⬜ Town area

0 kilometres   1
0 miles   0.5

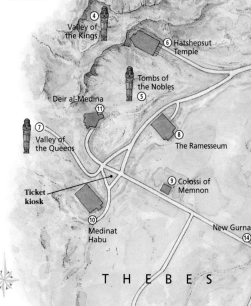

T H E B E S

Hatshepsut Temple ⑥
Discovered only in the mid-19th century, and still undergoing restoration, the Mortuary Temple of Hatshepsut rises out of the desert in a series of terraces that merge with the sheer limestone cliffs behind.

◁ **A flotilla of feluccas heading south down the Nile at Luxor**

GETTING AROUND
Luxor Temple is in the centre of town and easily accessible on foot; Karnak Temple can be reached by minibus, bicycle, taxi or caleche. Most Luxor hotels offer tours to the West Bank including the services of a guide, but a private arrangement may be cheaper. Alternatively, to get around Thebes, hire a taxi, donkey or bicycle (bikes hired in Luxor can be taken on the ferry) for the day.

The Ramesseum ⑧
Built to perpetuate the pharaoh's glory, the Mortuary Temple of Ramses II was part of a large complex that included a royal palace and a great many granaries and storerooms. Both pylons are decorated with scenes from the Battle of Qadesh.

⑬ Howard Carter's house

⑫ Temple of Seti I

RIVER NILE

Karnak Temple ③

Tourist ferry

Local ferry

Local ferry

② Luxor Museum

L U X O R

Car ferry

Tourist ferry

① Luxor Temple

Karnak Temple ③
The Karnak complex was known as "Ipet-Isut" ("the most perfect of places") to the ancient Egyptians.

Luxor Temple ①
Founded by Amenhotep III, Luxor Temple was dedicated to the Theban triad of Amun, Mut and Khonsu, who are celebrated at the annual Festival of Opet (see p186).

Street-by-Street: Luxor

BUILT ON THE SITE of the New Kingdom capital city of Thebes, Luxor has returned to prominence as the tourist mecca of the Nile Valley. The exciting excavations that were led by European archaeologists in the 19th and early 20th centuries, especially the discovery of Tutankhamun's tomb, aroused international interest in the town and visitors have been coming to marvel at the amazing concentration of ruins here ever since. Today the livelihood of Luxor's resident population depends almost entirely on tourism and visitors can expect to be approached by salesmen and touts at every turn. The bustling town is centred around the magnificent Luxor Temple, an enduring symbol of its glorious past.

Stone Ramses II at Luxor Temple

Felucca on the Nile at Luxor

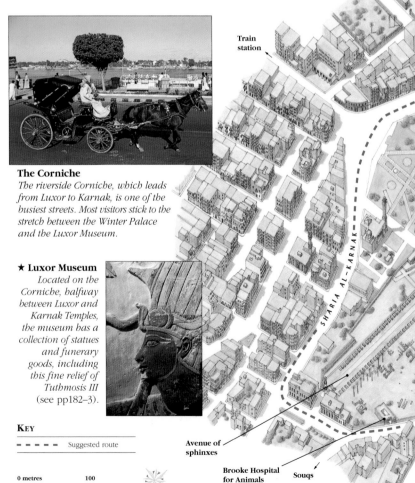

The Corniche
The riverside Corniche, which leads from Luxor to Karnak, is one of the busiest streets. Most visitors stick to the stretch between the Winter Palace and the Luxor Museum.

★ **Luxor Museum**
Located on the Corniche, halfway between Luxor and Karnak Temples, the museum has a collection of statues and funerary goods, including this fine relief of Tuthmosis III (see pp182–3).

Train station

SHARIA AL-KARNAK

KEY

- - - - - Suggested route

0 metres   100

0 yards   100

Avenue of sphinxes

Brooke Hospital for Animals *(see pp182–3)*

Souqs

Luxor Museum and Karnak

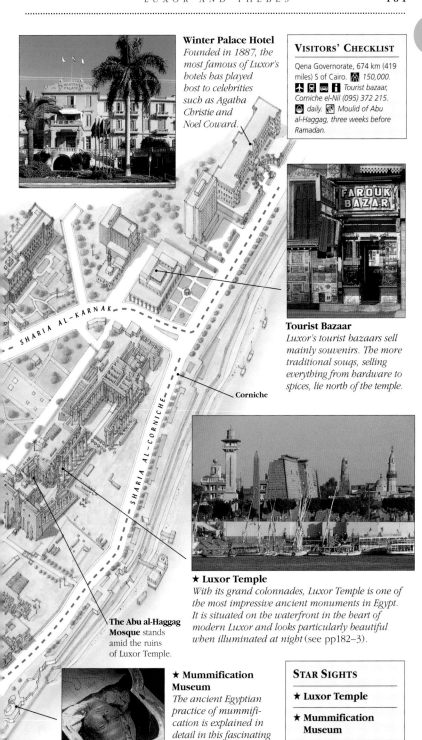

Winter Palace Hotel
Founded in 1887, the most famous of Luxor's hotels has played host to celebrities such as Agatha Christie and Noel Coward.

VISITORS' CHECKLIST

Qena Governorate, 674 km (419 miles) S of Cairo. 🏠 *150,000.*
✈ 🚉 🚌 ℹ *Tourist bazaar, Corniche el-Nil (095) 372 215.*
📷 *daily.* 🎎 *Moulid of Abu al-Haggag, three weeks before Ramadan.*

Tourist Bazaar
Luxor's tourist bazaars sell mainly souvenirs. The more traditional souqs, selling everything from hardware to spices, lie north of the temple.

Corniche

SHARIA AL-KARNAK

SHARIA AL-CORNICHE

★ Luxor Temple
With its grand colonnades, Luxor Temple is one of the most impressive ancient monuments in Egypt. It is situated on the waterfront in the heart of modern Luxor and looks particularly beautiful when illuminated at night (see pp182–3).

The Abu al-Haggag Mosque stands amid the ruins of Luxor Temple.

★ Mummification Museum
The ancient Egyptian practice of mummification is explained in detail in this fascinating museum close to the river (see pp182–3).

STAR SIGHTS

★ **Luxor Temple**

★ **Mummification Museum**

★ **Luxor Museum**

Exploring Luxor

SPREAD OUT ALONG the east bank of the Nile, Luxor today is a bustling town of some 150,000 inhabitants. The main tourist attractions are concentrated in the heart of town between Sharia al-Karnak and the Corniche. Luxor Museum is a short distance away on the Corniche in the direction of Karnak. Walking around town is a great way to soak up the atmosphere though it can also be fun to ride through the streets in a *caleche* (carriage).

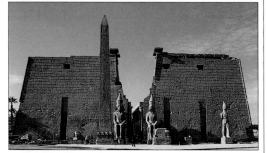

The first pylon, built by Ramses II, forming the façade of Luxor Temple

Luxor Temple

Corniche el-Nil. ⬤ winter: 6am–9pm daily; summer: 6am–10pm daily. 🏛

Dominating the banks of the Nile in the centre of town, Luxor Temple is an elegant example of Pharaonic temple architecture. Dedicated to the Theban triad of Amun, Mut and Khonsu, the temple was largely completed by the 18th-Dynasty pharaoh Amenhotep III and added to during the reign of Ramses II in the 19th Dynasty. Although the temple was further modified by later rulers, including Alexander the Great, its design remained strikingly coherent in contrast to the sprawling complex that developed at nearby Karnak. In the 3rd century AD the temple was occupied by a Roman camp and the site was subsequently abandoned. Over the centuries it was engulfed in sand and silt, and a village grew up within the temple walls. Then in 1881 archaeologist Gaston Maspero rediscovered the temple in remarkably good condition, but before excavation work could begin the village had to be removed. Only the **Abu al-Haggag Mosque**, built by the Arabs in the 13th century, was left intact, standing high on the layers of silt accumulated over the years.

The temple is approached by an avenue of sphinxes, which once stretched all the way from Luxor to Karnak, almost 2 km (1.2 miles) away. Fronting the entrance to the temple, the gigantic first pylon is decorated with scenes of Ramses II's victory over the Hittites in the battle of Qadesh. Two enormous seated colossi of Ramses and a huge 25-m (82-ft) high pink granite obelisk flank the gateway to the temple. The obelisk was originally one of a pair; the other was removed in the early 19th century and re-erected in the Place de la Concorde in Paris, a gift from the Egyptian ruler Mohammed Ali to the people of France.

Beyond the first pylon lies the Court of Ramses II, with the Abu al-Haggag Mosque towering incongruously over the courtyard to the east. The height of the mosque above the stone floor demonstrates the depth of debris that once buried the entire temple. The western corner of the court incorporates an earlier barque shrine (to house the gods' sacred boats) dedicated to the Theban triad. A double row of papyrus-bud columns encircles the court, inter-spersed with huge standing colossi of Ramses II.

More giant black granite statues of Ramses guard the entrance to the original part of the temple, which begins with the majestic Colonnade of Amenhotep III, with its avenue of 14 columns. The walls here were embellished during the reign of Tutankh-amun and depict the annual Opet festival, when the images of Amun, Mut and Khonsu were taken in procession from Karnak to Luxor (see p184). The western wall shows the outward journey to Luxor and the eastern wall the return journey to Karnak. The colonnade leads to the superb Court of Amenhotep III, which is noted for its double rows of towering papyrus

The Abu al-Haggag Mosque in Luxor Temple

The avenue of sphinxes leading to the entrance of Luxor Temple

Colonnade of Amenhotep III with its lofty papyrus columns

columns, the best preserved and most elegant in the temple. In 1989, work here on the foundations of the court led to the discovery of 22 New Kingdom statues, now on display in the Luxor Museum.

The hypostyle hall on the southern side of the court served as a vestibule to the main temple. It has 32 papyrus columns in four rows of eight, bearing the later cartouches of Ramses II, Ramses IV, Ramses VI and Seti I. The antechamber beyond was converted into a church by the Romans in the 4th century AD, its Pharaonic reliefs being plastered over and covered with Christian paintings. A second, smaller antechamber, the offerings chapel, leads on to another columned hall with the Sanctuary of the Sacred Barque in the centre. Rebuilt by Alexander the Great, this granite shrine was where Amun's barque ended its journey from Karnak in the Opet festival *(see p184).* It is decorated with scenes of Alexander making offerings to the Theban triad. The birth room to the east has reliefs depicting the divine birth of Amenhotep III, intended to validate his claim to be the son of Amun. Finally, behind the Sanctuary of the Sacred Barque, another hall leads to a small, damaged sanctuary that once housed a golden statue of Amun.

Pink granite obelisk

Mummification Museum

Corniche el-Nil, opposite Mena Palace Hotel. (*(095) 381 502.* ⬤ *9am–1pm and 4–9pm daily (5–10pm summer); 9am–3pm Ramadan.*

This small museum on the banks of the Nile houses a fascinating display describing the process of mummification performed by the ancient Egyptians *(see pp28–9).* Instruments for removing internal organs, substances to treat the body and items needed by the mummy on its journey to the afterlife are all displayed here. The intact mummy of Maseharti, a 21st-Dynasty high priest and general, was found at Deir el-Bahri along with Maseharti's painted coffin. A mummified cat, the symbol of the goddess Bastet, and a mummified ram, the symbol of the god Khnum, are among the other exhibits. Among the informative items on display is a cross-section of a mummified skull, stuffed with material where the brain has been removed. There is also a piece of a mummified toe.

Brooke Hospital for Animals

Montazah Sharia, next to Luxor Temple. (*(095) 381 305.* ⬤ *8:30am–1:30pm and 5–7pm daily.* In 1934, Dorothy Brooke, the wife of a major-general in the British army, established the Brooke Hospital for Animals in Cairo to care for the many starving and mistreated horses and mules that had been brought to Egypt from Britain during World War I. Further clinics opened throughout Egypt and the rest of the world. The Luxor branch opened in the 1960s and looks after dozens of sick horses. Visitors are welcome.

Luxor Museum

Corniche el-Nil, Luxor. (*(095) 370 569.* ⬤ *9am–1pm and 4–9pm daily (5–10pm summer); 9am–3pm Ramadan.*
Situated on the Corniche half-way between Luxor Temple and Karnak, this well-designed

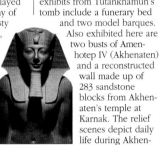

Statue of Tuthmosis III in the Luxor Museum

museum has an excellent collection of statues and artifacts found in temples and tombs in the Luxor area. Near the entrance is a stunning gilded head of Hathor, the cow-goddess, discovered in the tomb of Tutankhamun in the Valley of the Kings. Also on the ground floor look out for the large pink granite head of Amenhotep III and the beautiful carved figure of a youthful Tuthmosis III.

On the first floor further exhibits from Tutankhamun's tomb include a funerary bed and two model barques. Also exhibited here are two busts of Amenhotep IV (Akhenaten) and a reconstructed wall made up of 283 sandstone blocks from Akhenaten's temple at Karnak. The relief scenes depict daily life during Akhenaten's reign and show the heretical pharaoh and his wife Queen Nefertiti making offerings to the sun-god Aten.

The spectacular new hall near the exit on the ground floor is a highlight. It displays a collection of beautifully preserved New Kingdom statues, discovered at Luxor Temple in 1989. Priests are thought to have buried the stone statues in ancient times to make room for new statuary. Twenty-four pieces can be seen, including a near-perfect 2.5-m (8-ft) high statue of Amenhotep III and a statue of the gods Mut and Amun.

Painted relief from Akhenaten's Karnak Temple in Luxor Museum

Karnak: Temple of Amun

Statue of a scarab beetle

Aᴛ ᴛʜᴇ ʜᴇᴀʀᴛ of the immense Karnak complex lies the Temple of Amun, dedicated to the king of the gods. With its endless courts, halls and colossi and huge sacred lake, the scale and complexity of this sprawling temple is overwhelming. From its modest 11th-Dynasty beginnings, pharaoh after pharaoh added to and changed the existing buildings, seeking to make their mark on the country's most important temple. No expense was spared and during the 19th Dynasty some 80,000 men worked in the temple as labourers, guards, priests and servants. The temple lay buried under sand for more than 1,000 years before excavation work began in the mid-19th century. Today, the huge task of restoration continues.

★ Great Hypostyle Hall
The glorious highlight of Karnak, this cavernous hall was supported by 134 gigantic columns.

★ Colossus of Ramses II
An imposing granite statue of Ramses II, with one of his daughters at his feet, stands in front of the entrance to the Great Hypostyle Hall.

Tomb of Seti II
dedicated to the Theban Triad.

RECONSTRUCTION OF THE TEMPLE OF AMUN
The temple's brightly coloured exterior is visible in this reconstruction, which shows how the temple would have looked in around 1000 BC.

A row of sphinxes
led to the Nile.

Temple of Ramses III

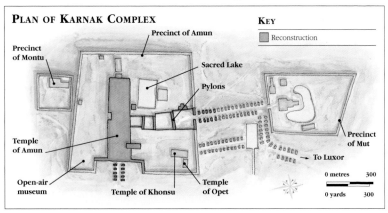

PLAN OF KARNAK COMPLEX

KEY

  Reconstruction

Precinct of Montu

Precinct of Amun

Sacred Lake

Pylons

Temple of Amun

Precinct of Mut

To Luxor

Open-air museum

Temple of Khonsu

Temple of Opet

0 metres	300
0 yards	300

Botanic Gardens
Part of the temple built by Tuthmosis III, this roof-less enclosure lies behind the Great Festival Temple. It is decorated with reliefs of exotic flora and fauna, brought back to Egypt by the pharaoh during his campaign in Syria.

★ **Great Festival Temple**
The central hall of this temple built by Tuthmosis III was supposedly designed to resemble the tent in which he lived whilst on campaign.

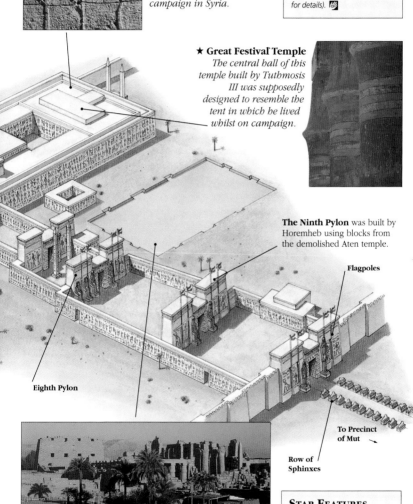

The Ninth Pylon was built by Horemheb using blocks from the demolished Aten temple.

Flagpoles

Eighth Pylon

To Precinct of Mut →

Row of Sphinxes

Sacred Lake
Priests purified themselves in the holy water of the Sacred Lake before performing rituals in the temple. North of the lake is a huge stone scarab of Khepri, built by Amenhotep III.

STAR FEATURES

★ **Great Hypostyle Hall**

★ **Colossus of Ramses II**

★ **Great Festival Temple**

Exploring Karnak

After the pyramids of Giza, Karnak is Egypt's most important Pharaonic site. Excavations over the years have gradually uncovered the original structure of the temple complex, which was built over a 1300-year period and covers a vast area just north of Luxor. As well as the colossal Temple of Amun, the 100-acre site comprises a fantastic array of temples, chapels, pylons and obelisks, all testifying to the importance of Thebes.

Statues of the lioness-goddess Sekhmet line up in the Precinct of Mut

Temples of Khonsu and Opet

Dedicated to the son of Amun and Mut, the well-preserved Temple of Khonsu was built largely during the reigns of Ramses III and IV. The main entrance is via a magnificent gateway, built by Ptolemy III, which is still virtually intact.

Close by is the smaller Temple of Opet (the goddesss thought to be the mother of Osiris). It contains some finely decorated reliefs dating from Ptolemaic and Roman times.

Open-air Museum

Located to the northwest of the Precinct of Amun, the open-air museum contains a fine collection of monuments that were discovered during an excavation of the Third Pylon. Among the museum's main attractions is the lovely, reconstructed, 12th-Dynasty White Chapel of Senusret I. This has delicate carvings of the king making offerings to Amun. The newly restored 18th-Dynasty Red Chapel of Hatshepsut can also be seen here; the chapel served as a shrine for the barque of Amun. Other attractions include the Alabaster Chapel of Amenhotep I and the Shrine of Tuthmosis III.

A separate ticket for the museum must be purchased before entering the complex.

Sound and Light

The sheer size of the Karnak complex means that one visit is seldom enough to take it all in. A good way to revisit the site is to attend the spectacular Sound and Light Show in the evening, which helps to unravel the complex 1500-year history of the building of the Temple of Karnak. The shows are performed in a number of languages, and there are three shows each evening. Check with the Luxor Tourist Office for details of times and prices.

Precinct of Mut

Built by Amenhotep III, the precinct contains the ruins of a temple dedicated to Amun's consort Mut. Huge, black granite statues of the lioness-goddess Sekhmet line the temple courts. To the west of the sacred lake surrounding the temple is the ruined 20th-Dynasty Temple of Ramses III. Relics of the Temple of Amenhotep III, dedicated to Amun, lie to the northeast.

Precinct of Montu

The Precinct of Montu is just north of the Temple of Amun. Montu, the warrior god, was the original deity of Thebes and was still worshipped after Amun rose to pre-eminence. The precinct contains Amenhotep III's Temple of Montu and the Temple of Amun, which was added during the 20th Dynasty. Both are closed to the public at present.

The Festival of Opet at Karnak

Amun was the principal god of Thebes who, along with his consort Mut and their son Khonsu, was worshipped as part of the Theban Triad. Once a year, during the flood season, the Festival of Opet celebrated the king's rebirth as the son of Amun. Accompanied by priests and revellers in a riotous festival, the images of Amun, Mut and Khonsu were carried on decorated barques to the Nile and then to Luxor Temple. Even today, elements of the Opet festival live on in the Islamic Moulid of Abu al-Haggag, a five-day event preceding Ramadan. Luxor stages a recreation of the festival for tourists on the 4th of November each year, the anniversary of the discovery of Tutankhamun's tomb.

Priests carrying the image of Amun in his barque during the Opet festival

Cruising the Nile

ALONG WITH the Grand Tour of Europe, a trip to Egypt was one of the most exciting journeys available to the 19th-century traveller. Having disembarked at Alexandria, wealthy European and American tourists were transported to Cairo – in the early days by boat, later by train. After several days visiting the sights of Cairo, often staying at the world-famous Shepheard's Hotel, passengers would board a *dahabiyya* (large sail boat) or steamer, and set off

Death on the Nile by Agatha Christie

for a trip up the Nile. The pace was languid: a steamer took three weeks to reach Aswan, while a sailing boat could take six to twelve weeks. Slow days on deck alternated with treks through the desert to marvel at the newly found secrets of ancient Egypt. It was not uncommon for tourists to come across or even fall into hitherto undiscovered tombs. Expeditions were led by local guides, while servants carried supplies of food and drink for picnics amid the ruins.

Thomas Cook, the founder of modern tourism, played a dominant role in the development of Egyptian travel. He once owned all the steamers plying the Nile.

Florence Nightingale described her 1848 trip up the Nile in a series of published letters. Other writers inspired by the trip include Agatha Christie, who wrote Death on the Nile.

THOMAS COOK & SON'S NILE FLOTILLA.

Cook's Steam Dahabeah "NITOCRIS", (For a Private Family).

Cook's New First Class Dahabeahs "OSIRIS", "HORUS", "ISIS", "HATHOR", "NEPTHIS", "AMMON-RA".

Cook's First Class Tourist Steamers "RAMESES", AND "RAMESES THE GREAT".

Cook's Mail Steamers "CLEOPATRA", "NEFERT-ARI", "AMENARTAS", AND "HATASOO".

Cook's First Class Tourist Steamers "TEWFIK", "PRINCE ABBAS", AND "PRINCE MOHAMMED-ALI".

CHIEF OFFICE: LUDGATE CIRCUS. LONDON

CAIRO * EGYPT *

SHEPHEARD'S * HOTEL *

Shepheard's Hotel was the focus of European life in Egypt from its founding in 1841 until it was burned down in 1952.

The highlight of a trip to Egypt for 19th-century travellers was then, as now, a visit to the Great Pyramids and the Sphinx at Giza. As seen in this illustration, these sites had yet to be fully excavated.

Exciting new discoveries from Egypt's ancient past provided an added thrill for early visitors to the country. Each year new finds were made.

Thebes: Valley of the Kings

TOMB OF TUT ANKH AMON NO. 62

The most famous tomb in Thebes

THE REMOTE, BARREN Valley of the Kings was the necropolis of the New Kingdom pharaohs. By digging their tombs deep into the Theban Hills, pharaohs from Tuthmosis I (c.1500 BC) on hoped to stop robbers stealing the priceless possessions buried with them. It was an unsuccessful strategy. Despite their hidden locations, every burial chamber was raided except for those of Yuya and Tuya (see p77), and Tutankhamun, discovered by Howard Carter in 1922, its glorious treasures still intact (see pp74–7). But for all that, the structures themselves remain, their dramatic corridors and burial chambers stunningly adorned with symbolic accounts of the journey through the underworld and ritual paintings to assist the pharaohs in the afterlife.

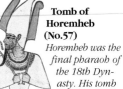

Tomb of Horemheb (No.57)
Horemheb was the final pharaoh of the 18th Dynasty. His tomb departs from the usual style of 18th-Dynasty tombs in that it consists of a single straight corridor with side-chambers. It is decorated with reliefs from the Book of Amduat.

Valley of the Kings, chosen as a burial ground because of its secluded location amid limestone hills

THE VALLEY TOMBS

Sixty-two tombs have been found in the Valley of the Kings and all are numbered on the map in the order of their discovery. The most significant tombs, some of which are described on p190, are marked with a red bullet. Of all the tombs, only a few are open at any one time.

Tomb of Tuthmosis III (No.34)
Dug 30 m (98 ft) above ground in a vain attempt to stop thieves, today the tomb is reached by a metal staircase. The walls are painted with rows of figures portraying the Book of Amduat (see p29), and a red granite sarcophagus is the sole remaining artifact.

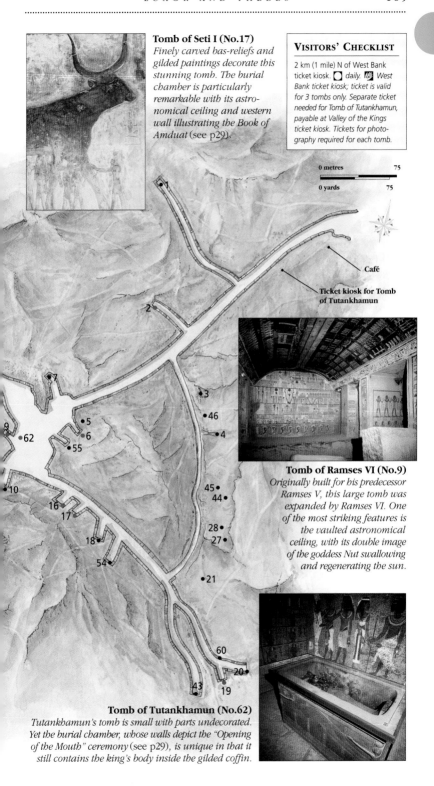

Tomb of Seti I (No.17)
Finely carved bas-reliefs and gilded paintings decorate this stunning tomb. The burial chamber is particularly remarkable with its astronomical ceiling and western wall illustrating the Book of Amduat (see p29).

VISITORS' CHECKLIST

2 km (1 mile) N of West Bank ticket kiosk. ◯ *daily.* West Bank ticket kiosk; ticket is valid for 3 tombs only. Separate ticket needed for Tomb of Tutankhamun, payable at Valley of the Kings ticket kiosk. Tickets for photography required for each tomb.

0 metres 75
0 yards 75

Café

Ticket kiosk for Tomb of Tutankhamun

Tomb of Ramses VI (No.9)
Originally built for his predecessor Ramses V, this large tomb was expanded by Ramses VI. One of the most striking features is the vaulted astronomical ceiling, with its double image of the goddess Nut swallowing and regenerating the sun.

Tomb of Tutankhamun (No.62)
Tutankhamun's tomb is small with parts undecorated. Yet the burial chamber, whose walls depict the "Opening of the Mouth" ceremony (see p29), is unique in that it still contains the king's body inside the gilded coffin.

Tomb of Ramses IV (No.2)

Although Greek and Coptic graffiti mar the walls of this 20th-Dynasty tomb, there are some beautiful, vividly coloured scenes from the Book of the Dead. In the burial chamber, the goddess Nut stretches across the blue ceiling. The enormous pink granite sarcophagus is covered with magical texts and carvings of Isis and Nephthys, designed to protect Ramses's mummy from danger.

Tomb of Ramses IX (No.6)

This typical late Ramesside tomb is long and steep, with interesting scenes on the sloping corridor walls taken from the Litanies of Ra, a religious work celebrating the solar deity's nightly journey. A four-pillared room precedes the burial chamber, which has an impressive astronomical ceiling, featuring the goddess Nut surrounded by sacred barques full of stars. Gods and demons are painted on the dark walls. Only the mark of the sarcophagus remains on the floor.

Tomb of Merneptah (No.8)

The tomb of 19th-Dynasty pharaoh Merneptah, son of Ramses II, was excavated by Howard Carter in 1903. Reliefs of Isis and Nephthys worshipping the solar disc decorate the tomb's entrance. From here the corridor descends steeply to the burial chamber, where the sarcophagus still lies. A false burial chamber did not fool robbers, who escaped with treasures but dropped the heavy sarcophagus lid in one of the corridors.

Tomb of Ramses III (No.11)

Discovered by the Scottish traveller James Bruce in 1768, the tomb of Ramses III is known as the "Tomb of the Harpists" after the bas-relief of two blind musicians in one of the side chambers. It is beautifully preserved and, unusually for a royal tomb, its colourful reliefs include scenes taken from everyday Egyptian life.

Tomb of Queen Tawsert/Sethnakht (No.14)

Originally built for the wife of Seti II, Queen Tawsert, this tomb was appropriated by 20th-Dynasty pharaoh Sethnakhte after he ran into difficulties building his own tomb. The well-preserved wall paintings include depictions of the "Opening of the Mouth" ceremony and, in the burial chamber, the gods greeting Sethnakhte.

Tomb of Ramses I (No.16)

The tomb of Ramses I, founder of the 19th Dynasty, is small but exquisitely decorated. Discovered in 1817 by the Italian explorer Giovanni Battista Belzoni, the walls are painted with scenes relating to the Book of Gates. A large granite sarcophagus remains in the burial chamber.

Tomb of Amenhotep II (No.35)

This is one of the deepest tombs in the valley, with 90 steps leading down to different levels. Although thieves made off with the treasure, Amenhotep's mummy was still in its decorative sarcophagus when the tomb was discovered by

Victor Loret in 1898. Nine other royal mummies, hidden in the tomb by priests, were also found. The pillared burial chamber is decorated with illustrations and texts from the Book of Amduat.

Colourful wall painting from the well-preserved Tomb of Siptah

Tomb of Siptah (No.47)

The Tomb of Siptah, who reigned briefly at the end of the 19th Dynasty, is one of the longest in the valley, stretching 106 m (350 ft) into the rock. Lightly coloured bas-reliefs decorate the walls and the ceiling is painted with a procession of vultures whose wings spread the width of the corridor.

KV5

In 1994 the American archaeologist Kent Weeks began excavating a tomb that had been considered unimportant by Egypt-ologists. What he found is the largest and most complex tomb in the Valley of the Kings. Known as KV5, the tomb is believed to be the burial site for Ramses II's 52 sons. A 16-pillared hall, several corridors and more than 100 chambers have so far been discovered and although no treasure has been found, thousands of important artifacts have been recovered from the rubble. Work is likely to continue for several years before the tomb will be open to the public.

Amenhotep II's burial chamber, containing the pharaoh's sarcophagus

Thebes: Tombs of the Nobles

EXTENDING OVER A LARGE AREA to the south of the Valley of the Kings, the Tombs of the Nobles is made up of more than 400 tombs of Theban nobles and high officials, mainly from the New Kingdom. While the royal tombs were hidden away in a secluded valley, these tombs are closer to the surface of the hills overlooking the Nile. Because of the poor quality of the limestone here, the tombs are painted and there are few carved reliefs. Vivid artworks cover the walls, providing an invaluable insight into daily life in the New Kingdom. The Sheikh Abd al-Gurna Tombs are clustered around the village of Old Qurna. Further east, tombs at the necropolises of Khokha, Assasif and Abu al-Naga are now open to the public.

Richly detailed paintings of life in ancient Egypt in the Tomb of Sennefer

Sheikh Abd al-Gurna Tombs
All the tombs here date from the 18th Dynasty. The **Tomb of Sennefer (No.96)**, mayor of Thebes and overseer of the gardens of Amun under Amenhotep II, is one of the best preserved. The ceiling is covered with brightly-coloured paintings of vines, and Sennefer is shown with his family and making offerings to the gods. The **Tomb of Rekhmire (No.100)**, a vizier during the reigns of Tuthmosis III and Amenhotep II, shows servants at work and Rekhmire collecting taxes and receiving gifts from foreign lands.

The **Tomb of Nakht (No.52)** is decorated with scenes of rural life, such as fishing, harvesting and hunting in the Nile delta. Nakht was the scribe and astronomer of Tuthmosis IV. The well-preserved **Tomb of Menna (No.69)**, an inspector of estates, shows Menna and his wife making offerings to the gods. It contains a detailed harvest scene and paintings of fishing and hunting.

Treading grapes – Tomb of Nakht

The **Tomb of Ramose (No.55)**, governor of Thebes before and during Akhenaten's reign, has reliefs showing both the old style of worship and the worship of Aten imposed by the heretic pharaoh. The **Tomb of Userhat (No.56)** has detailed scenes of everyday life, including a trip to the barber's. Userhat was one of Amenhotep II's scribes.

The **Tomb of Khonsu (No.31)**, an adviser to Tuthmosis III, is painted with colourful scenes of the Festival of Montu, while the **Tomb of Benia (No.343)** has vignettes of daily life and statues of the deceased and both his parents.

Khokha Tombs
Three tombs, discovered here in 1915, were opened for the first time in 1995. The **Tomb of Djehuty-Mes (No.295)** shows this 18th-Dynasty priest with his wife and family. The **Tomb of Neferronpet (No.178)**, a scribe during the reign of Ramses II, contains a painting of the scribe and his wife before Osiris. The **Tomb of Nefersekheru (No.296)**, another 19th-Dynasty scribe, shows a similar scene.

Assasif Tombs
The **Tomb of Kheruef (No.192)**, steward to Queen Tiy, contains scenes of the queen and 18th-Dynasty pharaoh Amenhotep III watching a dance in their honour. The nearby **Tomb of Anchhor (No.414)**, overseer of the priests of Amun, is an elaborate structure, but the decoration is not well preserved. The recently opened **Tomb of Pabasa (No.279)**, a 26th-Dynasty official, is noted for the pillared first court with its detailed bee-keeping and fruit-picking scenes.

Abu al-Naga Tombs
The first tombs in this area opened in 1999. The **Tomb of Roy**, a steward in the 18th Dynasty, and the **Tomb of Shuroy**, an 18th-Dynasty official, both have colourful tableaux of daily life.

Recording the harvest scene, Tomb of Menna

Thebes: Hatshepsut Temple

AGAINST ITS STARK mountainous backdrop, the partly rock-hewn Mortuary Temple of Hatshepsut at Deir al-Bahri is a breathtaking sight. It was designed by Queen Hatshepsut's architect Senenmut in the 18th Dynasty and is an extraordinary monument which rises from the desert plain in a series of imposing terraces.

Head of Hatshepsut

The temple was damaged by Ramses II and his successors, and Christians later turned it into a monastery (hence the name Deir al-Bahri, which means "Northern Monastery"). However, the ongoing excavation of the site continues to reveal much exquisite decoration. Adjacent to the main temple are the ruins of the much older Temple of Montuhotep II, the ruler of the 11th Dynasty who managed to unite Egypt, and the 18th-Dynasty Temple of Tuthmosis III.

Temple of Montuhotep II
The prototype for Hatshepsut's Temple, the older Temple of Montuhotep II now lies in ruins.

Temple of Tuthmosis III

The imposing Hatshepsut Temple, in its stunning setting at the foot of a sheer limestone cliff-face

RECONSTRUCTION OF THE TEMPLES AT DEIR AL-BAHRI

This reconstruction shows the Temples of Montuhotep II, Tuthmosis III and Hatshepsut as they would have looked during the reign of Tuthmosis III in the 18th Dynasty. Partly rock-cut and partly free-standing, the three temples are set into a natural amphitheatre and are given added majesty by the dramatic cliffs behind them.

STAR FEATURES

★ **Reliefs of Punt Expedition**

★ **Chapel of Hathor**

★ **Statues of Hatshepsut**

★ **Chapel of Hathor**
This chapel is noted for its Hathor-headed columns. The walls have retained much original colouring, including this relief of the ankh *and* djed *pillar, symbols of life and stability.*

★ **Statues of Hatshepsut**
The columns of the portico around the upper terrace were decorated with Osiride statues of Hatshepsut, character- istically represented as a male king with a beard. Although many statues were destroyed by later pharaohs, several have recently been reconstructed from their fragments.

The Shrine of Amun was dug into the cliff behind the temple.

Sanctuary of the Sun

VISITORS' CHECKLIST

2 km (1 mile) NE of West Bank ticket kiosk.
🚌 or on foot from other sites.
🕐 6am–5pm daily. 📷

Chapel of Anubis
This chapel contains brightly coloured murals, including a relief of Tuthmosis III making offerings to the sun god Ra-Harakhty.

Myrrh trees planted in the gardens yielded a gum that was burnt as incense.

Avenue of sphinxes led off in the direction of the temple complex at Karnak.

★ **Reliefs of Punt Expedition**
Stunning reliefs relate Hatshepsut's journey to the Land of Punt (Somalia). The king of Punt is seen here with his wife Ati (left), who is depicted suffering from obesity.

Birth Colonnade
Scenes along the Birth Colonnade portray the divine birth of Hatshepsut, designed to legitimize the queen's claim to the throne. On the right, the young queen is shown in the arms of the goddess Neith.

Thebes: Valley of the Queens

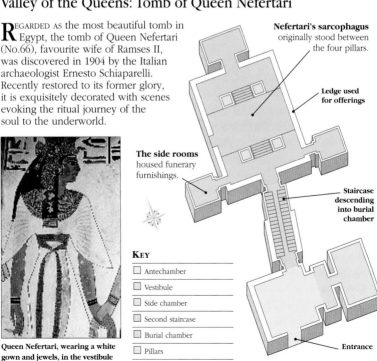

Celestial cow in Nefertari's tomb

Named by Champollion, the Valley of the Queens lies to the south-west of the Valley of the Kings and holds the tombs of many royal wives and children. Although it was used as a burial site in the 18th Dynasty, it was only from the reign of the 19th-Dynasty pharaoh Ramses I that royal wives were laid to rest here. Of the nearly 80 tombs populating the valley, the most famous is that of Queen Nefertari and only a handful are open to the public at any one time.

Tomb of Amunherkhepshep (No.55)

The elegant, well-preserved tomb of Prince Amunher-khepshep (Amun), son of Ramses III, was the highlight of the Valley of the Queens until the reopening of Nefertari's tomb. Amun would have succeeded his father as pharaoh but he died when he was a child and was buried in this royal tomb.

From the entrance, steps lead down to the tomb hall, which contains beautiful, brightly-coloured wall paintings of Ramses accompanying his young son on a visit to pay homage to the gods of the underworld. Amun is easily recognizable because he is wearing the characteristic braided hairstyle of a prince. From here, a corridor decorated with the Keepers of the Gates leads to the burial chamber, where the skeleton of a five-month-old foetus is on display in a glass cabinet. Foetuses have been found in other burial chambers and may have been placed there as part of the ritual of rebirth.

Tomb of Queen Titi (No.52)

Queen Titi was married to one of the Ramesside pharaohs of the 20th Dynasty, although it is unclear which one. Her tomb is small and damaged in parts, but certain sections have particularly colourful paintings. Some of the best scenes are in the burial chamber, where Hathor appears in bovine form in a mountainous landscape and again in human form, pouring water from the Nile to revive the queen. The tomb was closed at the time of writing.

Tomb of Prince Khaemweset (No.44)

This is the tomb of another of Ramses III's sons who died in infancy. Its intricate reliefs have preserved much of their colour. Ramses is shown introducing his son to the different deities and making offerings to them. The goddesses Isis, Nephthys, Neith and Selket are also depicted, addressing Osiris on behalf of the child prince.

Valley of the Queens: Tomb of Queen Nefertari

Regarded as the most beautiful tomb in Egypt, the tomb of Queen Nefertari (No.66), favourite wife of Ramses II, was discovered in 1904 by the Italian archaeologist Ernesto Schiaparelli. Recently restored to its former glory, it is exquisitely decorated with scenes evoking the ritual journey of the soul to the underworld.

Nefertari's sarcophagus originally stood between the four pillars.

Ledge used for offerings

The side rooms housed funerary furnishings.

Staircase descending into burial chamber

Entrance

KEY

☐ Antechamber
☐ Vestibule
☐ Side chamber
☐ Second staircase
☐ Burial chamber
☐ Pillars

Queen Nefertari, wearing a white gown and jewels, in the vestibule

Ra as a ram-headed deity between Isis and Nephthys, in the side chamber

ANTECHAMBER

Entrance to the tomb is
gained via a steep staircase,
hewn out of rock, which
descends into the antechamber.
Wonderful, brightly-coloured
paintings depicting Queen
Nefertari in the company of
various gods cover the walls
while the blue ceiling is
scattered with yellow stars
representing the heavens.
The paintings to the left of
the entrance relate to the
Book of the Dead and depict
Nefertari playing *senet*, an
early version of draughts.
On the eastern wall of the
antechamber, the entrance
to the vestibule is flanked by
pictures of Osiris, on the left
side, and Anubis, on the right.

VESTIBULE

On the left of this small
rectangular room, the goddess
Isis is shown introducing
Nefertari to the scarab-headed
god Khepri. On the right, the
falcon-headed Harsiesis (a
form of Horus), wearing the
double crown of Upper and
Lower Egypt, presents Nefertari
to the seated Ra-Harakhty and

Hathor-Imentit. The vulture
goddess Nekhbet spreads out
her wings above the narrow
doorway to the side chamber.

SIDE CHAMBER

Through the doorway, the
side chamber is ablaze with
stunning murals. To the left,
Nefertari is seen offering cloth
to the god Ptah, who is
wrapped in a white mummy
shroud in his shrine. On the
northern wall, Nefertari stands
before Thoth, while the large
eastern wall, which
faces the visitor on
entering the room,
shows Nefertari
making offerings
to Osiris and
Atum, on the
left and right
respectively.

Osiris in the
side chamber

SECOND STAIRCASE

A highly decorated stairway
corridor leads down into the
burial chamber. On the left,
the god Anubis, the black
jackal, welcomes Nefertari

into the kingdom of the
dead. On the right, Nefertari
is seen holding out ritual
pots, containing liquid offerings, to Hathor and Selket.
Lower down, the goddess
Maat spreads out her wings.

BURIAL CHAMBER

The burial chamber was where
the regeneration of Nefertari's
soul was designed to take
place. The wall paintings draw
inspiration from the Book of
the Dead, featuring Nefertari
with the guardians of the gates
of Osiris's kingdom, through
which she would have to
pass in order to proceed to
the underworld. By uttering
magic formulas and the names
of the guardians, Nefertari is
shown surmounting these
potential obstacles to rebirth.

PILLARS

The chamber's four pillars are
excellently preserved. Facing
the visitor on entering the
room, the first two pillars are
decorated with Horus wearing
the priestly leopard skin. Osiris
in typical pose adorns the four
inner faces of the pillars on
the north/south axis. Facing
where the coffin would have
been are the striped *djed* pillars
representing Osiris's spine and
a symbol of reincarnation.

REPAIRING NEFERTARI'S TOMB

Nefertari's tomb was carved from poor quality limestone and
over the years its reliefs were damaged by water, humidity
and crystallized salt. As a result, the tomb was closed in the
1950s. In 1986 the Supreme Council of Antiquities and the
Getty Conservation Institute embarked on an ambitious project
to restore the tomb. Salt-damaged plaster was removed, cleaned,
strengthened and replaced, and a solution of acrylic resin was
injected into cracks. The paintwork was carefully cleaned and
the colours returned to their original vibrancy. Work was completed in 1992 and the tomb was reopened in 1995. However,
to control humidity levels, visitor numbers are restricted.

**The interior of Queen Nefertari's
Tomb during restoration**

Thebes: The Ramesseum

PHARAOH RAMSES II, ruler of Egypt for 67 years in the 19th Dynasty, built his mortuary temple, the Ramesseum, as a statement of his eternal greatness and to impress his subjects. The huge complex, which took more than 20 years to complete, now lies largely in ruins. Dedicated to Amun, it once boasted an 18-m (60-ft) high, 1,000-tonne colossus of Ramses, parts of which lie scattered around the site. The complex also included a smaller temple dedicated to Ramses's mother Tuya and his wife Nefertari, as well as a royal palace and storehouses.

Wall relief of Amun in the hypostyle hall

★ Osiride Columns
Statues of Ramses as Osiris, god of the underworld, face into the second court. These figures, arms crossed bearing the crook and flail, signal the funerary nature of the temple.

★ Head of the Colossus of Ramses
The shattered head and shoulders of the immense colossus of Ramses now lie in the second court. An image of this evocative sight inspired Percy Bysshe Shelley to write his famous poem "Ozymandias".

Royal palace

Landing stage
provided mooring for boats from the Nile.

RECONSTRUCTION OF THE RAMESSEUM

This reconstruction shows how the Ramesseum would have looked when it was completed in around 1250 BC. The flooding of the Nile and earthquakes later took their toll, leaving today's atmospheric ruins.

STAR FEATURES

★ **Osiride Columns**

★ **Head of the Colossus of Ramses**

First Pylon
The imposing first pylon was decorated with scenes of Ramses in battle. Sadly, an earthquake badly damaged the pylon, and the gateway to the first court is now supported by concrete.

Hypostyle Hall Plant Capital
The hypostyle hall roof is supported by tall columns. The still colourful patterns of papyrus and lotus plants symbolize the union of Lower and Upper Egypt.

VISITORS' CHECKLIST

1 km (0.6 mile) NE of West Bank ticket kiosk.

🚌 or on foot from other sites.

🕐 7am–5pm daily.

Vestibules led to the sanctuary.

Mudbrick Stores
Innumerable vaulted mudbrick magazines once surrounded the temple, used as store-rooms, workshops and living quarters.

Huge mudbrick walls protected the entire temple complex.

Foundations of the Temple of Tuya
A small temple dedicated to Ramses's mother Tuya and his wife Nefertari stood to the north of the hypostyle hall.

BATTLE OF QADESH

Ramses II portrayed himself as a warrior pharaoh of great bravery and military prowess. Around 1275 BC, he led the Egyptian army into battle against the Hittites at Qadesh, an important trading town in the Orontes Valley in Syria. Although the battle was really a draw, Ramses paraded it as a victory on the walls of several of his great temples, including the Ramesseum. Ramses is depicted firing arrows at the fleeing Hittites and, in traditional pose, holding his enemy's head, about to inflict the fatal blow.

Wall relief on the inner face of the second pylon, depicting Hittites slain at the Battle of Qadesh

Exploring Other Sites in Thebes

SCATTERED AMID the wadis and hills of the West Bank are several other sites well worth a visit. Often by-passed in favour of the more famous Theban attractions, these additional sites can be visited in relative peace, well away from the tourist hordes. Medinat Habu, in particular, is one of the most underrated monuments on the West Bank, and Deir al-Medina provides a rare insight into the lives of ordinary people in ancient Egypt, as well as containing some exquisite tombs.

The awesome Colossi of Memnon on the flat desert plain of the West Bank

🏛 Colossi of Memnon

1 km (0.6 mile) E of West Bank ticket kiosk.

Soaring 18 m (60 ft) into the sky, the two enthroned statues of Amenhotep III are the first monuments most visitors see on arriving in the West Bank. They originally guarded Amenhotep's mortuary temple – thought to have been the largest ever built in Egypt – which was plundered for build-ing material by later pharaohs and gradually destroyed by the annual floods. All that remains are the two faceless colossi, which, despite the ravages of time, are an impressive sight.

During the Roman period the northernmost statue became a popular tourist attraction as it was heard to "sing" at sunrise.

Prominent visitors to the site to hear this peculiar phenomenon included the Emperor Hadrian, and the colossi are mentioned by classical authors such as Strabo and Pliny. The Greeks had earlier attributed the sound to the legendary figure of Memnon greeting his mother Eos, the goddess of dawn, with a sigh each morning. In fact, the statue had been badly damaged in an earthquake in 27 BC and its musical talent probably had a purely physical cause related to the damage it had sustained. Whatever the reason, once the statue had been repaired in AD 199 by the Roman emperor Septimius Severus, the singing stopped.

🏛 Medinat Habu

W of West Bank ticket kiosk.
◻ daily. 📷

Although second only to Karnak in size and detail, the beautiful temple of Medinat Habu is one of the less-visited sights in Thebes. The complex is dominated by the huge mortuary temple of Ramses III, modelled on Ramses II's mortuary temple at the Ramesseum *(see p196–7)*. During later invasions of Egypt in the 20th Dynasty, the entire population of Thebes took refuge within the temple's massive enclosure walls.

Ramses III's many military campaigns are recorded in detail on the temple's pylons and walls. In the second court, colourful reliefs depicting religious festivals are well preserved, partly thanks to the early Christians who converted the area into a church and covered the offending images with plaster.

To the west of the first court are the remains of Ramses's royal palace. Also within the enclosure walls is the smaller Temple of Amun, originally built by Hatshepsut but altered by Tuthmosis III and enlarged and modified up to Roman times.

🏛 Deir al-Medina

1 km (0.6 mile) NW of West Bank ticket kiosk. ◻ daily. 📷 (separate ticket needed for Pashedu's tomb).

The craftsmen, servants and labourers who worked on the royal tombs lived in the village of Deir al-Medina,

Painted relief from the Ptolemaic temple at Deir al-Medina

Sennedjem and his wife worshipping the gods of the underworld in his tomb at Deir al-Medina

also known as the Workmen's Village, to the south of the Valley of the Queens. They were buried in the nearby necropolis, in tombs that were intricately decorated and surmounted by a small pyramid. One of the most beautiful is the **Tomb of Sennedjem (No.1)**, a 19th-Dynasty servant. Discovered in 1886, its yellow ochre walls are in perfect condition; they show Sennedjem and his wife, Iyneferti, worshipping different gods and working in the fields of the underworld. The adjacent **Tomb of Inherkhau (No.359)**, the "foreman of the mayor of the Two Lands", is equally beautifully decorated with memorable scenes, including the Cat of Heliopolis killing the serpent Apophis under the holy tree. The small size of these tombs means that only ten people are allowed in them at one time. The recently opened **Tomb of Pashedu (No.3)**, a servant during the Ramesside era, is renowned for its delicate paintings and for a famous scene of Pashedu crouching next to a stream under a palm tree.

To the north of the village is a small Ptolemaic temple, dedicated to the goddesses Hathor and Maat. During the Coptic period it was turned into a monastery, which led to the site being named Deir al-Medina or "City Monastery".

Temple of Seti I
3 km (2 miles) E of West Bank ticket kiosk.
☐ daily.

Away from the popular tourist trail, the 19th-Dynasty mortuary Temple of Seti I, the northernmost of all the temples of Thebes, is dedicated to Amun and to the cult of Seti's father, Ramses I. After Seti's death, his son Ramses II completed the temple. Although the pylons and surrounding buildings are in ruins, the sanctuary, halls and antechambers of the main sandstone temple are well preserved and there are some interesting, high-quality reliefs, including those showing Seti and Ramses II making offerings to Amun. Part of the roof, featuring vultures and the winged sun disc, is still intact. The German Archaeological Institute is currently in the process of restoring the site.

The domed house of British archaeologist Howard Carter

Howard Carter's house
3 km (2 miles) E of West Bank ticket kiosk.
British archaeologist Howard Carter, best known for his discovery of the tomb of Tutankhamun in 1922 *(see pp20–1)*, lived for many years in this domed house on a barren hillside north of the Temple of Seti I. Plans to turn the house into a museum displaying Carter's personal belongings, pictures of his discoveries and letters to his patron, Lord Carnarvon, have yet to come to fruition.

The Villages of Gurna
Built on and around the Tombs of the Nobles *(see p191)* is Old Gurna. Despite its lack of basic infrastructure the village is alive with bright, mudbrick houses decorated with scenes of pilgrimages to Mecca. Old Gurna has long been considered a threat to the ancient tombs and in the 1940s New Gurna was built to rehouse its residents. Designed by architect Hassan Fathy and completed in 1948, New Gurna was inspired by the traditional domed, mudbrick style of Nubian architecture. Despite the innovative use of local materials it failed to lure the residents of Old Gurna who believe they safeguard both the monuments and tourists. Today, little more than New Gurna's mosque is intact and the government is intent on moving residents northeast to Taref, a purpose-built town.

New Gurna
2 km (1 mile) SE of West Bank ticket kiosk.

Old Gurna
1 km (0.6 mile) NE of West Bank ticket kiosk.

Part of the village of Old Gurna, nestling in the foothills of the Theban hills

Detail of the Temple of Khnum's astronomical ceiling at Esna

Esna ⑩

Qena governorate, 54 km (33 miles)
S of Luxor. 55,000.
from Luxor or Aswan.

THE SLEEPY FARMING town of Esna lies on the western bank of the Nile, just south of a sandstone dam across the river, built in 1906. Known as Latopolis by the ancient Greeks because the Nile perch (*lates* in Greek) was worshipped here, Esna is today best known for the **Temple of Khnum**. This Graeco-Roman structure was designed to resemble a much earlier temple on the site, built by 18th-Dynasty pharaoh Tuthmosis III (*see p49*). Both temples were dedicated to the ram-headed god Khnum, who, according to one of the Egyptian creation myths, fashioned mankind out of Nile clay using a potter's wheel.

Gradually, repeated flooding by the Nile buried the Graeco-Roman structure under layers of silt and mud, and the modern town of Esna was built on top of it. Excavation work on the site began in the 1860s but this has only cleared one part of the temple, the Roman hypostyle

hall, which was built during the reign of the Roman emperor Claudius (AD 41–54). Today this well-preserved hall stands in a huge excavation ditch 10 m (33 ft) below street level in the centre of town. Its roof, which remarkably is still intact, is on the same level as the foundations of the surrounding houses. The façade of the hall is inscribed with the cartouches of Roman emperors Claudius, Vespasian (AD 69–79) and Titus (AD 79–81). Inside the hall the last emperor mentioned is Decius, who died as late as AD 249. The roof is supported by 24 columns inscribed with hieroglyphs and fascinating texts describing the sacred festivals of Esna and recording hymns to the god Khnum. The bright colours of the astronomical ceiling have faded but it is still possible to make out the zodiac register, remarkable for its subtlety and detail.

Granite statue of the falcon god Horus

🔒 Temple of Khnum
⬜ daily. 📷

Edfu ⑪

Aswan governorate, 115 km (71 miles)
S of Luxor; 104 km (65 miles) N of
Aswan. 56,000.
from Luxor or Aswan.

EDFU STANDS beside the Nile almost exactly half-way between Luxor and Aswan. It was an important sacred site to the Egyptians because, according to ancient myth,

this was where the falcon god Horus fought a fierce battle with his uncle Seth, who had cruelly murdered Horus's father Osiris (*see p26*).

The **Temple of Horus** at Edfu, which was buried under sand and silt for nearly two thousand years, is the largest and best preserved Ptolemaic temple in Egypt. Construction of the temple began under Ptolemy III Euergetes in 237 BC and the main temple complex took 25 years to complete. However, construction continued up to the time of Ptolemy XII Neos Dionysus (80–51 BC). Despite its relatively recent construction, the temple is of particular interest to Egyptologists because it closely imitates much older Pharaonic designs. The imposing 36-m (118-ft) high first pylon is typically decorated with Pharaonic scenes of Ptolemy XII defeating his enemies in front of Horus and Hathor. Two elegant black granite statues of Horus flank the entrance to the pylon, which leads to a large colonnaded court and the first hypostyle hall. Behind this lies a second, smaller hypostyle hall with chambers off to the side. Gifts for the gods were stored in these rooms before being taken into the hall of offerings beyond. Stairs lead from the hall of offerings to the roof, which has glorious views of the Nile and the surrounding fields. The staircase walls are beautifully decorated with

Pylon of the Temple of Horus in Edfu with reliefs showing pharaoh Ptolemy XII

scenes from the New Year festival, a ritual celebrated in temples all over Egypt. On the first day of the year, in each temple, a procession of priests carried the statue of the temple god up to the roof to be revitalized by the sun. Beyond the hall of offerings is the sanctuary of Horus with its black granite shrine. Several chapels with excellent reliefs surround the sanctuary, one of which contains a model of Horus's sacred barque.

Southwest of the temple lie the remains of Horus's birth house. This was the focus of the annual Coronation Festival, a ritual celebrating the birth of Horus and his incarnation as the reigning pharaoh.

⌂ Temple of Horus
◻ *daily.* 📷

Postcard of Bedouin and camels – both at home in the desert

SHIPS OF THE DESERT

The *Camelus dromedarius* or one-humped Arabian camel has been an essential part of life in Egypt for thousands of years. Used primarily for transporting goods, the camel also provides milk, wool and meat. Contrary to myth, the camel's hump is not filled with water; it contains fat which allows the camel to survive for up to a week without food. Camels are ideally suited to desert life with their third, transparent eyelid that allows them to see in sand storms, nostrils that close between breaths and their unique body thermostat that minimizes unnecessary water loss through sweating. When they walk, camels move both legs on one side and then both legs on the other. This creates a rolling motion, hence their nickname "ships of the desert".

Relief of Sobek, the crocodile god, in the temple of Kom Ombo

Temple of Kom Ombo **⑫**

40 km (25 miles) N of Aswan. 🚌 🚗
🚆 🚉 *from Aswan or Luxor.*
◻ *daily.* 📷

SURROUNDED BY fields of sugar cane and corn, Kom Ombo is a pleasant agricultural town, home to many Nubians displaced by the creation of Lake Nasser *(see p206)*. The town's ruined yet imposing Graeco-Roman temple is in a particularly beautiful setting overlooking the Nile. The temple building is totally symmetrical with two entrances, two halls and two sanctuaries. This unusual structure is the result of the temple's dedication to two gods – the left side to the falcon god Haroeris (Horus the Elder) and the right side to Sobek, the local crocodile god. The construction of the temple was begun by Ptolemy VI Philometer in the 2nd century BC and mostly completed by Ptolemy XII Neos Dionysus during the 1st century BC. Finally the Roman emperor Augustus added the entrance pylon in around 30 BC. From the largely ruined forecourt, two doors lead to the hypostyle hall, which contains scenes relating to Haroeris on the left wall and Sobek on the right. The many columns are carved with the lotus or lily of Upper Egypt and the papyrus of the Delta. A series of halls and vestibules leads through to the sanctuaries of Haroeris and Sobek.

The Chapel of Hathor, just to the south of the temple, now houses a few crocodile mummies from the nearby crocodile necropolis.

Daraw **⑬**

8 km (5 miles) S of Kom Ombo.
👥 *31,000.* 🚉 *from Kom Ombo.*
🚌 *Tue.*

TRAVELLERS OFTEN combine a trip to Kom Ombo with a visit to the nearby village of Daraw for the famous Tuesday camel market, when hundreds of camels are up for sale. Most of the camels have been brought from Sudan on a month-long journey along "The Forty Days Road", an ancient droving route and former slave trail. The market is chaotic, colourful and very noisy. Traders travel from Cairo to haggle for camels to sell at the famous Birqash camel market, while locals come in search of a bargain.

Camels for sale in the famous Daraw camel market, held every Tuesday

Aswan

Relief from the Temple of Khnum

Situated downriver from the First Nile Cataract, Aswan is Egypt's southernmost city. From Old Kingdom times, this strategically important garrison town guarded Egypt's southern frontier and was a base for military incursions into Nubia and Sudan. Located at the crossroads of ancient trade routes between Egypt, Africa and India, the town was also a prosperous marketplace, where exotic goods were traded. Aswan stands on the most enchanting part of the Nile, where the desert comes right down to the water's edge and the river is dotted with islands. It is home to a large Nubian community, and the town's laid-back atmosphere makes it one of the most relaxing places in Egypt to visit.

The imposing Old Cataract Hotel overlooking the Nile at Aswan

Old Cataract Hotel

Corniche el-Nil. (097) 316 000.
The English crime-writer Agatha Christie penned part of her best-selling novel "Death on the Nile" in this impressive Moorish-style hotel, which opened in 1899. Set in beautiful gardens, with superb views over the Nile and Elephantine Island, it is one of the most famous hotels in Egypt. Past guests include the German Field Marshal Rommel, Sir Winston Churchill and King Farouk. It is the perfect place to soak up Aswan's romantic atmosphere while sipping afternoon tea on the verandah or watching the sun set over the Nile.

Nubian Museum

Off road to Aswan Dam, 1 km (0.6 mile) S of Aswan. (097) 319 111. 9am–1pm, 5–9pm daily (6–10pm summer); 9am–3pm Ramadan.
This well laid-out museum traces life in Nubia – the area between Aswan in Egypt and Khartoum in Sudan – from the earliest settlements to the present day. Nubian crafts such as basket making and pottery are featured and there

is a fascinating display about the UNESCO-backed projects to save Nubian monuments from submergence under Lake Nasser (see p206). The garden contains a reconstructed cave with prehistoric rock carvings, a Nubian house and a water feature showing the Nile's course and cataracts.

Unfinished Obelisk

1.5 km (1 mile) S of Aswan, next to Fatimid Cemetery. daily.
A gigantic obelisk, dating from the New Kingdom, lies semi-finished in an ancient granite quarry just south of Aswan. Had it been completed, it would have weighed a staggering 1.8 million kg (1,197 tons) and stood 41 m (134 ft) high. Three sides of the shaft were quarried before a flaw was discovered in the stone and the obelisk had to be abandoned, still partly attached to the parent rock. To the west of the quarry, the Fatimid cemetery contains several hundred mudbrick Islamic tombs, built between the 8th and 12th centuries.

Souq

Sharia as-Souq. daily.
From embroidered *galabiyyas* and coloured caps to aromatic spices, live chickens and fresh vegetables, there is a vast array of tempting goods on sale in Aswan's lively and extensive market. The chaotic, tightly packed network of narrow alleyways makes the souq a fascinating place to simply wander around and completes the exotic and colourful atmosphere. The market runs parallel to the Nile and becomes noticeably less tourist-orientated further inland from the busy main street, Sharia as-Souq.

Sharia as-Souq, the main thoroughfare in Aswan's famous market

◁ Detail of a relief showing the journey to the land of Punt – Hatshepsut Temple, Deir al-Bahri

A colourful Nubian village on the banks of Elephantine Island

⋔ Elephantine Island

Aswan. 🚢 ⛵

Known as Yebu (meaning "elephant") during the Old Kingdom, Elephantine Island is the oldest inhabited part of Aswan. It is not known whether the island was named after the huge granite boulders at the southern end of the island, which resemble bathing elephants, or because it was a major ivory trading post.

In ancient times, the island was the cult centre of the ram-headed god Khnum, creator of humankind and god of the Nile flood. Among the ruins of the ancient fortress town that once stood on the southern end of the island are the ruins of the **Temple of Khnum**, built by

Nectanebo in 4th century BC. An impressive gateway, added in the 1st century BC, showing Ptolemy XI worshipping Khnum, can be seen on the west side of the temple. Immediately to the north is the Graeco-Roman **Necropolis of the Sacred Rams**, and to the east, the **Temple of Satet**, built by Queen Hatshepsut. This area is being excavated by German archaeologists and some areas are out of bounds.

In the middle of the island, three traditional Nubian villages are distinguished by their brightly coloured homes.

⋔ Nilometer

Elephantine Island.

⭘ daily. 🖼

South of the Aswan Museum, the steep Nilometer steps descend into the river. The walls were calibrated to record the height of the annual flood and so indicate the likely crop yield for the next year. Dating from Pharaonic times, the Nilometer was briefly put back into use after its discovery in 1822.

Calibration on walls of Nilometer

🏛 Aswan Museum

Elephantine Island. ⭘ daily. 🖼

The Aswan Museum is set among pleasant, sub-tropical gardens near the southern end of Elephantine Island. It is home to a collection of well labelled artifacts found on digs in and around Aswan and Elephantine Island. Exhibits range from primitive prehistoric weapons to Graeco-Roman mummies and are labelled in chronological order. A new annexe displays recent finds from the island, including jewellery discovered at the island's Temple of Satet and a marriage contract dating from 350 BC.

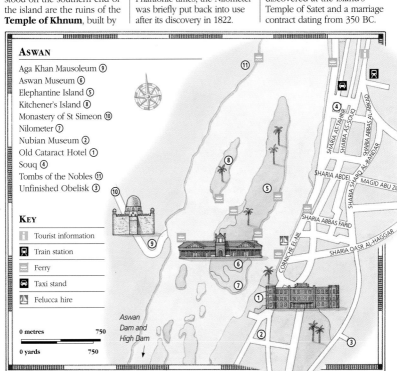

ASWAN

KEY

ℹ	Tourist information
🚉	Train station
	Ferry
🚕	Taxi stand
⛵	Felucca hire

0 metres   750

0 yards   750

Aswan Dam and High Dam

SHARIA AT-TAHRIR
SHARIA AS-SOUQ
SHARIA ABBAS AL-ABKAD
SHARIA ABDEL SHAMO AL-BANDAR
SHARIA SHAMO AL-BANDAR
MAGID ABU ZID
SHARIA ABBAS FARID
CORNICHE EL-NIL
SHARIA QASR AL-HAGGAR

Lush botanical gardens stocked with plants from all parts of the world on Kitchener's Island, Aswan

🚩 Kitchener's Island
Aswan. 🚤 🏛 ⭕ *daily.* 🅿

Situated in the Nile, west of Elephantine Island, the smaller Kitchener's Island (also known as the Island of Plants) is one of the most delightful places in Aswan. The lush botanical gardens that cover the island make it an ideal place to go for a peaceful stroll or simply relax in the shade of the trees.

The British general Horatio Kitchener was presented with the island in the 1890s as a reward for leading the Egyptian army's successful campaigns in Sudan. He made the island his home and indulged his passion for beautiful flowers by covering it with exotic plants imported from all around the world.

The huge sycamore trees, coconut palms and date palms that tower into the sky are filled with colourful birds and egrets, and as the sun begins to go down the entire island rings out with the sound of their calls.

🕌 Aga Khan Mausoleum
West bank, on the road to the Monastery of St Simeon.
⭕ *to the public.*

Standing on a barren hillside on the west bank of the Nile, opposite Aswan, is the Aga Khan Mausoleum. Aga Khan III (1877–1957), the 48th Imam, or leader, of the Ismaili sect of Shi'ite Muslims, fell in love with Aswan, where he spent the winter every year. After his death in 1957, his widow, the Begum, erected a mausoleum in his honour on the hillside behind their villa.

The domed and turreted sandstone construction is outwardly modelled on Cairo's Fatimid tombs *(see p102)*. Inside, there is a marble shrine and the Aga Khan's sarcophagus, inscribed with texts from the Quran. Until her

Mausoleum of the Aga Khan on a barren hillside opposite Aswan

death in 2000, the Begum spent part of each year in the villa and would visit the mausoleum every day to place a red rose on her husband's sarcophagus.

Lake Nasser, an enormous blue expanse in the desert

LAKE NASSER

Stretching south more than 500 km (310 miles) from the High Dam and reaching depths of over 180 m (590 ft), Lake Nasser is the largest artificial lake in the world. The lake was created by the construction of the High Dam. It flooded a huge expanse of land between Aswan and Abu Simbel, homeland of the Nubians since before Pharaonic times. About 800,000 Nubians were displaced, many settling in Aswan, and dozens of ancient temples had to be carefully relocated *(see p21)*.

**The imposing fortifications of the
Monastery of St Simeon, Aswan**

♦ Monastery of St Simeon

West bank. ▨ ▨ then by camel or
on foot. ○ daily. ▨

The desert Monastery of St
Simeon, on the west bank of
the Nile, was built in the 7th
century AD. Once home to a
community of around 300
monks, it was abandoned in
the late 12th century after an
attack by the famous Arab
leader Salah ad-Din.

The monastery was built as
a fortress and, though the
main buildings now lie
largely in ruins, the imposing
fortification walls remain. The
lower levels of the complex,
which comprised a church,
living areas for the monks,
stables and work quarters, are
made of stone, while the
upper levels are made of
brick. In the roofless basilica,
frescos of the Apostles are
still visible, their faces
scratched out by Muslims. In
the evening, the monastery
offers fantastic views of the
sun setting over the desert.

**The Tombs of the Nobles in the cliffs on the
west bank of the Nile near Aswan**

HARNESSING THE POWER OF THE NILE

The Aswan Dam was built to regulate the flow of the Nile
and so increase Egypt's cultivable land and provide hydro-
electric power. However, it soon proved too small to control
the river's unpredictable floods. President Nasser's solution
was the construction of the High Dam and the creation of
Lake Nasser. The resultant increases in agricultural production
and hydroelectricity have arguably saved Egypt from famine,
but there have been environmental consequences. The
rising water table is destroying ancient monuments and silt,
previously deposited in the Delta, is retained in Lake Nasser,
forcing Egypt's farmers to use potentially harmful chemicals.

The Aswan Dam, built by the British to regulate the flow of the Nile

♦ Tombs of the Nobles

Qubbet al-Hawwa, West bank.
▨ ▨ ○ daily. ▨

The hills on the west bank of
the Nile, north of Kitchener's
Island, are pock-marked with
the rock-hewn Tombs of the
Nobles. Dating from the Old
and Middle Kingdoms, many
of the tombs are decorated
with scenes of everyday life.
The largest and best preserved
tomb is that of Prince
Sarenput II (No. 31),
governor of southern
Egypt during the 12th
Dynasty. The burial
chamber is decorated
with statues of the
prince and paintings
of him and his son
hunting and fishing.
The tombs of Mekhu
(No. 25), a noble
from the 6th Dynasty
who was murdered
while on a military
expedition in Nubia,
and his son Sabni
(No. 26), are crudely
decorated with
funeral and family
scenes. The tomb of
Prince Sarenput I
(No. 36), Guardian
of the South during
the 12th Dynasty,
shows him with his
family and dogs.

The ancient necropolis is lit
up by spotlights at night and
looks particularly magical
when viewed from across
the river in Aswan.

♒ Aswan Dam

11 km (7 miles) S of Aswan. ▨ ∅

Stretching across the Nile, just
beyond the First Cataract, the
Aswan Dam was built by the
British between 1898 and 1902.
At the time of its construction
it was the largest dam in the
world, and its height was
twice raised again in an effort
to control the river. The roads
to Abu Simbel and the airport
cross the dam and the views
over the river and islands are
stunning. Photography around
both dams is strictly forbidden.

♒ High Dam

6 km (4 miles) S of Aswan Dam.
▨ ▨ ▨ ∅

Built between 1960 and 1971,
the immense High Dam is
3,830 m (12,562 ft) across,
111 m (364 ft) high and 980
m (3,214 ft) wide at its base.
At the eastern end of the dam
there is a visitors' pavilion
detailing the construction of
the dam and at the western
end there is a lotus-shaped
tower, built to commemorate
the Soviet Union's support in
the building of the dam.

The Temple of Kalabsha, dominating the shores of Lake Nasser close to the High Dam

Temple of Philae ⑮

Agilika Island, S of Aswan Dam. 🚗
from Aswan to Shellal. 🚤 *from Aswan.*
⬚ *daily.* 📷 **Sound and Light
Show** *6pm, 7:30pm, 9pm in winter;
8:30pm, 10pm, 11pm in summer.*

A S THE CENTRE of the cult
of Isis, the island of
Philae was an impor-
tant place of pilgrimage
for worshippers until
long into the Christian
era. From Philae, Isis
was said to watch
over the sacred island
of Biga, one of the
mythical burial sites of
her husband Osiris.
　After the building
of the Aswan Dam
(1898–1902), the
island's temples
were partly sub-
merged in water and visitors
took to rowing boats to peer
at the remains. With the
building of the High Dam
(1960–71), the monuments
were relocated to the nearby
island of Agilika. The UNESCO-
led project took from 1972 to
1980 to complete, during
which time Agilika was land-
scaped to look like Philae.
　Boats now drop visitors at
the southern end of Agilika,
near the oldest building on
the island, the **Kiosk of
Nectanebo II**, which dates
from the 4th century BC.
From here, a long courtyard,
flanked by colonnades, leads
to the magnificent **Temple of
Isis**, the main building in the
Philae temple complex. Built
in the late Ptolemaic and early
Roman periods, the huge
temple combines ancient
Egyptian and Graeco-Roman
architecture. Ptolemy XII

**Lion in the Temple
of Isis, Philae**

Neos Dionysos built the first
pylon, which has scenes of
him massacring his enemies,
watched by Isis, Horus and
Hathor. The birth house, built
by Ptolemy VI and altered by
later rulers, is dedicated to
Isis's son Horus. To the west
of the temple lies the **Gate of
Hadrian**, which was inscribed,
in 24th August AD 394, with
Egypt's last hieroglyphics.
On the eastern side of
the island, the small
Temple of Hathor
contains reliefs of
musicians, among
them Bes, the god
of singing. Further
south, close to
the edge of the
water, is the
classically grace-
ful, 14-columned
Kiosk of Trajan,
which has scenes of the Roman
emperor burning incense in
front of Osiris and Isis. At the
northern end of the island,
the **Temple of Augustus** and
Gate of Diocletian lie in ruins.

Temple of Kalabsha ⑯

W of High Dam. 🚗 *from Aswan.*
⬚ *daily.* 📷

T HE IMPOSING TEMPLE of
Kalabsha was built under
Emperor Augustus in the 1st
century AD on the site of
earlier buildings by Amenhotep
II and Ptolemy IX. Dedicated
to the fertility god Marul
(known as Mandulis by the
Greeks), it was moved 50 km
(31 miles) north of its original
location in 1970 in a German-
funded rescue operation
following the flooding of
Nubia. The temple now
dominates a stretch of Lake
Nasser's shore, just west of the
High Dam. The land here often
forms an island due to the
changing water levels.
　From the water's edge an
imposing causeway leads to
the temple's first pylon, beyond
which there is a colonnaded
court. The roofless hypostyle
hall is noted for its ornate

The well-preserved western colonnade leading to Philae's Temple of Isis

column capitals and its reliefs, which include Amenhotep offering wine to Marul.

ENVIRONS: Moved at the same time as Kalabsha Temple, the undecorated, battered remains of the Roman **Kiosk of Qertassi** lie to the northwest. Two Hathor-headed columns mark the entrance to this small kiosk, which commands fine views of Lake Nasser. The nearby **Temple of Beit al-Wali**, also relocated from Nubia, was built during the reign of Ramses II. Its walls depict Ramses's great battles, notably against the Nubians.

Avenue of sphinxes leading to the Temple of Wadi as-Sebua

Temple of Wadi as-Sebua ⓱

140 km (87 miles) S of High Dam.
🚌 🚢 from Aswan. ⭕ daily. 📷

APPROACHED BY the remains of an avenue of sphinxes, the Temple of Wadi as-Sebua was built by Ramses II and dedicated to the deified pharaoh, Amun-Ra and Ra-Harakhty. In the early 1960s the temple was moved a short distance west to its current site. Two colossi and statues of Ramses adorn the temple, which is partly carved directly into the rock. The inner sanctuary was converted into a Christian church and faint images of saints can be seen over the ancient reliefs.

ENVIRONS: Just to the north, the **Temple of Dakka** was begun by the Ethiopian king Arkamani in the 3rd century

BC and added to in the Ptolemaic and Roman eras. Dedicated to the god Thoth, it was originally 40 km (25 miles) further north. The huge pylon is still in good condition. Also relocated here, the **Temple of Maharraka** dates from Roman times. The best remains can be found in the hypostyle hall.

Temple of Amada ⓲

185 km (115 miles) S of High Dam.
🚌 🚢 from Aswan. ⭕ daily. 📷

DEDICATED TO Amun-Ra and Ra-Harakhty, the Temple of Amada was constructed by Tuthmosis III and Amenhotep II, and added to by Tuthmosis IV. Moved just 3 km (2 miles) from its original site, it is the oldest surviving Nubian temple. It also has some of the best preserved Nubian reliefs, including those on the sanctuary's back wall, which depict Amenhotep killing his Syrian prisoners of war.

ENVIRONS: A short distance across the desert is the re-located **Temple of Derr**. Built under Ramses II, it was later converted into a church. Although badly damaged, some colourful reliefs remain, particularly in the second pillared hall, where the pharaoh is seen presenting flowers and offering wine to the gods. The nearby rock-cut **Tomb of Pennout**, viceroy of northern Nubia under Ramses VI, was previously 40 km (25 miles) south of Amada in a necropolis of Old and New Kingdom tombs at Aniba. The

Finely preserved relief from the tomb of the Nubian viceroy Pennout, near Amada

tomb is decorated with scenes of Pennout and his family, and the "weighing of the heart" ceremony *(see p29)*.

Qasr Ibrim ⓳

60 km (37 miles) N of Abu Simbel.
🚌 ⭕ daily. 📷

THE RUINED FORTRESS of Qasr Ibrim is on its original site, although the flooding of the region means that whereas it once stood on a high plateau overlooking a valley it is now close to the water's edge. It is believed there was a fort here as far back as 1000 BC. By Roman times, seven temples stood within the fortified walls, including a temple dedicated to Isis and a 7th-century BC temple built by the Nubian king, Taharaqo. One of the last strongholds of paganism, Qasr Ibrim finally submitted to Christianity and a cathedral was built here in the 10th century AD. It resisted Islam until the 16th century, when Bosnians invaded the fort on orders from the Ottoman sultan and the cathedral was turned into a mosque. Still under excavation, the fort can only be visited by cruise boats on the lake.

The ruined fortress of Qasr Ibrim on the shores of Lake Nasser

Abu Simbel ⑳

Carved baboon at Abu Simbel

Hewn out of a solid cliff in the 13th century BC, the Great Temple of Abu Simbel and the smaller Temple of Hathor are a breathtaking sight. Although dedicated to the patron deities of Egypt's great cities – Amun of Thebes, Ptah of Memphis and Ra-Harakhty of Heliopolis – the Great Temple was built to honour Ramses II. Its 33-m (108-ft) high façade, with four colossal enthroned statues of Ramses II wearing the double crown of Upper and Lower Egypt, was intended to impress and frighten, while the interior revealed the union of god and king.

★ Temple Façade
Buried in sand for centuries, the façade was discovered in 1813 by Swiss explorer Jean-Louis Burckhardt.

Store rooms
held offerings to the gods and ritual items.

Baboons greeting the rising sun

Statue of Ra-Harakhty

Relocated Temples at Abu Simbel
In the 1960s, as Lake Nasser threatened to engulf the temples, UNESCO cut them from the mountain and moved them to an artificial cliff 210 m (688 ft) back from and 65 m (213 ft) above their original position.

Ramses II Colossi
Accompanied by carved images of captives from the north and south, the four colossi on the temple façade boast of a unified Egypt. Ramses's names adorn the thrones in cartouche form.

The broken colossus lost its head in an earthquake in 27 BC.

Entrance to temple

STAR SIGHTS

★ **Temple Façade**

★ **Hypostyle Hall**

★ **Inner Sanctuary**

The vestibule is adorned with scenes of Ramses and Nefertari making offerings to Amun and Ra-Harakhty.

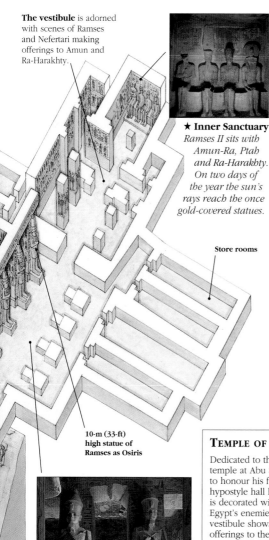

VISITORS' CHECKLIST

Aswan governorate, 280 km (174 miles) S of Aswan. 🚌 ✈ 🚪 6am–5pm (later when there are evening flights). **Sound and Light Show** 7pm, 8pm, 9pm in winter; 8pm, 9pm, 10pm in summer (see tourist office for details). ♿

★ **Inner Sanctuary**
Ramses II sits with Amun-Ra, Ptah and Ra-Harakhty. On two days of the year the sun's rays reach the once gold-covered statues.

Store rooms

Battle of Qadesh
Reliefs inside the hypostyle hall show Ramses II defeating Egypt's enemies including, on the right hand wall, the defeat of the Hittites in the Battle of Qadesh c.1275 BC.

10-m (33-ft) high statue of Ramses as Osiris

TEMPLE OF HATHOR

Dedicated to the goddess Hathor, the smaller temple at Abu Simbel was built by Ramses II to honour his favourite wife, Nefertari. The hypostyle hall has Hathor-headed pillars and is decorated with scenes of Ramses slaying Egypt's enemies, watched by Nefertari. The vestibule shows the royal couple making offerings to the gods, and the inner sanctuary holds a statue of Hathor in the form of a cow.

Statues of Nefertari as goddess Hathor alternate with Ramses II on the façade of Queen Nefertari's Temple

★ **Hypostyle Hall**
In Osiride form – carrying crook and flail – the colossi on the southern pillars wear the Upper Egypt crown, while the northern ones wear the double crown of Upper and Lower Egypt. The walls show Ramses II making offerings to his deified self.

SINAI AND THE RED SEA COAST

Treasured in pharaonic times *for its turquoise, copper and gold quarries, the region today is a magnet for tourists, attracted by the white, sandy beaches and fantastic marine life. Sinai is a region of great religious significance; its rugged interior was the setting for many important events in the Bible and remains a holy place for Jews, Muslims and Christians alike.*

Wedged between Africa and Asia, the Sinai peninsula is bordered by the Mediterranean Sea, the Gulfs of Aqaba and Suez, and Egypt's Suez Canal zone. The area has been plagued by conflict, most recently between 1967 and 1982 when it was occupied by Israel before being returned to Egypt in the Camp David peace treaty. However, since the late 1980s tourism has boomed along Sinai's eastern coast with resorts such as Sharm el-Sheikh becoming popular holiday destinations. Besides the dry, sunny climate, the main attraction of the region is the underwater world – the Red Sea coral reefs and teeming marine life make this area one of the world's richest dive sites. Yet despite the rapid growth of tourism, much of Sinai's stunning mountainous interior, inhabited by the nomadic, tribal Bedouin people, remains unexplored.

Egypt's Red Sea Coast stretches more than 1,250 km (777 miles) from the Suez Canal to the Sudanese border. Separated from the Nile Valley by the hills of the Eastern Desert, the coastline is famed for its brilliant turquoise waters. The area around the diving resort of Hurghada has developed along similar lines to Sinai's eastern coast and many new resorts and hotels are planned here.

The Suez Canal, a phenomenal feat of engineering when it opened in 1869, separates Sinai from mainland Egypt. In the past it was a cause of conflict; today it is one of Egypt's most important sources of revenue.

Shopping for fruit and vegetables in the Red Sea diving resort of Hurghada

◁ **Exquisitely coloured coral reef in the warm waters of the Red Sea**

Exploring Sinai and the Red Sea Coast

WITH ITS COMBINATION of mountains and sea, the natural beauty of the Sinai peninsula is awe-inspiring. Most visitors head for the sea, where there is an ever-growing string of tourist resorts from Nuweiba to Sharm el-Sheikh. St Catherine's Monastery in the interior can be visited as a day trip. On the western Red Sea coast, Hurghada is the main resort and from here the monasteries of St Anthony and St Paul make interesting excursions. The Suez Canal to the north is hardly picturesque, but the canal town of Ismailia is pretty and Port Said has good duty-free shopping.

Monastery of St Anthony, inland from the western Red Sea coast

KEY

▨	Motorway
▨	Major road
▨	Minor road
▨	Scenic route

0 kilometres   100

0 miles   50

Luxury resorts and diving centres around Naama Bay, to the north of Sharm el-Sheikh

SIGHTS AT A GLANCE

(map labels)
PORT SAID **3**
ISMAILIA **2**
AIN MUSA **4**
SUEZ **1**
GULF OF SUEZ
MONASTERY OF ST ANTHONY **15**
MONASTERY OF ST PAUL **16**

Camels and their Bedouin keepers at Assalah, to the north of Dahab, where camel treks into the interior can be arranged

GETTING THERE

The coastal roads of the Sinai peninsula are good and the main resorts can be reached by bus, car or service taxi. Exploring the interior is best done on organized trips with jeeps or camels and a Bedouin guide, though there is a bus service to St Catherine's Monastery. There is a good coastal road on the western Red Sea to Hurghada and Port Safaga, and also from Port Said to Suez. Inland sites are best visited on organized day trips or by taxi. A ferry service operates between Sharm el-Sheikh and Hurghada.

SEE ALSO

• *Where to Stay* pp269–73

• *Where to Eat* pp288–90

Ain Musa's springs, reputedly made drinkable when Moses, guided by God, threw in a branch

A fishing boat dwarfed by a cruise ship in the Suez Canal

Suez ❶

134 km (83 miles) E of Cairo.
🏠 418,000. 🛈 Sharia Suez Canal
(062) 331 141. 🚌 🚊 🚐

SITUATED at the southern end of the canal, Suez was a prosperous port in medieval times. In the 18th century, it was used by the British as a staging post on the route to India. Following the opening of the Suez Canal in 1869, it expanded further, but was severely damaged during the 1967 and 1973 wars with Israel. Thanks to money from Gulf states, however, Suez has been rebuilt and it continues to be one of Egypt's most important ports and a major industrial centre. Suez holds little of interest for the tourist but those travelling to or from Sinai will use the Ahmed Hamdi Tunnel, 12 km (7 miles) to the north of town.

Ismailia ❷

120 km (74 miles) NE of Cairo.
🏠 255,000. 🚌 🚊 🚐

NAMED after its founder Ismail Pasha, who ruled Egypt from 1863 to 1879, Ismailia was developed for foreign engineers and labourers working on the Suez Canal in the 1860s.
Ismailia is the prettiest and most populous of the canal towns. South of the railway line, huge European-style villas with lush gardens and large terraces line the wide boulevards. On Mohammed Ali Quay, the house of Ferdinand de Lesseps, director of the Suez Canal

Company and French vice-consul to Egypt at the time of its construction, is an impressive example of these grand houses. It now serves as a hotel for guests of the Suez Canal Authority.
The **Ismailia Museum** nearby is home to a large collection of Graeco-Roman artifacts as well as details of the canal's history. To visit the adjacent Garden of Stelae and its Pharaonic remains, permission is needed from the museum.
The Sweetwater Canal, built to bring fresh water from the Nile to the canal workers, leads to Lake Timsah (Crocodile Lake), which has some pleasant beaches. A ferry from Ismailia runs to the east bank of the canal, where Egypt launched its celebrated attack on Israeli forces in 1973.

🏛 **Ismailia Museum**
Sharia Salah Salem. ⬡ daily. 📷

A sphinx outside the Ismailia Museum

Port Said ❸

225 km (139 miles) NE of Cairo.
🏠 473,000. 🛈 8 Sharia Palestine
(066) 235 289. 🚌 🚊 🚐

ON THE COAST where the Suez Canal meets the Mediterranean, Port Said was founded in 1859 by Khedive Said Pasha to house workers on the canal. For years, the city was associated with drugs and smuggling but it has now shaken off its seedy past and is today mostly renowned as a tax-free shopping zone and minor beach resort.
Port Said, which is largely built on land reclaimed from Lake Manzila, is surrounded by water. It was heavily bombed during the 1956 Suez crisis and during the conflicts with Israel in 1967 and 1973, but most of the damage has since been repaired. The distinctive green domes of the Suez Canal Building, built in 1869 on Sharia Palestine, are one of the city's important landmarks.
Nearby, **Port Said National Museum** covers Egyptian history from ancient times; exhibits in the museum include Coptic antiquities and Pharaonic mummies.
A short walk away, the **Military Museum** on Sharia 23rd July presents a vivid account of the various conflicts that have chequered the history of the canal.

A 19th-century colonial-style villa in Ismailia

View across the Suez Canal from Port Said to Port Fuad

🏛 **Port Said National Museum**
Sharia Palestine. ☐ *daily.* 🞖
🏛 **Military Museum**
Sharia 23rd July. ☐ *daily.* 🞖

Ain Musa ❹

25 km (15 miles) SE of Ahmed Hamdi Tunnel. 🚌 *from Cairo or Port Said.*

ALSO KNOWN as the Springs of Moses, Ain Musa lies to the southeast of the Ahmed Hamdi Tunnel, which runs under the Suez Canal near its junction with the Gulf of Suez. According to the Old Testament, it was here that Moses, after leading the Israelites across the Red Sea, turned a bitter spring into sweet drinking water by throwing a branch into it, as instructed by God.

Although Ain Musa was a main source of fresh water for the local town until the 1860s, only one of the 12 springs mentioned in the Book of Exodus remains today. Ain Musa was used as a strategic stronghold by the Israeli army during their occupation of Sinai from 1967, but it was recaptured by Egyptian forces in October 1973. Surrounding palm groves were damaged during the Sinai conflicts.

Just over 3 km (2 miles) north of the springs is the Military Touristic Memorial of Ain Musa, a small museum dedicated to the achievements of the Egyptian army.

Serabit al-Khadim ❺

32 km (20 miles) E of Abu Zneima, Sinai.

BUILT DURING the 12th Dynasty, the rock temple of Serabit el-Khadim (Heights of the Slave) is perched on a 755-m (2,500-ft) summit to the east of the petroleum-industry town of Abu Zneima. In Pharaonic times the area was rich in copper and turquoise and thousands worked in the mines. The temple was dedicated to Hathor, goddess of love and "Mistress of the Turquoise". Some jeep safaris

from Naama Bay (near Sinai's southern tip) include Serabit al-Khadim in their tours of this beautiful part of Sinai's rugged interior. Hiring a four-wheel-drive vehicle is an alternative, but it is advisable to take a local guide with you.

Wadi Feiran ❻

60 km (37 miles) W of St Catherine's Monastery, Sinai. 🏠 *650.*

LYING HALFWAY between St Catherine's Monastery and the Red Sea coast, at the foot of the 2,000-m (6,560-ft) high Mount Serbal, Wadi Feiran is the largest oasis in south Sinai. A winding valley, thick with shady palms, tamarisks and orchards, the oasis is believed to be the *Rephidim* mentioned in Exodus – the last place of rest for the weary Israelites before they reached Mount Sinai.

An early Christian community flourished here and, in AD 451, it became the seat of a bishopric that governed St Catherine's Monastery (*see pp218–21*). The bishop's palace and convent were destroyed in the 7th century, but a small convent was rebuilt on the site with stone from the original Byzantine buildings. Today, the oasis belongs to the Tawarah tribes.

Palms flourishing in the oasis of Wadi Feiran, south Sinai

St Catherine's Monastery ❼

ESTLING AT THE FOOT OF MOUNT SINAI, the Greek Orthodox monastery of St Catherine is thought to be the oldest continuously inhabited Christian monastery in the world. Founded in AD 527 by Emperor Justinian, it replaced a chapel built by the Empress Helena in AD 337 on the site where it is believed that Moses saw the Burning Bush. The monastery was renamed St Catherine in the 9th or 10th century after monks claimed to have found the intact body of the saint on a nearby mountain.

Library
The collection of priceless early Christian manuscripts is one of the most important in the world.

★ Icon Collection
The monastery holds 2,000 icons, including this of St Peter. A selection is kept on view in the Basilica.

The Walls of Justinian, dating from the 6th century, are part of the complex's original structure.

The Burning Bush
This evergreen is said to be from the same stock as the bush from which God instructed Moses to lead his people out of Egypt to the Promised Land.

The Chapel of the Burning Bush, where the miraculous bush supposedly grew, is the most sacred part of the monastery.

★ Basilica of the Transfiguration
This richly decorated church owes its name to a rare 6th-century Mosaic of the Transfiguration in the apse. The mosaic is located behind the gilded 17th-century iconostasis.

STAR FEATURES

★ Basilica of the Transfiguration

★ Icon Collection

Bell Tower
Built in 1871, the tower houses nine bells donated by Tsar Alexander II of Russia. They are only rung on religious festivals.

The Mosque was built in 1106 by converting a chapel originally dedicated to St Basil. Its creation was an attempt to placate local Muslim rulers.

VISITORS' CHECKLIST

Sinai, 90 km (56 miles) W of Dahab and Nuweiba. ☎ (069) 470 032. ✈ 10 km (6 miles) NE of monastery. ☐ from Cairo, Taba, Dahab, Sharm el-Sheikh to St Catherine's village (Al-Milga), then taxi 3 km (2 miles). Petrol available at monastery. ☐ 9am–noon, except Fri & Sun. ● Greek Orthodox holidays. No admission charge but donations welcome.

Monks' quarters

St Stephen's Well

Dispensary

Guest house

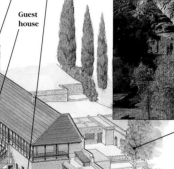

Monastery Gardens
A cemetery is located in the orchard from where monks' bones are periodically exhumed and taken to the Charnel House.

Charnel House

The elevated entrance, reached by a pulley system, used to be the only access.

The underground cistern was dug to store fresh water from the monastery's springs.

Visitors' entrance

St Catherine of Alexandria

St Catherine was one of the most popular early Christian saints. Supposedly born into a wealthy Alexandrian family in the early 4th century, she was tortured for her beliefs, first spun on a spiked wheel (hence Catherine wheel) and then beheaded by the pagan emperor. A marble sarcophagus in the monastery's Church of St Catherine contains two silver caskets said to hold part of her remains, found by monks 600 years after her death.

Detail of St Catherine from clerical vestments

Well of Moses
Inside the outer wall lies the monastery's main water source where Moses is said to have met his future wife, Zipporah, Jethro's daughter.

Exploring St Catherine's Monastery

COMPLETELY ISOLATED FOR MANY YEARS, and surrounded by red granite mountains, the monastery is now on the main tourist trail and busloads of visitors arrive each day. Around 20 or so monks (mostly from Greece) still live in the monastery, and hence its opening times are strictly controlled. The surrounding mountains are incredibly beautiful and most visitors climb the well-worn path to the top of Mount Sinai – where Moses is said to have received the Ten Commandments – to enjoy the spectacular view over this setting of profound biblical significance.

Ornately carved wooden inner door to the 6th-century Basilica

Inside the monastery

Entry is through a small postern or gateway in the north-eastern wall. The elevated entrance above it contains a pulley and used to be the only way into the monastery after the main gate was blocked as a defence against raiders in the Middle Ages. Parts of the huge granite walls date from the 6th century although they have been substantially rebuilt over the years – firstly, after an earth-quake in the 14th century and again in 1800 when Napoleon sent masons from Cairo to restore the stonework.

The monastery's main church, or Basilica, built by Emperor Justinian's architect Stephanos Ailisios in AD 527, is known as the Basilica of the Transfiguration. It is one of the few remaining churches in the region which survive from this period. Massive 11th-century wooden doors open onto the narthex (porch). Beyond is another door, carved with reliefs of animals, birds and flowers, which is believed to be the original from Justinian's church. The central nave is flanked by six pillars bearing Byzantine icons of saints worshipped in each month of the year. The marble floor and coffered ceiling are 18th century. A gilded iconostasis, painted in the early 17th century, separates the nave from the altar. Behind this, the roof of the apse is decorated with a superb 6th-century mosaic of the Transfiguration. Beyond the altar lies the Chapel of the Burning Bush, the holiest place of the monastery, which is usually closed to the public. The thorny, evergreen bush, reputedly a descendant of the original Burning Bush from which Moses heard the Lord speak, is of a species found nowhere else in Sinai.

Monks' skulls inside the Charnel House

The monastery's library, with over 3,000 ancient manuscripts in Greek and other languages, is second in importance only to that of the Vatican. One of the highlights is the *Codex Syriacus*, a 5th-century Syriac version of the New Testament. The priceless icons, dating from the early Byzantine period, are among the only survivors from the Iconoclast era (726–843) when such images were held to be heretical. They include a *St Peter* (5th–6th century), and the 7th-century *Christ in Majesty* and *Ladder of Paradise*. Some are on display in the narthex of the church and there are plans for a larger gallery outside.

In the garden, dense with olive and apricot trees, is the monastery cemetery and the Chapel of St Triphonius. The latter's crypt holds the Charnel House, which contains the bones of monks who have died here over the centuries. The robed skeleton is Stephanos, a 6th-century guardian of the path to Mount Sinai.

ENVIRONS: Rising to a height of 2,286 m (7,500 ft), **Mount Sinai** is held to be the Biblical Mount Horeb (Exodus 24) where Moses spent 40 days and nights before receiving the Ten Commandments. There are two paths to the top, both starting behind the monastery. The more gentle "Camel Path", created by Abbas Hilmi I, Pasha of Egypt from 1849–54, is the usual route up. Camels can be hired from the foot of the mountain, though the last 700 steps have to be

Chapel of the Burning Bush, viewable only by special dispensation

View of St Catherine's Monastery from path leading to Mount Sinai

undertaken on foot. The 3,700 steps of the "Stairs of Repentance" is a steeper route. Along it are several votive sites, including Moses' Spring, which gushes from a small cave, and St Stephen's Gate. Most visitors climb at night to reach the summit in time for sunrise.

Around 700 steps below the summit is **Elijah's Basin**, a sandy plain dotted with cypress trees, one of which is estimated to be 1,000 years old. This is where those who accompanied Moses are said to have waited while he climbed to the summit alone. Camping here, rather than at the summit, is recommended for those wanting to spend the night on the mountain.

At the summit, where God is believed to have spoken to Moses from a fiery cloud, is a 12th-century mosque and the small **Chapel of the Holy Trinity**, built in 1934 on the site of a 6th-century church. Neither of these is currently open to the public.

To the southwest of Mount Sinai, **Mount Catherine**, Egypt's highest mountain at 2,642 m (8,666 ft), offers a steep but picturesque climb. At the summit, which can be busy, there is a small chapel containing many icons, and a truly outstanding view, taking in the gulfs of Aqaba and Suez and the mountains of both Africa and Saudi Arabia.

St Catherine's Protectorate
Formally established in 1996, the Protectorate covers an area of 4,350 sq km (1,672 sq miles) around Mount Sinai. Its aim is to protect the area's plant and animal life and conserve historic and religious sites. A Trekkers' Code urges visitors to avoid leaving litter, removing rocks or plants and writing or carving graffiti.

A series of guides produced by the Protectorate details hikes in the area along **Wadi Arbaein** and **Wadi Shrayj**, taking in cultural sites and beauty spots. One describes the climb up **Abbas Pasha Mountain**, which leads to an incomplete 19th-century palace at 2,383 m (7,816 ft) – intended as a sanatorium for the sick Pasha. The books can be purchased and guides organized (walkers must be accompanied by a Bedouin guide) from the Visitors' Centre near the monastery and at the Protectorate Management Office in St Catherine's village.

THE BEDOUIN OF THE SINAI PENINSULA

The Bedouin of the Sinai, descendants of tribes from the Arabian peninsula, have lived a nomadic lifestyle in harsh arid regions for centuries, depending on sheep, goats and camels for a livelihood and sleeping in tents made of goatskin. Their name derives from the Arabic word *bedu*, meaning "desert dwellers". The Bedouin are distinctive in their traditional garb: the women don black garments with sequinned veils and the men wear long white robes. Their tightly wrapped figures invariably accompany images of bleak, sandswept landscapes. But life is rapidly changing for these denizens of the desert. With government resettlement programmes and tourism encroaching all over the Sinai, the old ways are under threat. TV aerials protrude from concrete houses and children are increasingly dressed in western-style clothes. While some Bedouin are still nomadic livestock breeders, many now work with jeeps not camels, and make a living from the tourist trade.

Bedouin woman in traditional dress

Naama Bay, Sharm el-Sheikh, showing the coral reefs just off shore

Sharm el-Sheikh ❽

300 km (187 miles) SE of Suez. ✈
🚌 🚢 🛈 *Ras Mohammed National Park (069) 660 559, (069) 660 668.*

THE POPULAR RESORT of Sharm el-Sheikh, north of Ras Mohammed, stretches over 20 km (12 miles) along the coast and is a renowned diving and snorkelling destination.

Sharm, as it is known to visitors, is divided into two parts – the town and port to the south and **Naama Bay**, the upmarket tourist enclave 7 km (4 miles) to the north.

After it was captured in the 1967 war, the port was developed by the Israelis who began to build hotels along the coast. The development which began in Naama Bay in the late 1980s is still booming. Europeans, and especially the Italians, favour it as a package holiday destination.

With diving schools and hotels lining the Corniche, Naama is far removed from the traditional Bedouin way of life. Nevertheless the water here is beautiful and there are many accessible dive sites along the coast – both for beginners and more experienced wreck divers. Excursions to St Catherine's Monastery and the Sinai interior are easily arranged from any good hotel in Sharm el-Sheikh.

ENVIRONS: Around 10 km (6 miles) north of Naama is **Shark Bay**, a cheaper, quieter and much smaller resort, although the recent building of a five-star hotel has changed the laid-back atmosphere and

more development is likely. The coral gardens and tropical fish here are beautiful – and despite its name, there are no sharks around. North of Shark Bay, where the Red Sea meets the Gulf of Aqaba, lie the Tiran Straits. Diving trips to **Tiran** and **Sanafir Island** leave from Naama, Sharm and Shark Bay. Further up the coast is the **Nabq National Park**. Popular with birdwatchers, the most northerly mangrove forests in the world are home to many birds such as grey and white herons, ospreys and storks. Animals suited to the arid conditions, such as gazelles, rock hyraxes and desert foxes, live inland.

🏕 Nabq National Park
29 km (18 miles) N of Sharm el-Sheikh. 🚗 🚌 ⏱ *daily.* 🏕 🎫

Ras Mohammed National Park ❾

20 km (12 miles) S of Sharm el-Sheikh.
🚶 🚌 *to Sharm el-Sheikh, then taxi.*
🛈 *Visitors' Centre (069) 660 559, (069) 660 668.* ⏱ *daily.* 🏕 🎫

COVERING THE southernmost tip of the Sinai peninsula, Ras Mohammed became Egypt's first marine National Park in 1989. The wealth of underwater life and extensive reefs dotted with brilliant corals and sponges make it one of the best places for diving and snorkelling in the world. Over 1,000 species of colourful fish populate the clear waters and barracuda, reef sharks, turtles and manta rays are among the more unusual creatures to look out for. Above water, the park is home to ibexes, gazelles and a wide range of birdlife. The

Turtle swimming in the Red Sea

mangrove forests here grow in a shallow channel south of the peninsula and are an important breeding area for birds. A visitors' centre in the park shows videos about the area and also offers a map of the colour-coded tracks which lead to the different beaches. Although thousands of tourists visit the park each year, considerable effort is made to protect the area from serious damage by not allowing any hotels to be built and

One of Sharm el-Sheikh's many diving centres

Coral Reefs of the Red Sea

CORAL REEFS ARE one of the richest ecosystems on earth. Coral is made up of colonies of tiny animals called polyps that need precise environmental conditions to grow. There are two types of coral: hard corals, which form hard outer skeletons for themselves, and soft corals, that do not. Most reefs are built over thousands of years from the accumulated skeletons of dead hard corals. In places, the Red Sea reefs form sheer walls covered with exotically shaped corals of pastel pink,

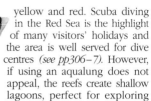
Colourful racoon butterfly fish

yellow and red. Scuba diving in the Red Sea is the highlight of many visitors' holidays and the area is well served for dive centres *(see pp306–7)*. However, if using an aqualung does not appeal, the reefs create shallow lagoons, perfect for exploring with a snorkel. These beautiful, calm lagoons serve as nurseries for schools of smaller fish. A word of caution: although the reefs seem robust, they are an extremely fragile environment and swimmers should look but not touch.

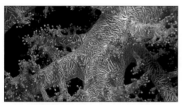

Soft corals *require salty, clear water and warm, gentle currents to bring them their food. At night the coral polyps use their fine tentacles to sting and capture plankton as it swims past.*

The jewel grouper *favours shady areas of the reef, for in the dim light this hunter's stunning colouring becomes surprisingly good camouflage as it waits for its smaller prey to swim past.*

Sea anemones *look like colourful plants but they are in fact animal predators. They use their stinging tentacles to stun their prey and feed it to their centrally located mouth.*

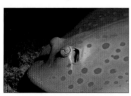

Blue-spotted rays *glide across the sea floor scooping up snails, worms and crabs before crushing them with special flattened teeth.*

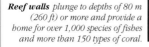

Reef walls *plunge to depths of 80 m (260 ft) or more and provide a home for over 1,000 species of fishes and more than 150 types of coral.*

Camels and their Bedouin keepers near Dahab

Dahab ➓

100 km (62 miles) N of Sharm el-
Sheikh. 🚌 🚗

THE WORD *dahab* means
gold in Arabic, and the
name of this popular resort
derives from its tawny golden
beaches. The resort grew up
around the Bedouin village
of Assalah, to the north of
the town, where the camp-
sites, beach huts, cheap hotels,
restaurants and market stalls
lining the waterfront cater
mostly for independent young
travellers on tight budgets.

To the south of the town,
the scene is distinctly upmarket, with luxury
holiday villages and
dive centres attract-
ing a very different
clientele. For all
tourists, however,
the sea is the main
attraction, and the
coral reef, with its
immensely rich
marine life, is close
to shore. A popular
dive site is the
Blue Hole, to the
north of Dahab.
This is almost
entirely surrounded by coral
reefs and drops to a depth of
80 m (260 ft) just a few
metres from the shore. The
Blue Hole and the nearby
Canyon can be dangerous for
inexperienced divers and
several lives are lost here
every year. A safe alternative
is to use snorkelling equipment
to admire the reef here.

Jeep and camel safaris into
the mountains can be easily
arranged from Dahab. These
are a great way to explore
Sinai's beautiful, rugged
interior and to see something
of the Bedouin way of life.

Nuweiba ➓

85 km (53 miles) N of Dahab. 🚌
🚢 from Aqaba (Jordan).

LOCATED MIDWAY along the
Gulf of Aqaba coast,
Nuweiba is divided into three
areas, spread over a 10-km
(6-mile) stretch. To the north
is the Bedouin settlement of
Tarabeen, where camp-
sites with bamboo
huts line the beach.
In the village are
the ruins of a 16th-
century fortress,
which was built
by the Mamluk
sultan Ashraf al-
Ghouri. About 1
km (0.6 mile) south
of Tarabeen, more
luxurious accom-
modation can be
found in Nuweiba
City. If you are
planning to catch the ferry to
Aqaba, there are several
hotels in the unattractive port
of Nuweiba, which is 8 km
(5 miles) further south.

All along the coast around
Nuweiba, hotels and camp
sites are being built, offering
a choice of 5-star and budget
accommodation. The setting
is particularly beautiful with

**Windsurfer on the Gulf
of Aqaba, Dahab**

the Sinai mountains providing
a hazy backdrop and those of
Saudi Arabia clearly visible
across the water.

For many tourists, the highlight of their visit to Nuweiba
is the chance to swim with a
dolphin at Mizela, a village
just south of the port. A local
fisherman, Abdullah, befriend-
ed a female dolphin who lost
her mate in 1992. Now he
leads the dolphin, named
Olin, to the bay where visitors
queue up to swim with her.

Also popular is a trip to the
ancient city of Petra, taking the
catamaran from Nuweiba port
to Aqaba. This spectacular
metropolis, 96 km (60 miles)
north of Aqaba, was carved out
of desert rock between the 3rd
century BC and 1st century AD.

ENVIRONS: Nuweiba is a good
base for exploring the interior
and jeep and camel trips are
easily arranged. The **Coloured
Canyon**, about 30 km (19
miles) inland from Nuweiba,
is a popular destination. It is
reached via the oasis of Ain
al-Furtaga, usually by four-
wheel-drive vehicle, though it
is possible to get there (more
slowly) by camel. The narrow
gorge gets its name from the
pink, brown, green and yellow
layers caused by the oxidation
of minerals, and looks like a
modern work of art.

South of Nuweiba is the
Abu Galum Nature Reserve,
a prime destination for dive
safaris. Inland from its lovely
deserted beaches is a maze
of wadis teeming with plants
and wildlife, including desert
foxes, ibexes and hyraxes.

**A new resort near Nuweiba, with
Saudi Arabia visible across the sea**

◁ **St Catherine's Monastery, founded in the 6th century AD in a valley at the foot of Mount Sinai**

Crusader castle on Pharaoh's Island, south of Taba, in the Gulf of Aqaba

Pharaoh's Island ⑫

7 km (4 miles) S of Taba. 🚗 🚌 *then ferry.*

Surrounded by fabulous reefs, Pharaoh's Island (known as Coral Island by Israelis) is very popular with divers. The island is just 250 m (820 ft) from the shore, close to the border with Israel, and boats leave from the Salah ad-Din Hotel on the coastal road opposite the island.

Worth exploring are the restored ruins of a 12th-century Crusader castle, strategically placed to ensure the safety of pilgrims to the Holy Land. The castle was captured by Salah ad-Din in 1170 and used as an Arab stronghold against the Crusaders until 1183, when it was eventually abandoned.

Taba ⑬

70 km (43 miles) N of Nuweiba. 🚌

On the border with Israel, Taba was only returned to Egypt in 1989 after international intervention. Egypt was determined to reclaim all its land from Israel and the dispute over this area lasted for seven years after the rest of Sinai had been recovered.

There are a few restaurants, cafés and a hotel at Taba, but most visitors are just crossing between the two countries.

The 70-km (43-mile) stretch between Taba and Nuweiba has been dubbed "The Egyptian Riviera" by the government. It is a priority development area with many hotels and resorts currently under construction.

If you are leaving Egypt at Taba, note that an Israeli stamp in your passport means that entry into some Arab countries, notably Lebanon and Syria, will be denied. Ask to have a separate piece of paper stamped.

Al-Arish ⑭

48 km (30 miles) SW of Rafah. 🚶 40,000. 🚉 *Sharia Fuad Zikry (068) 363 743.* 🚌 🚢 *Thu.*

Sinai's north coast is largely ignored by tourists, but there are some interesting places to visit, including the coastal town of Al-Arish. The palm-fringed white beaches and warm Mediterranean waters are the major attraction here, but Al-Arish is much more conservative than the laidback resorts along Sinai's Gulf of Aqaba coast.

On Thursdays there is a Bedouin market where women in traditional costume sell embroidered clothing and silver Bedouin jewellery. Outside Al-Arish, on the coastal road to Israel, the **Sinai Heritage Museum** exhibits Bedouin handicrafts and stuffed wildlife.

Popular with birdwatchers, the Zerenike Protectorate extends along the coast from the salt lagoon of Lake Bardawil, about 25 km (15 miles) east of Al-Arish.

🏛 **Sinai Heritage Museum**
Outskirts of Al-Arish, on road to Rafah. 🎫 (068) 324 105. 🕐 8:30am–2pm Sat–Thu. 🎟

Palm-lined promenade in the Mediterranean resort of Al-Arish

The distinctive façade of the Monastery of St Anthony with the Red Sea Mountains in the background

Monastery of St Anthony ⑮

47 km (29 miles) W of Zafarana.
🚌 from Cairo, Suez or Hurghada.
🕐 daily.

ISOLATED IN THE RED SEA Mountains, St Anthony's Monastery (AD 361–3), marked the beginning of the monastic tradition. It is the oldest Coptic monastery in Egypt. Legend has it that Anthony, orphaned at 18, retreated to the mountains to serve God. His disciples built the monastery on the site of his grave.

The monastery complex has retained much of its original appearance, despite attacks from Bedouin tribes in the 8th and 9th centuries, from Muslims in the 11th century and a murderous revolt by Bedouin servants in the 15th century. It is the largest in the country, with several churches and chapels and extensive living quarters, but only 25 resident monks. On the interior walls of the Church of St Anthony are some vivid 13th-century murals. Two kilometres (just over one mile) to the north-east of the monastery is the cave where St Anthony is said to have spent his last years.

Monastery of St Paul ⑯

80 km (50 miles) SE of St Anthony's Monastery. 🚌 from Cairo, Suez or Hurghada. 🕐 daily.

A WINDING ROAD leads to the Monastery of St Paul, hidden behind lofty walls. St Paul (AD 228–348) was from a wealthy Alexandrian family but became the earliest known hermit when he retreated to the Eastern Desert at the age of 16. The monastery's turreted walls were built around the cave where he lived for decades. The main Church of St Paul is painted with murals representing the Virgin and Child, and the archangels. The chapels contain scores of icons while ostrich eggs, a symbol of the Resurrection, hang from

Two of the monks at the Monastery of St Paul

the ceiling. A five-storey keep behind the church, supplied with water from a hidden canal, was used to protect the monks from Bedouin raids.

Hurghada ⑰

320 km (200 miles) S of Suez.
👥 36,000. ✈ 🚌 🚗 ⛴ daily catamaran and weekly ferry services from Sharm el-Sheikh. ℹ Sharia Banque Misr (065) 444 420.

HURGHADA, ON THE Red Sea coast, has undergone a complete transformation since the early 1990s when it was little more than a fishing village. Now a sprawling tourist town with resorts stretching 25 km (15 miles) along the coast, it is famous for its dive centres which offer scuba and snorkel trips to view the fantastic Red Sea marine life. There is a wide choice of accommodation with cheaper lodgings centred

Windsurfer at Sindbad Beach in Hurghada on the Red Sea coast

around Ad-Dahar, at the northern end of town, while Sigala to the south is more upmarket. Some hotels have good private beaches, and a variety of off-shore excursions are on offer, including day trips to **Giftun Island**. For those who wish to enjoy the wonders of the deep without getting wet, submarine tours are available from Sindbad Village or trips in a glass-bottomed boat from the Marine Sports Club. There is an **Aquarium** on the corniche and a **Marine Museum** north of town. In response to environmentalists' fears that the influx of tourists was damaging marine life, the Hurghada Environmental Protection and Conservation Association (HEPCA) was set up in 1992 to raise awareness and preserve the reef.

⚓ Aquarium
Al-Corniche. ⬤ *daily.* 📷

ENVIRONS: Just 30 km (19 miles) north of Hurghada, **Al-Gouna** is a new, luxurious resort. Set on a beautiful strip of coastline, the dome-roofed hotels and villas have a distinct Nubian theme.
    Soma Bay, 45 km (28 miles) to the south of Hurghada, is another recent tourist development with an 18-hole golf course, a marina, and upmarket hotels and villas.
    Remains of two Roman quarries in the Red Sea Mountains are accessible on day trips from Hurghada and the coast. **Mons Porphyrites**, 60 km (37 miles) north of town, was the site of ancient porphyry quarries. The pinky-purple stone was mined by the Romans for building and sent throughout the Empire. Parts of the Roman mining town are still in evidence. The mines at **Mons Claudianus**, around 50 km (31 miles) southeast of Hurghada, supplied the Romans with black granite columns – some of which still support the Pantheon in Rome today. Ruins of the fort and of the Roman town can also be visited.

⚓ Marine Museum
7 km (4 miles) N of Hurghada.
⬤ *daily.* 📷

Traditional ship-building at Port Safaga

Port Safaga ⓲

58 km (36 miles) S of Hurghada.
🏯 *23,500.* 🚗 🚌

JUST TO THE SOUTH of several upmarket resorts, Port Safaga is within easy range of some stunning reefs. Local weather conditions are ideal for wind-surfing and in 1993 the World Windsurfing Championships were held here. Apart from tourism, Port Safaga's principal activities are exporting locally-mined phosphates and ferrying travellers to Saudi Arabia.

Colourful house in a street of the Red Sea port of Al-Quesir

Al-Quesir ⓳

80 km (50 miles) S of Port Safaga.
🏯 *20,500.* 🚗 🚌

THE SMALL TOWN of Al-Quesir has a distinguished history. Queen Hatshepsut left from here on her famous expedition to the Land of Punt (*see p193*). Known in Ptolemaic times as *Leukos Limen* (White Harbour), it was the largest Red Sea port until the 10th century, popular with pilgrims travelling to Mecca. After the opening of the Suez Canal in 1869, Al-Quesir declined and today is little more than a quiet fishing village. The 16th-century Ottoman fortress of Sultan Selim still overlooks the town.
    As hotel development along the Red Sea coast continues, a growing number of excursions is available. Regular dive trips are offered to the islands of Big Brother and Little Brother, 67 km (42 miles) northeast of Al-Quesir. For those who prefer to sample more of the local life, however, the town has a traditional *souk*, and a Bedouin community. An ancient caravan trail to Qift in the Nile valley leads from the town through the mountains, passing several Pharaonic and Roman sites on the way.

Marsa Alam ⓴

132 km (82 miles) S of Al-Quesir.
🏯 *1,650.* 🚗 🚌

CURRENTLY A SMALL fishing village in phosphate mining country, and with a large army base, Marsa Alam also has good offshore coral reefs. Tourism in the region is expanding and an airport is being built between here and Port Safaga. 40 km (25 miles) to the south, a huge luxury resort is under construction at Wadi al-Gemel. A main road crosses the desert to link the town with Edfu, 230 km (143 miles) away in the Nile Valley.

THE DELTA AND THE NORTH COAST

FANNING OUT *between the two main branches of the Nile, the Delta is a green triangle in a desert landscape. Several Pharaonic dynasties ruled from here but, apart from the ruins of Bubastis and Tanis, most sites have long disappeared. The resorts of the North Coast are popular with Egyptians seeking relief from the summer heat.*

The Nile Delta, Egypt's most fertile and densely populated region, produces the bulk of the country's crops, helping to feed the huge and ever-increasing population. To the east of the Delta, beyond the Suez Canal, lies the Sinai peninsula; to the west is the legendary city of Alexandria and a sandy coastline that stretches for over 500 km (310 miles) to the Libyan border.

Although the north coast between Alexandria and Libya enjoys clear seas and beautiful beaches, many stretches are inaccessible because of landmines left over from World War II. However, there are dozens of holiday villages along the route to Marsa Matruh and more are planned.

Most visitors to Lower Egypt, as the north of the country is called, head straight for Alexandria, Egypt's cosmopolitan second city. Its rich history, links with Cleopatra's reign, moderate climate and pleasant beaches, make Alexandria the region's key attraction.

Although usually ignored by tourists, the Delta itself is worth exploring. This is the rural heart of the country: crisscrossed by irrigation canals, the flat land is rich with cotton, maize, sugar cane and vegetables. Buffalo plough the fields, donkeys pull carts, and mudbrick pigeon huts punctuate the picturesque landscape.

The lakes in the northeast attract an amazing variety of birdlife, especially during the annual winter migration south. Off the tourist trail, Rosetta's rich Ottoman architecture is one of the highlights of the area. Another is the cycle of lively *moulids* (religious festivals) that begin in October and transform the Nile Delta into a joyful place of celebration.

Colourful river taxis at Rosetta where a branch of the Nile flows into the Mediterranean

◁ Typical architectural motifs of stripes, porticos and balconies near Mosque of Abu al-Abbas Mursi, Alexandria

Exploring the Delta and the North Coast

ANNUAL FLOODING and plundering over the centuries have ensured that little remains to testify to the role of the Delta in ancient Egyptian history. However, the ruins at Tanis and near Zagazig hint at the area's importance in ancient times. Damietta and Rosetta have fine examples of Ottoman architecture, while Alexandria retains the faded grandeur of 19th-century colonial architecture and offers glimpses of its greatness as the Graeco-Roman capital of Egypt. Along the Mediterranean coast are a growing number of resorts, while the cemeteries at El-Alamein serve as reminders of the World War II battles that were fought here.

One of three sphinxes from a tomb near Pompey's Pillar, Alexandria

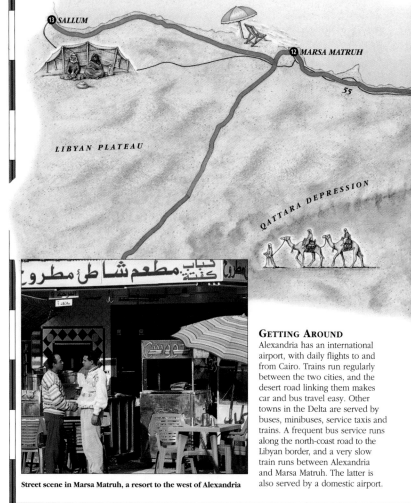

Street scene in Marsa Matruh, a resort to the west of Alexandria

GETTING AROUND

Alexandria has an international airport, with daily flights to and from Cairo. Trains run regularly between the two cities, and the desert road linking them makes car and bus travel easy. Other towns in the Delta are served by buses, minibuses, service taxis and trains. A frequent bus service runs along the north-coast road to the Libyan border, and a very slow train runs between Alexandria and Marsa Matruh. The latter is also served by a domestic airport.

Sights at a Glance

Abu Mina ⑩
Abu Qir ⑧
Agami ⑨
Alexandria pp236–43 ⑥
Damietta ①
El-Alamein ⑪
Marsa Matruh ⑫
Montazah Palace ⑦
Rosetta (Rashid) ⑤
Sallum ⑬
Tanis ④
Tanta ③
Zagazig ②

Fort Qaitbey, dating from the 1480s and occupying the site of
the Pharos – Alexandria's legendary lighthouse

ROSETTA ⑤
DAMIETTA ①
ABU QIR ⑧
⑦ MONTAZAH PALACE
ALEXANDRIA ⑥
⑨ AGAMI
TANIS ④
⑪ EL-ALAMEIN
⑩ ABU MINA
③ TANTA
② ZAGAZIG
Cairo

Babariyya Oasis

See Also

• *Where to Stay* pp260–3
• *Where to Eat* pp276–9

Key

▨ Motorway
▨ Major road
▨ Minor road
▬ Railway line
▨ Scenic route

0 kilometres   75

0 miles   40

Sidi Abdel Rahman, near the El-Alamein battlefield memorials

Detail of building in Damietta old town, illustrating Delta-style architecture

Damietta ❶

210 km (131 miles) NE of Cairo.
🚶 78,000. 🚌 🚗 🚆

D AMIETTA, an industrial port known for its furniture, textiles, sweets and fishing, lies on Egypt's north coast, next to the eastern branch of the Nile. A wealthy port in the Middle Ages, the town was frequently attacked by the Byzantines, occupied twice by Christian forces then completely destroyed in 1250 by the Mamluks, who held power in Egypt from the 13th century until the Ottoman conquest in 1517. Damietta was rebuilt by the Ottomans, whose pretty 'Delta-style' villas can still be seen today, and its importance as a port was restored. The completion of the Suez Canal in 1869, and the subsequent growth of Port Said, some 70 km (43 miles) to the east, seriously undermined Damietta's prosperity. Since the late 1980s, however, the port of Damietta has once again experienced an economic revival.

There is not a great deal to do in Damietta itself but nearby, to the east, the huge expanse of **Lake Manzila** – a salt-water lagoon that is separated from the sea by a narrow peninsula – is a popular destination for bird-watchers who come to observe the migrating flamingos, herons, pelicans and storks that stop here. Egypt is on one of the major migration routes for many species, and millions of birds pass through this region every autumn and spring.

To the north of Damietta is the popular small beach resort of **Ras al-Bar**, which has numerous restaurants, hotels and tea houses.

Zagazig ❷

80 km (50 miles) NE of Cairo.
🚶 268,000. 🚌 🚗 🚆

B UILT IN THE 1830s to house workers on the Nile Barrages (see p165), Zagazig's main claim to fame is as the birthplace of Colonel Ahmed Orabi, the nationalist who led the 1882 revolt against British rule, and whose statue stands outside the railway station. The town has a small museum that displays archaeological finds from the region.

Just to the southeast of Zagazig are the sparse ruins of **Bubastis**, capital of ancient Egypt in the 22nd and 23rd Dynasties and cult centre of the cat-goddess Bastet. It is believed that huge festivals in her honour were held at Bubastis and attracted thousands of revellers. The events involved dancing, vast quantities of alcohol and sacrifices to the goddess. Work began on the Temple of Bastet at Bubastis during the 6th Dynasty and, for nearly 1500 years, it was regularly added to; now, all that remains to be seen are scattered stones. Nearby, in the underground galleries of a cat cemetery where mummified cats were buried, bronze statues of the sacred animal have been discovered.

Cat worship near Zagazig

MOULIDS

Meaning "birth" in Arabic, a *moulid* commemorates the birthday of a local saint or holy person. Celebrated by Muslims and Christians alike, the moulid probably has its roots in the customs of ancient Egypt when, on festival days, a statue of the local god was paraded in a boat (see p174). Nowadays, big moulids in Cairo, Luxor and Tanta draw millions of people, allowing everyone a release from everyday concerns. After visiting the tomb or church, revellers might attend a *zikr*, a ritual chanting of Allah's name to induce a trance-like state. During the feast *tartours* (cone-shaped hats) and *fanous* (lanterns) are sold; traditional entertainment such as puppet shows and stick dancing take place alongside more modern funfair attractions. Usually lasting a week, moulids climax on the Great Night or *Leila al-Kebira* with a lively *zaffa* or procession.

Reeds of Lake Manzila (Damietta) providing cover for migrating birds

Tanta ❸

94 km (58 miles) N of Cairo.
🏛 373,000. 🚌 🚊

TANTA, EGYPT's fifth largest city and an important university town, is best known for its eight-day festival, or moulid, which is held each year after the October cotton harvest. Up to two million people take part in the event, which honours Sayyid Ahmed al-Badawi, the 13th-century founder of one of the largest Sufi brotherhoods in Egypt. Groups of Sufis from throughout Egypt camp in makeshift lodgings around the city and hold *zikrs* – lengthy sessions of chanting and swaying, intended to achieve unity with Allah. A procession led by the current sheikh tours the city, ending with a mass *zikr* outside the mosque where al-Badawi is buried.

Although fundamentally a spiritual occasion, this annual festival is also an important social event, allowing young Egyptians to let off steam in the boisterous atmosphere.

21st- and 22nd-Dynasty tombs at the royal necropolis at Tanis

Tanis ❹

70 km (43 miles) NE of Zagazig. 🚌

NEAR THE MODERN village of San el-Hagar, to the northeast of Zagazig, lie the jumbled ruins of the ancient Egyptian city of Djanet, known by the Greeks as Tanis. For several centuries, Tanis was one of the largest cities in the Delta and became the capital of Egypt during the 21st Dynasty. Flooding led to its decline, however, and by the 14th century the area was practically deserted. San el-Hagar grew up on reclaimed land during the 1820s.

Panelled wall in the Ottoman House of Amasyali in Rosetta

Excavations at Tanis have revealed ruins dating back to the 6th Dynasty: huge blocks and fragments of statues from the Ramessid Temple of Amun, as well as the foundations of many other temples, are among the remains on site. Several intact 21st- and 22nd-Dynasty tombs, including those of Psusennes I and Sheshonq III, were discovered at the royal necropolis, which lies to the south of the temple. The breathtaking treasures can be seen at the Egyptian Museum in Cairo *(see pp74–5)*.

Rosetta (Rashid) ❺

65 km (40 miles) E of Alexandria.
🏛 58,000. 🚌 🚉

FOUNDED IN THE 9th century by Ibn Tulun, the Muslim governor of Egypt, Rosetta (also known by the modern name of Rashid) became one of Egypt's most important ports, reaching its heyday during the 17th and 18th centuries. With Alexandria's revival in the 19th century, however, Rosetta fell into decline and today it is little more than an attractive fishing village surrounded by palm and orange groves.

Many beautiful Ottoman houses and mosques – reminders of Rosetta's more glorious past – can still be seen around the town and several are open to visitors. Among the most beautiful are the House of Amasyali on

Sharia Amasyali and Ramadan House on Sharia Port Said. The ornate 18th-century Azouz *hammam* (public baths) to the south of the town is almost entirely intact.

Rosetta is best known for the famous Rosetta stone *(see pp20–21)*, which was discovered here by French soldiers in 1799. Part of a black basalt stele dating from the 2nd century BC, the stone was carved with a decree by Ptolemy V, written in ancient hieroglyphics, Greek and demotic Egyptian. From these inscriptions, French professor Jean-François Champollion was able, in 1822, to formulate a system for deciphering hieroglyphics – a feat that was to unlock much of ancient Egyptian history.

Conceded to the British in 1801, the Rosetta stone is now on display at the British Museum in London.

Palm trees bordering the Rosetta branch of the Nile Delta

Alexandria

STRETCHING 20 km (12 miles) along the coast, Alexandria is Egypt's second largest city. Founded in 332 BC by Alexander the Great, the city grew to rival Rome before falling into decline in the 4th century AD. In the 19th century, the Pasha Mohammed Ali revived Alexandria's fortunes as a port by linking it to the Nile. This prosperity drew thousands of Europeans, who fostered the decadent atmosphere chronicled by writers such as Lawrence Durrell, E M Forster and Constantine Cavafy. This era ended in the 1950s as the foreigners fled Nasser's revolution. Little remains of Alexandria's ancient magnificence, but a few faded clues to its cosmopolitan heyday linger on.

Colourful fishing boats in Alexandria Harbour

⊞ Midan Saad Zaghloul
Situated on the seafront, Midan Saad Zaghloul is at the heart of modern Alexandria. From this square, a statue of Egyptian nationalist leader Zaghloul (1860–1927) *(see p62)* watches over the eastern harbour and the busy tram and bus stations in the adjacent Midan Ramla.

Sadly, nothing remains of the Caesareum, a magnificent temple built on the site more than 2,000 years ago. Begun by Cleopatra VII for Mark Antony and finished by Octavian after their deaths in 30 BC *(see pp54–5)*, only two obelisks survived its destruction in 912. Known as Cleopatra's Needles, they were relocated to London and New York in the 1800s.

Today the square consists of shops, hotels and three 1920s Art Deco cafés, Athineos, Délices and Trianon. South is Sharia Nabi Daniel, believed to be the ancient Street of Soma – a marble road lined with columns. Now lined

16th-century woodcut showing the Library of Alexandria on fire

with street vendors, its glory has faded.

⊞ Bibliotheca Alexandrina
Shatbi. 📞 *(03) 483 999, (03) 487 6024/8.* 🕐 *10am–7pm Wed–Thu & Sun–Mon, 3–7pm Fri–Sat (11am–2pm during Ramadan).*
Founded in the 3rd century BC, the Bibliotheca Alexandrina was the greatest library in the ancient world, attracting the best international scholars. The library and cultural centre was re-inaugurated in October 2002, more than two millennia after the original building was destroyed by fire.

The new Bibliotheca Alexandrina is striking in its architecture and also contains a Planetarium and Science Museum. The main library is encased in a giant cylindrical building at the far northern end of the corniche. The circular outer wall is made of Aswan granite engraved with letters from world alpha-

bets. The partly-glazed roof which tilts towards the sea is designed to angle sunlight on to the desks of the seven-tier 2,000-seat reading rooms. Eventually, the library will contain 8 million volumes.

⊞ Hotel Cecil
16 Midan Saad Zaghloul.
📞 *(03) 487 7173.*
One of the more obvious landmarks of Midan Saad Zaghloul is the Moorish-style Hotel Cecil which featured in Lawrence Durrell's *Alexandria Quartet*. Opened in 1929, it is reputed to be built on the site where Cleopatra VII committed suicide after her Egyptian fleet was defeated by Octavian in the Battle of Actium in 31 BC.

During World War II the hotel was used by the British Secret Service and later played host to politicians and writers such as Winston Churchill, Somerset Maugham and Noel Coward. Though restoration has not quite captured its past grandeur, the roof garden or sea-front terrace are pleasant places to enjoy a drink.

Elegant façade of Hotel Cecil

🏛 Cavafy Museum
4 Sharia Sharm el-Sheikh, off Sharia Nabi Daniel. 🕐 *Wed–Mon.*
The poet Constantine Cavafy (1863–1933) was born to Greek parents but spent most of his life in Alexandria. This small museum is housed in the flat where he spent the last 25 years of his life. Some of the rooms are arranged as they would have been when he lived here – the display of possessions includes his bed,

Marble benches capable of seating up to 800 Romans in the Amphitheatre at Kom al-Dikka

Kom al-Dikka (Mound of Rubble) after the remains of a Napoleonic fort were levelled for a housing project. The 13 tiered rows of marble seats, excavated by Polish archaeologists aided by the Graeco-Roman Museum, date from the 2nd century AD. Originally a small theatre, the building was altered over time and served as an assembly hall, possibly for the city council. A couple of sections of the original mosaic floor are on view in front of the amphitheatre.

Other excavations are still under way on the site. To the north lie the brick ruins of a Roman bathing complex. A series of basins and channels reveal how water would have

VISITORS' CHECKLIST

Alexandria governorate. 🏛 3.4 million. ✈ 5 km (3 miles) SE of the city. 🚇 Masr Station, Midan al-Gumhuriyya. 🚌 15th May Bus Station, Sidi Gaber. ℹ Midan Saad Zaghloul (03) 485 1556; Masr Station (03) 392 5985.

Roman mosaic at Kom al-Dikka

passed through the heating system to the marble covered baths. To the east lie the ruins of a residential area dating from the 1st century AD, but this site and the Roman baths are closed for excavation work.

Some items found at an underwater excavation near Fort Qaitbey, including part of an obelisk from the era of Seti I and a weather-beaten sphinx, are on show in the amphitheatre grounds.

desk, death mask, rare editions of his books as well as some of his letters. Cavafy is buried in the Greek Cemetery nearby.

Another room in the small museum is devoted to one of Cavafy's students, the Greek writer Stratis Tsirkas (1911–81).

🏛 **Roman Amphitheatre at Kom al-Dikka**
Sharia Yousef. ⭕ daily. 📷
In 1965, a semi-circular Roman amphitheatre was discovered under what was known as

---

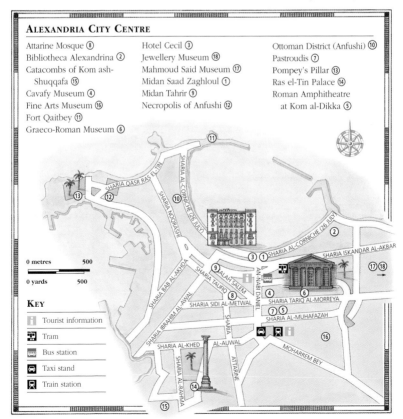

ALEXANDRIA CITY CENTRE

Attarine Mosque ⑧
Bibliotheca Alexandrina ②
Catacombs of Kom ash-Shuqqafa ⑮
Cavafy Museum ④
Fine Arts Museum ⑯
Fort Qaitbey ⑪
Graeco-Roman Museum ⑥

Hotel Cecil ③
Jewellery Museum ⑱
Mahmoud Said Museum ⑰
Midan Saad Zaghloul ①
Midan Tahrir ⑨
Necropolis of Anfushi ⑫

Ottoman District (Anfushi) ⑩
Pastroudis ⑦
Pompey's Pillar ⑬
Ras el-Tin Palace ⑭
Roman Amphitheatre at Kom al-Dikka ⑤

KEY

ℹ	Tourist information
🚋	Tram
🚌	Bus station
🚕	Taxi stand
🚉	Train station

Alexandria: Graeco-Roman Museum

Terracotta Pharos lantern

SITUATED IN THE HEART of modern Alexandria, the Graeco-Roman Museum contains around 40,000 artifacts, mostly covering around 1,000 years of history from the founding of the city in 331 BC to the Arab conquest in AD 640. The museum was established in 1892 by Khedive Abbas II. Its 25 rooms and central gardens are crammed with items found in Alexandria and the surrounding areas. The vast collection of artifacts from ancient Egyptian, Classical and Christian cultures testify to the complex history of Alexandria and provide an insight to the forces that influenced Western culture, even up to the present day.

Museum Gardens
In the museum's central gardens, amongst a wealth of tombs, statues and other artifacts, sits the head of a once huge statue of Mark Anthony.

Statue of Aphrodite (2nd-century AD)

Tomb Painting
Two oxen driving a waterwheel (an invention of Alexandrian scientists) are depicted in this tomb fresco dating from the 2nd century AD.

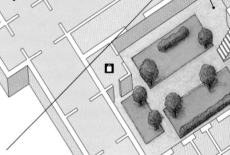

White Marble Sarcophagus
A bas-relief from the 2nd century AD depicts Dionysus and his retinue as they find Ariadne asleep on the island of Naxos before she was abandoned by her lover, Theseus.

Sacred Crocodile
This mummified crocodile was carried in processions honouring Sobek, the crocodile-god.

Terracotta models of town monuments are displayed in Hall 18.

★ **Tanagra Figures**
This intriguing collection of Graeco-Roman terracotta figures, found in the city's many necropolises, provides an insight into social life and the costume of the era.

VISITORS' CHECKLIST

5 Sharia al-Mathaf ar-Romani.
(03) 486 5820.
9am–5pm daily; 9am–3pm during Ramadan. 11am–1pm Fri. Extra charge for cameras and videos.

Emperor Hadrian
This 2nd-century AD bronze head has eyes of ivory and glass. Found at Qena, it was once part of a larger sculpture.

GALLERY GUIDE
The museum is organized in chronological order running clockwise from the entrance. This order is interrupted only by two large themed areas: the first contains handicrafts from all eras and the other a vast collection of coins. Also worth visiting is the garden, with some fine statues and a reconstructed temple of the crocodile-god from Fayoum.

Coptic artifacts from the 4th–7th centuries AD are displayed here.

KEY

	Coptic
	Ptolemaic
	Pharaonic
	Graeco-Roman
	Handicrafts (all periods)
	Coins
	Non-exhibition space

Entrance

★ **Antique Coins**
The magnificent collection of coins includes some bearing Cleopatra's profile (above right).

Alexander the Great (356–323 BC)
Sculpted from marble, this head of Alexander the Great is one of several portraits of the leader in the museum. He became the object of a cult worship that spread throughout the ancient world.

STAR EXHIBITS

★ **Antique Coins**

★ **Tanagra Figures**

Pastroudis, once a favourite with the Alexandrian literary crowd

Nasser as he gave a speech in 1954. This gave him the opportunity to remove any opposition to his rule. Two years later, in 1956, it was from Midan Tahrir that Nasser shocked the Western world and announced the nationalization of the Suez Canal.

To the north is Midan Orabi, a major transport hub with tram, minibus and bus depots. The grand Neo-Classical Monument to the Unknown Soldier, designed by the Italian architect Verucci and erected in 1937, stands on the corniche, facing out to sea.

⌘ Pastroudis
39 Sharia Horreya. **☎** *(03) 392 9609.*
The wood-panelled Pastroudis is an old-fashioned café from the early 20th century. Written about in Durrell's Alexandria Quartet, Pastroudis used to be a popular haunt of the poet Cavafy and the bohemian crowd. Although the café is no longer fashionable, its street-side tables still provide a good spot to watch the world go by and overlook the Roman amphitheatre and baths.

Sharia Horreya is believed to have been the colonnaded Canopic Way which ran from the Gate of the Sun in the eastern walls to the Gate of the Moon to the west. It is also thought that the intersection with Sharia Nabi Daniel was once the crossroads of the ancient city where the Great Library of Alexandria and Mouseion once stood.

⌘ Attarine Mosque
Sharia Attarine.
Topped by a pretty minaret, the Attarine Mosque lies just south of Midan Tahrir. It was built on the site of the fabled Mosque of a Thousand

Columns, which itself stood on the site of a church dedicated to St Athanasius in AD 370.

Napoleon's men removed a seven-ton sarcophagus from the mosque, believing it to be Alexander's. Handed over to the British it was found to be the sarcophagus of Nectanebo II, the last Egyptian pharaoh.

Around the Attarine Mosque, the sprawling antiques district begins. Antique shops, piled high with European furniture, and trinkets dating back to Napoleonic times, fill the backstreets. Here also, the intriguing belongings of many Europeans who fled the 1952 revolution are up for sale. However, the area is well known by international antiques dealers and genuine bargains can be hard to find.

⌘ Midan Tahrir
Originally known as Place des Consuls, the square was intended as the centrepiece of Pasha Mohammed Ali's new Alexandria in the 1830s. In 1873 his French-designed equestrian statue was set in its place on a high plinth and the square was thereafter known as Midan Mohammed Ali. After the destruction brought about by the British bombardment in 1882 *(see p59)*, the area was rebuilt as Midan Mansheiyya, before Nasser's revolution in 1952 renamed the square Midan Tahrir.

It was here that an assassination attempt was made on President

Detail of Andalusian-styled Mosque of Abu al-Abbas Mursi in Anfushi

⌘ Ottoman District (Anfushi)
The peninsula leading to Fort Qaitbey was home to the inhabitants of Alexandria in Ottoman times (1517–1914). The atmosphere here differs from the rest of the city and it is best experienced on foot. To the south, lively souqs sell medicinal herbs and perfume while Turkish-style houses overhang the narrow streets.

Ottoman mosques are also dotted throughout the area, with the El-Shorbagi Mosque Complex at the heart of the district. Built in the mid-18th century it has a distinctive gallery on the first floor with shops below. The Terbana Mosque on Faransa Street was originally built in 1685 and two antique columns, taken from another site, support the minaret. Further north, in Midan El-Gawamaa is a mosque, dedicated to the

Midan Tahrir at the centre of Alexandria

PHAROS LIGHTHOUSE

Built in the 3rd century BC on an island in the eastern harbour, the Pharos Lighthouse stood up to 150 m (492 ft) high and was one of the Seven Wonders of the ancient world. Built mainly of limestone to the design of the Asiatic Greek architect Sostratus, the lighthouse had three differently-shaped storeys. The base was square and used as lodgings for mechanics and for storing fuel. The second storey was octagonal and the third, which contained the lantern mechanism, was circular and topped with a huge bronze statue of Poseidon, god of the sea. Used for nearly 1,000 years, the lighthouse was neglected during the Arab occupation. The lantern collapsed in AD 700 and the lighthouse was later destroyed by a series of earthquakes in the 12th and 14th centuries. Recently, underwater excavation has discovered blocks of stone believed to be from the Pharos Lighthouse and a temple dedicated to Isis *(see pp26–7)* which stood nearby.

Reconstruction of the Pharos Lighthouse

13th-century Andalusian, Sidi Abu al-Abbas Mursi, the city's patron saint of fishermen. The current structure was designed in 1945 by Italian architect Mario Rossi. The octagonal-shaped building has a 73-m (240-ft) minaret.

Fort Qaitbey

Corniche. 🚌 15. ◻ daily. 📷
Although the turretted Fort Qaitbey situated on the tip of the Eastern Harbour looks like some kind of toy castle from the corniche, up close it is an imposing building. The fort was built in the 1480s by Sultan Qaitbey (1468–96) on the site of the Pharos Lighthouse, using stones from the dilapidated building. Within the keep there is a small mosque – the oldest in Alexandria – and a Naval Museum displaying relics from ships sunk nearby, the result of Roman and Napoleonic sea battles. These include bottles of wine and astronomical instruments retrieved from the French

ship L'Orient. The fort was badly damaged by the British bombardment in 1882 when the mosque's minaret was blown clean off. From its elevated position, set back from the corniche, the fort has fantastic views of Alexandria and out to sea.

⋔ Necropolis of Anfushi

Sharia Ras el-Tin, Anfushi. ◻ *daily.*
📷
The five rock tombs in the Necropolis of Anfushi date from around 250 BC and were discovered in 1901 and 1921. Cut into limestone, the tombs consist of a stairway leading down to a central courtyard with individual burial sites located off to the side. Tomb No. 2 is the most interesting and best preserved. The stairway walls are decorated with paintings of Osiris, Horus and Isis with the deceased as well as scenes of daily life and even an example of ancient Greek graffiti. The wall paintings and decoration are significant as they combine features of Greek and Egyptian art. There are also two vestibules with burial chambers; the one to the northeast is painted with black and white squares to resemble more expensive alabaster and marble tiling. The door to the burial chamber is flanked by two small stone sphinxes on stands, keeping watch over the tomb.

Fort Qaitbey from across the Eastern Harbour, built by recycling the stones from the Pharos Lighthouse

🏯 Ras el-Tin Palace

Sharia Ras el-Tin, Bahari. 🚇 🚌
Overlooking Alexandria's
Western Harbour, Ras el-Tin
Palace is surrounded by
elegant, formal gardens. The
palace was built originally by
Ottoman Pasha Mohammed
Ali (1805–48) so that he could
keep watch on his new fleet.
Under King Fuad I (1917–36),
it was redesigned by Italian
architects and served as the
government's summer seat.

During the 1952 revolution,
the palace was besieged by
Nasser's men and King Farouk
was forced to abdicate and
flee to Italy with his family
and retinue. The palace is
now Admiralty headquarters
and is reserved for state guests;
however its pleasant gardens
are open to the public.

🏛 Pompey's Pillar

Sharia Ahmoud al-Saweiri, Karmous.
🚇 16. ◯ daily. 📷
To the southwest of the city,
in the impoverished district of
Karmous, Pompey's Pillar is
a striking sight. Made of red
Aswan granite, the 27-m (89-ft)
high pillar was erected around
AD 297 in tribute to the Roman
emperor Diocletian. On its
base is written in Greek "To
the most just of emperors, the
divine protector of Alexandria,
Diocletian the invincible:
Postumus, prefect of Egypt."

The monument's popular
name may have come from
medieval travellers who
thought that the Roman
general Pompey, murdered
in Egypt in 48 BC, was buried
here; in fact, the pillar came
from the Serapeum complex
or Temple of Serapis, which
was built in the mid-3rd
century BC. (Serapis was an
Egyptian deity, very popular in
the Graeco-Roman period, who
combined aspects of the gods
Osiris and Apis). The pillar
would have been freestanding
and is all that remains of the
temple which was once an
important repository of religious texts and the "daughter
library" of that of Alexandria.

Enlarged by the Emperor
Hadrian in the 2nd century AD,
when it was described as
second only to the Capitol in
Rome, the temple was destroyed
by Christians in AD 391.

**Pompey's Pillar, once part of the
beautiful Temple of Serapis**

Nearby there are some underground galleries, where the
sacred Apis bulls (*see p160*)
were buried, as well as several
statues of the Sphinx that
originally stood at Heliopolis.

🏛 Catacombs of Kom ash-Shuqqafa

Sharia al-Nasserieh. 🚇 16. ◯ 9am–
5pm daily (Ramadan: 9am–3pm). 📷
Dating from the 2nd century
AD, the catacomb complex
of Kom ash-Shuqqafa is the
largest Graeco-Roman necropolis in Egypt. Just south of
Pompey's Pillar, the vast
burial site probably started
out as a much simpler private
family tomb but was subsequently expanded to hold
hundreds of bodies.

Dug into the rock to a depth
of about 35 m (115 ft), the
tomb complex has three levels.
However, flooding has made
the lowest level inaccessible.

The catacombs are reached
via a spiral staircase encircling
a shaft down which bodies of
the deceased were lowered.
On the first level there is a
central rotunda and a large
banquet hall, the Triclinium,
where friends and relatives
of the deceased gathered
to pay their last respects.

To the east of the rotunda
is the Caracalla Hall, an older
burial complex that became
accessible from the main
chamber when tomb robbers
broke through the wall. This
area is dedicated to Nemesis,
the goddess of sport. The
bones of horses found here
are thought to have belonged
to successful racehorses.

From the central rotunda,
stairs lead down to a second
storey with a vestibule and
burial chamber. Here the
decorated sarcophagi and wall
reliefs display a mixture of
Egyptian, Roman and Greek
styles: by the doorway, Anubis,
the god of the dead, is shown
as a Roman legionary with a
dragon's tail. On either side
of the burial chamber, below
heads of Medusa, are carved
two giant serpents, wearing
the double crown of Egypt.

From the burial chamber,
eerie passages lead off in all
directions to rooms containing
more than 300 loculi – small
chambers for bodies.

🏛 Fine Arts Museum

18 Sharia Menasce. 📞 (03) 393
6616. ◯ Sat–Thu. 📷
A short distance to the southeast of Masr station, the Fine
Arts Museum is housed in
a beautiful villa that was
donated in 1954 to the city

Relief of Anubis presiding over a mummification at Kom ash-Shuqqafa

of Alexandria by the wealthy Jewish Menasce family. The museum is used mainly for frequently changing exhibitions of contemporary foreign and Egyptian artists, so it is not possible to predict what will be on display, but the standard is usually very high.

The museum is also known for hosting the Alexandrian Biennial, a showcase for art from Mediterranean countries.

A statue by Mahmoud Mokhtar (1891–1934), who has been acclaimed as the first sculptor in the modern Egyptian art movement, stands in the gardens outside.

Mahmoud Said Museum Centre

6 Sharia Said Pasha, Gianaclis.
(03) 582 1688. 2.
10am–6:30pm Tue–Sun; 10am–1:30pm, 7–10:30pm Ramadan.

An Alexandrian aristocrat, Mahmoud Said (1897–1964) is one of Egypt's most important modern artists. The museum that bears his name is housed in what was the family villa. It contains a comprehensive selection of Said's work on the ground floor, including one of his earliest known works, a self-portrait painted in 1919.

Said trained originally as a lawyer and worked as a judge, but painting was his passion and in 1947 he gave up law to dedicate himself to art. He studied art in Paris and travelled widely in Europe. Said's work combines western techniques with Egyptian and Pharaonic themes to produce stunning, sensuous paintings. His 1924 self-portrait echoes a haunting Fayoum mummy portrait *(see p165)*.

As well as more formal portraits, Said produced a series of vivid and colourful street scenes from around Alexandria. In the late 1930s, he began to use a more impressionistic style in his landscapes, with a warmer, more direct use of colour.

The first floor of the museum contains works by the prolific Alexandrian painters, the Wanly brothers, Seif (1906–79) and Adham (1911–59). The eclectic choice of paintings includes portraits, landscapes, and even a few cartoons.

Montazah Palace, an eclectic mix of Turkish and Florentine architecture

The museum basement is filled with works by renowned modern Egyptian artists such as Sobhi Girgis and Ahmed Fuad Selim. There are also two areas used for displaying temporary exhibitions.

Royal Jewellery Museum

27 Sharia Ahmed Yehia Pasha, Zizinia.
2. (03) 582 8348.
9am–4pm daily; 9:30am–2:30pm Ramadan.

Housed in a building originally constructed for Mohammed Ali's granddaughter, Princess Fatima el-Zaharaa (1903–83), and later used as a palace by King Farouk, the museum has an extensive collection of jewels. The well-labelled exhibits date from Pasha Mohammed Ali's rule in the early 19th century to the end of King Farouk's reign in 1952.

Key pieces include a gold snuff box with Mohammed Ali's name spelled out in diamonds, King Farouk's gold- and diamond-studded chess set, and a fabulous platinum crown glittering with well over 2,000 diamonds. Some of the most peculiar items on display are the diamond-studded gardening tools.

The palace is lavishly, if not always tastefully, decorated with stained-glass vignettes of life in 18th-century France. The two bathrooms, the ladies' tiled with scenes of nymphs bathing in Alpine surrounds and the men's with pictures of French fishermen and sea-gulls, should not be missed.

Montazah Palace ❼

18 km (11 miles) E of Alexandria.
(03) 547 7152. daily.

Montazah palace is set in extensive gardens and overlooks a truly beautiful stretch of coast. Built at the beginning of the 20th century by Khedive Abbas II, a relative of King Farouk, the palace mixes Turkish and Florentine architecture: the central tower was inspired by the Palazzo Vecchio in Florence. Although the palace itself is closed to the public, the lush park and the semi-private beach are popular places to relax.

To the east lies the private beach resort of **Mamoura**. It has a more relaxed dress code than public beaches and the sand is relatively clean.

Mamoura

Sharia Abu Qir.

The elegant gardens and groves of Montazah Palace, Alexandria

Abu Qir ⓼

24 km (15 miles) E of Alexandria.
🚶 33,000. 🚌 🚐

Brightly painted fishing boats at Abu Qir

THE SMALL fishing town of Abu Qir, on the coast to the east of Alexandria, is renowned for two reasons: historic battles and excellent fish restaurants. It was at Abu Qir Bay that Admiral Nelson destroyed the French fleet in the dramatic Battle of the Nile in 1798. With the loss of his ships and army, Napoleon's plans for an eastern empire were effectively ruined. A year later the tables were turned slightly when Napoleon's troops repulsed a landing attempt by a British contingent of 15,000 Turkish soldiers and many thousands drowned.

Since 1998, underwater excavation work by teams of French and Egyptian divers has uncovered many artifacts from the sunken warships including gold coins, cannons, and plenty of everyday items. There are plans to build a new museum to display these finds.

Although the beach at Abu Qir is not suitable for bathing, at the weekend the streets are filled with Alexandrians who come to savour the delights of a small seaside town. These include eating in one of the many seafront restaurants that serve delicious seafood. Sitting right on the beach, the Zaphyrion *(see p290)* – the ancient Greek name for Abu Qir – is reputed to be one of the best restaurants in Egypt.

Agami ⓽

20 km (12 miles) W of Alexandria. 🚌

AGAMI WAS TRADITIONALLY the summer resort of the Cairene and Alexandrian elite during the 1950s. Known as the Egyptian St Tropez, it is far less exclusive these days. The semi-private beaches are less conservative and less crowded than in Alexandria, and the nightlife is livelier. High-rise apartment blocks have replaced most of the original resort architecture. Exceptions include the **Beit al-Halawa**, designed in 1975 by Abd el-Wahid el-Wakil and the extreme angular lines of **Villa Lashin**, built in 1962 by the architect Ali Azzam.

ENVIRONS: Other popular resorts nearby include the small village of **Hannoville**, 1 km (0.6 mile) to the west, notable for its inexpensive accommodation, and the private beach resort of **Sidi Kir**, which lies 14 km (8.5 miles) further west along the coast.

Abu Mina ⓾

63 km (39 miles) SW of Alexandria. 🚌

TO THE WEST of Alexandria, 15 km (9 miles) inland from Abu Sir on the coast, lies the Coptic Monastery of Abu Mina (Deir Mari Mina). St Mina was an Alexandrian-born Roman legionary who was tortured and killed in Phrygia (Asia Minor) at the end of the 3rd century for his Christian beliefs. His body is said to have been buried here after a camel carrying it home refused to go any further. Legend has it that a spring with miraculous powers immediately started flowing nearby and a church and basilica were built around the tomb. After the Emperor of Byzantium's daughter was cured by the waters in the 4th century its fame spread. The water was exported throughout Christendom and Abu Mina became a busy pilgrim town. However, after repeated sackings by the Bedouin, the town fell into decay as the water source dried up.

Today a modern monastery dominates the site and there are few impressive remains to see, although there are plans for a museum and archaeological park. The area is still important to pilgrims who visit the monastery, especially on 11th November, St Mina's day.

Monastery at Abu Mina built in 1959 on the site of a much older basilica

◁ Colourful fishing boats on the seafront at Abu Qir

El-Alamein ⓫

105 km (65 miles) W of Alexandria.
🏠 1,800. 🚌

E L-ALAMEIN, a small village on the coast to the west of Alexandria, was the site of a World War II battle which changed the course of the North Africa campaign in the Allies' favour. On 23rd October 1942, the British General Montgomery's Eighth Army attacked Field Marshal Rommel's German-Italian Afrika Korps at El-Alamein. After 11 days of fierce fighting, Rommel's troops retreated to Tunis to surrender six months later. More than 11,000 soldiers died and at least 70,000 were injured in the battle.

The **War Museum** to the west of town shows the stages of the North Africa campaign using electronic displays and many World War II mementoes. Tanks and artillery used during the battle are on display in the grounds. The **Commonwealth War Cemetery** to the east, where row upon row of Allied graves lie surrounded by the desert, is a chilling testimony to the war. A memorial here also lists the names of over 11,000 men whose bodies were never found. On the coast, 4 km (2.5 miles) west, lies the **German Cemetery**. This imposing fortress of a memorial overlooking the sea honours the 22,000 Germans who died in the North Africa campaign. The **Italian**

Gravestones at the Commonwealth War Cemetery at El-Alamein

Sherman tank outside the War Museum

Cemetery is just 3 km (2 miles) further west along the coast, with a marble tower in honour of the 22,000 Italian soldiers killed in the fighting. Further west, a string of resort villages line the coast. One with a particularly stunning beach is the up-market and unspoilt resort at **Sidi Abdel Rahman**, 23 km (14 miles) west of El-Alamein.

🏛 **El-Alamein War Museum**
⬜ daily. 📷

Marsa Matruh ⓬

290 km (180 miles) W of Alexandria.
🏠 52,000. ℹ Governorate Building, Al-Corniche (03) 493 1841. 🚌 🚗

T HE COASTAL TOWN of Marsa Matruh is a very popular summer resort for Egyptians.

However, although the coast is beautiful, the town itself and its beaches are pretty tatty and the resort lacks appeal for most tourists.

The town has a historical pedigree and was founded by Alexander on his way to the oracle at Siwa; later it served as a port for Anthony and Cleopatra's doomed fleet and this link is reflected in many of the place names.

West of town the sea is gorgeous. **Cleopatra Beach** is 7 km (4 miles) west, though rocks and a sudden drop in the sea bed make this a difficult place to swim. The royal queen herself is said to have bathed at Cleopatra's Bath nearby. The best place to swim is **Agibah Beach**, 28 km (17 miles) west on the coastal road. A steep path leads down to a cove where rock shelves make ideal plat-forms for diving into the sea.

Sallum ⓭

222 km (137 miles) W of Marsa Matruh. 🏠 6,000. 🚌

S ALLUM IS THE LAST Egyptian town before Libya and an important trading centre for the Bedouin. The town sits high up on a cliff looking out to sea, with a small harbour down below. This was the ancient Roman port of Baranis, and there are still some Roman wells in the area.

Sallum is not traditionally a tourist area, and although the beaches in town can be dirty, to the east there are stretches of golden sand and crystal waters that permit relatively secluded swimming. Visitors should check with the local Tourist Police first that bathing is allowed as some areas and beaches are out of bounds.

There is also a small **Allied War Cemetery** where soldiers killed fighting with Rommel's Afrika Korps lie buried.

A huge Palestinian refugee camp, 10 km (6 miles) east of town, houses those expelled from Libya in 1994.

Waves crashing into the rocks at Cleopatra's Beach, Marsa Matruh

THE WESTERN DESERT

EGYPT'S VAST WESTERN DESERT *stretches over nearly 3 million sq km (1.2 million sq miles), from the west bank of the Nile to Libya, and from Sudan towards the Mediterranean Sea. Despite covering over two-thirds of Egypt's total land area, the desert is virtually uninhabited, except for the fertile oases where communities and crops flourish amid barren desert surroundings.*

There are five oases in the Western Desert: Siwa, Kharga, Dakhla, Farafra and Bahariyya. Except for Siwa, the oases have been under the control of the rulers of the Nile Valley since Pharaonic times, when they were crucial stopping points on the busy caravan trading routes from Africa. The Ptolemaic temples and Roman forts dotted around the oases bear witness to their past importance and ongoing archaeological work is continually uncovering new finds.

Each of the Western Desert oases has its own unique character. While the main settlements of Bahariyya and Farafra are still villages, those of Dakhla and Kharga are large towns, surrounded by fascinating historical sites. In Siwa, isolated near the Libyan border, the inhabitants retain their own language and distinct culture.

In the late 1950s a plan was made to reclaim part of the desert and relocate thousands of people from the crowded Nile delta and valley. The area, covering Bahariyya, Farafra, Dakhla and Kharga oases, was named the New Valley. Although some building began, few people moved, and financial constraints together with the questionable sustainability of the water supply meant that the project was virtually abandoned.

The Western Desert today remains one of the few places in the world where travellers can experience a feeling of total isolation. Its sheer scale is overwhelming. From huge dunes to fantastical rock formations, the landscape varies dramatically and camping out overnight in such astonishing surroundings can be one of the highlights of a trip to Egypt.

Taking a break during the heat of the day in Dakhla, one of the Western Desert Oases

◁ **The boundless expanse of the Great Sand Sea, close to Siwa Oasis**

Exploring the Western Desert

THE WESTERN DESERT offers visitors the chance to escape the crowded sites of Cairo and the Nile Valley and sample the peace and tranquillity of the empty desert and its green oases. In the northwest, the remote Siwa is the perfect place to relax. Further east, Bahariyya is a picturesque oasis within easy reach of Cairo. The road leading on to Farafra, the least developed of the oases, passes through the Black Desert and the incredible White Desert, with its mysterious, wind-eroded rock formations. Pockets of fertile land growing fruit, rice and peanuts are dotted among the sand dunes between Farafra and the beautiful Dakhla oasis. For lovers of ancient monuments, Dakhla and the more built-up Kharga have the most to offer.

Statue in the Oasis Heritage Museum, Bahariyya

Marsa Matrub

5 SIWA OASIS

GREAT SAND SEA

Dakhla Oasis near Al-Qasr, showing the striking contrast between the fertile soil and the barren, inhospitable desert

GETTING AROUND

Travelling in the Western Desert is much easier than it used to be. Roads now link all the oases and buses run fairly frequently. Siwa Oasis is best reached by bus from Marsa Matruh, on the Mediterranean coast. Bahariyya and Farafra can be visited from Cairo, and Dakhla and Kharga can be reached quite easily from Asyut. There are airports at Dakhla and Kharga with twice weekly flights to and from Cairo. Depending on time pressure and your sense of adventure, the 1,000-km (620-mile) Great Desert Circuit of Bahariyya, Farafra, Dakhla and Kharga is an option. Usually starting at Cairo and ending at Luxor or Asyut, the trip can be taken either with an organized tour or hired transport. Exploring the area around each individual oasis is easy to arrange locally.

Siwa Oasis, with the salt lake Birket Siwa visible in the distance, viewed from the Mountain of the Dead

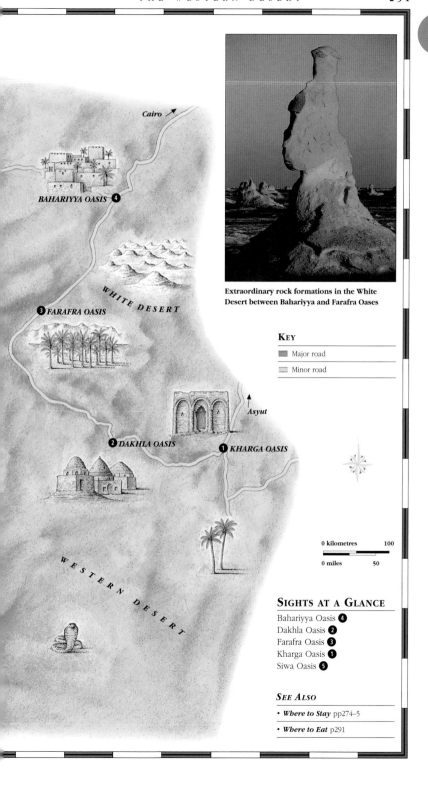

Extraordinary rock formations in the White Desert between Bahariyya and Farafra Oases

Cairo

BAHARIYYA OASIS ❹

WHITE DESERT

❸ **FARAFRA OASIS**

Asyut

❷ **DAKHLA OASIS**   ❶ **KHARGA OASIS**

WESTERN DESERT

KEY

▨ Major road

▨ Minor road

0 kilometres   100

0 miles   50

SIGHTS AT A GLANCE

Bahariyya Oasis ❹

Dakhla Oasis ❷

Farafra Oasis ❸

Kharga Oasis ❶

Siwa Oasis ❺

SEE ALSO

- *Where to Stay* pp274–5

- *Where to Eat* p291

Lush date groves surrounding the fertile fields of Dakhla, the prettiest of the Western Desert oases

Kharga Oasis ❶

233 km (144 miles) SW of Asyut.
🏠 65,000. ✈ 5 km (3 miles) N of
El-Kharga. 🚌 🛈 Government
building, Midan Nasser, El-Kharga
(092) 921 206.

K HARGA, THE LARGEST of the
oases, rose to prominence
as the penultimate stop on
"The Forty Days Road", the
infamous slave-trade route
between Sudan and Egypt.
Today the modern, sprawling
city of El-Kharga is capital of
the New Valley governorate,
which covers Kharga, Dakhla
and Farafra oases. The city
lacks charm but its **Antiquities
Museum** displays impressive
archaeological finds from
Kharga and Dakhla.
    Standing in palm groves
just north of the city, the well-
preserved **Temple of Hibis**,
built by Persian emperor
Darius I in the 6th century
BC, is the only sizeable
Persian temple left in Egypt.
Also north of the city is the
Necropolis of

al-Bagawat. This Christian
cemetery contains hundreds
of domed, mudbrick tombs
decorated with Coptic murals,
dating from around the 4th
to 6th centuries AD. The best
preserved paintings are in the
Chapel of the Exodus and
portray Moses leading the
Jews out of Egypt, away from
Pharaoh's pursuing troops.

ENVIRONS: Perched on a hill
on the road south to Baris are
the ruins of the 25th-Dynasty
Temple of al-Ghueita.
Further south, the villages of
Nasser and Bulaq are known
for their thermal springs,
reputed to treat rheumatism.

🏛 **Antiquities Museum**
Sharia Gamal Abdel Nasser. ◯ daily. 🖼
🛖 **Temple of Hibis**
2 km (1 mile) N of El-Kharga.
◯ daily. 🖼
🛖 **Necropolis of al-Bagawat**
3 km (2 miles) N of El-Kharga.
◯ daily. 🖼
🛖 **Temple of al-Ghueita**
18 km (11 miles) S of El-Kharga.
◯ daily. 🖼

Dakhla Oasis ❷

190 km (118 miles) W of Kharga.
🏠 70,000. ✈ 10 km (6 miles) SW
of Mut. 🚌 🛈 Sharia as-Sawra al-
Khadra, Mut (092) 821 686.

W ITH HUNDREDS of springs
set in a lush, verdant
landscape, Dakhla is regarded
as the prettiest of the oases.
A long band of pinkish rock
sits along the northern horizon,
and olives, dates, wheat and
rice thrive on the fertile farmland. The capital, Mut, has an
Ethnographic Museum
displaying figures sculpted
by a local artist, Mabrouk.
    Dakhla's ancient sites are
situated in the outlying parts
of the oasis. They can easily
be reached by hiring a pick-
up truck from Mut.

ENVIRONS: With its narrow,
winding streets and mudbrick
houses, **Al-Qasr**, 27 km (17
miles) northwest of Mut,
retains a strong medieval feel.
The town has a 12th-century
mosque and a 10th-century
madrassa (school) with
superb rooftop views. The **Al-
Muzawaka tombs** date from
Pharaonic times. The two best
tombs are those of Petosiris
and Sadosiris, which have vivid
coloured reliefs. To the west,
the remnants of **Deir al-Hagar**
temple, built by Emperor Nero
in the first century AD, stand
isolated in the desert. **Balat**
lies 35 km (22 miles) east of
Mut on the road to Kharga.
A medieval village, it is on
the site of an Old Kingdom
settlement that traded with
Kush (ancient Nubia).

Mudbrick tombs in the Necropolis of al-Bagawat, Kharga Oasis

🏛 **Ethnographic Museum**
Sharia as-Salem. ⬜ *ask at Tourist Office.*
⋔ **Al-Muzawaka tombs**
5 km (3 miles) W of Al-Qasr. ⬜ *daily.*
⋔ **Deir al-Hagar**
12 km (7 miles) W of Al-Qasr.
⬜ *daily.* 🖼

Farafra Oasis ❸

310 km (192 miles) NW of Dakhla.
👥 *2,800.* 🚌

T HE MOST ISOLATED and least
populous of the New
Valley oases, Farafra is an
extremely peaceful and
relaxing place to visit. Its
mainly Bedouin inhabitants
are well-known for their strong
traditions and religious piety.
The largest settlement, Al-
Farafra, is built like the other
oasis towns around a now
ruined fortress, where villagers
historically sheltered from
attacks. Though the traditional

**Bizarre rock formations caused by wind erosion in
the White Desert, near Farafra Oasis**

mudbrick, painted houses
remain, concrete developments
have sprung up due to government efforts to attract outsiders
to the area. Al-Farafra's **Town
Museum** displays sculptures
of oasis life by a well-known
local artist, Badr.

ENVIRONS: Farafra is an ideal
base for exploring the **White
Desert**, 41 km (25 miles) from
Al-Farafra on the road to
Bahariyya. Named after its
bright-white rock formations,
the White Desert resembles
a haunting lunar landscape.

Bahariyya Oasis ❹

185 km (115 miles) NE of Farafra.
👥 *33,000.* 🚌 ℹ *Town council
building, Bawiti (02) 847 3035.*

B AHARIYYA OASIS was a key
agricultural centre in
Pharaonic times, exporting
large quantities of wine to the
Nile Valley. Today it is famed
for its dates and olives. Bawiti,
the main village in the oasis,
is very picturesque, with palm
groves surrounding clusters
of mudbrick houses. The
Oasis Heritage Museum has

clay figure
displays by
the local artist
Mohammed
Eed. Hot and
cold springs
surround the
oasis and just
west of Bawiti
a hot spring,
Ain Bishmu,
is used by the
villagers for
washing and swimming.
Further afield, a few ruins
of the **Temple of Alexander
the Great**, built in 332 BC, lie
just north of the large discovery
of mummies. The nearby
26th-Dynasty **Temple of Ain
al-Muftela** is better preserved.
Bahariyya is surrounded by
hills, and the **Black Mountain**,
7 km (4 miles) northeast of
Bawiti, is worth a visit. Also
called the "English Mountain",
it is crowned with an old World
War I British outpost. Climbing
to the top takes about an hour
but the view is very rewarding.

ENVIRONS: The **Black Desert**,
created by wind eroding the
dark, rocky outcrops, begins
20 km (12 miles) south of
Bahariyya. Further south, the
mainly quartz rock formations
of **Crystal Mountain** sparkle
delightfully in the sun.

🏛 **Oasis Heritage Museum**
1 km (0.6 mile) N of Bawiti. ⬜ *daily.*
⋔ **Temple of Alexander
the Great**
6 km (4 miles) SW of Bawiti. ⬜ *ask at
Tourist Office.* 🖼
⋔ **Temple of Ain al-Muftela**
5 km (3 miles) W of Bawiti.
⬜ *ask at Tourist Office.* 🖼

Clay figures in the Oasis Heritage Museum, Bahariyya Oasis

A typical blue-painted mudbrick dwelling in Siwa Oasis

Siwa Oasis ⑤

550 km (341 miles) W of Cairo, 305 km (189 miles) SW of Marsa Matruh. 🏛 30,000. ℹ️ *Opposite Arous al-Waha, road to Marsa Matruh* (046) 460 2883. 🚌

Siwa Oasis seems to spring out of nowhere, its lush, green orchards glistening like a mirage in the surrounding barren and inhospitable desert. More than 300 fresh-water springs and streams sustain this remote desert oasis, feeding 300,000 date palms and 70,000 olive trees. Huge saltwater lakes add to the spectacular scenery. Isolated on the edge of the Great Sand Sea, Siwa remained unchanged and largely unvisited for centuries. Roads now link Siwa to Marsa Matruh on the Mediterranean coast and to Bahariyya Oasis in the southeast, bringing an influx of tourists to the area.

The ruins of the ancient mudbrick town of **Shali** tower above modern Siwa's main square. Built in 1203 to house the 40 survivors of a tribal attack on the nearby settlement of Aghurmi, this walled, hilltop town protected the entire Siwan population for centuries. Though the houses were abandoned in 1926 after heavy rain, the steep maze of streets can still be explored.

Close to Siwa's town centre, the **House of Siwa Museum** displays a collection of typical Siwan clothing, jewellery and handicrafts. The museum was the brainchild of a Canadian ambassador who feared the threat posed by tourism to Siwa's traditional way of life.

A short distance north of the town, the limestone **Mountain of the Dead**, or Jebel al-Mawta, is riddled with tombs from the 26th Dynasty and Ptolemaic era. When fighting spread to Siwa during World War II, the Siwans sheltered in the tombs from bombing attacks. The 3rd-century BC **Tomb of Si-Amun** contains scenes depicting the deceased – a Siwan of Greek origins – with his family and the gods.

Detail from the Tomb of Si-Amun on the Mountain of the Dead, Siwa

About 3 km (2 miles) east of Siwa, the **Temple of the Oracle**, built between 663 and 525 BC, stands on a rock that was once at the heart of the ancient settlement of Aghurmi. The Oracle's fame was widespread and Alexander the Great came here to consult it in 332 BC after liberating Egypt from Persian rule. Though the temple currently lies largely in ruins, the steep climb to the top is worthwhile for the stunning views it affords over the palm trees and lakes below.

Further east, all that remains of the huge 30th-Dynasty **Temple of Amun** is a wall decorated with bas-reliefs and a large pile of rubble. The temple was probably built by Nectanebo II during the 4th century BC. A short distance away is **Cleopatra's Pool**. Despite the name, Cleopatra never bathed here, but many people do venture into the circular pool for a swim, undeterred by algae floating on the surface of the water and onlookers watching from the busy path.

A better place for swimming can be found on **Fatnis Island** (also known as Fantasy Island), on the salt lake Birket Siwa, 6 km (4 miles) west of the town. A narrow causeway leads to the island, which is covered in lush palm trees and has an idyllic, secluded, freshwater pool in the centre. The island can be reached by bike or donkey cart from Siwa.

🏛 **House of Siwa Museum**
Siwa. ◯ *Sat–Thu.* 📷
⋒ **Tomb of Si-Amun**
1 km (0.6 mile) N of Siwa. ◯ *daily.*

SIWAN CULTURE

Far removed from the rest of Egypt, Siwans have their own distinct culture and way of life, although these are increasingly threatened by tourism. Siwi, a Berber language, is spoken alongside Arabic, and Siwan women, who are rarely seen in public, dress in costumes decorated with coins. The oasis is renowned for its silver jewellery and handwoven baskets. Siwans are very conservative and visitors should dress modestly.

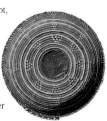

Traditional handwoven Siwan basket

◁ **Mural on a Siwan house encouraging pilgrims to make the journey to Mecca**

Oases in the Egyptian Deserts

A WELCOME SIGHT for tired and weary travellers, oases have sufficient water to allow permanent plant growth and human settlement. The major depressions beneath Egypt's Western Desert give rise to a chain of oases west of the Nile, for here the water table is near the earth's surface. The oasis of Siwa, for example, lies 18 m (59 ft) below sea level. Oases vary considerably in size and can be anything from just a few palms around a spring to large expanses of water capable of sustaining cities. As well as supporting human population, they also offer ideal conditions for many species of wildlife, such as the striped hyena, the Egyptian mongoose and the little green bee-eater. However, the combination of a growing population and increasingly intensive farming is threatening the water supply. The oasis of Fayoum *(see p164)* now has to channel water from the Nile to supplement its inadequate natural resources.

Little green bee-eater

Saltwater lakes are formed over thousands of years by evaporation. As the water evaporates dissolved minerals are left behind and the salinity of the lake slowly increases.

Human settlements *have developed around many oases. These isolated, self-sufficient communities are typically surrounded by green patches of cultivation and separated from each other by areas of dry desert.*

Agriculture *thrives on the fertile land of the oases. Rice, wheat, olives, dates, figs, mangoes and apricots are some of the crops grown.*

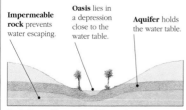

Date palms *have always been a multi-purpose crop, providing food, timber and leaves for thatching.*

THE FORMATION OF OASES

Rain falling a long way from the oasis seeps into porous rocks, known as aquifers, through which it slowly flows. This water emerges at an oasis, either where the water table is at or near the surface, or where pressure created by the flow of water in the aquifer forces it up through a fault in the rock.

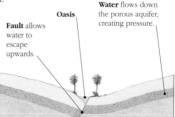

Impermeable rock prevents water escaping.

Oasis lies in a depression close to the water table.

Aquifer holds the water table.

Fault allows water to escape upwards.

Oasis

Water flows down the porous aquifer, creating pressure.

Oasis formed by a natural depression

Oasis resulting from a fault in the rock layers

TRAVELLERS' NEEDS

WHERE TO STAY

IN COLLOQUIAL EGYPTIAN, the word for hotel *(funduq)* derives from a verb meaning "to leave wide open" – as in leaving a door ajar – and this phrase reflects the traditional Egyptian sense of hospitality. Visitors will find "open doors" throughout the country, with hotels offering accommodation at a wide range of prices and an even wider range of quality. At the top end are grand old colonial hotels, along with a growing array of modern, four- and five-star high-rises and resort complexes. Even at such expensive places,

Egyptian hospitality doesn't always translate into good service, but hotel managers and tourism officials are beginning to realize that employees need training to keep guests happy. At the other end of the scale, cheap doesn't have to mean squalid: you can still find simple but clean accommodation in some of the country's most picturesque settings. However, always look closely at what you are getting before handing over your money: demanding customers are more likely to end up as satisfied customers.

Doorman at Old Cataract Hotel, Aswan

WHERE TO LOOK

TOURISM HAS LONG been a major industry in Egypt and, as a result, you will find hotels just about everywhere. In Cairo, the luxury hotels are clustered in three main areas, catering to the different purposes and needs of visitors to the city. Several are situated to the northeast of the city, around the airport and the suburb of Heliopolis, making them convenient for air travel but rather far away from the city's major tourist attractions. Then there are the downtown luxury hotels, which are found mainly along the banks of the Nile. These

offer great views and are a more convenient base for getting around the city sights, but they leave the traveller right in the thick of downtown Cairo, which can be a daunting prospect. Finally, there are hotels around the pyramids in Giza. For many visitors, staying right next to what they consider to be Egypt's biggest tourist attraction may outweigh the disadvantage of being further away from other sights in central and Islamic Cairo, such as the Egyptian Museum and Khan al-Khalili. Alternatively, you can find smaller and cheaper hotels throughout the city. Many low-budget, backpacker hotels are located in the downtown area near Midan Talaat Harb and Midan Opera, with some truly disreputable premises around the Ramses train station. The leafy island of Zamalek has a few pleasant mid-range hotels and, though the area has few sights of its own, it is handy for the rest of the city.

The same general pattern can be found in most towns in Egypt, with large five-star hotels in the town centre, low-budget places clustered around

Marble-floored foyer of the Old Winter Palace, Luxor

the train station, and mid-range options scattered throughout. Except for the most important tourist destinations, most towns in Upper Egypt and the Delta do not have a five-star hotel.

HOTEL TOUTS

THE NEWLY arrived traveller in Cairo may fall prey to hotel touts who attach themselves to the unwary, using every trick in the book to get them to the hotel for which they are hustling. Some taxidrivers are part of the scam, earning a commission from the hotels to which they take their fares. To avoid being taken in by these tricksters, be alert to their strategies and be very firm about your plans. If possible, book a room in advance and don't be diverted from going there, whatever claims are made. If a taxidriver says he hasn't heard of your hotel, don't get in his cab. Never let anyone go into the hotel with you.

The Sheraton Hotel on Gezira island, Cairo

BOOKING A ROOM

HIGHER-CATEGORY hotels follow standard international procedures for reservations, with customers often being asked to give their credit card number as confirmation of a booking. Hotels lower down the scale may do the same, but with slightly less reliable results. The more popular inexpensive hotels usually operate on a first-come, first-served basis and do not accept reservations.

HOTEL GRADING AND FACILITIES

EGYPTIAN HOTELS are graded on a star-rating system with up to five stars, which are allocated by the government. Large, internationally run chain hotels generally get into the four- and five-star class, while locally owned premises fill out the middle and lower ranges.

Hotel gradings can appear a little arbitrary at times and, in many cases, seem to owe more to influence than to actual quality and service. Sometimes the only tangible difference between two stars and no stars is price – and five-star hotels are certainly not all equal in the facilities or service offered. A five-star hotel will, however, always include several restaurants, a bar, and some form of nightclub or disco. There will also always be a swimming pool and health-club facilities. Five-star hotels at resorts are likely to include facilities such as riding stables, diving centres, tennis courts and similar amenities.

Siwa Safari Paradise Hotel, set in palm groves near the Temple of Amun

A four-star hotel will usually have a coffee shop, restaurant, a bar of sorts, and usually a smaller swimming pool that is good enough for a cooling-off dip.

Hotels at the lower end also usually have some kind of eating establishment, but alcohol will rarely be served in such premises. It is rare to find telephones in the rooms of smaller establishments, but most will have a telephone at the front desk and a fax machine that guests may use.

HIDDEN EXTRAS

APART FROM some of the Red Sea resorts, where guests pay a single price to enjoy all the amenities, normal practice is to pay for extras as you use them. Up to 20 per cent tax may be added to your hotel bill, along with charges for phone calls and other services. In smaller, two- and three-star hotels, check exactly what is included in the price: you may find that you are charged extra for breakfast and for having a fridge and TV in your room.

Tipping *(baksheesh)* is a way of life in Egypt: many hotel workers survive on the tips they get for carrying out minor tasks for guests, such as carrying bags or flagging taxis.

DISCOUNTS

DISCOUNTS on hotel rooms are rarely offered and are available only through travel companies. In low season (July–September) in Upper Egypt, however, it may be possible to bargain down room prices, especially in hotels in the lower price categories. Egyptians and foreigners with residence permits, however, qualify for vastly cheaper rates.

CHAIN HOTELS

THE FAMILIAR international chain hotel names can all be found in Egypt: Hilton and Sheraton are predominant, but Marriott, Sofitel, Meridien, Mövenpick, Swissôtel and Four Seasons are also all present. The big chain hotels are the most luxurious and the most expensive in the market and they generally offer a dependable level of service, despite the occasional variation from international standards.

There is no established chain of cheap or budget hotels in Egypt: the vast number of mid-level and inexpensive hotels in the country are usually family-owned and independently run.

The Taba Hilton, set against the magnificent backdrop of the Sinai mountains

The Nile Hilton Hotel, Cairo, built in the 1950s on the site of the Qasr el-Nil (Palace of the Nile) *(see p72)*

SMALLER HOTELS

O NE OF EGYPT'S drawbacks for the independent traveller is that it does not have a strongly developed system of mid-range hotels. With most tourism in Egypt being of the five-star or the budget backpacker variety, there is a great deal of choice at either end of the scale but little in the middle.

Every major destination in Egypt has a wide selection of small, cheap hotels catering for the young traveller. For those willing to forsake private bathrooms and air conditioning, the price can be amazingly low. Many small hotels offer a variety of rooms, including those with or without bathrooms and air conditioning. Some have the option of more than one bed in the room. In Cairo and Alexandria, most small hotels are located on the upper floors of old apartment buildings, which can provide an intimate setting that is full of character. At most places, the price includes a simple continental breakfast.

Two- and three-star hotels, when they can be found, are more likely to take up a whole building. Such establishments often include a coffee-shop and a small restaurant, and their rooms always have bathrooms and air conditioning; they may even have a small swimming pool. Quality varies widely and, while some mid-range hotels are excellent and quite charming, others are not even remotely worth the price. When negotiating for a room in a two- or three-star hotel, check the room to see whether facilities such as hot water and clean bed linen are provided, and confirm with the proprietor whether breakfast is included in the price.

BUSINESS TRAVELLERS

C AIRO IS RAPIDLY turning into a major business centre and its hotels are adapting to the new market. New, ultra-luxury, five-star hotels are springing up with the

Hotel Metropole, Alexandria

requirements of the travelling business executive in mind, distinguishing themselves by the extra services and facilities that such clients expect. Well-trained concierges and an efficient, well-equipped 24-hour business service are becoming standard in Cairo's new hotels, such as the Four Seasons at the First Residence, on the west bank of the Nile, and the Conrad, on the Nile Corniche. These have rooms furnished with computers, fax, voice mail, and internet connections. Well-equipped meeting rooms and conference facilities are available, as are chauffeur-driven limousines to ferry guests to and from Cairo's international airport.

DISABLED TRAVELLERS

E GYPT IS NOT the easiest destination for the disabled visitor. With many cheaper hotels located on the fairly inaccessible upper storeys of tall buildings, wheelchair-bound travellers are usually restricted to the modern five-star hotels. Even many of those still have stairs instead of ramps at vital places, though that is starting to change. What Egypt does have in its favour, however, is friendly people for whom disability carries no stigma and who will be more than ready to assist travellers with extra needs with a minimum of fuss.

CHILDREN

EGYPTIANS LOVE children and consider them a blessing, so bringing them should not present any particular problems. This is not to say that Egyptian hotels make any special provisions in terms of extra activities – the exception being some of the luxury resort hotels, which organize daily programmes for children. Even if you are not staying at a four- or five-star hotel, either in Cairo or at a resort, most of the bigger hotels have swimming pools that they allow non-residents to use, often without charge for children, and this can provide an excellent way of soothing frazzled youngsters when the heat and bustle get too much.

BUDGET OPTIONS

EGYPT CAN BE a paradise for travellers on low budgets, as witnessed by the generations of young backpackers who visit the country, whether seeking Pharaonic ruins, exotic culture, or a bit of sun and surf in the Sinai peninsula.

No matter where you are in Egypt, there will always be hotels offering fairly

The luxury As-Salamlek Hotel in Montazah Palace grounds, Alexandria

decent accommodation at fairly low prices. Youth hostels exist, but comparing their poor quality with the other available options, they are best avoided: why settle for a three-tier bunk bed when a clean room can be found closer to the city centre for only a few pounds more?

In any case, most of Egypt's cheaper hotels, which are not by any means frequented only by young backpackers, offer the camaraderie familiar in youth hostels worldwide. Camping in Egypt is a little more problematic and is not particularly recommended in most towns. There is a kind of camping

YHA sign at youth hostel in Aswan

area by the Giza pyramids in Cairo and sites can be found in Luxor and some of the other southern cities, but the facilities are rudimentary at best.

Rather better opportunities exist for camping elsewhere in the country, however. There are some beautiful places in the Sinai, including the Ras Mohammed National Park *(see p222)*, near Sharm el-Sheikh, and a night under the stars in the Western Desert is an experience not to be missed.

Safaris, consisting of a guide with a large four-wheel-drive, can be organized out of any of the oasis towns. It should be borne in mind that camping in the Western Desert is mainly a winter activity, and that the nights can be cold. Desert camping is not recommended during high summer and, in fact, few guides will be interested in venturing out during that time. Wherever you camp, follow commonsense rules and keep all your valuables with you, in your tent. Even in well-patrolled national parks, thefts are not unknown.

Choosing a Hotel

THE HOTELS IN THIS GUIDE have been selected across a wide range of price categories for the excellence of their facilities, location or character. The chart below first lists hotels in Cairo by area, and this is followed by a selection of places to stay in the rest of Egypt. The price ranges are given in US $. For a detailed listing of recommended restaurants see pages 282–291.

	Number of Rooms	Credit Cards	Air Conditioning	Swimming Pool	Restaurant
CAIRO					
CENTRAL CAIRO: *Ismailia House Hotel* $ 8th Floor, 1 Midan Tahrir, Downtown. **Map** 1 C5, 5 B4. 📞 *(02) 796 3122.* This popular budget hostel has fantastic views over Midan Tahrir that make up for sometimes grubby facilities. Some rooms have adjoining bathrooms. 🛠	27				
CENTRAL CAIRO: *Mayfair Hotel* $ 9 Sharia Aziz Osman, Zamalek. **Map** 1 A3. 📞 *(02) 735 7315.* **FAX** *(02) 735 0424.* Located in the upmarket neighbourhood of Zamalek, this budget hotel is popular with backpackers, so reserve in advance.	38	▦	●		
CENTRAL CAIRO: *Pension Roma* $ 4th Floor, 169 Sharia Mohammed Farid, Downtown. **Map** 2 D4, 6 D2. 📞 *(02) 391 1088.* **FAX** *(02) 579 6243.* One of Cairo's great bargains, this hotel comes with antique furniture, shiny wooden floors and an old-world elegance that belies its price. Five of the rooms have bathrooms attached. Very popular – reserve in advance. 🛠	32				●
CENTRAL CAIRO: *Berlin Hotel* $ 2 Sharia el-Shawarby, 4th Floor, Qasr el-Nil. **Map** 1 C5, 5 C3. 📞 *(02) 395 7502.* **FAX** *(02) 395 7502.* @ berlinhotelcairo@hotmail.com Characterful rooms and an attentive owner more than make up for a rather unprepossessing exterior. The hotel can usually organize Pyramid tours and has e-mail facilities. 🛠 TV	7		●		
CENTRAL CAIRO: *Carlton Hotel* $$ 21 Sharia 26th July, Downtown. **Map** 1 C4, 5 C2. 📞 *(02) 575 5022.* **FAX** *(02) 575 5323.* @ carlton@menanet.net This pleasant old Downtown hotel is entered from a side street off Sharia 26th July. Built in 1935, it has newly renovated rooms, some with minibar, plus a rooftop bar and restaurant. 🛠 ▮ TV	62		●		●
CENTRAL CAIRO: *Fontana Hotel* $ Midan Ramses, Downtown. **Map** 2 D3. 📞 *(02) 592 2321.* **FAX** *(02) 592 2145.* This comfortable mid-range hotel has great views over the bustle of Midan Ramses, a small rooftop pool and a disco. 🛠 ▮ TV	87		●	▦	●
CENTRAL CAIRO: *Horus House Hotel* $$ 4th Floor, 21 Sharia Ismail Mohammed, Zamalek. **Map** 1 A3. 📞 *(02) 735 3634.* **FAX** *(02) 735 3182.* Small three-star hotel in a Zamalek apartment building. Few facilities, but this is made up for by friendly staff and reasonable prices. 🛠 ▮ TV	35	▦	●		●
CENTRAL CAIRO: *Lotus Hotel* $$ 12 Sharia Talaat Harb, Downtown. **Map** 1 C5, 5B3. 📞 *(02) 575 0966.* **FAX** *(02) 575 4720.* A clean and comfortable mid-priced option in the heart of Downtown with the same owners as the nearby Windsor Hotel. Most rooms have their own bathrooms, but those with shared bathrooms are much cheaper. 🛠 ▮ TV	50	▦	●		●
CENTRAL CAIRO: *New Star Hotel* $$ 34B Sharia Yehia Ibrahim, Zamalek. **Map** 1 A3. 📞 *(02) 735 0928.* **FAX** *(02) 736 1321.* Comfortable and quiet hotel, despite being close to the intersection of Sharia Hassan Sabry and 26th July. Large rooms are actually suites, making them good value; some have balconies and Nile views. 🛠 TV	26	▦	●		●
CENTRAL CAIRO: *Windsor Hotel* $$ 19 Sharia al-Alfy, Downtown. **Map** 2 D4, 6 D2. 📞 *(02) 591 5277.* **FAX** *(02) 592 1621.* @ wdoss@link.net This quirky former British Officers' club was immortalized by Michael Palin in the TV series *Around the World in 80 Days*. The hotel still retains its old-colonial atmosphere, particularly in the bar. 🛠 ▮ TV	50	▦	●		●

Price categories are per night for two people, occupying a standard double room, with tax, breakfast and service included:
$ under $25
$$ $25–$50
$$$ $50–$100
$$$$ $100–$200
$$$$$ $200 plus

CREDIT CARDS
Major credit cards accepted (including: American Express, MasterCard, Visa).

AIR CONDITIONING
Some or all of the rooms have air conditioning.

SWIMMING POOL
Private swimming pool for hotel guests.

RESTAURANT
Good restaurant, open to non-residents.

	NUMBER OF ROOMS	CREDIT CARDS	AIR CONDITIONING	SWIMMING POOL	RESTAURANT
CENTRAL CAIRO: *Atlas Zamalek Hotel* $$$ 20 Sharia Gamiat ad-Dowal al-Arabiyya, Mohandiseen. ((02) 346 6569. FAX (02) 347 6958. This friendly highrise, located on one of Mohandiseen's major thoroughfares, has a swimming pool and a popular disco.	74	●	●	●	●
CENTRAL CAIRO: *Cosmopolitan Hotel* $$$ 1 Sharia Ibn Tahlab, Downtown. **Map** 1 C3, 5 C3. ((02) 392 3663. FAX (02) 393 3531. This characterful mid-range hotel is set in a lovely Art Deco building. Some rooms have antique furniture and original bathroom fittings.	84	●	●		●
CENTRAL CAIRO: *Flamenco Hotel* $$$ 2 Sharia Gezirat al-Wusta, Zamalek. **Map** 1 A2. ((02) 735 0815. FAX (02) 735 0819. @ sales@flamencohotels.com A mid-range hotel, this is popular with business professionals looking for something more intimate than the large five-star hotels. The best rooms have Nile views.	162	●	●		●
CENTRAL CAIRO: *Odeon Palace Hotel* $$$ 6 Abdel Hamid Said, Downtown. **Map** 1 C4, 5 C2. (& FAX (02) 577 6637. This comfortable mid-range hotel is located on a quiet Downtown side-street. The 24-hour rooftop bar is very popular with Cairo intellectuals.	30	●	●		●
CENTRAL CAIRO: *The President Hotel* $$$ 22 Sharia Taha Hussein, Zamalek. **Map** 1 A2. ((02) 735 0652. FAX (02) 736 1752. @ preshotl@thewayout.net Popular three-star hotel occupying a somewhat characterless highrise on a quiet Zamalek street. The staff are very friendly.	117	●	●		●
CENTRAL CAIRO: *Cairo Marriott Hotel* $$$$ PO Box 33, Zamalek. **Map** 1 B3. ((02) 735 8888. FAX (02) 735 6667. @ reservation@cairomarriott.com This opulent Orientalist residence was built for the opening of the Suez Canal in 1869 *(see pp60–61)*. It has one of Cairo's only garden terraces, making it popular with visitors and local residents.	1124	●	●	●	●
CENTRAL CAIRO: *Sheraton al-Gezira* $$$$ Al-Gezira, Gezira. **Map** 3 A1. ((02) 736 1555. FAX (02) 735 5056. @ gzsher@rite.com This round tower stands on the southern end of Gezira, adjacent to the upmarket neighbourhood of Zamalek. All rooms have fabulous views and there are a number of Nileside restaurants and bars.	460	●	●	●	●
CENTRAL CAIRO: *Conrad International Hotel* $$$$$ 1191 Corniche el-Nil, Bulaq. **Map** 1 B3. ((02) 580 8000. FAX (02) 580 8080. @ reservation@conradcairo.com.org The latest luxury chain to hit Cairo offers good Nile views and luxurious rooms. It is conveniently located close to some of Cairo's newest shopping malls and upmarket restaurants.	617	●	●	●	●
CENTRAL CAIRO: *Nile Hilton* $$$$$ Midan Tahrir, Downtown. **Map** 1 B5, 5B3. ((02) 578 0666. FAX (02) 578 0475. @ nhilton@brainy1-ie.eg.com This 1950s lowrise is situated on Cairo's chaotic central square. Its refurbished rooms are comfortable and surprisingly quiet. It also has a secluded garden pool and tennis courts.	431	●	●	●	●
CENTRAL CAIRO: *Royal Nile Tower* $$$$$ Corniche el-Nil, Garden City. **Map** 3 B1, 5A5. ((02) 362 1717. FAX (02) 368 1555. w royalniletower.com This hotel changed hands in 2001 and is now a branch of the sumptuous Royal Nile. The fabulous Nile views remain a feature.	714	●	●	●	●

Price categories are per night for two people, occupying a standard double room, with tax, breakfast and service included:	**CREDIT CARDS** Major credit cards accepted (including: American Express, MasterCard, Visa).	
⑤ under $25	**AIR CONDITIONING** Some or all of the rooms have air conditioning.	
⑤⑤ $25–$50		
⑤⑤⑤ $50–$100	**SWIMMING POOL** Private swimming pool for hotel guests.	
⑤⑤⑤⑤ $100–$200		
⑤⑤⑤⑤⑤ $200 plus	**RESTAURANT** Good restaurant, open to non-residents.	

	NUMBER OF ROOMS	CREDIT CARDS	AIR CONDITIONING	SWIMMING POOL	RESTAURANT
CENTRAL CAIRO: *Semiramis Intercontinental* ⑤⑤⑤⑤⑤ Corniche el-Nil, Garden City. **Map** 1 B5, 5 A4. (02) 795 7171. FAX (02) 796 3020. cairo@interconti.com One of Cairo's major five-star hotels, this has all the amenities you would expect, as well as fabulous views from its Nileside rooms. The hotel is very popular with Gulf Arabs in the summer.	730	■	●	■	●
ISLAMIC CAIRO: *Al-Hussein Hotel* ⑤⑤⑤ Midan Hussein, Hussein. **Map** 2 F5. (02) 591 8089. FAX (02) 591 8479. Basic, comfortable rooms, 28 with air conditioning and attached bathrooms, the remainder with fans only. Great views of medieval Cairo, but its location close to Khan al-Khalili means that noise levels are high.	56		●		●
GIZA AND HELIOPOLIS: *Novotel Cairo Airport* ⑤⑤⑤ Cairo Airport, Heliopolis. (02) 291 8520. FAX (02) 291 4794. This is a good option if you have a short stopover in Cairo. The hotel is bland but comfortable, with a pool, sauna and bar.	207	■	●	■	●
GIZA AND HELIOPOLIS: *Mövenpick Jolieville* ⑤⑤⑤⑤ Cairo-Alexandria desert road, Giza. (02) 385 2555. FAX (02) 383 5006. This comfortable, family-oriented option is located near the Pyramids and has extensive gardens, a large swimming pool and tennis courts. It is also conveniently close to the Sharia 26th July corridor into the city.	240	■	●	■	●
GIZA AND HELIOPOLIS: *Mena House Oberoi* ⑤⑤⑤⑤⑤ Sharia al-Ahram (Pyramids Road), Giza. (02) 383 3222. FAX (02) 383 7777. obmhobc@oberoi.com.eg Built in 1860 as a hunting lodge, this was transformed into a hotel in 1890. It has unparalleled views of the Pyramids, Egypt's first golf course, a casino and one of the city's best Indian restaurants.	523	■	●	■	●
GIZA AND HELIOPOLIS: *Sheraton Heliopolis* ⑤⑤⑤⑤⑤ Sharia Uruba, Heliopolis. (02) 267 7730. FAX (02) 267 7600. shhelio@gega.net Situated on a main road close to the airport, this hotel is very convenient for central Cairo, and useful for a five-star stopover. Its restaurants are very popular with Heliopolis residents.	588	■	●	■	●

AROUND CAIRO

	NUMBER OF ROOMS	CREDIT CARDS	AIR CONDITIONING	SWIMMING POOL	RESTAURANT
FAYOUM OASIS: *Auberge du Lac Hotel* ⑤⑤⑤⑤ Lake Qarun, Fayoum. (084) 572 001/2. FAX (084) 572 003. This one-time hunting lodge of King Farouk has been turned into a luxury hotel on the edge of Lake Qarun. Excellent facilities in an ideal location for sightseeing, birdwatching or just relaxing.	76	■	●	■	●

THE NILE VALLEY

	NUMBER OF ROOMS	CREDIT CARDS	AIR CONDITIONING	SWIMMING POOL	RESTAURANT
ABU SIMBEL: *Kariat Abu Simbel* ⑤⑤ Abu Simbel. (097) 400 170. FAX (097) 400 770. This is the reasonably priced alternative for Abu Simbel, a quiet, comfortable hotel which opened in 2001. Built in the domed Nubian style, it offers traditional comforts and a terrace overlooking Lake Nasser.	26		●		●
ABU SIMBEL: *Nefertari Hotel* ⑤⑤⑤⑤ Abu Simbel. (097) 400 508 or (097) 400 510. This is the closest hotel to the Temple of Ramses II. Room prices are 30 per cent cheaper in summer; in the winter, reservations are recommended. They allow non-guests to pitch tents in the garden.	120	■	●	■	●
ASWAN: *Keylany Hotel* ⑤ Sharia Keylany, off Sharia Souq. (097) 317 332. FAX (097) 317 332. This very clean, very cheap hotel has to be one of the best bargains in town. All rooms have ensuite bathroom and fan, but no air conditioning.	28				●

ASWAN: *Orabi Hotel* ⑤ 13
Sharia Keylany, off Sharia Souq. 【 *(097) 317 578.* 🅵🅰🆇 *(097) 317 578.*
This is a good, centrally located budget hotel with communal bathrooms, friendly staff and air conditioning in some rooms.

ASWAN: *Al-Amir Hotel* ⑤⑤ 36
Off Corniche el-Nil. 【 *(097) 314 735.* 🅵🅰🆇 *(097) 304 411.*
A very clean and comfortable hotel, it is primarily targeted at the Gulf Arab market and therefore no alcohol is served. 🔼 📺

ASWAN: *Happi Hotel* ⑤⑤ 64
Off Corniche el-Nil. 【 *(097) 314 115.* 🅵🅰🆇 *(097) 307 572.*
This lean and friendly establishment has large rooms, some with views over the Nile. Guests can use the pool at the Cleopatra Hotel at a discount. 🔼 📺

ASWAN: *Hathor Hotel* ⑤ 64
Corniche el-Nil. 【 *(097) 314 580.* 🅵🅰🆇 *(097) 303 462.*
This small hotel has good Nile views and a roof terrace with a small pool. Nile-view rooms tend to be in better shape than the others. 🔼

ASWAN: *Ramses Hotel* ⑤⑤ 112
Sharia Abtal al-Tahrir. 【 *(097) 304 000.* 🅵🅰🆇 *(097) 315 701.*
A good-value hotel, the Ramses has modern, carpeted rooms with telephone, fridge and Nile views. Popular with European tour groups. 🔼 📺

ASWAN: *Basma Hotel* ⑤⑤⑤ 200
Sharia Abtal al-Tahrir. 【 *(097) 310 901.* 🅵🅰🆇 *(097) 310 907.*
@ basma@rocketmail.com
This friendly, comfortable hotel is next to the Nubian Museum and has a pleasant garden terrace overlooking Elephantine Island. 🔼 🍸 🛎 📺 🎱 🍴

ASWAN: *Cleopatra Hotel* ⑤⑤⑤ 109
Sharia al-Souq. 【 *(097) 314 003.* 🅵🅰🆇 *(097) 314 002.*
A well-located and comfortable, if somewhat gloomy, hotel with a rooftop pool. Most rooms come with a mini-bar. 🔼 🍸 🛎 📺

ASWAN: *Ile d'Amoun Hotel* ⑤⑤⑤⑤ 50
Amun Island. 【 *(097) 313 800* or *(02) 574 7991.*
🅵🅰🆇 *(097) 317 190.* @ rashab@starnet.com.eg
With modest, comfortable rooms in a beautiful, lush, island setting, this hotel is good for families if you don't mind the Club Med group ambiance. It has its own launches to ferry guests to and from the Corniche. 🍸 📺 🎱 🍴

ASWAN: *Isis Hotel* ⑤⑤⑤⑤ 100
Corniche el-Nil. 【 *(097) 315 100.* 🅵🅰🆇 *(097) 315 500.*
Although slightly ramshackle this is the only riverside hotel in the centre of town, making it a handy base for exploring the souq. 🍸 🛎 🎱 📺 🎱 🍴

ASWAN: *Old Cataract* ⑤⑤⑤⑤ 131
Sharia Abtal al-Tahrir. 【 *(097) 316 001.* 🅵🅰🆇 *(097) 316 011.*
@ h1666@accor-hotels.com
Opened in 1899, this hotel was rated one of the best in the world by *The Times* in 1999. It featured in Agatha Christie's *Death on the Nile* and combines colonial grandeur with Orientalist motifs. The Nileside rooms have fine views and a sundowner on the terrace is one of the highlights. 🍸 🛎 🎱 📺 🎱 🍴

ASWAN: *Aswan Oberoi* ⑤⑤⑤⑤⑤ 244
Elephantine Island. 【 *(097) 314 666.* 🅵🅰🆇 *(097) 313 538.*
@ aswan_res@oberoi.com.eg
As well as spacious comfortable rooms and extensive gardens, this hotel offers spa facilities, including sandpit therapy, from May to September. It is famous for its huge modernist tower, which somewhat diminishes the picturesque Elephantine Island landscape. 🔼 🛁 🍸 🛎 🎱 📺 🎱

ASYUT: *YMCA* ⑤ 30
Sharia Salah ad-Din al-Ayyubi. 【 *(088) 323 218.* 🅵🅰🆇 *(088) 313 118.*
This is a surprisingly comfortable budget hotel. All the rooms have carpeting, television, fridge and attached bathroom. 🔼 📺

ASYUT: *Assiutel Hotel* ⑤⑤ 28
Sharia al-Thawra. 【 *(088) 312 121.* 🅵🅰🆇 *(088) 312 122.*
A mid-range hotel that is the top establishment in town. It is well located on the Corniche and has great views from some of its rooms. 🔼 📺

For key to symbols see back flap

Price categories are per night for two people, occupying a standard double room, with tax, breakfast and service included:

$ under $25
$$ $25–$50
$$$ $50–$100
$$$$ $100–$200
$$$$$ $200 plus

CREDIT CARDS
Major credit cards accepted (including: American Express, MasterCard, Visa).

AIR CONDITIONING
Some or all of the rooms have air conditioning.

SWIMMING POOL
Private swimming pool for hotel guests.

RESTAURANT
Good restaurant, open to non-residents.

	Price	NUMBER OF ROOMS	CREDIT CARDS	AIR CONDITIONING	SWIMMING POOL	RESTAURANT
LUXOR: *Amon al-Gezira Hotel* Bayarat al-Gezira, West Bank. ((095) 310 912. FAX (095) 311 205. This small, clean, family-run hotel is situated close to the ferry landing in the village of Al-Gezira. The owners are helpful, there are ensuite bathrooms in five rooms and a pleasant roof terrace overlooks the sugar cane fields.	$	12		●		
LUXOR: *Happyland Hotel* Sharia al-Kamar. ((095) 371 828. FAX (095) 371 140. @ happylandluxor@hotmail.com A hotel with cheap, clean and simply furnished rooms with mosquito coils. A few rooms have their own bathrooms; most share spotless toilets and showers.	$	24		●		
LUXOR: *Marsam Hotel* Al-Gurna, West Bank. ((095) 372 403. Built in the 1920s for archaeologists and later patronized by Egyptian artists, this hotel has been recently renovated. 13 of its rooms are in the original mud-brick building while ten are in the modern concrete addition. All are simply and tastefully furnished, with clean shared bathrooms. No alcohol served.	$	23				●
LUXOR: *St Mina Hotel* Sharia Cleopatra. ((095) 375 409. FAX (095) 376 568. A small, friendly family-run hotel situated in the centre of town. Half of the rooms have their own bathrooms and some are equipped with air conditioning units. The shared facilities are kept very clean.	$	20		●		●
LUXOR: *Venus Hotel* Sharia Yussef Hassan. ((095) 372 625. This central budget hotel is popular with backpackers. Most of the rooms have air conditioning and a bathroom and there is a rooftop bar and restaurant with satellite TV. There are bikes for rent and donkey trips to the West Bank.	$	25				●
LUXOR: *Al-Gezira Hotel* Bayarat al-Gezira, West Bank. ((095) 310 034. FAX (095) 310 034. Situated close to the river, this small, two-storey hotel boasts a rooftop bar/restaurant that serves very good Egyptian food. The owners are friendly and the rooms clean with bathrooms and fans. Some also have great Nile views.	$$	11		●		●
LUXOR: *Flobater Hotel* Sharia Khaled Ibn al-Walid. ((095) 374 223. FAX (095) 370 618. A good budget hotel, with a small pool, carpeted rooms and friendly staff. Some rooms have Nile views.	$$	40	▣	●	▣	●
LUXOR: *Nur al-Gurna* Beside Gurna Antiquities Inspectorate, West Bank. ((095) 311 430. This intimate new hotel looks out over the hills of Gurna. Each room is individually decorated and has a fan and its own bathroom. It is a good base from which to visit the tombs and temples of the West Bank.	$$	9				●
LUXOR: *Pharaoh's Hotel* Bayarat (close to Antiquities Inspectorate), West Bank. ((095) 310 702. FAX (095) 311 205. A concrete low-rise hotel with clean, air-conditioned rooms, a garden bar and some fantastic views over the Gurna Hills.	$$	29		●		●
LUXOR: *St Joseph Hotel* Sharia Khaled Ibn al-Walid. ((095) 381 707. FAX (095) 381 727. Situated in the newer part of Luxor, this clean and economical hotel has friendly staff and a basement bar.	$$	75	▣	●	▣	●
LUXOR: *Emilio Hotel* Sharia Yousef Hassan. ((095) 373 570. FAX (095) 370 000. This mid-range hotel in the town centre boasts a rooftop pool and comfortable rooms. Popular with tour groups so book ahead in the winter.	$$$	48	▣	●	▣	●

LUXOR: *Gaddis Hotel* $$$ 55
Sharia Khaled Ibn al-Walid. (095) 382 838. FAX (095) 382 837.
@ gaddislxr@yahoo.com
Located about 1 km (0.6 mile) south of the Corniche is this small, four-star
hotel with extremely comfortable rooms.

LUXOR: *Windsor Hotel* $$ 120
Sharia Nefertiti. (095) 375 547. FAX (095) 373 447.
Popular with Europeans, this is the largest three-star hotel in Luxor. Before
checking in, inspect the rooms as some are better than others.

LUXOR: *Novotel Luxor* $$$$ 185
Corniche el-Nil. (095) 380 925. FAX (095) 380 972.
This unprepossessing high-rise, at the southern end of the Corniche, has a
disco, floating pool and good Nile views.

LUXOR: *Luxor Hilton* $$$$$ 261
Sharia Karnak. (095) 374 933. FAX (095) 376 571. W www.hilton.com
Set in lush Nileside gardens, north of town, this hotel is close to Karnak
Temple and a bus ride away from the city centre.

LUXOR: *Mövenpick Jolieville Crocodile Island* $$$$ 332
Crocodile Island. (095) 374 855. FAX (095) 374 936.
@ jollie.ville@movenpick/lxr.com.eg
The eight-room bungalows of this hotel are set in lush gardens surrounded
by a banana plantation. The food is good and guest facilities include feluccas,
a jogging track, bicycles, a playground and a small zoo.

LUXOR: *Sheraton Luxor* $$$$ 290
Sharia Khalid Ibn al-Walid. (095) 374 544. FAX (095) 374 941.
W www.sheraton.com
Situated 3 km (2 miles) from the town centre, this three-storey hotel has 14
chalets and a pleasant garden setting. It offers good sports facilities, bike rental
and daily yacht excursions to Dendara Temple.

LUXOR: *Sofitel Winter Palace Hotel* $$$$$ 354
Corniche el-Nil. (095) 380 422. FAX (095) 374 087.
The hotel's grand old wing was built in the 19th century when Thomas
Cook first ran package tours up the Nile. The modern block does not combine
well with the old, but its rooms are much cheaper.

MINYA: *The Akhenaten* $$ 48
Corniche el-Nil. (086) 365 917/365 918.
FAX (086) 365 917. @ kingakhanaton@hotmail.com
This hotel has clean, carpeted rooms, some with great Nile views.

MINYA: *The Palace Hotel* $ 29
Midan Tahrir. (086) 364 071.
Although this hotel is very basic, the shabby rooms off a central lobby, the
enormous Nefertiti mural at the entrance and other Pharaonic motifs which
look as if they date back to colonial times give the place lots of character.

MINYA: *The Nefertiti & Aton Mercure Hotel* $$$ 54
Corniche el-Nil. (086) 341 515. FAX (086) 366 467.
W www.accoregypt.com
Despite its musty rooms and the need for some improvements this hotel
is run by friendly staff and is the best in town.

SOHAG: *Cazalovy* $ 31
East Bank. (093) 601 185. FAX (093) 601 170.
Comfortable rooms and low prices make this hotel excellent value.

SOHAG: *Merit Amoun Hotel* $$ 28
Madinet Naser, East Bank. (093) 601 985. FAX (093) 603 222.
This is a large, three-star hotel with simple but comfortable rooms.

SINAI AND THE RED SEA COAST

AIN SUKHNA: *Hilton Ain Sukhna Resort* $$$$ 41
Ain Sukhna Road. (062) 290 500. FAX (062) 290 515.
This is the best of a cluster of resorts around Ain Sukhna and because of its
proximity to Cairo it is a prime weekend destination for Cairene families
escaping the city. It is advisable to book in advance.

Price categories are per night for two people, occupying a standard double room, with tax, breakfast and service included:

$ under $25
$$ $25–$50
$$$ $50–$100
$$$$ $100–$200
$$$$$ $200 plus

CREDIT CARDS
Major credit cards accepted (including: American Express, MasterCard, Visa).

AIR CONDITIONING
Some or all of the rooms have air conditioning.

SWIMMING POOL
Private swimming pool for hotel guests.

RESTAURANT
Good restaurant, open to non-residents.

	NUMBER OF ROOMS	CREDIT CARDS	AIR CONDITIONING	SWIMMING POOL	RESTAURANT
AL-GOUNA: *Sheraton Miramar* $$$$$ Al-Gouna Resort. ((065) 545 845. FAX (065) 545 885. W www.sheraton.com With a lighthouse, an art island with sculptures and a variety of accommoda-tion, including 25 VIP rooms with their own butler service, this hotel is the jewel in the crown of Al-Gouna Resort.	338	■	●	■	●
DAHAB: *Bishbishi Camp* $ Mashraba. ((069) 640 727. Of the 50 or so beach camps that make Dahab so popular with young travellers, this is one of the cleanest. The camp's bamboo huts all have screened windows and some have their own fans.	18				●
DAHAB: *Jasmine Pension* $ Mashraba. ((069) 640 110. The rooms of this budget-priced pension, situated on the seafront, are all equipped with fans and bathrooms and tend to be more comfortable than those of the camps. The pension's simple restaurant serves good food.	17				●
DAHAB: *Blue Beach Club* $$ Lighthouse. ((069) 640 413. FAX (069) 640 413. @ bbeach@menanet.net North of the main part of Asilah is this small, Swiss-run, beachfront hotel. It is quiet at night and the rooms have fans and fridges as well as good views.	22	■		■	●
DAHAB: *Club Red* $$ Mashraba. ((069) 640 380. FAX (069) 640 380. @ club-red@club-red.com This is a well-established beachfront dive centre with simple rooms. The shared rooms are the cheapest option while the others have fans and adjoining bathrooms. A 15 per cent discount is offered to divers.	134	■	●		●
DAHAB: *Nesima Hotel and Diving Centre* $$$ Mashraba, Asilah. ((069) 640 320. FAX (069) 640 321. W www.nesima-resort.com One of Dahab's most attractive hotels, it boasts domed rooms and a beau-tiful pool overlooking the sea. The hotel offers some of the best food in town as well as childcare services and is popular with dive groups.	40	■	●	■	●
DAHAB: *Hilton Resort* $$$$ Dahab Bay. ((069) 640 310. FAX (069) 640 424. W www.hilton.com This family-oriented resort has whitewashed rooms gathered around a lagoon and a good stretch of sandy beach on the sheltered Dahab Bay. It offers good watersports, including its own windsurfing and diving centres and runs organized games for children.	163	■	●	■	●
HURGHADA: *Four Seasons Hotel* $ Ad-Dahar. (& FAX (065) 545 456. Situated close to the beach in central Ad-Dahar, all the rooms of this hotel have balconies and six rooms have air conditioning. For a small additional charge guests can use the beach at the nearby Geisum Village Resort.	14		●		
HURGHADA: *El-Khan Hotel* $$ Kafr al-Gouna, Al-Gouna Resort. ((065) 545 060. FAX (065) 545 061. The simple domed and vaulted rooms here are in keeping with Kafr al-Gouna's fanciful Orientalist architecture. Some first-floor rooms offer good views and guests have use of Al-Gouna's sports facilities.	25	■	●	■	●
HURGHADA: *Empire Hotel* $$ Sharia Hospital & Sayed Korayem. ((065) 549 200. FAX (02) 347 5643. @ sales@empire.hotels.com A well-priced, mid-range hotel in the heart of Ad-Dahar. Although it doesn't have its own beach, it is only 200 metres from the waterfront and guests have the use of the nearby Village Beach.	396	■	●	■	●

HURGHADA: *Jasmine Village Hotel*　$$$　446
Hurghada. 【 (065) 446 442. FAX (065) 446 441. @ jasminevillage@hotmail.com
This family resort has 460 bungalows and good children's facilities, including
a playground and a zoo. It is used as a base for one of Hurghada's dive cen-
tres and has its own glass-bottomed and snorkelling boats. ▮▮▮▮▮

HURGHADA: *Dawar al-Umda*　$$$$　64
Kafr al-Gouna, Al-Gouna Resort. 【 (065) 545 060. FAX (065) 545 061.
This beautifully designed boutique hotel, with Arabesque-stencilled walls
and domed restaurants, is small and intimate. Nevertheless, it does have
use of Al-Gouna's sports and beach facilities. ▮▮▮▮▮▮

HURGHADA: *Iberotel Arabella*　$$$$　294
Al-Sakala. 【 (065) 545 086. FAX (065) 545 090. @ gm@iberotelarabella.com
This is one of the nicer looking resort hotels in this area. It is close to the
centre of town and home to one of Hurghada's popular discos. Rooms are
offered on a half-board basis. ▮▮▮▮▮▮

HURGHADA: *Sheraton Soma Bay Resort*　$$$$　310
Soma Bay, 48 km (30 miles) south of Hurghada. 【 (065) 545 845.
FAX (065) 545 885. @ reservationsomabayegypt@stanwoodhotels.com
Built to resemble an ancient Egyptian temple, this resort also has an
18-hole championship golf course, a wide range of watersports and is run
according to environmentally-friendly guidelines. ▮▮▮▮▮▮▮▮

HURGHADA: *Hurghada InterContinental*　$$$$$　244
Hurghada. 【 (065) 446 911. FAX (065) 446 910. @ hurghada@interconti.com
One of Hurghada's most luxurious resorts, it comes complete with its own
marina and extensive fitness and watersports facilities. ▮▮▮▮▮▮▮

ISMAILIA: *Nefertari*　$　32
41 Sharia Sultan Hussein. 【 (064) 912 822. FAX (064) 910 940.
Comfortable and clean air-conditioned rooms make this hotel the best
value in Ismailia. In addition to its own bar, there is a disco. ▮

ISMAILIA: *Mercure Forsan Island*　$$$$　152
Gezirat al-Forsan. 【 (064) 918 040. FAX (064) 918 043.
▮ www.accoregypt.com
About 1 km (0.6 mile) from the city centre, this modern low-rise sits on a quiet
shady island in Lake Timsah and is the town's top hotel. ▮▮▮▮▮▮

MARSA ALAM: *Red Sea Diving Safari*　$$　50
Marsa Shagra, 18 km (10 miles) north of Marsa Alam. 【 (02) 337 1833.
FAX (02) 749 4219. @ redseasaf@hotmail.com
Popular with dive groups, this hotel consists of ten tents and ten huts, with
shared bathrooms, and ten chalets with private facilities. The price includes
meals and soft drinks and all accommodation overlooks a stunning bay. ▮

MARSA ALAM: *Shams Allam*　$$$　159
50 km (30 miles) south of Marsa Alam. 【 (02) 417 0046. FAX (02) 417 0158.
@ info@shamshotels.com
This is the most southerly resort on Egypt's Red Sea coast specializing in diving
trips to local and less frequented southern reefs. Comfortable rooms in domed
and vaulted two-storey chalets are offered on a half-board basis. ▮▮▮

NUWEIBA: *Basata*　$　16
Ras al-Burqa. 【 (069) 500 481. FAX (069) 500 480.
This eco-resort, some 23 km (14 miles) north of Nuweiba, consists of
16 bamboo or mudbrick huts on a private sandy beach. It has its own
generator, bakery and desalination plant. Despite the fact that scuba diving,
alcohol, drugs, TV and loud music are not allowed, it is extremely popular
and advance booking is recommended. ▮

NUWEIBA: *La Sirene*　$$$　40
Nuweiba City. 【 (069) 500 701. FAX (069) 500 702.
Situated on a beautiful stretch of beach, between Nuweiba City and the port,
this hotel has its own dive centre and is popular so book in advance. ▮▮

NUWEIBA: *Coral Hilton Resort*　$$$$　200
Nuweiba City. 【 (069) 520 320. FAX (069) 520 327.
@ rm_nuweiba@hilton.com
Very popular with Israeli families, this is one of the older beach resorts
in the area. It has 20 villas in addition to the regular rooms and offers a
nightly disco and extensive watersports as well as other sports. ▮▮▮

For key to symbols see back flap

<table>
<tr><td colspan="2">

Price categories are per night for two people, occupying a standard double room, with tax, breakfast and service included:
$ under $25
$$ $25–$50
$$$ $50–$100
$$$$ $100–$200
$$$$$ $200 plus

</td><td>

CREDIT CARDS
Major credit cards accepted (including: American Express, MasterCard, Visa).

AIR CONDITIONING
Some or all of the rooms have air conditioning.

SWIMMING POOL
Private swimming pool for hotel guests.

RESTAURANT
Good restaurant, open to non-residents.

</td></tr>
</table>

	NUMBER OF ROOMS	CREDIT CARDS	AIR CONDITIONING	SWIMMING POOL	RESTAURANT
PORT SAID: *Hotel de la Poste* $ 42 Sharia al-Gumhuriyya. (066) 224 048. FAX (066) 221 473. Built in the 1940s and situated in the centre of Port Said's old town, this hotel has a faded elegance. Its high-ceilinged rooms, equipped with fans and baths, are comfortable and some have balconies.	44		●		●
PORT SAID: *Sonesta Port Said* $$$$ Sharia Sultan Hussein. (066) 325 511. FAX (066) 324 825. An unremarkable high-rise with comfortable rooms and views over the Suez Canal and the Mediterranean.	110	●	●	●	●
QUESIR: *Quesir-Sirena Beach Mövenpick* $$$$$ Al-Qadim Bay. (065) 332 100. FAX (065) 332 129. @ resort@movenpick-quesir.com.eg Run by an environmentally-friendly management, this is one of the most peaceful hotels on the Red Sea. It offers excellent diving and snorkelling, desert trips and horse-riding. Under 16s stay for free.	250	●	●	●	●
RAS SUDR: *Moon Beach Resort* $$$ Ras Sudr. (02) 336 5103. FAX (02) 336 5103. This is a mid-priced, simple beach resort with a famous, British-run windsurfing centre. The rooms are in small domed huts and the resort is a popular weekend destination for Cairo expats and Egyptian families.	50	●	●		●
SAFAGA: *Holiday Inn Safaga Palace* $$$ Safaga. (065) 252 821. FAX (065) 252 825. @ holidayinnsafaga@yahoo.com A half-an-hour drive from Hurghada airport, this mid-priced resort sits on a bay famous for its windsurfing. The resort offers extensive watersports, a large children's playground, volleyball and other sports.	327	●	●	●	●
SHARM EL-SHEIKH: *Pigeon House* $ Naama Bay. (069) 600 996. FAX (069) 600 995. @ pigeon@access.com.eg Sharm's favourite budget option, this hotel consists of a variety of huts or rooms, 36 of which have air conditioning. There is no beach access but a discount is offered at the nearby Anemone dive centre. Book in advance.	68		●		●
SHARM EL-SHEIKH: *Shark's Bay Camp* $$ Shark's Bay. (069) 600 943. FAX (069) 600 941. A Bedouin-run beach camp with its own reef and dive centre, some 10 km (6 miles) from Naama Bay. It has a quiet atmosphere, spotless shared bathroom facilities and is very popular during Israeli holidays.	96		●		●
SHARM EL-SHEIKH: *Amar Sina* $$$ Sharm el-Sheikh. (069) 662 222. FAX (069) 662 233. This is a mid-range hotel in Sharm el-Sheikh's clifftop area. It is pleasantly designed by its owner with domes and arches.	91	●	●	●	●
SHARM EL-SHEIKH: *Camel Hotel* $$$ Naama Bay. (069) 600 700. FAX (069) 600 601. @ info@cameldive.com This small hotel, close to Naama Bay, has extensive facilities for the disabled and is attached to the Camel Dive Centre, one of the few centres offering diving courses for the disabled.	38	●	●	●	●
SHARM EL-SHEIKH: *Sanafir Hotel* $$$ Naama Bay. (069) 600 197. FAX (069) 600 196. @ sanafir@access.com.eg One of the first hotels to be built in this area, it has air-conditioned rooms, a number of bars and restaurants, and one of Naama Bay's most popular nightclubs.	60	●	●	●	●

SHARM EL-SHEIKH: *Ritz-Carlton Resort* $$$$$ | 307
Ras Umm Sid. ((069) 661 919. FAX (069) 620 500.
@ ritzcarltonssh@sinainet.com.eg
This is the first Ritz-Carlton in Africa and has all that you would expect of a luxury resort, as well as its own reef and great views.

SHARM EL-SHEIKH: *Sofitel Coralia Sharm el-Sheikh* $$$$$ | 302
Naama Bay. ((069) 600 083. FAX (069) 600 085.
@ sofitel@sofitelsharm-redsea.com
Built in tasteful Moorish style, this is a top Sharm hotel with stunning views over Naama Bay and a superb Indian restaurant.

ST CATHERINE'S MONASTERY: *Auberge St Catherine* $$$ | 52
St Catherine's Monastery. ((069) 470 353. FAX (069) 470 353.
Situated next to the monastery and at the foot of Mount Sinai, this hotel has spartan but comfortable rooms with heaters and plenty of extra blankets. The price is on a half-board basis and the restaurant serves beer and wine.

ST CATHERINE'S MONASTERY: *St Catherine Tourist Village* $$$$ | 118
St Catherine Village. ((069) 470 333. FAX (069) 470 326.
Located just off the main road, a short distance from the monastery, this is the most upmarket hotel in the area.

SUEZ: *Red Sea Hotel* $$$ | 75
13 Sharia Riad, Port Tawfiq. ((062) 334 302. FAX (062) 334 301.
This is a top hotel in Suez with decent rooms and a sixth-floor restaurant offering great views over the Suez Canal.

TABA: *Sea Star Hotel* $$$ | 171
Taba Heights Resort. ((069) 530 190. FAX (069) 530 192.
@ seastar@link.net
One of the lower-priced options at the new Taba Heights Resort, the *Sea Star* offers its own amenities, as well as access to the resort's restaurants, diving centre, casino and watersports facilities.

TABA: *Hilton Taba Resort* $$$$ | 410
Taba Beach. ((069) 530 140. FAX (02) 578 7044.
W www.hilton.com/TBAHITW
This hotel sparked ten years of bitter negotiation when Israel claimed it was not covered by the Camp David Accords. Returned to Egypt in 1989, it boasts a casino and a large watersports centre.

ZAAFARANA: *Windsor Zaafarana* $$$$ | 160
Coast road, Zaafarana. ((02) 414 5602. FAX (02) 419 9999.
A five-star beach resort useful for its proximity to the monasteries of St Paul and St Anthony. Popular around Egyptian holidays.

THE DELTA AND THE NORTH COAST

ALEXANDRIA: *Acropole Hotel* $ | 33
Midan Saad Zaghloul. ((03) 480 5980.
This small, modest hotel located in the downtown area of Alexandria won't break your budget. The art deco building and high-ceilinged rooms have plenty of charm and the balconies give great town and sea views.

ALEXANDRIA: *Union Hotel* $ | 40
5th floor, 164 Sharia 26th July. ((03) 480 7350. FAX (03) 480 7350.
Housed in an Art Deco building, three blocks from Midan Saad Zaghloul, this popular hotel is excellent value. The staff are friendly, the facilities clean and the rooms, with their own bathrooms, comfortable.

ALEXANDRIA: *Le Crillon Hotel* $$ | 36
4th Floor, 5 Sharia Adib Ishaq. ((03) 480 0330.
A very good, two-storey budget hotel, housed in a graceful old building. Some rooms have ensuite bathroom and the rooms with harbour views have large French windows and balconies. Book well in advance.

ALEXANDRIA: *Intercontinental Metropole Alexandria Hotel* $$$$ | 66
62 Sharia Saad Zaghloul. ((03) 486 1465. FAX (03) 486 2040.
@ metropole@interconti.com
Recently renovated, this elegant building was where the poet Constantine Cavafy supposedly worked. It is centrally located with comfortable rooms and friendly staff. All that is missing is a sea view.

For key to symbols see back flap

Price categories are per night for two people, occupying a standard double room, with tax, breakfast and service included:
$ under $25
$$ $25–$50
$$$ $50–$100
$$$$ $100–$200
$$$$$ $200 plus

CREDIT CARDS
Major credit cards accepted (including: American Express, MasterCard, Visa).

AIR CONDITIONING
Some or all of the rooms have air conditioning.

SWIMMING POOL
Private swimming pool for hotel guests.

RESTAURANT
Good restaurant, open to non-residents.

	Price	Number of Rooms	Credit Cards	Air Conditioning	Swimming Pool	Restaurant
ALEXANDRIA: *As-Salamlek Hotel* Montazah Palace. (03) 547 7999. FAX (03) 547 3585. @ salamlek@sangiovanni.com This sumptuously renovated palace was built by Khedive Abbas Helmi II in 1892 as a hunting lodge for his mistress. The hotel offers uniquely decorated suites, a cinema, a casino and magnificent views.	$$$$$	20	■	●		●
ALEXANDRIA: *Cecil Hotel* Midan Saad Zaghloul. (03) 487 7173. FAX (03) 485 5655. This hotel was the setting for Lawrence Durrell's *Alexandria Quartet*. The rooms are large with unbeatable sea views.	$$$$	84	■	●		●
ALEXANDRIA: *Helnan Palestine Hotel* Montazah Palace. (03) 547 4033. FAX (03) 547 3378. @ resp@helnan.com Overlooking Montazah's Royal Beach, the hotel offers a jogging track, children's playground, fishing and windsurfing.	$$$$$	231	■	●		●
DAMIETTA: *Al-Manshy Hotel* 5 Sharia an-Nokrashy. (057) 323 308. FAX (057) 334 884. One of the only hotels in town, it is basic, but clean and convenient for viewing Damietta's famous architecture.	$	20		●		●
MARSA MATRUH: *Reem Hotel* Corniche, Marsa Matruh. (046) 493 3605. FAX (046) 493 3608. Situated on the waterfront in the centre of town, this small budget hotel is one of the better options for a quick stopover in Matruh.	$$	51	■			●
MARSA MATRUH: *Beau Site* Corniche, Marsa Matruh. (046) 493 2066. FAX (046) 493 3319. @ beausite@hiba.com This large holiday village has a private beach and is popular with Egyptian families during the summer months, so book in advance.	$$$$	170	■	●	■	●
SIDI ABDEL RAHMAN: *El-Alamein Hotel* Sidi Abdel Rahman. (046) 468 0140. FAX (046) 468 0341. A popular choice among Egyptians, this ordinary resort sits on a stunning pure-white beach fringing unbelievably turquoise water.	$$$$	228	■	●		●
TANTA: *Arafa Hotel* Midan al-Mahatta. (040) 340 5040. FAX (040) 335 7080. This is the best option in town but does fill up during the famed Moulid of Sayed Ahmed al-Badawi in October. Check dates and book ahead.	$$	58	■	●	■	●

THE WESTERN DESERT

	Price	Number of Rooms	Credit Cards	Air Conditioning	Swimming Pool	Restaurant
BAHARIYYA: *Ahmed's Safari Camp* Bawiti. (02) 847 3399. FAX (02) 847 3090. Located 4 km (2 miles) west of Bawiti's town centre, this camp is a popular budget-traveller haunt. Accommodation ranges from domed rooms with private bathrooms to reed huts. All rooms are cheap and reasonably clean.	$	25				●
BAHARIYYA: *Alpenblick Hotel* Bawiti. (02) 847 2184. FAX (02) 847 2184. A pleasant hotel that is popular with travellers. Some of the rooms have private bathrooms and breakfast is included in the price.	$	22				●
BAHARIYYA: *Al-Beshmo Lodge* Bawiti. (02) 847 2177. FAX (02) 847 2177. This pleasant and comfortable hotel is beautifully located beside one of Bahariyya's springs overlooking acres of palm groves. 12 of the rooms share spotless facilities while the remainder are equipped with air conditioning and ensuite bathrooms.	$$	25		●		●

BAHARIYYA: *International Health Centre* $$ 36
Bawiti. (02) 847 3014. FAX (02) 847 2322. W www.whitedeserttours.com
This three-star spa is built around a sulphuric hot spring. Its half-board price includes the use of the spring and a small gym. TV

DAKHLA: *Bedouin Camp* $ 21
Sharia Mut al-Qasr. (092) 850 480.
Run by Bedouin, this hilltop camp is 7 km (4 miles) north of Mut. The restaurant consists of a tent with carpets and cushions and the rooms, with shared bathroom facilities, are simple but clean.

DAKHLA: *Mebarez Hotel* $ 33
Mut. (092) 821 524. FAX (092) 821 524.
Popular with overland tour groups, the rooms of this hotel, 18 of which have their own bathrooms and air conditioning, are simple but comfortable. TV

DAKHLA: *Mut Talata* $$$ 11
Mut. (092) 821 530. FAX (092) 927 983.
This hotel comprises a combination of chalets, a five-room villa and canvas tents, all clustered around a hot spring. The rooms are simple but clean.

FARAFRA: *Al-Badawiyya Safari & Hotel* $$ 30
Farafra. (092) 510 060. FAX (092) 510 400. @ badawya@link.net
This tastefully-designed hotel is one of the best in the Western Desert. Rooms range from large dormitories to suites, the facilities are clean and the food good. Desert safaris can be arranged and advance booking is essential. TV

KHARGA: *Hamad Allah Hotel* $ 54
Kharga. (092) 920 638. FAX (092) 925 017.
Rooms here are gloomy but comfortable and some have fridges and balconies. The hotel is popular with budget travellers and groups on desert safari. TV

KHARGA: *Kharga Oasis Hotel* $$ 30
Kharga. (092) 921 500. FAX (092) 921 615.
A modernist high-rise with simple, comfortable rooms and a palm-filled garden. All but six rooms have air conditioning and beer is available.

KHARGA: *Pioneers Hotel* $$$ 102
Kharga. (092) 927 982. FAX (092) 927 983.
The food at this low-rise, five-star hotel is about the best you'll find in Kharga. Rooms are comfortable and prices are on a half-board basis. TV

SIWA: *Alexander Hotel* $ 17
Siwa. (046) 460 0512. FAX (046) 460 0006.
This is the newest of Siwa's budget hotels and offers clean rooms with fans and a roof terrace. The hotel also operates a laundry service.

SIWA: *Palm Trees Hotel* $ 26
Siwa. (046) 460 2304.
A budget favourite just off Siwa's main square, with somewhat shabby rooms but a lovely palm garden and friendly staff.

SIWA: *Arous al-Waha Hotel* $ 20
Siwa. (046) 460 2100. FAX (046) 460 0006.
Despite the uninspired architecture, the rooms at this central hotel are clean and the staff friendly and helpful.

SIWA: *Shali Lodge* $$$ 8
Siwa. (046) 460 2399. FAX (046) 460 1799.
@ info@eqi.com.eg
A beautiful hotel with huge rooms around a narrow pool and a restaurant set around date palms for which advance booking is essential.

SIWA: *Siwa Safari Paradise* $$$ 70
Siwa. (046) 460 2289. FAX (046) 460 2286.
Various styles of room are offered at this hotel from bungalows to basic huts. The hotel is conveniently located close to the town centre. TV

SIWA: *Adrere Amellal* $$$$$ 32
Sidi Jaafar. (02) 735 1924. FAX (02) 735 5489.
@ info@eqi.com.eg
At Egypt's first true ecolodge, the traditional architecture, organic food, lack of electricity and swimming pool created from a Roman spring make this a very special hotel. The price includes meals and desert excursions.

For key to symbols see back flap

WHERE TO EAT

Staff at central Cairo's Café Riche

ACCORDING TO an Egyptian proverb, "the best food is that which fills the belly". Traditional Egyptian cooking combines Arabic and Turkish with European and African influences. The result is sometimes described as bland, but this is unjust. Hearty main dishes are usually accompanied by a selection of pickles and dips, so you can spice up or cool down your meal as you wish. The cuisine is dominated by *semna* (clarified butter), which ensures a rich taste and a heavy impact on the arteries. Egyptians often say no meal is complete without meat, yet *fuul* (mashed fava beans), *taamiyya* (deep-fried patties filled with fava bean paste and green herbs, otherwise known as *falafel*) and *koshari* (a mixture of noodles, rice, lentils and onions) – the meatless staples of the poor – are consumed by all classes. Most large Egyptian towns have a few old-fashioned European restaurants, along with growing numbers of fast-food outlets and restaurants serving a wide range of ethnic cuisines. Even better, restaurants are increasingly serving a variety of traditional local dishes.

RESTAURANTS AND BARS

IN MUCH OF EGYPT, the idea of dining out is quite new. As a result, the wide range of dishes that Egyptians eat at home is simply not available in restaurants. Their delicious meat and vegetable stews, for example, are hard to find in a restaurant, except during the month of Ramadan. There is, however, a distinct Egyptian cuisine that adapts remarkably well to modern demands for fast food. *Fuul* sandwiches or roasted chicken *(firakh)*, for example, are likely to be sold in any settlement bigger than a hamlet. Most towns have at least one *kebabgi*, offering a selection of kebabs and a choice of several salads. These are often accompanied by dips such as *hummus* (made from fava beans and herbs),

The interior of L'Aubergine, a vegetarian restaurant in Zamalek

tahina (made from sesame paste) and *babaghanoush* (grilled aubergine and *tahina*). Quality varies, but eating out at a good kebab place is an experience not to be missed.

Pigeon is another popular dish in Egypt. It is stuffed with rice and spices and roasted, or cooked in a stew *(tagine)* with onions and tomatoes.

The culture of dining out is most deeply rooted in the cosmopolitan Mediterranean city of Alexandria, where a number of Greek, Italian and French restaurants and cafés still thrive. Alexandria is also rightly famous for its seafood, which can be eaten at an open-air grill or in one of the town's restaurants. Either way it will be fresh and delicious.

In Cairo, the foreign embassy community alone is enough to keep several old European-style restaurants in business. Younger expatriates and upper-class Egyptians tend to frequent Cairo's trendier restaurant-bars, with flashy décor, loud music and some variation on *nouvelle* Mediterranean fare. More and more ethnic restaurants are opening, and now it is possible to get a full range of Asian food, from Korean and Chinese to Thai and Indonesian.

Many fashionable restaurants double as bars, so going for an evening meal can easily turn into a full-scale night out. Cairo has the remnants of a colonial café scene and some of these places, such as Café Riche, are enjoying a revival. Cairo also has a few traditional-style pubs, which often provide some form of food. Bars usually display signs stating a minimum drinking age of 21, but this guideline is not applied very strictly.

The entrance to Che Omar's Restaurant, Luxor

OPENING HOURS

STREET STALLS selling snacks of *fuul* and *taamiyya* open at the crack of dawn for a basic breakfast. Juice bars are usually open from 8am–10pm, serving freshly squeezed juice. *Koshari* restaurants and shops selling *baladi* sandwiches (*baladi* is a flat, round, country bread) open around 10am. Most other restaurants, unless specifically serving breakfast, open at midday. Very few establishments open before 1pm on Fridays, except those that cater specifically for foreign visitors.

Egyptians tend to eat their main meal in the afternoon, and most restaurants close around 11pm to 1am.

PRICES AND PAYING

IN EGYPTIAN restaurants, dishes are usually ordered individually rather than as fixed combinations. In many establishments, *mezzes (see pp280–81)* will be brought to your table, whether or not you order them. These will be charged for, so send them back if you do not want them and make sure that they are not included on your bill.

A service charge of 12 per cent is added automatically to every restaurant bill, but customers are expected to pay a small tip as well – usually an additional 10 per cent, but not more than LE 10. So once the sales tax of 5 per cent is added on, diners are paying more than 20 per cent over the price of their food.

BOOKING

RESERVATIONS are required only at the most upmarket restaurants. Such places will have a telephone, and most of them will have at least some staff who speak English. Attempts to book a table at less upmarket establishments can prove frustrating, however, and it is likely that there will be no record of your call when you arrive at the restaurant. Nevertheless, the staff will probably be most accommodating and make every effort to find you a table.

Selection of snacks available from an Egyptian fast-food outlet

ETIQUETTE

AS IS THE CASE generally in Egypt, shorts and short skirts are not appropriate attire for restaurants. Other than that, however, most places are quite relaxed as far as dress code is concerned. Egyptians like to dress smartly when going out – including visits to fast-food outlets, which are considered trendy by young Egyptians. Foreign visitors can usually get away with wearing fairly casual clothing, but in more upmarket establishments a shirt with a collar, and shoes rather than sandals, would be advisable. On the other hand, it is not unusual to see women dressed in cocktail dresses in such restaurants, especially late in the evenings.

In Egypt, smoking is inescapable in bars and pervasive in restaurants. Some of the more expensive restaurants in Cairo have established no-smoking sections, but these areas tend to be small and tucked away in a corner, surrounded by smoking tables. Fast-food places are now smoke-free, thanks to a recent campaign by the environment ministry.

CHILDREN

CHILDREN ARE welcome in most restaurants and cafés before about 11pm, though it would not be appropriate to bring them along to places that are primarily drinking establishments. Some restaurants have gardens with play equipment. The Felfela chain, for example, has several branches, including one on the Corniche and another in the Pyramids area, that are geared to children.

A Cairo juice bar, offering a variety of freshly squeezed fruit juices

Stall in Aswan selling deep-fried fava bean and herb patties, known as *taamiyya*

DISABLED CUSTOMERS

FEW EGYPTIAN establishments have facilities for disabled customers, such as wheelchair access, though staff will be willing to help customers overcome any obstacles. Public toilets with wheelchair access are unheard of, but at least the traditional hole-in-the-floor type is almost extinct.

FAST-FOOD OUTLETS

WHILE THERE HAS BEEN some form of international fast-food in Egypt since the 1970s, the last few years have seen a proliferation of international brand names. All the big

American chains (except for Burger King) are here, as well as some less well-known South African outlets. As in the rest of the world, these places have become favourite haunts of the young.

Apart from these international chains, Egypt has its own indigenous fast-food tradition. As well as the ubiquitous street stalls selling snacks of bread *(aish)* stuffed with *fuul* and *taamiyya*, there are stalls that specialize in other traditional snacks. *Koshari*, a mixture of rice, noodles and crispy fried onions in a spicy tomato sauce, is sold at stand-up stalls, also called *koshari*, while more expensive, café-like establishments known as *fatatri* specialize in *fatir*. A cross between pancakes and pizzas, these are made from flaky filo pastry and come with sweet or savoury fillings.

VEGETARIAN FOOD

VEGETARIANISM is extremely rare in Egypt and, as a result, vegetarian restaurants are almost unheard of – L'Aubergine in Zamalek *(p283)* is one of the few exceptions.

However, many Egyptian dishes contain no meat, and restaurants in the cheaper range frequently serve only meatless dishes. More expensive restaurants will usually have a few vegetarian dishes on the menu. Strict vegans could have a harder time, but staples such as *fuul*, *taamiyya* and *koshari* should be acceptable to almost anyone. Obviously, places to avoid are those specializing in kofta and kebab or rotisserie chicken.

A starter of blue-cheese salad with baguette at a Cairo restaurant

HYGIENE

SUFFERING SOME degree of gastric ailment in Egypt seems to be fairly inevitable for anyone spending more than a few days there, but experienced travellers have come up with a few rules of thumb. Some suggest you avoid raw vegetables and salads, particularly lettuce, because these are often not properly washed. (Pickled

Cairo's Café Riche – a reminder of Egypt's colonial café scene vegetables that come as an appetizer should be safe, however). Others believe that the real problem is with the meat. Although it might seem that eating only at the more expensive restaurants would minimize the risk, there are stories of people getting sick everywhere. Fast food is usually safer but, once again, there are exceptions and people have got just as sick from the big chains' burgers as from kofta sandwiches.

In major towns and cities, tap water is safe to drink though heavy chlorination does little for the taste. New arrivals should stick to mineral water *(mayya maadaniyya)*, which is readily available. When buying bottles of mineral water, always check that the seal is intact. *(See also Health Precautions, pp316–7).*

RAMADAN

RAMADAN is an interesting (though also potentially frustrating) time to be in Egypt. The ninth month of the Islamic calendar, Ramadan is a period akin to Lent in the Christian church, with a fast that involves abstention from food, drink and smoking during daylight hours. The fast is strictly observed and days revolve around waiting for sunset. Then the sunset call to prayer is made, lamps are lit on the minarets and everyone gets down to eating the first meal of the day and enjoying the night-time celebrations.

During Ramadan, restaurants may be open during the day, but only tourists will be eating

Restaurant housed in what was once a Nile cruise ship on Zamalek

and fewer options will be available. Travellers may prefer to postpone their meal until after sunset, especially since the cooks making the food and the waiters serving it will not have eaten all day. At sunset, most restaurants are packed, and many set up huge tents so they can fit in as many customers as possible. These feasts provide a good opportunity to get to meet a cross-section of Egyptian society. Everyone sits together at long tables and will probably be quite friendly – once they've eaten.

A wider, more interesting range of traditional dishes will be available during Ramadan, and restaurants will be open throughout the night, in order to serve *sohour*, the last meal before sunrise. In addition, certain drinks, such as apricot juice *(amar el din)*, and foods are specific to this time of the Islamic calendar.

Fish restaurant sign in Abu Qir

ENTERTAINMENT

IF YOU ARE KEEN to combine dining out with some form of entertainment, then your best bet is to book a table at one of Cairo's five-star hotels. Most of these have nightclubs where a flat charge covers an excellent four-course meal and a floor show featuring some of Egypt's most popular dancers and traditional musicians. Smart dress and reservations are required at these venues.

For a variation on this idea, you might like to try one of Cairo's floating restaurants. Many of these offer cruises on the Nile, during which lunch or dinner is served to the accompaniment of live Egyptian music or a floor show complete with belly dancers and band. At Zamalek there are also luxury Nile Cruisers from a bygone era that remain moored, serving food in opulent surroundings. These restaurants often also have live entertainment.

If five-star hotels are beyond your means, there are less expensive nightclubs, where dinner is served and entertainment is provided – though both food and performances are likely to be of variable standard. Several of these nightclubs are located on Pyramid Road.

Remember that nightlife in Cairo doesn't really begin until after midnight, with the floor shows going on as late as 3 or 4 in the morning.

L'Aubergine restaurant in Zamalek, offering a mainly vegetarian menu

What to Eat in Egypt

EGYPT'S CUISINE REFLECTS its position at the crossroads of several cultures – African, Arabic and Mediterranean – whose dishes have been adapted to the fresh local produce. Although the souqs are filled with a colourful assortment of spices, Egyptian dishes are rarely very spicy. Despite being a Muslim country, alcohol is widely available at restaurants and bars, but do not miss out on the delights of the freshly squeezed juices.

Pickled vegetables

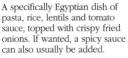

MEZZES
Egyptian meals usually start with a selection of *mezzes*, small tasty dips, snacks and *torshi* (pickled vegetables), which can even serve as a main meal. Although mostly meat free, vegetarians should make sure that any stuffed vegetables do not contain meat.

KOSHARI
A specifically Egyptian dish of pasta, rice, lentils and tomato sauce, topped with crispy fried onions. If wanted, a spicy sauce can also usually be added.

Taamiyya
These delicious deep-fried patties of fava bean paste and herbs have a crunchy coating.

Aish (Bread)
An essential accompaniment to dips, fresh-cooked baladi *(flat bread) is puffed up and soft.*

Lentil Soup
Lentils and beans form a staple part of the Egyptian diet and make a tasty filling soup.

Fuul
This is a traditional Egyptian dish of fava beans mashed with lemon juice, herbs and oil.

Hummus
Middle Eastern dip of cooked chickpeas and oil flavoured with tahini (sesame seed paste).

Babaghanoush
This smooth dip made from grilled aubergines and tahini has a wonderfully smoky taste.

Cheese
Domiati is a white, slightly salty Egyptian cheese that is perfectly suited to juicy tomatoes.

Stuffed Vine Leaves
These are usually filled with rice, vegetables and herbs but they can also contain meat.

Salad
The Egyptian sun and fertile soil produce truly succulent salads with real taste.

MAIN DISHES

Egyptian food is simple and hearty. Most restaurant menus feature meat dishes served with bread or rice and either cooked vegetables or a crisp salad. *Samak* (fish), *firakh* (chicken) or *hamaam* (pigeon) are usually chargrilled with lemon, herbs and spices.

Bamiyya
As a main dish, this is a stew of okra, tomatoes – and often meat – served with rice.

Molokhiyya
This Egyptian speciality is a glutinous green vegetable stew served with or without meat.

Chicken

Kofta

Cubes of lamb

Grilled Meats
Lamb, chicken or kofta *(patties of minced lamb) are often simply grilled as a kebab.*

Stuffed Vegetables
Peppers, aubergines, tomatoes and even potatoes are stuffed with rice, onions and herbs.

Stuffed Lamb
Lamb may be stuffed with onions, sultanas and nuts and served in a tomato sauce.

DESSERTS AND FRUIT

Fruit makes a refreshing and tasty dessert. *Baklawa* is made of different shapes and textures of filo pastry, filled with an assortment of nuts and soaked in a sweet syrup. *Umm Ali* is a special Egyptian dessert of flaky pastry layers stuffed with nuts and raisins soaked in sweet milk and baked.

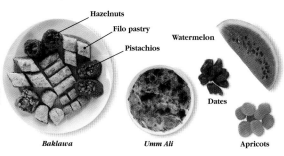

Hazelnuts

Filo pastry

Pistachios

Watermelon

Dates

Apricots

Baklawa   **Umm Ali**

EGYPTIAN DRINKS

The local Stella lager is good and Egyptian wines have improved greatly recently. Hot drinks include *chai* (mint tea) and *ahwa* (Arabic coffee) which is strong and either *ziyada* (sweet), *mazboota* (medium) or *saada* (bitter). *Karkade*, an infusion made from hibiscus leaves, is served hot or cold and fresh fruit juices are also widely available.

Ahwa (coffee)

Apricot juice   **Karkade**

Sugarcane Juice
Sugarcane pulp is squeezed to give asab, *a sweet, light-green drink with a foamy head.*

Egyptian produced wines   **Stella lager**   **Chai (mint tea)**

Choosing a Restaurant

THE RESTAURANTS IN THIS GUIDE have been selected across a wide range of price categories for their good value, good food, atmosphere and interesting location. The adjacent chart highlights some of the factors that may influence your choice. Restaurants are listed region by region, starting with Cairo. The Street Finder for Cairo can be found on pages 140–149.

	CREDIT CARDS ACCEPTED	OUTSIDE DINING	VEGETARIAN CUISINE	WINE LIST	OPEN LATE

CENTRAL CAIRO					
ABOU TAREK $\textcircled{S}$ Sharia Champollion, Downtown. **Map** 1 C4 & 5 C2. Garishly decorated on the outside, this basic restaurant reputedly has the best *koshari* in the city. A wide range of Egyptian sweets is also available.			▦		
KOSHARI GOHA $\textcircled{S}$ Sharia Emad ad-Din. **Map** 2 D4 & 6 D2. Neo-Baroque plasterwork on the ceiling of this famous downtown *koshari* shop is a reminder of former splendour and elegant living.			▦		
KOSHARI HILTON $\textcircled{S}$ Midan Tahrir, Downtown. **Map** 1 C5 & 5 B4. Named after the nearby five-star Nile Hilton hotel, this conveniently located *koshari* shop is a good choice for a quick, cheap, nutritious meal and an escape from the papyrus and perfume hustlers in the square.			▦		
ALFI BEY $\textcircled{S}\textcircled{S}$ 3 Sharia Mohammed Alfy, Downtown. **Map** 2 D4 & 5 C2. ▐ *(02) 577 4999.* A venerable restaurant serving kebab, *kofta*, pigeon and chicken, plus traditional salads and starters, in a setting of faded elegance.			▦		
AN-NIL RESTAURANT $\textcircled{S}\textcircled{S}$ 25 Sharia al-Bustan, Downtown. **Map** 1 C5 & 5 B3. ▐ *(02) 354 0042.* This friendly seafood restaurant is located in the Bab al-Louq market district. A wide variety of grilled fish is sold by weight.					
ALY HASSAN AL-HATY & ALY ABDOU $\textcircled{S}\textcircled{S}$ 3 Midan Halim Pasha, Downtown. **Map** 2 D4 & 6 D2. ▐ *(02) 591 6055.* Once the haunt of cabinet ministers and movie stars, this high-ceilinged meat and kebab house evokes the atmosphere of Cairo's pre-revolutionary days.					
ANDREA $\textcircled{S}\textcircled{S}$ Sharia Abu al-Fida, Zamalek. **Map** 1 A2. ▐ *(02) 737 0523; 737 0525; 737 0529.* At the northern tip of Zamalek, this waterside terrace offers a unique view of the Cairo suburbs Imbaba and Rod Al Farag, and the century-old railway bridge that connects them. Try Andrea's special grilled chicken. ▮	▦	●	▦	●	▦
CAFÉ OLÉ $\textcircled{S}\textcircled{S}$ Nile Hilton Hotel, Midan Tahrir, Downtown. **Map** 1 C5 & 5 B4. ▐ *(02) 578 0444.* Overlooking the bustle of Midan Tahrir, this café serves a good breakfast special every morning, while coffee and pastries are available all day. ▦ ▮	▦		▦	●	
CAFÉ RICHE $\textcircled{S}\textcircled{S}$ 17 Sharia Talaat Harb, Downtown. **Map** 1 C5 & 5 C3. ▐ *(02) 391 8873.* This historic café is decorated with portraits of former regulars who include many of Egypt's most famous stars of stage and screen. ▤ ▦ ▮	▦		▦	●	
DIDO'S AL-DENTE $\textcircled{S}\textcircled{S}$ 26 Sharia Bahgat Ali, Zamalek. **Map** 1 A2. ▐ *(02) 735 9117.* A cramped space with backless stools, Al-Dente serves good pastas at good prices. When the big windows are open, the place feels like a patio.			▦		
FATATRI PIZZA TAHRIR $\textcircled{S}\textcircled{S}$ 165 Sharia at-Tahrir, Downtown. **Map** 1 C5 & 5 B4. ▐ *(02) 795 3596.* Open 24 hours, this restaurant serves meat, fish and cheese *fateers* or "pizzas", (very different from their Italian equivalents). Sweet *fateers* are also available.			▦		▦
THE GREEK CLUB (LE CLUB HELLENIQUE) $\textcircled{S}\textcircled{S}$ Qasr el-Nil, Downtown. **Map** 1 C5 & 5 C3. ▐ *(02) 575 0759.* Most of the year, eating and drinking is done in a refurbished colonial dining hall, but everything moves out to the terrace for the summer months. ▮		●	▦	●	

Price categories are for a three-course meal for one person, including coffee, tax and service:

$ under $5
$$ $5–$10
$$$ $10–$15
$$$$ $15–$20
$$$$$ $20 plus

CREDIT CARDS
Major credit cards accepted (including: American Express, Diners Club, MasterCard, Visa).

OUTSIDE DINING
Garden, courtyard or terrace with outside tables.

VEGETARIAN CUISINE
A selection of vegetarian dishes available.

WINE LIST
A choice of wines available.

OPEN LATE
Restaurant serves meals until 2am.

	$	Credit Cards Accepted	Outside Dining	Vegetarian Cuisine	Wine List	Open Late
JO SUSHI — 47 Sharia Mohammed Mazhar, Zamalek. Map 1 A2. *(02) 735 7746.* The plainly furnished Jo Sushi is Cairo's best-value Japanese/Chinese restaurant. Meals begin with a free round of starters.	$$	■		■	●	
MAISON THOMAS — 157 Sharia 26 July. Map 1 A3. *(02) 735 7057.* Maison Thomas makes the city's best European-style pizzas and is open 24 hours. However, it is mainly a delivery place, with no toilet for customers.	$$			■	●	■
ANGUS — 34B Sharia Yehia Ibrahim, Zamalek. Map 1 A3. *(02) 735 1865; 735 0928.* Located inside the New Star Hotel in Zamalek, this Argentine-themed steakhouse has an inevitably meat-based menu. Nevertheless, the food is good and the portions are large.	$$$	■		■	●	■
L'AUBERGINE — 5 Sharia Sayed al-Bakry, off Sharia Hassan Sabry, Zamalek. Map 1 A3. *(02) 738 0080.* A popular haunt of foreign journalists, this top restaurant specializes in well-presented vegetarian food; some meat dishes are also available.	$$$	■		■	●	■
ESTORIL — 12 Sharia Talaat Harb, Downtown. Map 1 C5 & 5 B3. *(02) 574 3102.* This renowned Franco-Levantine restaurant and bar provides a welcome escape from the bustle of the city centre. The *mezes* are outstanding.	$$$			■		
FELFELA — 15 Sharia Hoda Shaarawi, Downtown. Map 1 C5 & 5 C3. *(02) 392 2751.* With an English-speaking staff and tasty, reasonably priced Egyptian specialities, this restaurant caters blatantly to the tourist market. It was once strictly vegetarian, but now serves meat dishes too.	$$$			■		
LE GRILLON — 8 Qasr el-Nil, Downtown. Map 1 C5 & 5 C3. *(02) 574 3114.* This old leftist haunt, decorated with paintings by local artists, serves old-fashioned continental and Egyptian fare in an indoor garden setting.	$$$	■	●	■	●	■
ROY'S COUNTRY KITCHEN — Cairo Marriott Hotel, Sharia Saray al-Gezira, Zamalek. Map 1 B3. *(02) 735 8888.* The breakfast buffet is the high point of this would-be US truckstop, open 24 hours a day. A comfortable place to pass a Friday morning.	$$$	■		■	●	■
ASIA HOUSE — Helnan Shepheard Hotel, Corniche el-Nil, Garden City. Map 3 B1 & 5 A5. *(02) 795 3801.* The restaurant serves excellent Indian, Chinese and other Asian dishes in a spacious hall decorated like an Islamic palace.	$$$$	■		■	●	
LA BODEGA — 157 Sharia 26 July. Map 1 A3. *(02) 735 6761.* Located in Zamalek's historic Art Deco Baehler Mansions, this elegantly trendy restaurant caters to Cairo's young upper-class. Reservations required.	$$$$	■		■	●	■
CINZANO — Sharia Amerika al-Latineya, Garden City. Map 3 B1 & 5 A5. Popular with Cairo's young upper-class crowd, Cinzano serves good pasta in an intimate Mediterranean-style cellar room. However, ordering wine can make dining here surprisingly expensive.	$$$$	■			●	
FIVE BELLS — 13 Sharia Ismail Mohammed, Zamalek. Map 1 A3. *(02) 735 8980 or 735 8635.* This popular restaurant-bar serves a mix of French and Levantine dishes in an elegant indoor area, or in a garden with a cherub-covered fountain.	$$$$	■	●	■	●	

For key to symbols see back flap

<table>
<tr><td colspan="2">

Price categories are for a three-course meal for one person, including coffee, tax and service:

$ under $5
$$ $5–$10
$$$ $10–$15
$$$$ $15–$20
$$$$$ $20 plus

</td><td>

CREDIT CARDS
Major credit cards accepted (including: American Express, Diners Club, MasterCard, Visa).

OUTSIDE DINING
Garden, courtyard or terrace with outside tables.

VEGETARIAN CUISINE
A selection of vegetarian dishes available.

WINE LIST
A choice of wines available.

OPEN LATE
Restaurant serves meals until 2am.

</td></tr>
</table>

	CREDIT CARDS ACCEPTED	OUTSIDE DINING	VEGETARIAN CUISINE	WINE LIST	OPEN LATE
HA NA $$$$ 21 Sharia Aziz Abaza, at Midan Sidki, Zamalek. **Map** 1 A3. ((02) 738 2972. This dim, comfortable semi-basement dining room offers a mainly Korean menu, with food cooked at your table if you wish. ▤ 🗲 🍷	■		■	●	
HARRY'S PUB $$$$ Cairo Marriott Hotel, Sharia Saray al-Gezira, Zamalek. **Map** 1 B3. ((02) 735 8888. For visitors feeling a little homesick for English food, the Harry's Pub menu features traditional dishes such as steak and kidney pie. Big-screen TVs make this a popular venue for watching sports. ▤ 🗲 🍷 P	■		■	●	■
IL PICCOLO MONDO $$$$ Le Pacha 1901, moored off Sharia Saray al-Gezira, Zamalek. **Map** 1 B5. ((02) 735 6730. Part of a multi-restaurant complex in a boat moored near the Cairo Marriott Hotel, this Italian diner offers a well-organized and attractive salad bar. Be sure to get a window seat. ▤ 🍷 P	■		■	●	■
KOWLOON $$$$ Cleopatra Hotel, 2 Sharia al-Bustan, Downtown. **Map** 1 C5 & 5 B3. ((02) 575 9831. Dine on delicious Chinese and Korean food in a slightly surreal dining room set around a big, glowing fish tank. The dumplings are especially good. ▤ 🍷	■		■	●	
PAPRIKA $$$$ 1129 Corniche el-Nil, Maspero. **Map** 1 B4 & 5 A2. ((02) 578 9447. Situated near the Arab Television Building, this restaurant is popular with Egyptian media types. The Mediterranean-influenced menu features everything from Italian pasta dishes to Egyptian game fowl. ▤ 🗲	■		■	●	
LE STEAK $$$$ Le Pacha 1901, moored off Sharia Saray al-Gezira, Zamalek. **Map** 1 B5. ((02) 735 6730. Excellent steaks and Middle Eastern specialities with a fine Nile view on this floating restaurant. A jacket is obligatory for men. ▤ 🍷 P	■		■	●	
CIAO ITALIA! $$$$$ Sheraton al-Gezira. **Map** 3 A1. ((02) 736 1555. A small intimate restaurant, Ciao Italia! offers Cairo's most authentic Italian fare. The food is superb and there is an impressive Nile view. ▤ 🗲 🕭 🍷 P	■	●	■	●	
THE FISH MARKET $$$$$ Sharia Saray al-Gezira; boat docked in front of the Cairo Marriott hotel. **Map** 1 B3. ((02) 737 4833. The highlights of this floating restaurant are its delicious sea bass and shrimps, as well as the dessert trolley. Unfortunately, the view of the Nile is blocked by another boat. ▤ 🗲 🍷 P	■		■	●	
TROPICANA GARDEN $$$$$ Nile Hilton Hotel, Midan Tahrir, Downtown. **Map** 1 C5 & 5 A3. ((02) 578 0444. Enjoy finely prepared grilled dishes and Egyptian specialities in the pleasant setting of the Nile Hilton garden. 🍷 🕭 P	■	●	■	●	

ISLAMIC CAIRO

	CREDIT CARDS ACCEPTED	OUTSIDE DINING	VEGETARIAN CUISINE	WINE LIST	OPEN LATE
KOSHARI GOMHOURYA $ Sharia al-Azhar, Midan Hussein. **Map** 2 F5. This *koshari* shop, plainly fitted out and with sawdust on the floor, is a good place to fill up before a walk around the Khan al-Khalili.			■		
ABU BASSEM GRILL $$ 2 Al-Gahini Alley, Midan Hussein. **Map** 2 F5. ((02) 593 7935. The medieval surroundings are the star feature of this restaurant, which serves *kofta*, kebab, roasted lamb and grilled chicken, along with the usual *mezes*.		●	■		■

Egyptian Pancake House $$
Just off Midan Hussein. **Map** 2 F5.
This unassuming restaurant's speciality is the *fateer,* an envelope of flaky pastry holding either a sweet or savoury filling. Here they are prepared in front of you with a technique that recalls the dance of a whirling dervish.

Ar-Rifai $$
Just off Midan Sayyida Zeinab, at the top of Sharia al-Barrani. **Map** 4 D2.
This restaurant, consisting simply of tables set up in an alley, offers authentic Cairo atmosphere and grilled meat sold by weight. Popular with clubbers.

Felfel Restaurant $$
9 Sharia Mohammed Farid, Al-Nasariyya, Sayyida Zeinab. **Map** 4 D1 & 6 D5.
The highlight in this tiny, white-tiled restaurant is grilled meat, but good salads are also served. The service is fast and friendly.

Khan al-Khalili Restaurant & Cafe $$$
5 Al-Badistan, Khan al-Khalili. (02) 593 2262. **Map** 2 F5.
Catering for tourists by serving Egyptian food in a theatrical Eastern salon setting, this restaurant provides a welcome refuge from the bazaar. Run by the Oberoi Hotel group, it can get crowded with tour groups.

GIZA AND HELIOPOLIS

Abu Haidar $
15 Sharia Ibrahim al-Laqqani, Roxy, Heliopolis. (02) 570 871.
This streetside grill in historic Heliopolis is famous for juicy, tender *shawarma* and fresh, lumpy mango juice.

Al-Kods $
52 Sharia Haroun al-Rashid, Heliopolis. (02) 632 3467.
Abu Riyadh has run this little piece of East Jerusalem in Heliopolis since the late 1960s. The *falafel, hummus* and home-made yoghurt are delicious.

Koshari Hind $
Sharia Thawra, near Midan Korba, Heliopolis.
The best *koshari* in Heliopolis is just up the street from the Baron's Palace. Single men eat in the front part, but there is also a family area in the back.

Tut Express $
1 Sharia al-Saad al-Aali, Doqqi. (02) 335 0915.
Mainly a drive-in juice bar, Tut Express also serves straightforward Egyptian fast-food favourites like *shawarma* and baked macaroni. **P** on the street.

Al-Amoudi $$
4 Sharia Zamzam, Mohandiseen. (02) 749 9694.
This hole-in-the-wall Yemeni restaurant features Bedouin food at its best, but brace yourself for huge portions of less-familiar parts of a lamb's anatomy.

Andrea's $$
4–5 Sharia Saqqara, Al-Maryutiya. (02) 381 0205.
Located in the Pyramids area, this branch of Andrea's is a good choice after a day of visiting antiquities. Fresh-baked bread makes the meal. **P**

Ataturk $$
20 Sharia al-Riyadh, Mohandiseen. (02) 347 5135.
The menu seems to be a familiar combination of *mezes,* soups and grilled meat, but Turkish cuisine differs in the details. Try the grilled chicken.

At-Tekkia $$
12 Midan Ibn al-Walid, near the Shooting Club, Doqqi.
(02) 749 6673.
Restaurants rarely do a good imitation of Egyptian home cooking, but Al-Tekkia is a delicious exception. The service is slow but friendly.

Chantilly $$$
11 Sharia Baghdad, Korba, Heliopolis. (02) 290 7303; 290 5213.
Here you can enjoy a continental breakfast and read the English-language papers in a Swiss-chalet dining room with a bakery attached.

Chopsticks $$$
23b Sharia Syria, Mohandiseen. (02) 304 8568.
Cairo's most delicious and authentic Chinese food is served here.
Downstairs is a casual, friendly karaoke bar.

Price categories are for a three-course meal for one person, including coffee, tax and service:

💲 under $5
💲💲 $5–$10
💲💲💲 $10–$15
💲💲💲💲 $15–$20
💲💲💲💲💲 $20 plus

CREDIT CARDS
Major credit cards accepted (including: American Express, Diners Club, MasterCard, Visa).

OUTSIDE DINING
Garden, courtyard or terrace with outside tables.

VEGETARIAN CUISINE
A selection of vegetarian dishes available.

WINE LIST
A choice of wines available.

OPEN LATE
Restaurant serves meals until 2am.

	CREDIT CARDS ACCEPTED	OUTSIDE DINING	VEGETARIAN CUISINE	WINE LIST	OPEN LATE
JAITTA 💲💲 120 Sharia al-Thawra, Heliopolis. ☎ *(02) 415 2326; 417 3135.* This Lebanese restaurant serves excellent *kofta*. Try a water-pipe. ▤	■	●	■		■
THE CAIRO JAZZ CLUB 💲💲💲💲 197 Sharia 26 July, near Midan Sphinx, Agouza. ☎ *(02) 345 9939.* The cover charge is steep and the room is smoky, but it's the only place in Egypt to hear decent live jazz. The *nouvelle* Egyptian food is good, too. ▤ 🍸	■		■	●	■
KANDAHAR 💲💲💲💲 Sharia Gamaat al-Dawal al-Arabiya (2nd floor), off Midan Sphinx, Mohandiseen. ☎ *(02) 303 0615.* A cosy little space, this restaurant serves delicious starters and a wide range of Indian main courses – spicy if requested. ▤ 🍸	■		■	●	
LE TABASCO 💲💲💲💲 8 Midan Amman, Mohandiseen. ☎ *(02) 336 5583.* A very fashionable night spot, Tabasco provides attentive service and top Mediterranean cuisine, including home-made pasta. ▤ 🍸	■		■	●	■
MOGHUL ROOM 💲💲💲💲💲 Mena House Oberoi Hotel, Al-Haram. ☎ *(02) 383 3222.* Ornately decorated in high Moghul style, the restaurant serves Cairo's best, subtly spicy, Indian cuisine. Reservations recommended. ▤ 🌠 ♿ 🅿	■		■	●	

AROUND CAIRO

	CREDIT CARDS ACCEPTED	OUTSIDE DINING	VEGETARIAN CUISINE	WINE LIST	OPEN LATE
FAYOUM: *Queen Hotel* 💲💲 Sharia Lotfallah Hassan. ☎ *(084) 346 819.* This hotel restaurant is located in the town of Fayoum and serves a wide range of food. Try the grilled chicken. ▤		●	■		
FAYOUM: *Auberge du Lac-Fayoum* 💲💲💲💲💲 Lake Qarun. ☎ *(084) 572 001.* This luxury hotel once served as a hunting lodge for King Farouk. Its setting makes it a popular lunch-stop for upmarket tour groups. ▤ 🌠 ♿ 🅿	■	●	■	●	■

THE NILE VALLEY

	CREDIT CARDS ACCEPTED	OUTSIDE DINING	VEGETARIAN CUISINE	WINE LIST	OPEN LATE
ASWAN: *Hamam* 💲 Corniche el-Nil Open 24 hours a day, this café offers an excellent variety of roasted and stewed meats, all served on great mounds of rice.					■
ASWAN: *Sayida Nafisa* 💲 Sharia al-Souq. Locals and tourists pack this simple restaurant in the heart of the market area. Typical Egyptian dishes are complemented by fresh fruit juices.		●	■		
ASWAN: *Aswan Moon* 💲💲 Next to the felucca quay at the north end of the Corniche. Hard to miss, thanks to its blazing neon lights, this place offers decent Egyptian and European food in a riverside setting. ▤		●	■		
ASWAN: *Aswan Panorama* 💲💲 Corniche el-Nil, in front of the courthouse. ☎ *(097) 306 169.* As well as hearty meat and fish *tagines* (stews), this riverside restaurant serves delicious grilled chicken and fish in a pleasant garden setting. ▤		●	■		
ASWAN: *Darwish* 💲💲 Sharia Saad Zaghloul. Three-course meals of Egyptian specialities, including fish fresh from Lake Nasser, are offered in this spotlessly clean restaurant.			■		

ASWAN: *Emy* $$
Corniche el-Nil, in the centre of town.
A boat-restaurant on the Corniche serving grilled fish and typical Egyptian fare at reasonable prices, Emy provides a spectacular view of Lake Nasser and Elephantine Island, particularly as the sun is setting.

ASWAN: *Al-Masry* $$
Sharia al-Matar. *(097) 302 576.*
Located in the centre of town, Al-Masry offers an extensive selection of Egyptian and European dishes in a clean, bright, indoor setting. 🍴

ASWAN: *Medina* $$
Sharia al-Souq, across from the Cleopatra Hotel.
Well-prepared *kofta* and kebab, as well as fresh fish, are the highlights at this restaurant, which is conveniently located near the market.

ASWAN: *Mona Lisa* $$
Corniche el-Nil.
This riverside restaurant serves basic but decent Italian main courses along with a range of typical Egyptian dishes and delicious fruit-juice cocktails. The best feature is the view of Elephantine Island. 🍷

ASWAN: *Nubian Restaurant* $$$
Essa Island, free transport from ferry dock opposite EgyptAir.
Often busy with groups, this restaurant on a tiny island just south of Elephantine Island serves good food, with live entertainment each night.

ASWAN: *The Terrace Bar & Restaurant* $$$
Old Cataract Hotel. *(097) 316 000.*
This luxurious colonial hotel is an excellent location for an elegant dinner or drink overlooking the Nile, with good views of the temples at the southern end of Elephantine Island. 🛗🍷🅿

ASYUT: *Akhnaton Hotel* $$
Akhnaton Hotel Restaurant. *(088) 337 723.*
Continental dishes and pizzas are the highlights of the menu at this busy hotel restaurant in Asyut, 400 km (250 miles) south of Cairo. 🍴

EDFU: *New Egypt Restaurant* $
Midan Maabad (Temple Square).
The grilled meat or chicken with rice and vegetables served at this restaurant is virtually the only option for a full meal out in Edfu.

KOM OMBO: *Venus Cafeteria & Restaurant* $
On the bank of the Nile on the way to the temple.
The food is not that special, consisting largely of *kofta* sandwiches and ice cream, but the riverside setting is soothing, the restaurant is open 24 hours a day, and there are not many other options in Kom Ombo.

LUXOR: *Abu Haggar* $
Sharia Abdel Moneim al-Adasi. *(095) 376 306.*
The ornately decorated Abu Haggar is a favourite late-night destination in Luxor. The reasonably priced menu features chicken, kebab, stuffed vegetables and other traditional Egyptian specialities.

LUXOR: *Khased Khear* $
Sharia al-Mahatta, near the train station. *(095) 384 580.*
A cramped little kebab house that nevertheless provides respite from the heat. The restaurant serves both beef and lamb kebabs. 🍴

LUXOR: *Mensa* $
Sharia al-Mahatta.
A good place to fill up before boarding a train north, this no-frills restaurant specializes in roasted chicken and stuffed pigeon.

LUXOR: *Sultana* $
Sharia Television. *(095) 325 450.*
This brightly painted, air-conditioned café offers European-style pizzas and sandwiches along with Egyptian *mezes* and *kofta*. 🍴

LUXOR: *Amoun* $$
Sharia Karnak.
Its location in the tourist bazaar and inexpensive menu (kebabs and Mediterranean fare) ensure that this uninspiring-looking restaurant is always busy.

For key to symbols see back flap

	CREDIT CARDS ACCEPTED	OUTSIDE DINING	VEGETARIAN CUISINE	WINE LIST	OPEN LATE
Price categories are for a three-course meal for one person, including coffee, tax and service: **$** under $5 **$$** $5–$10 **$$$** $10–$15 **$$$$** $15–$20 **$$$$$** $20 plus **CREDIT CARDS** Major credit cards accepted (including: American Express, Diners Club, MasterCard, Visa). **OUTSIDE DINING** Garden, courtyard or terrace with outside tables. **VEGETARIAN CUISINE** A selection of vegetarian dishes available. **WINE LIST** A choice of wines available. **OPEN LATE** Restaurant serves meals until 2am.					
LUXOR: *Al-Gezira Hotel* **$$** West Bank, 250 m on the left from ferry dock, on the way into town. One of the few West Bank restaurants that sell beer, this is a popular hotel serving good Egyptian food. Eating on the rooftop terrace under the stars, with the lights of Luxor across the Nile, is an atmospheric experience.		●	■		
LUXOR: *Al-Houda* **$$** Sharia Television. Friendly service and decent Egyptian-Mediterranean food at average prices make this a bright spot on Luxor's restaurant landscape.					
LUXOR: *King's Head Pub* **$$** Sharia Khaled ibn al-Walid, behind the Isis Hotel. A popular traditional English pub, complete with dart boards and billiards tables, the King's Head serves an authentic British Sunday lunch of roast beef and Yorkshire pudding, as well as soup and sandwiches.	■				■
LUXOR: *Marhaba* **$$** Sharia Karnak, above the Tourist Bazaar. At this rooftop restaurant offering a view of the Nile and Luxor Temple, the menu includes a mix of Egyptian and Mediterranean food.		●	■		
LUXOR: *Tutankhamun Restaurant* **$$** Just S of local ferry dock, West Bank. Hidden in the reeds beside the Nile, this excellent restaurant combines copious amounts of good food with genuine hospitality. If you ask him nicely, the owner will set your table literally on the bank of the Nile.		●	■		
LUXOR: *Anubis* **$$$** Corniche el-Nil, next to the Museum of Mummification. This riverside restaurant offers a vegetarian-friendly interpretation of Egyptian cuisine: roasted chicken, kebab, stuffed vegetables and a variety of *mezes*. More adventurous diners may be disappointed, however.	■	●	■	✓	
LUXOR: *Class* **$$$** Sharia Khalid Ibn al-Walid. (095) 376 327. A range of continental dishes along with a few Egyptian standards is served at this relatively upmarket restaurant. Service is courteous and efficient.	■		■	●	
MINYA: *Cafeteria Aly Baba* **$** Corniche el-Nil, north of Sharia Port Said. The Aly Baba is a good place to fill up cheaply on chicken, kebabs and *mezes* in a town that struggles a little in the way of restaurants.					

SINAI AND THE RED SEA COAST

AL-ARISH: *Maxim* **$$$$** On the beach, off Sharia Fouad Zakry. Ideally located among the shady palms on the beach, Maxim is a class above most other restaurants in town. Only open in summer.		●	■		■
DAHAB: *Crazy House* **$$** Al-Masbat. Eating at a dive camp restaurant is an essential part of the Dahab experience and although Crazy House is more expensive than the competition, it is clean, has chairs and sells beer.		●	■		■
DAHAB: *INMO Divers Home Restaurant* **$$$** Al-Mashraba. (069) 640 370. This pleasant, domed restaurant, attached to a diving centre and hotel, serves a typical range of Egyptian food alongside international cuisine. Recommended for vegetarians and, obviously, divers.	■	●	■		

DAHAB: *Nesima Restaurant* $$$$
Al-Mashraba. (069) 640 320.
Set within a hotel, this restaurant has a good-quality international menu.
Watch the sun go down from the restaurant's rooftop bar.

HURGHADA: *Felfela Hurghada* $$
Sharia Sheraton. (065) 442 411.
This successful chain of Egyptian restaurants sells good food in clean, pleasant
surroundings and this branch has the added attraction of a superb sea view.

HURGHADA: *Young Kang* $$
Sharia Sheikh Sebak.
Set in the heart of Downtown Hurghada, this Chinese/Korean restaurant
serves better food than its slightly tatty decor would suggest.

HURGHADA: *Red Sea I* $$$
Off Sharia Tariq Nasr, Ad-Dahar. (065) 547 704.
One of the best restaurants in Hurghada for seafood, this restaurant also serves
pizzas and traditional Egyptian dishes. The rooftop terrace can get crowded.

HURGHADA: *Portofino* $$
Sharia General Hospital. (065) 546 250.
Serving good Italian food, this restaurant stands out among the many Red Sea
coast Italian restaurants because of the enthusiasm of the owner, Mr Hakim.

ISMAILIA: *King Edward Restaurant* $$
171 Sharia at-Tahrir. (064) 369 611.
One of the better eating establishments in Ismailia, it is also very clean. Try
the grilled chicken. Not terribly good for vegetarians.

NAAMA BAY: *Bua Khao* $$$$
Sharm Holiday Resort. (069) 601 391.
Part of a large holiday complex, this excellent Thai restaurant makes a nice
change for palates jaded by the Italian food on offer everywhere else.

NUWEIBA: *Blue Bus* $$
Tarabeen.
This is one of the original dive camps, located on Tarabeen beach. The
restaurant serves good quality food (fish, pasta and pizza) at fair prices.

NUWEIBA: *Ibn Hamido* $$
Nuweiba City.
Situated near the Helnan Nuweiba Hotel, this restaurant serves standard
local fare as well as pizzas with nice, fresh toppings.

NUWEIBA: *Helnan Restaurant Panorama* $$$$
Helnan Nuweiba Hotel, Nuweiba City. (069) 500 402.
One of the few licensed restaurants in Nuweiba City, this upmarket
establishment serves standard hotel fare in its main air-conditioned
restaurant and cheaper snacks at its more relaxed beachside bar.

PORT SAFAGA: *Al-Fayrouz* $$$$
Hurghada–Safaga road. (065) 252 821.
This huge 600-seat restaurant is set within the Holiday Inn Safaga Palace
and may not be to everyone's taste. However, air conditioning and reliable
food may be just what is needed after a few days at dive camps.

PORT SAID: *Hotel de la Poste* $$
42 Sharia al-Gumhuriyya. (066) 224 048.
This is actually more of a café and bar than a restaurant, and it sells lighter
meals such as sandwiches, salads, hamburgers and pizzas. The terrace is a
popular place to relax while the rest of the world bustles past.

PORT SAID: *Maxim* $$$$
Sharia Palestine. (066) 238 628.
Actually located in the shopping centre next to the Sonesta Hotel, this is
the most expensive restaurant in Port Said. However, the price is merited by
the combination of excellent fish dishes and a view over the Suez Canal.

SHARM EL-SHEIKH: *Al-Fanar Restaurant* $$$
Ras Um Sid beach. (069) 662 218.
Located at the foot of the lighthouse on the beach, the beautiful location of
this open-air restaurant makes it an idyllic place for a spot of lunch or even
a dinner under the stars. Serves excellent Italian food.

For key to symbols see back flap

<table>
<tr><td colspan="6">

Price categories are for a three-course meal for one person, including coffee, tax and service:

$ under $5
$$ $5–$10
$$$ $10–$15
$$$$ $15–$20
$$$$$ $20 plus

</td></tr>
</table>

CREDIT CARDS
Major credit cards accepted (including: American Express, Diners Club, MasterCard, Visa).

OUTSIDE DINING
Garden, courtyard or terrace with outside tables.

VEGETARIAN CUISINE
A selection of vegetarian dishes available.

WINE LIST
A choice of wines available.

OPEN LATE
Restaurant serves meals until 2am.

	CREDIT CARDS ACCEPTED	OUTSIDE DINING	VEGETARIAN OPTIONS	WINE LIST	OPEN LATE
SHARM EL-SHEIKH: *Safsafa* $$$ Asia Mall, Downtown Sharm el-Sheikh. [(069) 660 474, (069) 603 418. A good supply of fresh fish and an unpretentious clientele ensure this small family-run restaurant, now one of several branches, remains popular.			▩		
SHARM EL-SHEIKH: *La Luna Restaurant* $$$$ Ras Um Sid. [(069) 661 919. Located in the Ritz-Carlton Hotel, this restaurant serves good quality Italian food and makes its own pasta on site.	▩	●	▩	●	
SUEZ: *Fish Restaurant* $$ Sharia as-Salaam. Not surprisingly, this restaurant's speciality is fish, sold by weight and delicious when grilled. It is situated near the White House Hotel.			▩		
THE DELTA AND THE NORTH COAST					
ABU QIR: *Zaphyrion* $$ 41 Sharia Khaled Ibn al-Walid, Abu Qir. [(03) 562 1319. Eat fine seafood, grilled meats and *mezes* in a stunning setting overlooking the bay where Nelson fought the Battle of the Nile. ▮		●	▩		
ALEXANDRIA: *City Café* $ 21 Salah Salem. [(03) 484 7994. This Mediterranean-style café in downtown Alexandria serves one of the best cappuccinos in town, as well as pastries, sandwiches, pizza and pasta. The glass-walled decor is sleek and simple.			▩		
ALEXANDRIA: *Fuul Mohammed Ahmed* $ 17 Sharia Shakour. [(03) 487 3576. Often touted as the best place for *fuul* in the whole of Egypt, Mohammed Ahmed serves quite a number of variants of the bean staple, including the spicy *Fuul Iskandarani*, as well as *falafel*, omelettes and *mezes*.			▩		
ALEXANDRIA: *Elite* $$ 43 Sharia Safia Zaghloul. [(03) 486 3592. The Elite offers good continental cuisine in one of the city's best spots for people-watching. On one side, the wall is decorated with art posters; on the other, wide picture windows open onto the street. ▮			▩	●	
ALEXANDRIA: *Gezirat al-Malika* $$ 48 Sharia Safr Basha, Ras el-Tin. [(03) 480 4996. *Kofta* and kebab are served by weight here, in a room decorated like an Egyptian rural village. The stuffed vegetables are worth trying too.			▩		
ALEXANDRIA: *Pastroudis* $$ 39 Sharia al-Huriya, west of Sharia Safia Zaghloul. [(03) 392 9609. This famous café was established in 1923 and is known mainly for its pastries, its atmosphere and its literary past. However, it also does decent, if slightly over-priced sandwiches and main dishes such as pasta.			▩	●	
ALEXANDRIA: *Taverna* $$ Sharia Mahattat al-Ramla, across from the tram terminal. [(03) 486 8189. This is the best of a chain of four Taverna restaurants. The pizzas and *fateers* here are served straight out of a brick oven. The chicken and lamb *shawarma* and the *mezes* are also excellent.			▩		
ALEXANDRIA: *Trianon* $$$ Sharia Saad Zaghloul. [(03) 486 0986. An essential component of the city's pre-revolution café scene, the Art Deco Trianon has been restored to its former glory. The high points of the menu are the coffees and desserts, especially the fantastic *Umm Ali*.	▩		▩		

ALEXANDRIA: *China Restaurant* $$$
Cecil Hotel, Midan Saad Zaghloul. █ *(03) 487 7173.*
This rooftop restaurant has a fairly decent menu of authentic Chinese
dishes to complement the stunning view of Alexandria's Western Harbour.

ALEXANDRIA: *Eddoura* $$$
33 Sharia Bayrim at-Tonsi. █ *(03) 480 0405.*
A 24-hour, open-air fish and seafood grill situated close to the Qaitbey fort.

ALEXANDRIA: *Santa Lucia* $$$$
40 Sharia Safia Zaghloul. █ *(03) 486 0332 or 486 4240.*
This wood-panelled, candle-lit restaurant serves the fish and seafood for
which Alexandria is famous. Intimate ambience with resident pianist. 📋 ▼

ALEXANDRIA: *Al-Farouk* $$$$$
As-Salamlek Palace Hotel, Montazah Gardens. █ *(03) 547 7999.*
King Farouk's former hunting lodge, recently renovated and converted,
now houses several elegant dining rooms and a bar. 📋 ⚡ ▼ 🅿

ALEXANDRIA: *Saraya San Giovanni Restaurant* $$$$$
█ *(03) 546 7773.*
This upmarket hotel-restaurant serves European cuisine, including fish dishes,
and offers an outstanding view of Stanley Bay. 📋 ▼

THE WESTERN DESERT

BAHARIYYA: *Popular Restaurant* $$
Bawiti, al-Bahariyya Oasis.
One of the few restaurants in the oasis not based within a hotel. It sells
falafel in the mornings and grilled meats all day – also good for cold beer.

DAKHLA: *Ahmed Hamdy's Restaurant* $$
Mut. █ *(092) 820 767.*
Ahmed Hamdy's Restaurant is the best known restaurant in Mut and good
for chicken or meat kebab or *kofta* with rice. The manager is very helpful.

DAKHLA: *Garden's Hotel Restaurant* $$
Mut. █ *(092) 821 577.*
Situated near the Old Town area of Mut, this restaurant is good value and
popular with travellers. The restaurant has a pleasant garden location.

FARAFRA: *Hussein Restaurant* $
Qasr al-Farafra.
This restaurant is centrally located, inexpensive and therefore popular with
budget travellers. Open for breakfast, lunch and early dinner.

FARAFRA: *Al-Badawiyya Safari and Hotel* $$
On the road to Bawiti, Qasr al-Farafra. █ *(092) 510 060.*
One of the best restaurants in the oasis, although the competition is not so
fierce. It is busy and serves genuinely good food as well as beer.

KHARGA: *Kharga Oasis Hotel* $$
El-Kharga. █ *(092) 921 500.*
Conveniently located in the centre of town, this drab concrete hotel
actually has a pleasant garden and and a terrace bar. ▼

KHARGA: *Pioneers Hotel* $$$
El-Kharga. █ *(092) 927 982.*
This five-star hotel restaurant may not provide the authentic desert experience,
but it does provide a refuge from the heat and an international menu. 📋 ▼

SIWA: *Alexander Restaurant* $
Alexander Hotel, Siwa.
Inside the Alexander Hotel, this friendly restaurant offers good local food.

SIWA: *Abdu Restaurant* $
Siwa. █ *(046) 460 2243.*
This restaurant has an expanded repertoire of dishes – it serves pizzas
alongside the ubiquitous grilled meats and chicken and spicy stews.

SIWA: *Siwa Safari Paradise Hotel* $$$
Siwa. █ *(046) 460 2289.*
In the most upmarket hotel in Siwa, this restaurant serves excellent food and
arranges traditional Siwan feasts with entertainment and dancing every week.

SHOPPING IN EGYPT

When it comes to shopping, the souqs and bazaars are undoubtedly Egypt's main attraction. The biggest and most famous is Cairo's Khan al-Khalili *(see pp88–90)*, a 500-year-old maze of commerce at the heart of the old Islamic city. While on first encounter it can seem to cater excessively to tourism, explore deeper and the narrow alleys become a bustling hive of small workshops turning out attractive jewellery, glass-, copper- and brassware. Here you can buy direct

Souq trader in Luxor smoking a water pipe

from the artisans and cut out the middleman. Most other towns and cities throughout the country also have souqs, with particularly good ones in Alexandria, Aswan and Port Said. For visitors intending to shop in these places it is essential to become acquainted with the art of bargaining. In contrast to the traditional nature of the souq, larger cities, such as Cairo and Alexandria, also possess modern shopping precincts, as well as shopping centres filled with globally recognized brand names.

OPENING HOURS

There are no strictly defined opening hours in Egypt – it depends on each individual proprietor. Generally, however, except for local grocery stores, which open early, business activity begins at around 9 or 10am. Businesses tend to close for a siesta from around 2 to 5pm, except in Cairo, where shops remain open all day. They then typically stay open until 9pm or later. In summer, in busy commercial areas, and especially Khan al-Khalili, the shutters often do not come down until 10 or 11pm, as people prefer to shop when it is cooler. Other souqs keep shorter hours, with stalls and businesses packing up around sunset. Friday is the official day off, although in Cairo many shops are open seven days a week. Those open on Friday may still close for a couple of hours in the middle of the day for noon prayers. Businesses owned by Christians may close on Sunday. During Ramadan shops close 30 minutes before sunset but reopen a couple of hours later. The whole country shuts down on major feasts, which include the Prophet's Birthday, Eid al-Fitr and Eid al-Adha *(see p39)*.

HOW TO PAY

Although their use as a form of payment is increasing, credit cards are typically still only accepted at larger or tourist-oriented shops, such as

those found in hotel complexes or shopping malls. Likewise, traveller's cheques are hardly accepted anywhere. In most places, it is necessary to pay in cash. Egyptian pounds are the country's only legal currency and purchases cannot usually be made in dollars.

SOUQS AND MARKETS

Besides Khan al-Khalili there are numerous other souqs and markets in Cairo, many worth a visit irrespective of whether you intend buying anything. Fruit and vegetables are sold at the many street markets scattered throughout the city. Every neighbourhood has one. In central Cairo there is the Tawfiqiyya market, one block north of Sharia 26th July, open so late that many stall-holders don't bother going home; they simply sleep beside their carts. On the east bank of the Nile, opposite Zamalek, again just north of Sharia 26th July, is Bulaq market selling textiles, second-hand clothing, car parts and military surplus.

Cairo's Downtown bookshops are excellent for books on Egypt

An even stranger mix is presented at the weekly Souq al-Gomaa, or Friday market, held just south of the Citadel, where the trade is in bric-à-brac and animals. It must be one of the few markets where you can buy both a set of 1930s crockery and a squawking cockatoo. Next to Ataba metro station, just north of Midan Opera, is Al-Azbakiyya Gardens. Here, second-hand books and magazines, many of them in English, are sold from a collection of cabins.

In Alexandria, Attarine is not so much a market as a maze of narrow alleyways lined with antique shops that spill their goods out on to the street. Al-Arish in northern Sinai also has a colourful Thursday-morning market frequented by local Bedouin who sell embroidered dresses and distinctive, hand-crafted jewellery.

Stacked merchandise in one of Cairo's markets

Examining the brass- and copperware in Khan al-Khalili

SHOPPING CENTRES

C AIRO – AND ALEXANDRIA to a lesser extent – has a rapidly growing number of large shopping centres or malls. These are filled with standard arcade-type outlets that sell everything from greetings cards to electrical goods, most of which are US and European imports. They also usually incorporate fast-food outlets and multi-screen cinemas. In Cairo, one of the city's most exclusive malls is the **World Trade Centre**, on the Corniche el-Nil, Bulaq, which houses a large number of outlets for clothes, fashion accessories and designer items. It has several upmarket restaurants and clubs, and one of the city's newest and most comfortable cinemas. Similarly chic is the **First Residence Mall** in Giza, which overlooks the zoo and forms part of an accommodation complex for the rich. The **Ramses Hilton Mall**, adjacent to the Ramses Hilton hotel in the city centre, is more family friendly and offers value-for-money shoes and clothing. On the top floor is a cinema and a snooker hall. Out in Heliopolis (see pp136–7) beside the Basilica is the **Horreyya Mall**, which has become a popular place for local kids to hang out.

BUYING ANTIQUES

M OST ANTIQUITIES offered to visitors are anything but antique. "Old" papyrus may well have been painted just last week and probably not on papyrus (which has all but vanished) but on dried banana leaves. Similarly, so-called ancient scarabs are often made by carving them from old bone and then feeding them to turkeys – the birds' gastric juices create a realistic ageing effect. However, in some respects this is all just as well because genuine antiquities (in general, anything over 100 years old) can only be exported with a licence from the Department of Antiquities.

HOW TO BARGAIN

B UYING AND SELLING in Egypt is traditionally a highly ritualized affair, in which bargaining is far more than just haggling for a cheap price. The aim of the exercise is to establish a fair price that both vendor and buyer are happy with. As part of the process, a shop-owner may well invite you to have a cup of tea or coffee and may literally turn the place upside down to show something. You should not feel obliged to buy because of this, as it is a common sales practice and all part of the ritual.

Bargaining even happens in city-centre shops over goods which appear to have a fixed price. It is in the souq, however, that it becomes a necessity if you want to avoid paying greatly over the odds.

Once you have identified an article that interests you, especially if it is an expensive one, be brave enough to offer half the price quoted by the shop-owner. Don't be put off by feigned indignation or mockery on the shop-keeper's part, and only raise your next offer by a small amount. Through a process of offer and counter-offer you should eventually arrive at a mutually agreeable price. If you don't reach a price you think is fair then simply say thank you and leave. Making to walk away can often have the effect of bringing the price tumbling down.

In theory, although you may feel uncomfortable, no one gets cheated. You, the buyer, have set the price yourself, so it follows that you are happy with what you have agreed to pay. The shop-keeper, for his part, will never sell at a loss, so he will certainly have made a profit on the deal.

The Sindbad Shopping Mall at Sindbad Beach Resort, Hurghada

Where to Shop in Egypt

Cairo's khan al-khalili (*see pp88–90*) is the first place to look for Egyptian souvenirs, while city-centre shopping focuses on the triangle of Sharia Talaat Harb, 26th July and Qasr el-Nil. The island suburb of Zamalek is a great hunting ground for boutiques specializing in ethnic crafts, designer wear and antiques. Elsewhere in Egypt, only the most determined shopaholics will find much to buy – perhaps colourful textiles and spices in Aswan and pottery and jewellery in the oases.

SOUVENIRS

Khan al-khalili in Cairo and other tourist bazaars in Upper Egypt are crammed with incredibly kitsch items, such as Nefertiti reading lamps, alabaster pyramids, stuffed leather camels and Tutankhamun baseball caps.

There are more worthwhile items to be found, however: attractive backgammon boards, like those used in Egyptian coffeehouses, at least have a practical purpose. Or you could buy your own *sheesha* (waterpipe), though you will also need to stock up on the special tobacco and the small clay pots that the tobacco is stuffed into. Small boxes inlaid with mother-of-pearl are pretty and very inexpensive. Inlaid chessboards are also popular buys. Almost everyone visiting Egypt picks up some papyrus – often cheap and poor quality, shoddily painted with scenes copied from pharaonic wall paintings. For better quality work, visit one of the **Dr Ragab Papyrus Institutes**, where you can get the genuine article, which will not crack or have the paint flake off when it is rolled.

Souvenir figure of Anubis

BRASS- AND COPPERWARE

Plates, coffeepots and trays of brass and copper are made in the workshops around Khan al-Khalili. For good examples, have a look at the Coppersmiths Market (Souq an-Nahassin) in Sharia al-Muizz li-Din Allah, south of the great mosques on Bein al-Qasreen.

Stallholder selling leather belts in Midan Ataba

HANDICRAFTS

Different parts of Egypt are associated with their own particular crafts, but much of the best of this work makes its way to Cairo. For example, **Al-Khatoun**, which is based in a restored Ottoman house behind the Mosque of al-Azhar, sells wrought-iron furniture that is made in a village just outside Cairo, as well as soft wall hangings, glassware and locally-made leather goods.

The nearby **Wikala of al-Ghouri**, an early 17th-century merchants' hostel, plays host to a number of artisans, whose work is sold on the premises. Opposite the entrance to the Mosque of Ibn Tulun, also in Islamic Cairo, **Khan Misr Touloun** is a beautiful gallery selling handicrafts from the villages and oases of Egypt. These include wooden chests, bowls and plates, blown glass, clay figurines, scarves and woven clothing. Based in Zamalek, **Egypt Craft** has Bedouin rugs and embroidery from Sinai and the northern Western Desert, hand-made paper from Muqattam and shawls from Upper Egypt. Also in Zamalek, located on the first floor of an apartment block overlooking the Nile, **Nomad** specializes in jewellery and traditional Bedouin craft and costumes.

CARPETS AND RUGS

Unlike morocco, Turkey or Iran, Egypt is not a big carpet producer. What you will find, however, are hardwearing, brown and beige striped, camel-hair rugs of Bedouin origin. The biggest selection is to be found in the Haret al-Fahhamin, a tight maze of alleys behind the Mosque of Al-Ghouri, across the road from Khan al-Khalili in Islamic Cairo. Many of the places mentioned in the Handicrafts section also stock Bedouin rugs. Connoisseurs might want to visit the weekly markets at Al-Arish, in northern Sinai, and in Dahab. In the area of the Pyramids,

Coppersmith's workshop in Sharia al-Muizz li-Din Allah

Locals gather at one of Cairo's colourful carpet bazaars

just off the road to Saqqara, the **Wissa Wassef Art Centre** specializes in very distinctive woollen rugs and wall hangings depicting rural and folkloric scenes. These can also be bought at **Senouhi**, a fascinating little shop on the fifth floor of an apartment block in Downtown Cairo. Senouhi also sells good quality jewellery, antiques, Bedouin rugs and art.

CLOTH AND TEXTILES

COTTON IS EGYPT's biggest cash crop, and department and clothing stores in central Cairo and Alexandria carry excellent quality, plain cotton shirts, T-shirts and underwear. Look out, in particular, for branches of **Safari**, found in all the big malls and in some hotel shopping complexes. Down in Middle Egypt, just across the Nile from Sohag, the village of Akhmim is the centre of an ancient weaving tradition. Legend has it that pharaohs were buried in shrouds of Akhmim silk. Still in production, but now in factories rather than the local workshops, the cloth comes in deep, rich colours, with elaborate floral and paisley-style patterns. It is extremely beautiful, but hard to find. The best bet is to go direct to the factories; otherwise some of the hotel shops in Luxor carry a small selection.

BELLYDANCING COSTUMES

SEQUINNED BRAS, beaded hip-bands, veils and flimsy skirts are sold in a couple of specialist shops in Khan al-Khalili. One is in the small passageway leading from Muski to Fishawi's coffee house. Serious practitioners should pay a visit to the studio of **Amira al-Khattan** in Mohandiseen, who tailors costumes to order.

JEWELLERY

EGYPT'S GOLD and silver shops are concentrated in the centre of Khan al-Khalili. Jewellery is sold by weight, with a little extra added for workmanship. The current gold prices are listed each day in the *Egyptian Gazette*. The most popular souvenirs are gold or silver cartouches with a given name engraved in hieroglyphics. Most of the shops in Khan al-Khalili can arrange to have this done.

SPICES AND HERBS

KHAN AL-KHALILI in Cairo and the souk in Aswan are both excellent for spices. Generally these are fresher and of better quality than any of the packaged variety sold in the West. They are also much cheaper, especially saffron. The stalls that sell spices often also have heaps of purplish, dried hibiscus leaves. When boiled up, strained and sugared, these make *karkade*, the excellent deep red, iced drink served in coffee houses. Some of the shop owners in the Spice Bazaar are also herbalists, who prepare traditional remedies for a variety of ailments.

A colourful display of aromatic spices in the Spice Bazaar

What to Buy in Egypt

Box inlaid with mother-of-pearl

EGYPT'S MAGICAL SOUQS and bazaars offer the visitor an eclectic mix of trinkets and souvenirs. The quality can vary greatly so always inspect the items closely and be prepared to haggle over the price *(see p293).* Sheesha (waterpipes), backgammon boards, decorative boxes and an array of kitsch paraphernalia fill the market stalls alongside traditional handicrafts often made by local artisans. Egyptian copperware and Muski glass are produced in Cairo's Khan al-Khalili *(see pp88–9),* while Bedouin jewellery traditionally comes from Sinai. The best hand-woven silk and cotton is made in Akhmim in Middle Egypt, famous for the quality of its weaving.

Sheesha
A fixture in every coffee house, a waterpipe makes an excellent gift. Decorated with stainless steel or brass fittings, the pipes use a special fragrant tobacco loosely packed into a clay pot.

Backgammon Board
Backgammon and chess are popular pastimes in Egypt. Sets of varying quality are readily available with the cheaper boards being crudely made and with little inlay. The better sets are made out of hard woods and inlaid with intricate designs of mother-of-pearl, bone or ivory.

Sandals
Reasonably-priced leather items such as bags, wallets and hand-crafted sandals are sold in most bazaars.

Glass and Pottery
Hand-blown, blue Muski glass is uniquely Egyptian and fashioned into plates, vases, glasses and candle-holders. Good hand-made pottery, like this rustic alabaster vase, is also easily found.

Perfume Bottles
These delicate glass perfume bottles are fashioned into intricate shapes. They come in various sizes and make wonderful gifts.

Bedouin Jewellery
Bedouin jewellery traditionally comes from Sinai and Siwa Oasis, and often features coins in its designs. While truly authentic Bedouin jewellery is hard to find, its styles have been widely imitated. Other popular designs include those based on Pharaonic, Islamic and Nubian motifs.

Copperware
A wide range of copper and brass goods is sold through-out Egypt but the Cairo souqs and workshops offer the widest selection. Typical buys include Arabic coffeepots, trays and hanging lamps as well as decorative pieces such as plates embossed with classic arabesques.

Clothes and Textiles

Cotton is one of Egypt's major crops and cotton clothes are popular. Plain and embroidered cotton shirts, trousers and galabiyyas (loose, all-in-one robes) are usually of high quality and good value. The brightly-coloured fabrics are excellent as scarves, cushion covers, wall hangings and throws. Garish belly-dancing outfits are also popular purchases.

Embroidered cotton shirts   **Brightly-coloured woven scarf**   **Sequined belly-dancing costume**

Tourist souvenirs

A myriad of kitsch reproductions of Pharaonic art, alabaster pyramids, stuffed leather camels, busts of Nefertiti and sheets of papyrus painted with scenes from temples or tombs are sold in all tourist areas. These items, along with trinket boxes, ashtrays, chessboards and sheesha *make popular and inexpensive gifts.*

Stuffed leather camel

Papyrus with Pharaonic scenes

Carved figurines of ancient gods

Bust of Nefertiti   **Alabaster ashtray**

Egyptian Music

The easiest way to recreate the Egyptian experience is to buy some Egyptian CDs or tapes. The choice ranges from traditional folk music and the mournful sounds of Umm Kolthum (see p125) to modern, bouncy Egyptian pop.

Spices and Flavourings

Colourful and fragrant, Egyptian spices can be located easily in the bazaars. Spices are sold loose by weight and are often far cheaper, fresher and of better quality than the pre-packaged ones sold in the west. One word of caution, however, Egyptian saffron is very cheap but it may not be top quality.

Carob   **Cinnamon**

Cloves   **Chillies**   **Turmeric**

Cayenne Pepper   **Cardamon pods**   **Saffron threads**

ENTERTAINMENT IN EGYPT

MOST PEOPLE FIND that the range of entertainment options in Egypt, especially outside Cairo, is surprisingly limited. Locals tend to fill their free time with visits to friends or family, or, in the case of the menfolk, whiling away the hours in a coffeehouse. A few major, well-attended cultural events punctuate the calendar, notably the Cairo International Book Fair in spring and the Cairo Film Festival in November and December *(see p41)*. Otherwise the annual high spots are tied

Passing time at a street-side coffeehouse in Cairo

into religion – the feast days of Eid al-Adha and Eid al-Fitr *(see p33)*, and the holy month of Ramadan. On these occasions, temporary fairgrounds are often set up in main squares, and there are plenty of performances of traditional music and folk dancing. Recent years have even seen a revival of the age-old art of story-telling, with actors and actresses half-performing, half-narrating tales from the likes of *The Thousand and One Nights* to enraptured audiences.

Cairo by night, its bright lights reflected in the calm waters of the Nile

Cairo, particularly during Ramadan, there are often music evenings and theatre productions held at the **Beit Zeinab Khatoun** and the **Al-Ghouri Palace for Traditional Culture**, part of the historic Al-Ghouri Complex *(see pp91–2)*. It is worthwhile trying to attend one or more of the performances at the Al-Ghouri Complex even if it is only to savour the atmosphere of the superb historic setting.

INFORMATION

THERE IS no shortage of entertainment guides in Egypt. Each month a glossy magazine called *Egypt Today* is published and includes extensive coverage of artistic and cultural events taking place throughout the country. It is available from bookstands and newsagents everywhere. The weekly English-language newspapers *Al-Ahram Weekly, The Middle East Times* and *The Cairo Times* also carry good listings information on what is showing at cinemas, galleries and the theatre, although their coverage is limited solely to Cairo. *The Big Croc,* a small, quarterly, pocket-sized magazine covering the city's nightlife and entertainment scene has now folded but may start up again in the future. Their website at www.ecroc.com is still operational.

There is no central booking office for shows and concerts, and it is generally necessary

to buy tickets from the relevant theatre or concert hall box office. It is also a sensible precaution to book tickets several days in advance.

ARABIC MUSIC

MUCH OF THE programming at the **New Cairo Opera House** and Alexandria's **Sayed Darwish Theatre** involves live performances of Arabic classical music. In Islamic

WHIRLING DERVISHES

THE AL-GHOURI COMPLEX in Islamic Cairo also stages whirling dervish performances every Wednesday and Saturday, starting at 9pm. The shows last for about an hour and are free. There is fairly limited seating, so it is always advisable to get there early to avoid having to stand. It is permitted to take photos but not to film on video.

Whirling dervish putting on a spectacular performance in Cairo

Belly Dancing

DESPITE A HERITAGE THAT dates back to Pharaonic times, modern-day belly dancing owes more to the European experience of Egypt in the 18th and 19th centuries. The sensual movements of the Egyptian dancers, who blended folk, gypsy and Ottoman dances, fired the imaginations of repressed Europeans. It is largely due to their descriptions that the dancing was associated with prostitution. Even

A belly dancer's backing musician

dedicated, professional belly dancers, who prefer the term "oriental dancer", get tarred with this brush. The advent of cinema put belly dancing on the big screen, increasing its popularity and making stars of the performers.

Today, despite its popularity, belly dancing still carries a social stigma which discourages Egyptian women from entering the profession and the gap is increasingly being filled by foreign dancers.

Dancers played an important part in ancient Egyptian ritual and celebration. Their poses, as shown here, clapping or using castanets are very similar to modern Egyptian dancing.

Salome, in the Bible, asked Herod for the head of John the Baptist as reward for her dancing. Late 19th-century writers added eroticism to the story, resulting in a series of scantily-clad cabaret acts as depicted in this 1909 music sheet cover.

Superstar Amira dances at the Giza Pyramids. Although belly dancing's popularity has been hit by the rise of Islamic fundamentalism, its top stars are among Egypt's highest earners.

Belly dancers at nightclubs in Central Cairo perform before mainly male audiences, who look but most definitely do not touch.

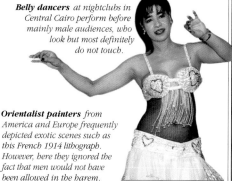

Orientalist painters from America and Europe frequently depicted exotic scenes such as this French 1914 lithograph. However, here they ignored the fact that men would not have been allowed in the harem.

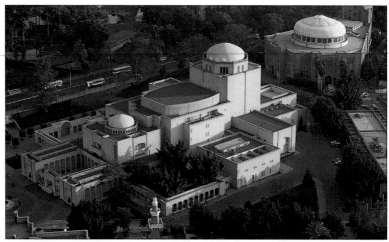

View of the Cairo Opera House from the top of the 185-m (606-ft) Cairo Tower *(see p84)*

BELLY DANCING AND FOLKLORIC DANCE

WHILE THE best dancers perform at the nightclubs attached to Cairo's five-star hotels, such as the **Haroun al-Rashid Club** and **Auberge du Nil**, where a seat costs about US $50 a head (buffet included), for pure entertainment visit the much cheaper **Palmyra**. The main act generally does not appear until at least 1am and the band will not call it a night until the sun is rising. Dancers can be seen at most hotels and tourist restaurants in the country. Venues in Luxor and Aswan, such as the **Aswan Cultural Palace**, often feature Egyptian folkloric dance troupes.

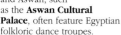

Billboards advertising forthcoming cultural events in Cairo

SOUND AND LIGHT SHOWS

EVERY MAJOR SITE in Egypt feels compelled to present a sound and light show. These begin once the sun goes down, and involve the monument being illuminated by coloured floodlights while a recorded voice narrates snippets of history and mythology. The narration often leaves a lot to be desired, but it is worth going just to revisit some of Egypt's sights by moonlight. The Pyramids at Giza, Luxor, Karnak, Philae and Abu Simbel all offer several shows a night in various languages.

WESTERN CLASSICAL MUSIC

EGYPT'S MAIN classical music venue is the **New Cairo Opera House**, on the island of Gezira. Its main hall hosts regular performances from a variety of visiting international artists. On such occasions a jacket and tie is compulsory for men. The small hall has nightly recitals by quartets, soloists and ensembles and is also used by the Cairo Symphony Orchestra, which gives concerts here every Saturday from September to mid-June. The Cairo classical music scene is well covered in *Al-Ahram Weekly*. In Alexandria, both the **Alexandria Conference Hall** and **Sayed Darwish Theatre** host classical concerts organized by the French, Italian or German consulates. Details of what's on are posted in the window of the Elite restaurant *(see p289)*. Otherwise, you are unlikely to hear much Western classical music in Egypt.

OPERA AND BALLET

THE PREMISES of the **New Cairo Opera House** are shared by both the Cairo Ballet Company and the Cairo Opera Company. The season is limited, and productions are few, although they are sometimes supplemented by visiting companies. There are also occasional dance performances at Cairo's **Gumhuriyya Theatre**. Almost every year now, the Ministry of Culture also mounts a grand production of *Aida*, the opera written in honour of the opening of the Suez Canal *(see pp60–61)*. Previous performances have been held at the temples of Hatshepsut and Karnak in Luxor, but most recently the venue has been the Pyramids. It is a very high-profile occasion, drawing opera-lovers from all over the world. Egypt's overseas tourist offices will be able to provide full details on when the next grand event takes place.

Inside a young and fashionable bar in upmarket Mohandiseen, Cairo

BARS AND DISCOS

Despite being predominantly Islamic, there are plenty of bars in Egypt beyond those in the hotels – look for signs for "cafeterias". Some of the best are to be found in Alexandria, notably the **Cap d'Or** and **Havana**, two beautiful old places that feel like real Mediterranean tavernas. In Cairo, nightlife centres on the upmarket neighbourhoods of Zamalek and Mohandiseen. Bars such as **Deals**, **L'Aubergine**, **Le Tobasco** and **Bull's Eye** cater mainly for young wealthy Egyptians, as well as the city's large expatriate community. Later on, those with the energy move on to the busy Downtown discos which play hip-hop and dance music. These include **Space Disco**, Egypt's only purpose-built dance venue, part of a large, modern entertainment complex called Cairo Land.

Red Sea and Sinai resorts such as Sharm el-Sheikh, Naama Bay and Hurghada are also packed full of bars and discos. But the scene is constantly changing, so pick

A hotel disco at Agami, on the North Coast, west of Alexandria

up *Sinai Today* or *Red Sea Today* from bookshops or newsstands to get all the details on what's happening.

The resorts along the north coast have few good bars or discos. Typically these are attached to hotels like the **Summer Moon** at Agami, the so-called St Tropez of Egypt.

ROCK, JAZZ AND POP

Rock, jazz and pop concerts are virtually unheard of. A handful of artists, such as The Grateful Dead, Shirley Bassey and, at the Millennium

celebrations, Jean-Michel Jarre, have played the Pyramids but such events happen very rarely. Egyptian pop stars don't do concerts either. Practically the only place to hear live contemporary music is in hotel lounges and bars. Every major five-star establishment has a resident cabaret singer or jazz quartet, but don't expect to recognize any names. About the only dedicated live venue in the country is the **Cairo Jazz Club**, a small, suitably smoky joint, with a band every night, usually drawn from the tiny but enthusiastic local scene.

DIRECTORY

ARABIC MUSIC AND WHIRLING DERVISHES

Alexandria Conference Hall
International Conference Centre, Shatby, Alexandria.
((03) 487 8093.

Al-Ghouri Palace for Traditional Culture
Sharia al-Muizz li-Din Allah, Cairo. **Map** 2 F5.
((02) 510 0823.

Beit Zeinab Khatoun and Beit al-Harawi
Harat al-Azhar, Cairo.
Map 2 F5.
((02) 735 7001.

New Cairo Opera House
Sharia at-Tahrir, Gezira, Cairo. **Map** 1 A5.
((02) 739 8114.

Sayed Darwish Theatre
22 Tariq al-Horreyya, Alexandria.
((03) 486 5106.

BELLY DANCING

Aswan Cultural Palace
Corniche, Aswan.
((097) 313 390.

Auberge du Nil
Royal Nile Tower Hotel, Corniche el-Nil, Cairo.
Map 5 A5.
((02) 362 1717.

Haroun al-Rashid Club
Semiramis Hotel, Corniche el-Nil, Cairo.
Map 5 A4.
((02) 795 7171.

Palmyra
Just south of Sharia 26th July, between Sharia Sharif and Mohammed Farid, Cairo.
Map 2 D4, 6 D2.

SOUND AND LIGHT SHOWS

For all sites
((02) 386 3469.
w www.sound-light. egypt.com

OPERA AND BALLET

Gumhuriyya Theatre
12 Sharia al-Gumhuriyya, Cairo. **Map** 2 D3.
((02) 390 7707.

BARS AND DISCOS

L'Aubergine
5 Al-Sayyid al-Bakri, Zamalek, Cairo. **Map** 1 A3.
((02) 738 0080.

Bull's Eye
32 Sharia Jedda, Mohandiseen, Cairo.
((02) 361 6888.

Cap d'Or
4 Sharia Adib, Alexandria.
((03) 487 5177.

Deals
Al-Sayyid al-Bakri, Zamalek, Cairo.
Map 1 A3.
((02) 736 0502.

Havana
Sharia Tariq al-Horreyya, Alexandria.

Space Disco
Cairo Land, 1 Sharia Salah Salem, Cairo. **Map** 3 C4.
((02) 365 6913.

Summer Moon
Summer Moon Hotel, on the beach front, Agami.
((03) 433 0367.

Le Tabasco
8 Midan Amman, Doqqi, Cairo.
((02) 336 5583.

ROCK, JAZZ AND POP

Cairo Jazz Club
197 Sharia 26th July, Mohandiseen, Cairo.
((02) 345 9939.

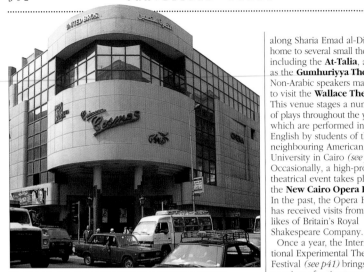

The Cosmos cinema, one of many local movie houses in Cairo

CINEMA

IN RECENT YEARS, cinema in Egypt has had an overhaul. Large, modern multiplexes have been opened in Cairo and Alexandria and old movie houses have been refurbished. Programming is usually split between Arabic films and the latest Hollywood releases, with foreign films screened in their original languages and subtitled in Arabic. All films suffer censorship except those screened during the Cairo International Film Festival *(see p41)*, where the possibility of seeing exposed flesh on the big screen ensures packed houses.

A trip to the cinema is an experience in itself. Audiences are extremely animated, greeting screen events with cheers, boos or applause. In Downtown Cairo, particularly around the Sharia Talaat Harb area, there is a plethora of old, single-screen cinemas, several of which, including the **Metro, Miami** and **Radio**, show English-language films. Better equipped cinemas are found in the modern shopping malls and include **Horreyya I & II** in Heliopolis, the **Ramses Hilton I & II**, and the **Renaissance** at the World Trade Centre. In

Colourful advertising for the Diana Palace cinema

Alexandria, the **Amir** and **Metro** are outstandingly beautiful period cinemas, which are worth a visit for the architecture alone. But by far the most luxurious cinema in Alexandria is the **Renaissance**, attached to the Smouha Mall, to the east of the city centre.

Up-to-date details of all the films currently being screened are published in *The Egyptian Gazette, Middle East Times* and *Al-Ahram Weekly*.

THEATRE

THE NUMEROUS local theatres in Cairo are testimony to a strong dramatic tradition in Egypt. Productions are performed in Arabic and are of local fare, typically slapstick comedy with a bit of belly-dancing thrown in. Cairo's Downtown area, particularly along Sharia Emad al-Din, is home to several small theatres including the **At-Talia**, as well as the **Gumhuriyya Theatre**. Non-Arabic speakers may wish to visit the **Wallace Theatre**. This venue stages a number of plays throughout the year which are performed in English by students of the neighbouring American University in Cairo *(see p72)*. Occasionally, a high-profile theatrical event takes place at the **New Cairo Opera House**. In the past, the Opera House has received visits from the likes of Britain's Royal Shakespeare Company.

Once a year, the International Experimental Theatre Festival *(see p41)* brings in a variety of acting troupes from all around the world to perform at venues throughout Cairo. The *Al-Ahram Weekly* newspaper is an excellent source of information on all such events. The newspaper also lists details of all the regular theatre performances taking place in Cairo.

CASINOS

MANY OF EGYPT's five-star hotels have casinos, open to non-Egyptians only (passports must be shown at the door). All games are conducted in US dollars or other major foreign currencies, with a minimum stake of US $1. The dress code is smart casual. Hotels with casinos include the **Semiramis Intercontinental**, the **Marriott Cairo** and the **Nile Hilton** in Cairo and the **As-Salamek Palace** in Alexandria. Note that in Egypt the word "casino" is sometimes used to denote a bar – this is usually the case when it is encountered outside a hotel.

Billboard advertising an Arabic theatre production

SPECTATOR SPORTS

FOOTBALL RULES in Egypt. A big match is one of the few times when the country is silent – at least until the final whistle, when the streets fill with flag-waving, horn-honking fans. Footballing life is dominated by Cairo, home to the country's two biggest clubs, Ahly and Zamalek. These clubs, along with Alexandria's Ittihad team, boast players of international standard. Games between Cairo's big clubs are the highlight of the sporting calendar and take place at the **Cairo Stadium** in Medinat Nasr. Tickets for all major games are in high demand and can be difficult to obtain.

Media sports coverage focuses almost entirely on football, even in summer when there are no matches. Of other sports, the most prominent is squash. The annual August Al-Ahram International Squash Tournament draws competitors from all over the world to play in glass-enclosed courts

Football fans cheering on the Egyptian national soccer team in Cairo

set up next to the Pyramids. The Pyramids also feature as the start and finishing point in the annual Pharaoh's Rally, a four-wheel-drive and trail-bike desert race in October. Other spectator sports include rowing races on the Nile every Friday between November and April, and horse racing at the **Gezira Sporting Club** and the **Alexandria Sporting Club** from October to May. Since

the year 2000, there has also been an annual showjumping competition held in the second two weeks of February at the Alexandria Sporting Club. For something more unusual, watch local Bedouin participate in inter-tribe camel racing as part of the annual Sharm el-Sheikh festival *(see p38)*.

Details of all sporting fixtures are in *The Egyptian Gazette* and *Al-Ahram Weekly*.

Coffee House Culture

FOUND ON ALMOST every street corner, the ubiquitous coffee house *(ahwa)* plays an important role in the everyday life of Egyptians. Like the cafés of continental Europe, *ahwas* are social places where Egyptians can meet to talk with friends, idle away an hour reading a newspaper, or watch football on TV. Frequented predominantly by men, coffee houses are busy at all hours of the day and many remain open around the clock.

Card players with *sheeshas* concentrate on their game

As well as tea *(shai)* and coffee *(ahwa)*, most serve fresh lemon juice *(lamoon)*, iced *karkade*, a refreshing crimson drink made from boiled hibiscus leaves, *zabaady*, a yoghurt drink and *sahleb*, a warm drink made with semolina powder, milk and chopped nuts. No coffee house would be complete without the *sheesha* (waterpipe) through which tobacco is smoked.

A typical coffee house, such as Fishawi's in Khan al-Khalili, is often little more than a collection of old tables and chairs placed in a narrow alleyway.

Chess is not particularly common in Egypt but a few coffee houses are venues for fans of the game, including the popular Horreyya situated in Downtown Cairo.

Backgammon and dominoes are the most popular of the coffee house games with animated players slamming down their pieces.

Sheeshas (waterpipes) are offered in coffee houses as an accompaniment to drinks. The tobacco is soaked in molasses or sometimes apple juice.

Coffee houses, like Horreyya, are often all-male environments but foreign women are usually welcomed.

CHILDREN'S ENTERTAINMENT

WHEN THE HEAT of Cairo becomes too much, **Dr Ragab's Pharaonic Village** can provide a welcome break and keep children thoroughly entertained. The village is an ancient Egypt theme park situated on the southern tip of Al-Qorsaiah Island which lies on the west bank of the Nile, 10 km (6 miles) south of the city centre. Visitors take small boats through the reed beds viewing scenes of Pharaonic daily life recreated by costumed actors. The park also boasts a replica temple.

The **Cairo Puppet Theatre**, just north of Midan Opera, gives performances of traditional tales like Sindbad and Ali Baba. The plays take place most mornings from October to May and although in Arabic, they are highly visual and easy to follow. Another alternative is the **Cairo Zoo** in Giza. The zoo is set in pleasant grounds on the west bank of the Nile opposite Rhoda Island. Although it has promised to concentrate on improving conditions, some may find the animal enclosures distressing.

On the outskirts of Cairo are several recently built amusement parks. **Dream Park**, northwest of Cairo, has Disney-type rides, go-karts and games arcades, as well as golf and tennis courts. **Aquapark**, 32 km (20 miles) east of Cairo, offers waterchutes, a wave pool and a playground area. The nearby theme park **Gero Land** also has rollercoasters, go-karts and other thrill rides.

Children enjoying themselves at the fairground of a local festival

Elsewhere in Egypt there are few concessions made to children's entertainment. However, activities are often laid on for children during *moulids* (saints' days) and other festivals. At the coast, many of the bigger resort hotels now run activity centres designed to keep younger guests amused.

COFFEE HOUSES

THERE IS an abundance of coffee houses *(ahwas)* in Egypt, each one filling its own niche and frequented by its own particular clientele. Several of the more interesting coffee houses are tucked away down tight alleys and include the Downtown **Ash-Shams**, notable for its garishly painted walls. One of the oldest and most famous of all the coffee houses is **Fishawi's** *(see p90)*. Buried in the narrow lanes of Khan al-Khalili, it is open 24 hours and is as much a

must-see sight for visiting out-of-town Egyptians as it is for foreigners. In Alexandria, coffee houses line the Corniche, while in Aswan and Luxor there are several dotted around the busy souq areas.

WEDDINGS

THURSDAY NIGHT is the end of the Muslim week and the traditional night for weddings in Egypt. Throughout the country celebrations are heralded with drums, tambourines, honking cars and women wailing. Weddings are very public affairs, where musicians, dancing processions and showers of rose petals fill the streets, and foreign spectators are often invited to join the celebrations.

A young child enjoying the beach at the resort of Dahab

Sports and Adventure Holidays

Sign for horse riding in the desert around Cairo

WITH THE RUGGED MOUNTAINS of Sinai, the spectacular coral reefs of the Red Sea and the wide expanse of its desert plains, Egypt is well-equipped to offer the visitor a wide range of outdoor activities. Exploration by camel or on horseback is a favourite pastime, while diving and snorkelling in the Red Sea is among the finest in the world. Numerous resorts also offer sailing, windsurfing, parasailing and water-skiing. In Cairo, the luxury hotels offer golf, tennis and health-club facilities, which are usually open to non-residents.

GOLF

ONCE CONFINED to a few courses in Cairo and Alexandria, golf is now a booming industry in Egypt. In Central Cairo, **The Gezira Club** offers a nine-hole course while, at the **Mena House Oberoi** course, built in 1902, enthusiasts can play in the shadow of the Giza Pyramids. New courses east of Cairo include **Katameya Heights** with 27 holes and **Mirage City** near the airport. The **Jolie Ville Golf Resort** in Sharm el-Sheikh has excellent facilities in a superb setting.

DIVING AND SNORKELLING

THE RED SEA is renowned for the clarity of its waters and the variety of its spectacular corals and fish. The southern tip of the Sinai Peninsula, the Gulf of Aqaba and the coast near Hurghada are popular destinations and all the large resorts here have dive clubs. As well as short trips, clubs organise dive safaris, on "live-aboards" – vessels on which divers can spend up to two weeks at sea, visiting dive sites. Clubs also run a variety of courses for all levels of divers, including the popular five-day, open-water PADI course. When choosing a dive centre, it is important to check that the instructors speak your language fluently, are fully certified, and have equipment that is in first-rate condition. Reputable centres include

the **Aquarius Diving Centre** in Hurghada, the **Canyon Dive Club** in Dahab, and the **Camel Dive Club** in Naama Bay which also has facilities for disabled divers.

Snorkelling in the Red Sea is a great alternative to diving and is offered by most diving centres. However, rental gear can be of poor quality so it is best to bring your own gear or buy it in Cairo. Wear a T-shirt and use waterproof sunscreen. Hotels and dive centres can advise on the reefs best suited to your ability.

Sign advertising boat hire in Cairo

HORSE AND CAMEL RIDING

STABLES HIRING OUT horses are basic affairs and it is best to use recommended ones. **MG** stables at the Pyramids of Giza

have well-kept horses. A five-hour round-trip between Giza and Saqqara *(see pp158–9)* can be taken from Giza or, in reverse, from stables at the **Saqqara Country Club**. Horses can also be hired from **Al-Ferousseya** at the Gezira Sporting Club in Zamalek and the **Az-Zahraa Stud Farm** near Heliopolis, famous for breeding Arabian horses.

Camel rides are popular, particularly at the Pyramids and around Aswan. Be wary of unscrupulous owners who may try to charge a lot more than the going rate of LE 20–30 per hour. Long treks in the Western Desert and to traditional Bedouin villages in Sinai can be arranged with local operators.

HIKING

THE SPECTACULAR interior of the southern Sinai peninsula is a hiker's paradise of jagged mountains, natural springs and forgotten ruins. The area is known as the **St Catherine Protectorate** and hikers must be accompanied by a Bedouin guide. Treks include the well-trodden Mt Sinai, the 2,383-m (7,900-ft) summit of Jebel Abbas Pasha and two gentler walks along wadis. Treks can be arranged at St Catherine's village and information obtained from the Visitors' Centre at St Catherine's Monastery *(see pp218–21).*

A crown of thorns, one of many fascinating encounters on a Red Sea dive

Hot-air balloons drifting gracefully above the Valley of the Kings

ADVENTURE HOLIDAYS

ALTHOUGH MOST visitors to Egypt are likely to spend a day or two snorkelling or diving or an afternoon camel riding, many of the activities that Egypt has to offer can also be enjoyed as part of an organized adventure holiday lasting a week or more.

Specialist holidays can be organised in the US and UK before departure using reputable travel agents such as **Abercrombie & Kent Travel, Guerba Adventure & Discovery Holidays** or, in the US, **Overseas Adventure Travel.** There are also several established, Cairo-based organisations, including the **Egypt Exploration Society**, that offer a wide range of tours for the visitor. Dive packages and most adventure holidays can also be booked through large hotel resorts and local travel agents. Such trips are often an unforgettable experience, taking visitors beyond the usual tourist trail.

The rugged interior of the Sinai Peninsula is popular for climbing and hiking tours while the potentially hazardous environment of the Western Desert offers a different type of adventure. An organized desert safari is the easiest way to experience the thrill of desert driving and camping. Trips exploring the desert around oases such as Kharga or Bahariyya (*see pp252–3*) are easy to arrange locally.

Hot-air balloon flights over the Valley of the Kings in Luxor are organised by **Balloons Over Egypt** and offer magnificent views of the ancient site.

SURVIVAL
GUIDE

Practical Information

EGYPT HAS MADE significant progress in improving its tourist infrastructure and the provision of services and security to visitors. Nevertheless certain obstacles remain. Major cities usually have adequate signposting, but most of the monuments still lack proper on-site information panels, signs and labelling. One of ancient Egypt's gifts to the world was bureaucracy and modern-day

Sign for the Temple of Amun, Siwa

visitors must now contend with a sometimes bewildering and frustrating number of formal and informal procedures. With six millennia of history behind them, Egyptians are not in as much of a hurry as the rest of the world. Problems can often be avoided by allowing extra time for even the most minor tasks. However, patience and a good sense of humour are definite assets on a trip to Egypt.

A tourist sign providing general information at Saqqara

Passports and Visas

VISITORS TO EGYPT should possess a passport valid for six months beyond their planned date of entry. All North Americans, Australians, New Zealanders and most Europeans need a tourist visa to enter the country. These can be obtained in advance from Egyptian consulates abroad, but it usually only takes a few minutes to buy one on arrival at Cairo, Hurghada or Luxor airport. Note that general visas cannot be purchased at the overland crossings of Rafah and Taba, nor can they be obtained at Aswan, Suez or Nuweiba.

Both the single-visit and multiple-entry types of visa allow visitors to stay in Egypt for one month; multiple-entry visas allow the bearer to go in and out of the country three times during that period. Visas that are valid only for Sinai can be purchased at the border crossing at Taba, at Sharm el-Sheikh airport

and at the ports of Sharm el-Sheikh and Nuweiba. These visas last for only two weeks and restrict visitors to the Aqaba coastline as far as the main resort of Sharm el-Sheikh and the vicinity of St Catherine's Monastery.

Be prepared for individual officials to introduce new regulations or to be generally obstructive. In such an event, try to keep calm and friendly.

Customs and Duty-Free Allowances

IF YOU WISH to bring personal supplies of cigarettes and alcohol into Egypt, it is best to purchase them when you arrive at either Cairo or Luxor airport. Both have duty-free shops, before and after the Customs checkpoint. The shops before Customs are generally better stocked and less crowded than those after.

Semiramis Hotel, Cairo, which offers duty-free facilities

Upon arrival, visitors can purchase 4 litres of alcohol, or 3 litres and a case of beer, and 200 cigarettes. If visitors elect not to purchase these items upon arrival, they have 24 hours to get to a duty-free shop elsewhere, where they can purchase 3 litres of alcohol and 200 cigarettes.

There are duty-free shops in Cairo at the Semiramis Hotel, the Giza Sheraton and at the end of Sharia Gamiat ad-Dowal al-Arabiyya in Mohandiseen. There are also duty-free shops in the centre of Luxor and Hurghada. Bring your passport, as you will be asked for it in these shops. You may also be approached by Egyptians asking if they can borrow your passport to visit the shop themselves.

The allowance for visitors bringing cigarettes or alcohol that have been purchased in another country is 1 litre of alcohol and 200 cigarettes.

If you bring a video camera or computer into Egypt, it must be declared on "Form D" upon arrival. If either of those items is stolen, be sure to obtain a police report. Otherwise when you are leaving, it will be assumed that you have sold them and a duty of 100 per cent will be levied.

Language

MOST URBAN and professional Egyptians speak a little English and sometimes some French as well. Egyptians working in the tourist sector are accustomed to visitors who cannot speak Arabic and will speak enough English to

Ticket kiosk at Philae – vendors usually understand some English

take care of your needs. It is still worth mastering a few Arabic words and phrases. Recognizing Arabic numerals can help in getting around and dealing with money, while being able to convey a polite greeting will inevitably delight the recipient. If you are planning to travel off the beaten tourist track, a little knowledge of basic Arabic can be useful, if not essential.

PUBLIC CONVENIENCES

Public toilets are rare in Egypt, although major tourist sites often have some type of provision. Facilities in petrol stations, bus and train terminals and cafés in the poorer quarters are likely to be unpleasant, squat toilets. Toilet paper is unlikely to be provided, so it is a good idea to carry tissues with you. Small packets are available from kiosks, stores and street vendors everywhere. Better hotels and restaurants usually have flush toilets. These are often staffed by an attendant who will provide toilet paper and turn on the tap for you. *Baksheesh* of 25–50 piastres is customary for this service.

Electric plug adaptor with two round pins

ELECTRICAL ADAPTORS

The electric current is 220V and sockets take two-pin plugs. A travel converter will enable you to use appliances from abroad. Brief power cuts are common, so it is a good idea to carry a torch with you.

TIME

As well as being two hours ahead of the standard GMT, Egypt often uses its own concept of time – what Egyptians and foreigners alike call "IBM" time, which stands for *Inshallah, Bokra, Maalesh*.

Inshallah (God willing) is a way of remembering Allah in every action, but sometimes, in the context of tourism, it suggests that something might or might not happen. *Bokra* literally means "tomorrow", but it might be used to mean two days, two weeks or perhaps never. It definitely means "not today". *Maalesh* means "Never mind, don't worry, forget about it."

Egyptians do not like to say no or disappoint guests, so you must be persistent and good-humoured in trying to establish when, or if, a desired outcome is likely to occur.

CONVERSION CHART

Imperial to Metric
1 inch = 2.54 centimetres
1 foot = 30 centimetres
1 mile = 1.6 kilometres
1 ounce = 28 grams
1 pound = 454 grams
1 pint = 0.6 litre
1 gallon = 4.6 litres

Metric to Imperial
1 millimetre = 0.04 inch.
1 centimetre = 0.4 inch
1 metre = 3 feet 3 inches
1 kilometre = 0.6 mile
1 gram = 0.04 ounce
1 kilogram = 2.2 pounds
1 litre = 1.8 pints

DIRECTORY			

EGYPTIAN EMBASSIES ABROAD

Australia
112 Glenmore Road,
Paddington, Sydney,
NSW 2021.
☎ (02) 9332 3388.

Britain
2 Lowndes Street,
London SW1X 9EG.
☎ (020) 7235 9777.
W www.egypt-embassy.org.uk

Canada
454 Laurier Avenue East,
Ottawa, ON K1N 6R3.
☎ (613) 234 4958.

Ireland
12 Clyde Road,
Dublin 4.
☎ (01) 606 566.

Israel
54 Rehov Basel,
Tel Aviv.
☎ (03) 546 5151.

Egyptian Consulate
68 Afraty Street,
Bna Betkha, Eilat.
☎ (07) 597 6115.

Jordan
3rd Floor, Jebel Amman
Zahran Street, Amman.
☎ (06) 641 375.

Egyptian Consulate
Al-Wahdat al-Jarbiyya,
Sharia al-Istiqlal, Aqaba.

United States
2310 Decatur Place NW
Washington DC 20008.
☎ (202) 234 3903.

Egyptian Consulate
1110 Second Ave,
New York, NY 10022.
☎ (212) 759 7120.

EGYPTIAN TOURIST OFFICES

In the UK
170 Piccadilly,
London W1V 9DD.
☎ (020) 7493 5283.

In the US
630 Fifth Avenue,
Suite 1706,
New York, NY 10111.
☎ (212) 332 2570.

In Canada
1253 McGill College Ave,
Suite 250, Montreal,
Quebec, H3B 2Y5.
☎ (514) 861 4420.

Tips for Visitors

ALTHOUGH PRACTICAL INFORMATION is sometimes hard to obtain from the Egyptian tourist board, the major offices are worth visiting as most of the staff usually speak good English and are knowledgeable about the sites. Travel agencies and hotel receptionists are often more helpful and can usually offer up-to-date advice on accommodation, transport and other practicalities.

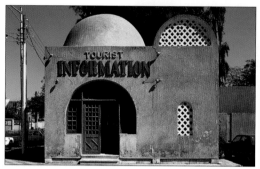

Tourist information office at Aswan with Nubian-style domes

OPENING HOURS

THE MAJOR HISTORIC sites and museums are open daily from 9am until 5pm (6pm in summer). During Ramadan, they may open a little later than the advertised time and will close around 3pm.

Government and administrative offices generally close on Fridays, while shops and stores sometimes close on Sundays. Most stores are open from 9am until 2 or 3pm, then again from 5 to 9pm. However, shops in tourist areas usually stay open all day and late into the night.

During Ramadan, offices and shops open later than normal and close around 3pm. They re-open around 8 or 9pm, and remain open until quite late.

VISITING RELIGIOUS SITES

EGYPT GENERALLY welcomes non-Muslim visitors to its mosques *(see pp32–3)*. It is, however, advisable to seek permission before visiting any mosque outside Cairo and Alexandria, where residents may be less accustomed to seeing tourists.

With the exception of the mosques of Al-Hussein and Sayyida Zeinab, most religious sites in Cairo are seen as historic monuments, open to non-Muslims from 9am until 4pm. However, tourists should not intrude in any way on worshippers and avoid visiting at prayer times.

Modest dress is essential at all mosques. In some places, women may be asked to cover their hair (a scarf will be provided). You must also remove your shoes before entering the mosque. There is sometimes a shoe custodian (who will expect a small *baksheesh*) or you can leave them outside the door. If you want to climb the minaret, carry your shoes, with the two soles pressed together.

Similar rules apply when visiting monasteries, though you will not have to remove your shoes. With the exception of St Catherine's, which is

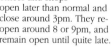

Modestly dressed women visiting a mosque

Greek Orthodox, monasteries in Egypt are Coptic. All the monasteries quite readily admit visitors during the day, except during Lent.

DISABLED TRAVELLERS

FEW TOURIST SITES in Egypt are equipped for disabled visitors. Steep flights of stairs, deep sand and the poor condition of streets combine to make life difficult for those who are less able. On a more positive note, Egyptians are not embarrassed by disability and museum and hotel staff are always willing to help.

The Egyptian national travel company, **Misr Travel**, has tours and accommodation suited for disabled travellers, while **ETAMS Tours** organizes trips specifically for people with physical disabilities. For those who wish to experience the magic of swimming and diving in the Red Sea, the **Camel Dive Club** has facilities and training geared towards those with special needs.

STUDENTS

FULL-TIME STUDENTS can enjoy discounts at museums and historical sites, and reduced air, rail and bus fares with an International Student Identity Card (ISIC). If you arrive in Cairo without one, you can obtain a card at the Egyptian Scientific Centre, 23 Sharia al-Manial on Rhoda Island. A student card can also be purchased at several down-town hotels, but beware of shops offering forgeries.

International Student Identity Card

ETIQUETTE

EGYPT IS ONE of the most liberal Muslim countries in the Middle East, and its citizens are justifiably famous for their tolerance, generosity and warmth. However, the presence of five-star hotels,

Visitor about to engage in the ancient art of haggling in Aswan's souk

beach resorts, casinos and other trappings of Western culture, such as mobile phones, luxury cars and bars serving alcohol, may lead the casual visitor to conclude that Egypt is more open and liberal than it really is. At its heart, Egypt is still a deeply conservative country and the dominant values are Islamic. To get closer to a truly welcoming people, visitors need to be aware of these values and modify their dress and behaviour accordingly.

Modest dress is essential if one wishes to avoid giving offence or, for women, attracting undue attention. Shorts and swimwear are really only acceptable at beach resorts, primarily along the Aqaba coast on the Red Sea, and the private beaches of certain hotels in Hurghada. In other areas, use your discretion, but remember that, for both sexes, bare shoulders are considered offensive.

Boorish behaviour, such as arrogance or bluntness, can create problems, so remain patient and polite when confronted with bureaucratic hassles or persistent touts. A gentle sense of humour helps to ameliorate difficult circumstances, and is the approach most often deployed by Egyptians themselves.

Egyptians of the same sex frequently hold hands and kiss in public, but open displays of affection between the sexes are rare and can cause deep offence.

If invited to someone's home, a small gift of flowers or sweets is appropriate. For men, sitting with legs crossed and showing the sole of your foot is seen as rude. Shopkeepers will offer tea or soft drinks during negotiations, but this incurs no obligation to buy. When bargaining, however, once you have agreed a price, it is rude to refuse to purchase the item.

Egyptians are aware of their country's weaknesses but do not appreciate it when foreigners point them out.

Avoid criticizing religion or the president, and issues such as *baksheesh* or the condition of the streets or buildings.

PHOTOGRAPHY

Museums and major tourist sites charge for the use of video and still cameras. The use of a flash is often forbidden, so bring some fast film with you (400 ASA or higher) as it is hard to find in Egypt. Always ask permission before taking someone's photograph, especially of women or religious figures and in rural areas. Taking photographs that show Egypt as backward or poor may also cause offence. Visitors should remember that it is forbidden to take pictures of army bases, airports, government buildings, dams, bridges or anything considered vital to security.

Tourists photographing the Sphinx near the Pyramids of Giza

Security

IN SPITE OF THE SIZE and population density of its cities, Egypt is one of the safest countries in the world for travellers. The most serious crime that most visitors are likely to encounter is minor theft, which is rare, especially away from congested tourist areas. Visitors should, of course, take the usual precautions of wearing a money belt and keeping a close watch on cameras and bags. In fact, tales abound of taxi drivers, hotel personnel and ordinary citizens returning lost property and keeping a look-out for the welfare of guests.

POLICE

VISITORS TO EGYPT are often surprised by the numbers of police posted on street corners, at intersections and outside government buildings and historic sites. This is not a sign of imminent or recent trouble, but has simply been the status quo since the 1960s.

Different police forces deal with different aspects of law and order. The Municipal Police handle crime and are recognizable by their uniforms – khaki in winter and tan or white in summer. Traffic Police wear similar uniforms, with the addition of striped cuffs. Both forces deal with accidents and can help in emergencies, but few speak English.

The Tourist Police are the agency visitors should turn to in times of trouble. Ordinary ranks wear khaki uniforms, while officers wear black in winter, white in summer. Easily identified by "Tourist Police"

armbands, they are stationed at ports, airports, stations, tourist sites and museums and usually speak some English.

The Central Security Police guard embassies, banks and highways. Dressed in black uniforms and armed with Kalashnikovs, their appearance can be very intimidating. In general they are no cause for concern, but if you do find yourself caught up in a demonstration, get right away immediately.

Unless drugs or espionage are suspected, foreigners are usually treated with extreme politeness by the police.

Sign for police guarding antiquities

PETTY CRIME

EGYPT IS PROUD of its low crime rate and in general visitors should have little trouble as long as they take sensible precautions and avoid travelling alone when away from tourist areas. As in any large city, crowded areas, such as the Khan al-Khalili, provide the ideal conditions for pickpockets and petty thieves. Keep your money and passport in a money belt or pouch and your camera and other valuables out of sight. Security on camp sites, hostels and cheap hotels is likely to be poor, so leave valuables at the reception desk, or take them with you. If travelling by car, do not leave anything of value visible or accessible.

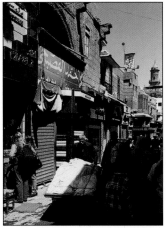

Crowded street near Khan al-Khalili, where it is wise for visitors to mind their valuables

TRAVEL AND TERRORISM

THE AREA COMMONLY known as Middle Egypt – which includes the cities of Minya, Asyut and Sohag and the historic sites of the Tombs of Beni Hassan, Tell al-Amarna, Abydos, Dendara and several monasteries – is a potential hot spot for trouble *(see p172)*. Because of this, the Egyptian authorities are reluctant to allow visitors into the area. There is heavy security and the movements of tourists are very tightly controlled.

It is possible to arrange day trips as part of a group from Cairo and Luxor, but only under strict security. If you try to go alone by local bus or by service taxi, you will eventually be discovered at one of the many police checkpoints and either given an escort into the sites or back to where you started from, depending on the situation. Information about the causes and extent of the unrest is hard to come by and often conflicting. The threat is not always directed at tourists, but visitors do run the risk of being caught up in local violence.

Terrorist attacks on tourists in general have ceased since the massacre at the Temple of Hatshepsut in Luxor, on 17 November 1997. Since then, the Egyptian government has expressed its determination to prevent further attacks on tourists and has increased security, particularly at the major historical sites.

The situation is likely to change, so visitors intending to travel to Egypt should keep in touch with developments. Up-to-date advice on foreign travel can be obtained from your ministry of foreign affairs (in the UK, the Foreign and Commonwealth Office).

IN CASE OF FIRE

HOSTELS, cheap hotels and even some of the more expensive establishments are unlikely to have adequate fire exits or even fire extinguishers. Therefore, it is a good idea at

Distinctive Egyptian fire engine, equipped for the rough terrain

least to familiarize yourself with the layout of the building and possible escape routes in case a fire does occur.

WOMEN TRAVELLERS

Egypt has become more conservative in recent years, as witnessed by the increasing numbers of women wearing the *hijab* or head-scarf. Women tourists are not expected to wear scarves, but may feel more at ease doing so in mosques or rural areas.

The social norms for women in Egypt are very different from those in the West and this, combined with images of women in Hollywood films, creates misconceptions. For example, women travellers unaccompanied by a man are often regarded as morally loose. While serious sexual assaults are rare, verbal harassment and groping does occur. The risk of harassment can be reduced by dressing modestly. Wear long, loose, opaque clothes that cover your chest, shoulders, upper arms and your legs below the knees. Many single women wear wedding rings, which signal respectability. Sit with other women on trains and buses and in the front car of the Cairo Metro, which is reserved for women. Avoid eye contact and smiling at strange men as these can be misconstrued. If you are harassed, the best response is to ignore the offender. Using phrases such as *haram* (shame), or *sibnee le wahdi* (leave me alone) may bring help. Women in Islam are highly respected and help is frequently extended to female travellers in distress.

EMBASSIES

If you find yourself in trouble, contact your embassy or consulate who will give legal advice and replace lost passports. They are unsympathetic to drug offenders and will not lend you money to get home,

although, as a last resort, they will arrange repatriation. It is as well to remember that although you are a welcome visitor to the country, you are still subject to Egyptian laws.

DIRECTORY

EMERGENCY SERVICES

Fire 125.
Tourist Police 126.

EMBASSIES

Australia
World Trade Centre (11th floor), Corniche el-Nil, Bulaq, Cairo.
Map 1 A3.
(02) 578 0650.

Canada
26 Sharia Kamel el Shenawi, Garden City, Cairo.
Map 5 A5.
(02) 794 3110.

Ireland
3 Sharia Abu al-Feda, Zamalek, Cairo.
Map 1 A3.
(02) 735 8264.

UK
7 Sharia Ahmed Ragheb, Garden City, Cairo.
Map 5 A4.
(02) 794 0850.

USA
5 Sharia Amerika al-Latineya, Garden City, Cairo.
Map 5 B4.
(02) 797 3300.

A police escort accompanying tourists taking a camel ride at Aswan

Health and Insurance

Distinctive Egyptian pharmacy logo

Aᴌᴛʜᴏᴜɢʜ travelling in Egypt might be thought to pose serious health risks, these can be minimized by careful pre-planning, taking sensible precautions while in the country and by the reassurance offered by taking out appropriate travel insurance before leaving home. The most common problems are mild gastric disturbances – simply caused by bacteria in food and drink to which the traveller has yet to acquire immunity – plus the range of ailments induced by a careless attitude to extreme heat and sunshine.

Egyptian pharmacy shop front, with name in Arabic and English

GENERAL ADVICE

Fᴏʀ ᴍᴏsᴛ ᴠɪsɪᴛᴏʀs to Egypt, stomach upsets and over-exposure to the sun constitute the greatest health risks. It is a good idea, however, to pack a first-aid kit with plasters, bandages, antiseptic ointment and some painkillers. Insect repellent is vital, especially in the Western Desert oases, on the Sinai coast, in the Delta, and for felucca rides at sunset. Include some oral rehydration salts in your kit: these will help replace lost minerals if you do suffer a bad bout of diarrhoea.

Pack supplies of prescription medicines and contact lens solution. Lens wearers may find that desert dust causes problems: it is advisable to wear glasses instead of lenses for at least part of the time to avoid constant irritation.

The sun is strong throughout Egypt, even in winter, and particularly in Upper Egypt, where there is very little shade. Wear a sunhat and sunglasses and use a sunscreen with a protection factor of at least 15.

VACCINATIONS

Vɪsɪᴛᴏʀs ᴛᴏ ᴇɢʏᴘᴛ do not require any vaccinations unless they are coming from an infected area. However you may like to ask your GP for the current World Health Organization (WHO) health bulletin on Egypt before travelling. As well as ensuring that your polio and tetanus cover is up to date, the most common recommendations include vaccinations against typhoid and Hepatitis A and B. A meningitis vaccination may also be advised.

Rabies is a serious problem throughout the country. Avoid touching any stray animals, including cats, dogs, bats and monkeys. If you think you have been exposed to the disease, seek help urgently.

PHARMACIES

Eɢʏᴘᴛɪᴀɴ ᴘʜᴀʀᴍᴀᴄɪsᴛs are a good source of help for minor health complaints. They generally speak English and can be trusted to advise on remedies for most common ailments. Pharmacies carry a wide range of drugs, which are cheap and can often be dispensed without a doctor's prescription. Pharmacists can also help you find a doctor.

A dive trip in the Red Sea, with fierce sun, intense heat and lack of shade posing potential health hazards

STOMACH UPSETS

MILD DIARRHOEA is a common ailment for visitors to Egypt. However, a few simple precautions can reduce your chances of falling ill, or at least lessen the effects.

While tap water is generally safe, it is heavily chlorinated and rather unpleasant tasting. Bottled water is available everywhere – but make sure that the seal is unbroken when you buy it. Avoid raw vegetables and unpeeled fruit, or wash them thoroughly in purified water. Do not buy food from a street stall that has no running water, and beware of ice-cream that may have melted, then been refrozen. Choose budget restaurants with care and always check that meat has been cooked thoroughly.

If you do feel unwell, bottled water with a little added fresh lime juice can help settle an upset stomach.

Local brand of Egyptian bottled water

OTHER HAZARDS

DEHYDRATION, sunburn and heat exhaustion are of particular concern, especially in Upper Egypt. Lack of shade at archaeological sites, plus wind-blown sand and dust, can make for an uncomfortable experience. Sweat evaporates quickly in these dry conditions and you may become dehydrated without realizing it. Drink plenty of bottled water and add a little extra salt to your food to replace salts lost in sweat. Wear a sunhat and loose-fitting clothes made of natural fibres, and wear a T-shirt when swimming.

Heatstroke is a potentially fatal condition that occurs when the body temperature rises to dangerous levels. Symptoms include flushed skin, severe headaches and confusion. Immediate medical attention is essential.

Bilharzia, or schistosomiasis, is another hazard in Egypt. This disease is transmitted by water-borne flukes that infest the stagnant water found in canals or in slower-moving stretches of the Nile. Do not wade or bathe in such water or walk barefoot on the muddy banks. Never drink water from such a source.

HOSPITALS AND EMERGENCIES

PRIVATE HOSPITALS provide the best medical care in Egypt, but they still fall short of standards found in the West. The most reliable private hospitals are in Cairo and Alexandria, and those attached to universities are generally competent and well equipped. Irrespective of whether the patient is insured, both private and state-run hospitals will probably ask for a cash payment before providing treatment of any kind. If you do not have sufficient funds to cover this, contact your embassy who may be able to arrange for relatives or your insurance company to cover the fees in advance of your claim. Be sure to obtain receipts for all the expenses you incur, since these will be required by your insurance company to support your claim for reimbursement.

With the exception of the private service run by As-Salaam Hospital in Cairo, ambulances do not carry paramedics or life-support equipment. Since telephone lines in Egypt are seriously overloaded, it is best, in a real emergency, to take a taxi to the nearest hospital rather than trying to call an ambulance.

DIRECTORY

EMERGENCY NUMBERS

Tourist Police (*126.*
Public Ambulance (*123.*

CAIRO HOSPITALS

Anglo-American Hospital
Sharia al-Hada az-Zuhriya,
Gezira. **Map** 1 A5.
(*(02) 735 6162, 735 6163.*

As-Salaam Hospital
3 Sharia Syria, Mohandiseen.
(*(02) 302 9091 or (02) 303 0502.*

As-Salaam International Hospital
Corniche el-Nil, Maadi.
(*(02) 524 0250.*

CAIRO PHARMACIES

Isaaf
38 Sharia 26 July, Downtown.
Map 1 C4, 5 B2. ○ *24 hours.*
(*(02) 574 3369.*

Ataba Pharmacy
17 Midan Ataba, Downtown.
Map 2 D4, 6 D2.

Victoria Pharmacy
6 Sharia al-Brazil, Zamalek.
Map 1 A3. ○ *until 11pm.*
(*(02) 735 1628.*

TRAVEL INSURANCE

MOST TRAVEL policies cover you for lost belongings and cancellation as well as medical emergencies, and are strongly recommended. Be sure to inform the insurance company if you intend to take part in any dangerous sports, such as diving, otherwise your cover may be invalid. Keep the documents with you so that you can readily contact the company if necessary.

A typical red and white Egyptian ambulance

Communications

Egyptian telephone and internet services have improved dramatically in recent years. An entirely new public card phone system is now in place and internet cafés are opening in the more tourist-orientated areas. Unfortunately the same cannot be said of the postal service. Overseas letters sent from Egypt can still take weeks to arrive, if they do at all. Egypt has eight television channels and several English-language newspapers and magazines.

Postage stamps celebrating Egypt, past and present

PUBLIC TELEPHONES

Two companies – Menatel and Nile Telephone – offer public card phone services, replacing the decades-old coin-operated system. Menatel, identified by its green and yellow half-booths, is the more widespread of the two systems. Cairo is especially well served, with Menatel phones on nearly every street – a welcome relief in a city where not every house has a phone. Phonecards can be obtained from pharmacies, newspaper stands, tobacco shops and kiosks displaying the green and yellow Menatel sign. The LE 10 cards are for local calls and the LE 30 cards for international calls. Local calls cost 25 piastres for every three minutes. The Nile Telephone booths, which are red and blue, are fewer. Their cards for calls within Egypt cost LE 10, while international cards come in LE 20 and 40 denominations. You can dial mobile phones from either system and both companies' booths have instructions in Arabic and English.

While these improvements are welcome to Egyptians and travellers alike, the phone system as a whole remains overloaded and it can take numerous attempts to reach the person you are calling. Numbers change frequently

Nile Telephone and Menatel phonecards

and in such cases, a recorded message both in Arabic and English will provide you with the new number.

MAIL SERVICES

Most post offices in Egypt are open from 9am to 3pm daily, except Friday. They are often overcrowded and difficult to use if you don't speak Arabic. Overseas postboxes are painted blue and red ones are used for domestic post. However, it is probably simpler to purchase stamps and send letters from hotels. To send important mail or packages, it is strongly advised to use one of the

Typical blue and red postboxes for international and domestic mail respectively

international courier services, such as Federal Express or DHL. Both companies have offices in Cairo. This is a more expensive option but the only way of guaranteeing that items will reach their intended recipient quickly.

Receiving letters *poste restante* at the post office is not always reliable and it is a better idea to have letters sent to your hotel. In addition, the main American Express office in Cairo at 15 Sharia Qasr el-Nil holds mail for people who have American Express cards or Amex traveller's cheques. Receiving packages or over-stuffed envelopes from overseas is best avoided as all such parcels are inspected by customs and censors. Items such as compact discs, video tapes and computer games arrive very late or not at all. If they do arrive, expect to pay duty worth more than the package's contents.

USEFUL DIALLING CODES

- To dial locally: dial 6 or 7 digit telephone number.
- To dial within Egypt: dial 0 + area code + telephone number.
- Area codes: Cairo and Giza: 2; Alexandria: 3; Aswan: 97; Fayoum: 84; Luxor: 95; Ismailia: 64; Hurghada: 65; Sharm el-Sheikh: 69.
- To dial internationally: dial 00 + country code + telephone number.
- Country codes: US and Canada: 1; France: 33; Germany: 49; Italy: 39; Netherlands: 31; Spain: 34; Switzerland: 41; UK: 44; South Africa: 27; Australia: 61.
- To dial mobile phones: dial 0 + 12 (or 0 + 10) + telephone number.

TELEVISION AND RADIO

Television channels 1 and 2 are the national channels, with the latter broadcasting news in English and French. Channel 3 is the local Cairo channel. Channels 4 to 8 are broadcast from Ismailia, Alexandria, Tanta, Minya and Aswan respectively. All the channels broadcast foreign language programmes with Arabic subtitles, and the better hotels provide cable or satellite television.

Foreign-language radio programmes are rare outside Cairo and Alexandria. In Cairo, FM 95 broadcasts programmes in English and French and a few other stations mix Western classical and pop music with Arabic music and news. Check the *Egyptian Gazette* for TV and radio schedules or *Egypt Today* magazine for satellite and cable TV highlights.

Newspaper stand selling foreign papers in Mahattat Ramla, Alexandria

A selection of English-language newspapers and magazines

NEWSPAPERS AND MAGAZINES

The daily *Egyptian Gazette* and the weekly *Middle East Times* and *Al-Ahram Weekly* cover international and domestic news; the latter two provide good coverage of television, films and cultural events. The weekly *Cairo Times* is a mix of local and regional news, features and reviews. Outside Cairo, the *Egyptian Gazette* is the only local English-language paper.

There are a number of English-language magazines. The monthly *Egypt Today* contains comprehensive

cultural and restaurant listings. Other English-language magazines include *Egypt's Insight*, and *Egypt Today*'s sister publications *Business Today* and *Sports and Fitness*, which is useful for health clubs, sports and recreation listings. A broad range of Western newspapers is usually on sale the day after publication at street-side newspaper stands in affluent areas of large cities and at major hotels. *Time* and *Newsweek* are also available.

INTERNET AND FAX

Fax machines can be found in the business centres of most major hotels. However, rates are usually high. Faxes are also available in long-distance and international phone centres, but these machines have a reputation for being less reliable, if cheaper.

There is currently an internet boom taking place in Egypt and internet cafés are a fast-growing phenomenon, especially in the tourist centres of Cairo, Alexandria and Luxor. Most major hotels also offer internet access.

One of the latest Egyptian internet cafés: glob@l net Alexandria

Banking and Currency

EGYPT IS STILL VERY MUCH a cash economy. Both banks and exchange offices will change cash and traveller's cheques, but exchange offices usually offer better hours, shorter queues and more favourable rates. Credit cards, while accepted at most major hotels and some tourist shops, are not much use anywhere else. Automated Teller Machines (ATMs) are now often found outside many banks and can be used for cash withdrawals, although some credit cards charge heavily for this service. Egypt prohibits the exportation of its currency, which, in any case, is useless outside the country.

**Logo of
Banque de Caire**

Standard ATM with instructions in a range of languages

BANKS

THE USUAL OPENING HOURS for banks in Egypt are Sunday to Thursday 8:30am to 2pm. Exchange offices are also open in the evenings from 6:00pm to 9:00pm. Most banks are closed on Friday and Saturday. As well as Egyptian banks, which include Banque Misr, there are a few well-known international names such as Barclays and Citibank. The best time to go is just as the bank opens – to avoid crowds.

Thomas Cook exchange office on the Corniche, Luxor

EXCHANGE OFFICES

EXCHANGE OFFICES can be found throughout major cities and tourist areas and are preferable to banks, shops and hotels for changing money. The black market for hard currency is now in decline and scarcely worth the risk.

It is a good idea to change some money on arrival; both terminals at Cairo Airport have 24-hour exchange offices.

TRAVELLER'S CHEQUES AND CREDIT CARDS

MOST BANKS and exchange offices accept American Express, Barclays, Citibank and Travelex traveller's cheques. Eurocheques are not recommended for use in Egypt. A passport is required to change traveller's cheques. Always keep the receipt and a record of the serial numbers separate from the cheques in case they are lost or stolen. It is difficult outside tourist areas to use either traveller's cheques or credit cards. The most widely used credit cards are Visa, MasterCard and American Express.

BAKSHEESH AND TIPPING

PEOPLE DEMANDING *baksheesh* without rendering a service can be irritating, but calm and good-humoured refusals will eventually meet with success. Most Egyptians are paid such low salaries that *baksheesh*, in the form of a tip for service, is a vital part of their income. It is usual, in restaurants, to round up the bill or give an extra 10 per cent directly to the waiter. Small tips, in the 25 pt to LE 1 range, should be given to people who help you in some small way, such as lavatory attendants, and the people who park cars, carry luggage or unlock tombs. Offers to bend the rules a bit, such as letting you into a site after hours or opening one supposedly closed, will cost a little more. However, don't assume money will buy you

everything. Do not risk offence by refusing to pay small sums for even minor assistance, but also do not throw money at people to get your way.

CURRENCY

T HE BASIC UNIT of currency in Egypt is the Egyptian pound or *ginee*, written as £E or LE. The Egyptian pound is divided into 100 piastres (pt) or *irsh*. The 50 and 100 LE notes can sometimes be difficult to change, so always carry some smaller notes. It is also advisable to keep a separate supply of lower denomination notes for *baksheesh* and for taxis who invariably have no change. Avoid accepting ragged or mutilated notes because taxi drivers and vendors will also refuse to take them.

Coins

Coins come in denominations of 5, 10, 20 and 25 piastres, and are mainly used for tipping. There are two versions of the 10 piastres coin.

5 piastres (5 pt)

10 piastres (10 pt)

10 piastres (10 pt) **20 piastres (20 pt)** **25 piastres (25 pt)**

Banknotes

Banknotes are issued in 1, 5, 10, 20, 50 and 100 pounds denominations as well as 50 and 25 piastres. There are also notes worth 5 and 10 piastres, although these are getting rare. Smaller in size than pound notes, they are often refused by vendors and taxi drivers alike. Most smaller shops round prices up or offer sweets or matches in lieu of exact change.

50 piastres (50 pt)

25 piastres (25 pt)

5 Egyptian pounds (LE 5)

1 Egyptian pound (LE 1)

10 Egyptian pounds (LE 10)

20 Egyptian pounds (LE 20)

50 Egyptian pounds (LE 50)

100 Egyptian pounds (LE 100)

TRAVEL INFORMATION

MOST VISITORS TO EGYPT fly to Cairo, but flights are also available to Luxor, Alexandria, Hurghada and Sharm el-Sheikh. A holiday in Egypt can also be combined with a visit to another Middle Eastern or North African country, but flying within the region is comparatively more expensive than flying direct from the US or Europe.

EgyptAir logo

Another popular method of entry into Egypt is overland from Jordan, via Israel, although this entails some extra effort and time because of having to cross two borders on the way. An easier route from Jordan is on the regular ferry or catamaran service that runs between Aqaba and Nuweiba on the Gulf of Aqaba coast of Sinai.

Cairo International Airport, to the northeast of the city

ARRIVING BY AIR

DIRECT FLIGHTS to Egypt are regularly available from most European capitals. Both British Airways and EgyptAir fly daily from Heathrow (with a flight time of approximately 5 hours) while Air France flies daily from Paris (4.5 hours). Other daily flights include CSA from Prague, KLM from Amsterdam, Lufthansa from Frankfurt, Malev from Budapest, Olympic from Athens, TAROM from Bucharest and Turkish Airlines from Istanbul. Charter flights are available to Luxor, Sharm el-Sheikh and Hurghada.

EgyptAir flies direct to Cairo from New York's JFK airport five days a week. The flight time is approximately 12 hours. Currently, there are no American airlines operating flights to Egypt. EgyptAir also flies once a week to Los Angeles, with a flight time of 17 hours. There are no direct flights to Egypt from Canada.

Travellers from Australia and New Zealand usually get to Egypt via London, or add on Cairo as part of a Round the World Ticket. However, Singapore Airlines offers three flights a week from Sydney to Cairo, with a flight time of 19 hours. Fares vary according to the time of year.

TRANSPORT FROM CAIRO AIRPORT

CAIRO INTERNATIONAL Airport is 20 km (12 miles) to the northeast of the city and has two terminals. Western European and US airlines use Terminal 2 (also known as the New Airport), while Egyptian carriers, El-Al, and most Arab, African and Eastern European airlines land at the Old Airport – Terminal 1.

Both of these terminals are connected to the city centre by bus and minibus, but the fastest and most comfortable transfer is by taxi. (For more general information regarding buses and taxis, see pp325–9.)

There is no difficulty in finding a taxi at the airport, as drivers descend on new arrivals the minute they have cleared Customs. The time of day, number, gender and appearance of the passengers, amount of luggage, volume of traffic and bargaining skills all factor into the fare. A trip from the airport to downtown Cairo typically costs between LE 25 and 35 per car load, not per person. New arrivals may also be offered a "limousine" service – the fixed rate for the trip in a decent saloon is around LE 40 to 50.

Both terminals have duty-free and tourist shops, cafés offering meagre fare and currency exchange booths.

TRANSPORT FROM OTHER AIRPORTS

THE AIRPORT IN Alexandria is 5 km (3 miles) south of the city and is served by buses and minibuses. A taxi to the centre of town costs approximately LE 10 to 20. Most visitors arriving at Luxor are met at the airport by representatives from their hotels or cruise boats. If not, a taxi into town costs around

Black and yellow taxi serving Alexandria airport

LE 10 to 15. Similarly, most visitors to Sharm el-Sheikh are met by hotel transportation. Taxis from the airport, located north of Naama Bay, test the skills of the best bargainers. Expect to pay around LE 25 to 30 per trip. The situation at Hurghada airport is similar, but a taxi into town should cost only LE 15 to 20.

ARRIVING BY LAND FROM ISRAEL AND JORDAN

BUSES RUN DAILY from Tel Aviv and Jerusalem to Egypt, crossing at Rafah or Taba. Taba is the gateway to the Sinai coast while Rafah is more convenient for getting to Cairo. The journey between Jerusalem and Cairo takes 12–14 hours, depending on how long it takes to cross the border. In recent years the process has been streamlined slightly at the Taba crossing, which serves both the Israeli resort of Eilat and Egyptian resorts on the Gulf of Aqaba and the rest of the Sinai.

It is also possible to enter Egypt by land from Jordan through Israel. The journey involves a 5-km (3-mile) taxi or "service" taxi from Aqaba to the border, followed by a short walk to the Israeli side. From there, visitors can take a taxi into Eilat. Buses and taxis

Cruise ship passing through the Suez Canal

run from the centre of Eilat to the border with Egypt at Taba. Departure taxes must be paid when leaving Jordan and Israel, even if one is just passing through the latter.

Bear in mind that having Israeli stamps in your passport may preclude you from visiting other Arab countries.

ARRIVING BY SEA

ALTHOUGH EGYPT is served by several ports on both its Mediterranean and Red Sea coasts, the advent of cheap air fares and package holidays has inevitably seen the decline of passenger ferries bringing travellers to the country. There

is one exception to this – the crossing from Aqaba, in Jordan, to Nuweiba, in the Sinai. This route is served by both a ferry, which takes 3–5 hours, depending on the weather, and a high-speed catamaran service that does the trip in an hour.

There are no longer any direct ferries from Greece or Cyprus, but two cruise ships sail from Limassol to Port Said, taking passengers on a two-day group visa to Egypt.

Otherwise the only other arrivals by sea are passengers from the cruise ships in the surrounding waters, who come ashore on daytrips to visit some of the sights.

Travelling in Egypt

Egyptian tour bus logo

THE OVERALL STANDARDS of plane and train travel in Egypt are pretty good, but both services can be frustrating in terms of booking and scheduling. The rail network links the Nile Valley, the Delta and the Canal Zone, while EgyptAir and Air Sinai, the national carriers, serve the major cities. Costs for air travel, however, are substantially higher than trains and long-distance buses, so it is not an option for budget travellers. The bus service in Egypt is extensive and, for short trips, often preferable to trains, both in cost and transit time. For longer journeys, night buses are often available.

Train bound for Aswan departing from Ramses station in Cairo

Sign for the Abu Simbel airport in the Nile Valley

DOMESTIC FLIGHTS

FLYING WITHIN EGYPT entails flying with EgyptAir as the company has a monopoly on air travel within the country. Air Sinai is part of the same company and was formed to serve Israel and the Sinai, thus protecting the mother carrier from losing its landing rights in other Arab countries. EgyptAir operates frequent daily flights between Cairo, Luxor, Hurghada and Aswan, and a slightly reduced service to Alexandria. All domestic flights leave from Terminal 1, the Old Airport, in Cairo. There are several flights a day between Aswan and Abu Simbel. Air Sinai offers daily flights between Cairo, Luxor, Hurghada, Sharm el-Sheikh and St Catherine's Monastery.

FLIGHT RESERVATIONS

FARES ARE AVERAGE by international standards and are calculated in US dollars. It is possible to pay in Egyptian pounds, backed up by an exchange receipt. Reservations should be made as far in advance as possible, especially during winter or important Muslim festivals such as Eid al-Adha and Eid al-Fitr (see p39).

Overbooking is common on EgyptAir and Air Sinai: always confirm your flight reservation and make a note of the confirmation reference number. Delays are also common and Egypt's domestic airports are dreary places. It is a good idea to have something to read or to otherwise fill the time you may spend waiting. The baggage allowance for domestic flights is 20 kg (44 lb), but this rule is often flouted, especially with regard to hand luggage. It is important to arrive at the airport at least one hour before domestic flights and two hours before international flights.

TRAINS

TRAINS ARE THE BEST option for long trips between major cities, offering a much more pleasant alternative to buses and taxis. For short journeys, however, trains tend to be slower and less reliable. Trains in Egypt fall into two

categories: air-conditioned (A/C), which includes the luxury wagons-lits, and non-A/C, or local stopping trains. A/C trains usually offer first- and second-class cars. First-class cars are less crowded and the seats are more comfortable. Second-class travel is not significantly worse and costs quite a bit less. Seats can be reserved up to a week in advance. Round-trip bookings are not possible, so it is best to book for the return journey when you arrive at your destination. There are 16 A/C trains a day between Cairo and Alexandria and five daily between Cairo and Luxor and Aswan. Two overnight express trains run between Cairo and Luxor and Aswan.

Wagons-lits provide a fast, comfortable, but expensive overnight service between Cairo and Luxor and Aswan. Carpeted compartments have

Façade of the Masr train station in central Alexandria

One of the buses used by the West Delta Bus Company

two bunks and a washbasin. There is a lounge car, and breakfast and dinner are served in the compartments. Wagons-lits must be booked at least a day in advance: this is best done through Thomas Cook or American Express. In Cairo, bookings can be made at the Helnan Shepheard Hotel.

Non-A/C trains have only second- and third-class seats, the latter with open doors and windows for ventilation. Both classes are very dirty and crowded and are rarely used by foreign travellers.

Logo of the Superjet bus run by the Arab Union Transport Company

LONG-DISTANCE BUSES

THERE ARE THREE main bus operators in Egypt. The Upper Egypt Bus Company operates services to the Nile Valley, Al-Fayoum, the Western Desert oases and towns along the Red Sea Coast down to Quesir. It also runs a luxury bus service every evening to Luxor and to Aswan. The East Delta Bus Company covers services to the Sinai beach towns of Sharm el-Sheikh, Dahab, Nuweiba and Taba, as well as to St Catherine's Monastery and the Suez Canal towns of Port Said, Ismailia and Suez. Alexandria, Marsa Matruh, Siwa Oasis and the Delta towns are served by the West Delta Bus Company. Travellers have a choice between air-conditioned (A/C) buses, which are usually newer, and non-A/C vehicles

which are generally in worse shape and can take much longer to arrive at their destination. Be aware that just because a bus is advertised as having air-conditioning does not mean that it will actually work; nor will passengers necessarily obey the "no smoking" signs.

The Arab Union Transport Company operates the super-comfortable Superjet and Golden Arrow buses along the main Cairo to Alexandria, Luxor, Hurghada, Sharm el-Sheikh and Aswan routes. Superjet buses also serve Port Said with around nine trips a day. The buses are air-conditioned, with toilets, videos and hostesses offering highly priced snacks.

All long-distance buses from Cairo now depart from the bus terminal behind Ramses train station. In Alexandria, Port Said and Ismailia several different terminals are used. Bus schedules, usually posted in Arabic, are erratic and change frequently so it is advisable to ask travel agencies, hotels and tourist offices to help check the departure times. Tickets are sold from small kiosks at city terminals, up to 24 hours in advance for A/C and long-haul services. In smaller towns, tickets may only be available an hour or so before departure. Ticket prices vary according to the type of service and time of day you want to travel. For popular trips, it is wise to book as early as possible to be sure of a seat and to catch the bus at the main departure terminal.

DIRECTORY

AIRPORTS

Alexandria
(03) 427 1036.

Aswan
(097) 480 333.

Cairo
(02) 291 4266.

Hurghada
(065) 442 831 or 442 592.

Luxor
(095) 374 655.

Sharm el-Sheikh
(069) 601 140.

BUS COMPANIES

East Delta
(02) 419 8533.

Superjet
(02) 579 8188.

Upper Egypt
(02) 431 6723.

West Delta
(02) 414 1318.

TRAIN STATIONS

Alexandria
Masr Station,
Midan al-Gumhuriyya.
(03) 392 3207.

Cairo
Ramses Station, Midan Ramses.
Map 2 D3. (02) 575 3555.

Imposing entrance to Ramses train station, on Midan Ramses, Cairo

Road Travel in Egypt

Typical petrol pump

DRIVING IN EGYPT IS NOT for the faint-hearted. Traffic in Cairo is continually busy and horrendous and the main roads out of the metropolis are hazardous. In Alexandria, traffic is no more orderly than in Cairo, but it is less dense, except for summer when millions of Egyptians relocate to Alexandria and the Mediterranean coast. Service (pronounced *servees*) taxis go just about anywhere in the country, providing a fast, cheap form of transport. However their relative discomfort and lack of safety limit their usefulness on all but a few routes. For day-trips, hiring a driver with car may be the best option.

One of several international car rental agencies in Egypt

SERVICE TAXIS

AS IN OTHER Middle-Eastern countries, service taxis form an important part of Egypt's internal transport system. The vehicles are usually either large Peugeot estates or minibuses, but they all operate in the same way and provide a fast and cheap method of getting around the country. Drivers congregate at recognized locations – usually near bus and train stations – and tout for passengers by shouting out their destination. They leave when their vehicle is full up. They will not leave before it is full unless the passengers are prepared to pay the extra fares. There is no need to book a seat: just show up at the "terminal" and look for a vehicle that is going to your destination.

Alternatively you may like to hire a whole service taxi for your group if you wish to undertake a day trip to a destination that is not easily accessed by other means. This can be a cheaper option than hiring a car to drive yourself or using other forms of public transport.

There is a downside to this service, however. Because the vehicles are always full to capacity, the ride can be hot and uncomfortable, especially over long distances. There is little room for luggage, though there is usually a roofrack

where luggage can be stowed. More worryingly, the drivers are notorious for their reckless driving and their vehicles are often in poor condition.

CAR RENTAL

INTERNATIONAL vehicle rental companies such as Hertz, Budget and Avis have offices at the airports and in major hotels in tourist areas. To rent a car, you must be between 25 and 70 years old and hold a valid International Driver's Licence. Cairo and the larger towns are well served by petrol stations but in rural and desert areas long distances can separate them, so always fill the tank to the limit. If driving off-road, always carry spare fuel, water and tools. Most petrol stations can perform minor repairs and Egyptian mechanics are quite good at solving problems, sometimes resorting to more creative or less orthodox measures.

DRIVING IN EGYPT

THERE ARE NO FIXED rules for driving in Egypt and in the cities anarchy prevails. Drivers ignore lane markings, drive the wrong way up one-way streets, back up in the face of oncoming traffic if they miss a turn and ignore red lights and non-signposted intersections. Drivers' intentions are often communicated by horns or hand gestures rather than by conventional signals. A common gesture of drivers

Large estate car operating as a service taxi for longer trips

Minibus holding up to 12 passengers, operating as a service taxi

and pedestrians alike is raised fingers, tips pinched together. This means "Wait". A flip of the hand forward means "Pass". Drivers will sometimes signal turns by pointing with their whole arm out the window. The honking of horns may at first seem senseless, but it is often relevant. One or more short beeps means "Watch out." A long, unbroken blast means "I'm not stopping".

Other hazards in the cities include people jumping from moving buses, overloaded motorbikes, donkey carts and flocks of sheep, not to mention pedestrians who also do not seem to follow any obvious rules of road etiquette.

Hazards on roads between cities are even more serious and numerous. Cars and trucks routinely overtake in the face of oncoming traffic or on the hard shoulder. Roads are in poor condition, with potholes, rough patches and drifting sand. Children often play alongside and in the road, and all manner of livestock, including camels, wander across. Motorists will stack rocks or construction

Typical heavy traffic near Midan Ramses in Cairo

debris in the road in lieu of hazard warning signs when they have pulled in because of a breakdown.

Driving at night is best avoided. Egyptians tend not use their lights at night, except to flash them at oncoming vehicles. Off-road driving without a local guide in the Sinai, along the North Coast near El-Alamein and in the Canal Zone can be especially dangerous because of the presence of land mines, left over from World War II and the Arab-Israeli wars.

Police checkpoints are a frequent occurrence. Foreign drivers are usually waved through, but be prepared to show your passport.

Hiring a private car with a driver can work out cheaper than renting a car. Check with travel agencies and hotels. Regular taxis can also be hired for the day at negotiable rates.

MAPS

THE BEST GENERAL map of Egypt is one published by Freytag & Berndt, which is available in most major tourist areas. Mobil's *Motoring Guide to Egypt* is a good choice if you are going to drive. It is sold in Mobil stations and tourist bookstores. Egyptians themselves seldom refer to maps and map coverage of cities other than Cairo is poor.

Stop sign

Uneven road

No car horns

DIRECTORY

CAR RENTAL

Avis
Cairo International Airport.
((02) 265 2429.

Nile Hilton,
Corniche el-Nil, Cairo.
Map 5 A3.
((02) 579 2400.

Budget Rent-a-Car
Cairo International Airport.
((02) 265 2395.

Cairo Marriott,
Sharia Saray al-Gezira.
Map J B4.
((02) 735 8888.

Hertz
Cairo International Airport.
((02) 265 2430.

Ramses Hilton,
Corniche el-Nil,
Cairo. **Map** 5 A3.
((02) 577 7444.

195 Sharia 26th July,
Mohandiseen,
Cairo.
((02) 347 2238.

7/1 Sharia El Laselki,
Maadi.
((02) 754 9413.

J-Car
Cairo International Airport.
((02) 265 2340.

33 Sharia Mesiah,
Dokki.
((02) 335 0521.

MOTORING ORGANIZATIONS

Automobile Association (AA)
Fanum House,
Basingstoke,
Hants RG21 2EA.
((01256) 201 123.

Automobile and Touring Club of Egypt
10 Sharia Qasr el-Nil,
Cairo.
Map 1 C5.
((02) 574 3355.

Royal Automobile Club (RAC)
PO Box 100, RAC House,
7 Brighton Road,
South Croydon, CR2 6XW.
((020) 8686 0088.

MAP OUTLETS

In UK
Stanfords
12–14 Long Acre,
London WC2E LP.
((020) 7863 1321.

In Egypt
AUC Bookshop
AUC, Mohammed Mahmoud Gate, Cairo.
Map 1 C5, 5B4.
((02) 797 5929.

Getting Around Cairo and Alexandria

Metro sign at Midan Opera

THE TRAFFIC IN CAIRO is notorious, both for its congestion and its chaos. Driving in the city is impractical for the visitor and many areas, such as the narrow streets and alleys of Islamic and Coptic Cairo, are best explored on foot. The city's public transport includes an extensive bus system, which is cheap but extremely overcrowded, and a clean and efficient metro, which is of limited use to visitors. Taxis are the easiest way to get around and are plentiful, inexpensive and simple to use once the fare system is understood.

Alexandria's main form of transport is its tram system which covers most areas around the city centre. Downtown is compact enough to negotiate on foot but while distances are short the area has not yet been properly mapped and street names appear in French and Arabic.

Tram in front of the Basilica in Heliopolis (see pp136–7)

WALKING

WALKING IN Cairo is the best way to experience the richness and diversity of this vibrant city. Tackling the streets for the first time, however, can be an intimidating prospect and care should be taken. Drivers do not obey lane markings, road signs or traffic lights. They will slow down to give you time to cross the street, but do not hesitate partway across as this confuses the dodge-and-dash flow of traffic and pedestrians and can increase the chances of an accident. Where possible, cross with groups of other people. Walking in the poorer quarters is remarkably safe, but be wary of petty thieves in crowded areas like the Khan al-Khalili.

Women may also encounter verbal harassment and gropers downtown, on the bridges and in the Khan al-Khalili.

TAXIS

THE BEST FORM of transport to use in Cairo is the black and white taxi. To hail one, stand on the side of the road and signal with your hand. State your destination by district or landmark and be prepared for the driver to pick up other people travelling in the same direction.

By law, taximeters must be switched on but they are never used. Drivers will leave the fare up to you, so it is best to know the going rate in advance to avoid overpaying. In general, most trips within the Downtown-Doqqi-Mohandiseen-Zamalek area cost between LE 3–5. From Downtown to Heliopolis or Maadi charges are LE 10–15 and from Downtown to the

airport, LE 25–35. Expect to pay a little more late at night. Taxis at five-star hotels charge higher fares but are good for day hire as they are in better condition and the drivers speak some English.

Single women passengers are generally safe, but should ride in the back of cabs and not talk or make eye contact with the driver, both of which can attract unwanted attention.

RIVER BUSES AND FELUCCAS

AN ALTERNATIVE means of getting around is by river bus. These are inexpensive and run approximately every half-hour from near Coptic Cairo to the Arab Television Building north of the Egyptian Museum, stopping at Rhoda Island (see pp124–5). At weekends, the buses are full of revellers heading for the Nile Barrages (see p165) north of the city. River buses only run until 4pm.

Feluccas (sailing boats) are found along the river and can be hired out for short cruises (about LE 35–45 per hour). This is a great way to see Cairo from the Nile and cruises at sunset are particularly popular. One of the main departure points is in Garden City by the Meridien Hotel. Feluccas can also be hired out for longer cruises (see p330).

METRO

THE CAIRO METRO is clean, safe and inexpensive but visitors will find it useful for only a few stops, the most prominent of which is the

One of Cairo's ubiquitous black and white taxis

Felucca on the Nile in Central Cairo – a sedate mode of travel

Mar Girgis station opposite Coptic Cairo. There are two lines, identified by direction. The al-Marg to Helwan line follows the east bank of the Nile for most of its length and the recently opened Shubra to Giza line runs north to southwest, via Midan Tahrir. The last stop on the line is displayed on the front of each train and maps of the network can be found at each station.

Tickets are available at all stations and are valid for one trip, including transfers. Ticket-operated turnstiles control access to all platforms so you will need to keep your ticket in order to exit at your destination. The metro is extremely crowded during the morning and evening rush hours.

The first car on each train, and sometimes the second as well, is reserved for women only, but women can and do ride on any car.

BUSES

CITY BUSES ARE red, blue and white with route numbers displayed in Arabic on the front. The buses are often overcrowded and are not really recommended. However, they do cover almost all destinations and are extremely cheap. The city-run minibuses (orange and white) are a slightly more pleasant experience and also very inexpensive. These have

fixed routes and a flat fare, paid as you board. Buses leave from Midan Tahrir or from where you see metal shelters, signs mounted on lamp posts, or more commonly, crowds of people waiting alongside the road. Two useful minibus routes are numbers 82 and 83 which run from Midan Tahrir to the Pyramids at Giza. The city also has microbuses and service taxis that operate on fixed routes and stop on request. However, like the local buses, they are overcrowded and used mainly by workers and residents.

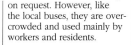
Local bus providing an authentic Cairo experience for the visitor

GETTING AROUND ALEXANDRIA

ALEXANDRIA STILL relies on an aged tram system. The cars are worn and the pace is slow, but fares are cheap. The service runs from 5:30am to midnight, and to 1am during

the summer months. Ramla is the main downtown terminal, located east of the bus depot on Midan Saad Zaghloul. Trams headed east from Ramla are blue, while those travelling west are yellow. Note that on trams that are made up of three cars the middle car is normally reserved for women.

Useful tram routes for visitors include No.15 for the Mosque of Abu al-Abbas Mursi (see pp240–41) and Fort Qaitbey (see p241), and No.16 for Pompey's Pillar (see p242). Heading east, route No.2 travels two-thirds of the way to Montazah Palace (see p243). All tram and route numbers are in Arabic script only.

As in Cairo, buses are old and overcrowded. Minibuses are a better option, following most of the same routes and operating hours as the tram. City minibuses are white while private ones are blue or grey. Both cost under LE 1.

Useful minibus routes for visitors include No.706 and No.707 to Fort Qaitbey via the Corniche, No.703 and No.710 from Midan Orabi to the airport, and No.728 and No.729 from Masr Station to Abu Qir (see p246).

City taxis are black and orange, or yellow, and the rules that apply to taxis in Cairo (see p328) apply here.

Horse-drawn carriages, or caleches, ply the Corniche and Masr Station and can be a relaxing way of getting around the city, providing the traffic is light. The price, as elsewhere in the country, is negotiable. An hourly rate of LE 10–15 is reasonably equitable to all involved.

A westbound tram on a busy thoroughfare in Alexandria

Nile Cruises

A CRUISE ON THE NILE offers one of the best ways to experience the lush countryside of the Nile Valley and visit the magnificent monuments that line its river banks. The Nile is home to over 200 cruise boats and many more feluccas, and numerous tour operators offer cruises as part of a package holiday to the region. Nile excursions can be booked in the UK and US before departure or upon arrival, at Cairo-based tour operators or in Luxor *(see pp180–81)* and Aswan *(see pp204–5)* where there are local agents.

Tourists on a felucca

cruises since the mid-19th century *(see p187)*. Their fleet includes three specially designed river vessels.

NILE CRUISING AS A PACKAGE DEAL

CRUISING ON THE NILE has been a popular tourist pastime since the 19th century, when visiting Egypt's ancient sights was a highlight of the Grand Tour. Although this has now developed into a hugely profitable industry, with some 240 boats plying the river between Aswan and Luxor, the combination of shipboard life and Pharaonic treasures, romanticized by countless films and novels, still has an irresistible appeal to travellers.

One of the simplest ways of organizing such a cruise is to book an inclusive package holiday from home. This will include flights to Egypt where you will join the cruise boat. A typical seven-day trip might head for Aswan, stopping at Esna, Edfu and Kom Ombu *(see pp200–1)* en route. Excursions are made from the ship

Passengers awaiting the departure of a river bus from Cairo

to the monuments along the way, and may include Dendara *(see pp174–5)* or Philae *(see pp208–9)*. Some excellent deals are available on such holidays, which include accommodation in comfortable cabins, meals and transportation to and from the sights. When booking, check what is included in the cost – for example transfer from and to the airport, entrance fees to the sights, entertainment on board, and so on. Cruises offered as part of package holidays are generally reliable and of a consistent standard.

Thomas Cook Holidays is one of the longest-established tour companies operating in the area, having been organizing Nile

ARRANGING A NILE CRUISE IN EGYPT

R IVER BUSES TRAVEL regularly up and down the Nile and are good for day trips to Qanater *(see p165)*. However, if you are planning a holiday based in Cairo, Alexandria or the Sinai Peninsula, but still want to visit the ancient monuments of the Nile Valley, you may decide that a cruise is the best way of doing this. Because of the proliferation of boats offering such excursions, this is easy to arrange through hotels such as the Sheraton, Oberoi and Hilton. The best deals, however, are generally offered by local agents or through dealing directly with the boatmen in Luxor or Aswan. Prices vary greatly, depending on the level of luxury offered. Shop around and check out the facilities on board before confirming the booking. As always, ensure that you know what is included in the fare.

It is possible to cruise from Cairo to Aswan (about 10–12 days) but most people either fly or take the train to Luxor, where they join a boat for the four-day trip to Aswan.

FELUCCA TRIPS ON THE NILE

N O TRIP TO EGYPT would be complete without a trip in a felucca. These ancient sailing boats cruise the Nile throughout the day and for popular sunset tours, and are available for short trips or longer cruises. The most popular felucca trips are between Aswan and Luxor. Travellers can sail from Aswan to Kom Ombo *(see p201)* or Edfu *(see p200)* and continue on to Luxor by road. Some boats do travel further down the Nile to Esna *(see p200)* and Luxor, but this often depends on the security measures in operation along this stretch of water. In winter, when the weather is most favourable, the journey to Kom Ombo takes two nights, while the trip to Edfu and Esna takes

The shore at Aswan, lined with elegant feluccas

Nubian sailor steering his felucca on the Nile at Luxor

at least three nights. Since the journey upstream from Luxor to Aswan depends heavily on the wind, which can die, most travellers start the journey in Aswan and travel downstream.

Felucca cruises require a minimum of five people. If your group is smaller, enquire at the tourist office for others who may like to join you. The tourist office can also recommend good captains, as can hotels, although the latter charge a commission. Before deciding on a boat, ensure that it is stocked with the following vital equipment: a water container of some kind (usually a jerry can); a shade awning; a kerosene stove and lamp; utensils and cutlery; a luggage hold with a lock. Nights are very cold so make certain that the felucca has plenty of blankets or take a sleeping bag with you.

Tourist offices quote rates for all-inclusive cruises. Since prices vary according to the season and demand, these rates should be taken as a starting point for negotiation. Note that in some cases "all inclusive" may not guarantee that water, or even food, is included, so double check exactly what the cruise is offering. Three litres of drinking water per person per day is a minimum standard, and does not include water for cooking if the group decides on this option for meals.

Hygiene is a serious issue on a felucca journey. Treat the Nile water used for washing up with sterilizing tablets and take extra care to

wash your hands thoroughly before handling food. Any rubbish should be burned and excrement buried to avoid polluting the banks of the Nile any further.

For a pleasant experience on the Nile, hats, sunscreen and bug repellent are essential and swimming not advised since the Nile is infested with the parasitic fluke, bilharzia.

WHEN TO GO

THE PEAK TIME for cruises on the Nile is from December to February, with the result that resorts such as Luxor and Aswan become unpleasantly overcrowded at that time. In March/April and October/early November there are fewer visitors but the weather is still very pleasant.

From October to May, the water level in the Nile can be low because of the need to conserve water at the Aswan Dam. This can occasionally make it difficult for feluccas and cruise boats to navigate.

Tour group from a Nile cruise taking in the splendours of Abu Simbel

General Index

Acknowledgments

DORLING KINDERSLEY would like to thank the following people whose contributions and assistance have made the preparation of this book possible.

PUBLISHING MANAGER
Jane Ewart.

MANAGING EDITOR
Anna Streiffert.

**DIRECTOR OF PUBLISHING –
TRAVEL GUIDES**
Gillian Allan.

PUBLISHER
Douglas Amrine.

PRODUCTION
Joanna Bull, Sarah Dodd.

MAIN CONTRIBUTORS
Jane Dunford, Dr Joann Fletcher, Andrew Humphreys.

ADDITIONAL CONTRIBUTORS AND CONSULTANTS
Robin Gauldie, Kyle Pakka, David Stone.

ADDITIONAL ILLUSTRATIONS
Rebecca Milner.

ADDITIONAL PHOTOGRAPHY.
Jo Doran, Clive Streeter.

DESIGN AND EDITORIAL ASSISTANCE
Samira Mahmoud, Dale Harris.

PROOF READER
Stewart J Wild.

INDEXER
Hilary Bird.

SPECIAL ASSISTANCE
Ben Faulks, Gamal, Peter Sheehan, Shehad, Hisham Youssif.

ADDITIONAL PICTURE RESEARCH
Nicole Kaczynski.

PHOTOGRAPHY PERMISSIONS
The publisher would like to thank all the churches, museums, hotels, restaurants, shops, galleries and sights too numerous to thank individually, for their co-operation and contribution to this publication.

PHOTOGRAPHY PERMISSIONS
t=top; tl=top left; tlc=top left centre; tc=top centre; tr=top right; cla=centre left above; ca=centre above; cra=centre right above; cl=centre left; c =centre; cr=centre right; clb=centre left below; cb=centre below; crb=centre right below; bl=bottom left; b=bottom; bc=bottom centre; bcl=bottom centre left; br=bottom right; (d)=detail.

The publisher would like to thank the following individuals, companies and picture libraries for permission to reproduce their photographs:

AFP, London:
Amr Mammoud-STR 299cr; AMR NABEEL-STR 42t; Manoocher Deghati-STF 39clb; Marwan Naamani-STF 38cr; Mohammed al-Sihiti-STR 40bl, 38t, 41t, 303tr; Narwan Naamani-STR 40b; Patrick Hertzog-STF 42b; STR 39tr; STR-STR 41b.

AKG London:
55tc; 179t, 236bl, 241ca; François Guenet 170b; Erich Lessing 24tl, 83cl, 171tr, 179t, 193bl, 234tr; Gilles Mermet 110bl.

Ancient Art & Architecture Collection:
22tr, 24cl, 26–27, 26br, 28tr, 29cl, 31tl, 45ca, 48br, 49b, 50crb, 51b, 52clb, 52bc, 56bc, 70cb, 77tl, 105tl, 132br, 164cr, 170tr, 171cl, 186br, 189cr, 189br, 191br; Dr. S Coyne 207tr, 207cl, 207br; Muhammed al-Agsarai 56crb; R Sheridan 20tl, 22br, 34br, 242b.

The Ancient Egypt Picture Library:
30bl, 74cl, 170cr, 171br, 173tr, 174bl, 190cra, 190bl, 235cl.

Jon Arnold:
1c.

The Art Archive:
Mander & Mitcheson Theatre Col/
Eileen Tweedy 61ca; Museo Civico
Revoltella Trieste/Dagli Orti 60–61c;
Museum Correr, Venice/Dagli Orti
58cb, 211cra; Dagli Orti 58t; The
Egyptian Museum, Cairo/Dagli Orti 3c,
27tr, 74clb, 76tl, 76br, 77bc.

Axiom:
Heidi Grassley 211bl, James Morris
31crb, 160br, 173cb, 173bl, 211tc,
235br, 256cb.

Bildarchiv Preußischer Kulturbesitz:
Johannes Laurentius 54cl.

**Bridgeman Art Library, London /
New York:**
30tr, 30cr, 32ca, 55tr, 57br, 59bc, *The
Flight into Egypt* by Jean-Leon Gerome
123t, 128tr; Bargello, Florence 57bc;
Magdelen College, Oxford 57br; Musée
des Beaux-Arts, Beziers 54–5 c; Musée
du Louvre 22cl, 22–23, 26bl, 174br;
Stapleton Collection 24b, 65inset,
132bl, 210tr, 299bl; The British Library,
London 58bc; The British Museum,
London 46bl; Whitford & Hughes 123t.

Jean-Loup Charmet:
53bl.

Bruce Coleman Ltd:
Franco Banfi 37bl; Charles and Sandra
Hood 223br, 306br.

Thomas Cook Archive:
187cr.

Corbis:
60tr; Bettman 55ca; Bettmann 18c; Galen
Rowell 257cbr; Hulton Deutsch
Collection 20br; Julia Waterlow/Eye
Ubiquitous 18b; KM Westermann 64–5,
304cl; Reuters New Media Inc, 54c,
253cl; Sandro Vannini 258–9; Stephane
Compoint/Sygma 19t; Sygma 20/21c;
Vanni Archive 118–119; Yann Arthus-
Bertrand 15b.

G. Dagli Orti:
110cl; Graeco-Roman Museum,
Alexandria 55tl, 238tl, 238clb, 239cra;
Graeco-Roman Museum, Alexandria.

CM Dixon:
24tr.

DK Picture Library:
60b, 296tr, 296br; Alan Hills 296bl;
Alistair Duncan 21t, 25b, 25cra; British
Museum 23cb, 31br; British Museum/
Peter Hayman 122t, 122tr; Dave King
297br; Frank Greenaway 55cb; Geoff
Brightling 21br, 31clb; Peter Hayman
30cbl; Philip Dowell 297br; Philip
Enticknap 187cl.

**DK Picture Library/British
Museum, London:**
28cla, 28cl, 28cr, 28crb, 28br, 28bcl, 29tl,
29tr, 29cla, 29ca, 29crb, 29bl, 48t, 55bl.

Jo Doran:
115b, 197t.

Edimedia, France:
34c.

Mary Evans Picture Library:
56tc, 57tl, 59tr, 59cr, 59clb, 59br, 60cl,
187crb, 187br, 299cbl.

Werner Forman Archive:
51ca, 134cr, 159tc, 160cl, 188tr, 191cb,
195crb; British Museum London 26tl,
30ca; Dr. E Strouhal 31bl, 31c, 194bl,
194tl, 195tl, 199tl; Graeco-Roman
Museum, Alexandria 53tc, 238cl, 238bl,
239bl; J Paul Getty Museum, Malibu
165bc; Metropolitan Museum of Art,
New York 77c, Musée du Louvre
31cla; Schimmel Collection New York
23tl, 122cl; The Egyptian Museum,
Cairo 20clb, 50ca, 51cb, 74tl, 74bc,
75tr, 75cra, 75cr, 75cb, 76cr, 76cla.

Kenneth Garrett:
190b.

Genesis Space Photo Library:
10bl.

© J. Paul Getty Trust:
Guillermo Aldana 195br.

Patrick Godeau, Egypt:
14fp, 114b.

Ronald Grant Archive:
55b.

© Michael Holford:
23tr, 25crb, 117tc, 193br, 202–203.

Angelo Hornak Library:
34tl, 35ca, 93cr.

Hulton Getty:
Hulton Getty 54tr.

Hutchison Library:
Liba Taylor 162–163.

Jurgen Liepe:
5bl, 45bl, 46tl, 47tc, 47crb, 47bl, 49cb, 122bl, 132tc, 299cla.

Magnum:
Bruno Barbey 63bc.

Richard T Nowitz:
110tr, 114ca, 116bl, 125c, 180b, 181b, 183cr, 183br, 306c.

Oronoz Archivo Fotográfico:
British Museum 22bl.

Lesley Orsen:
233cla.

Christine Osborne:
25tl, 31cra, 35cb, 92bl, 103br, 106tr, 106cl, 107t, 111bl, 114cb, 120bl, 121bl, 123b, 172tl, 172c.

Oxford Scientific Films:
Mark Webster 212; Mike Brown 257tc.

Pa Photos:
61br; EPA European Press Agency 63cb, 63t.

Popperfoto:
20tr, 20cla, 20cl, 21cr, 60tl, 61bl, 62tl, 62cb, 63br, 122br, 125br, 135bc; Donald McLeish 73tr.

Retrograph Archive Ltd:
187bl.

Scala Group S.p.A.:
30tl, 116cr; Archaeological Museum, Palestine 44a; Coptic Museum, Cairo 114t, 116t; The Egyptian Museum, Cairo 15t, 45bc, 66crb.

Topham Picturepoint:
20bl.

Art Directors & TRIP:
D Saunders 222tl.

Wawson Wood:
223t, 223cra, 223clb, 223bl.

Jacket
FRONT – DK PICTURE LIBRARY: British Museum/Peter Hayman bc, cbr; Peter Wilson cbl; GETTY IMAGES: Hugh Sitton main image.
BACK – DK PICTURE LIBRARY: Jon Spaull t; OXFORD SCIENTIFIC FILMS: Mark Webster b.
SPINE – GETTY IMAGES: Hugh Sitton.

All other images © Dorling Kindersley. For further information see:

www.dkimages.com

Phrase Book

The official language of Egypt is Arabic. While it is not an easy language for newcomers to learn, it is well worth taking the time to practise and memorize a few key words and phrases. Most urban Egyptians speak a little English but they will greet any attempt to speak Arabic with delight and encouragement.

The Arabic given here is the Modern Standard Arabic. This is the Arabic written in newspapers, spoken on the radio and recited in prayers in the mosque. This varies somewhat from the language spoken on the street (Egyptian Colloquial Arabic), which is in fact a dialect of the standard language. Nevertheless if you speak slowly and clearly, you should have no difficulty being understood.

Transliteration from Arabic script to the Roman alphabet is a difficult task. Although many attempts have been made, there is no satisfactory system and you will repeatedly come across contradictory spellings in Egypt.

In this phrasebook we have given a simple phonetic transcription only. The underlined letter indicates the stressed syllable.

PRONUNCIATION

a, -ah	as in "mad"
aa	as in "far"
aw	as in "law"
ay	as in "day"
e	as in "bed"
ee	as in "keen"
i	as in "bit"
o	as in "rob"
oo	as in "food"
u	as in "book"
A	pronounced as an emphasised "a" as in "both of us – you And me!"
D	a heavily pronounced "d"
gh	like a French "r" – from the back of the throat
H	a heavily pronounced "h"
kh	as in the Scottish pronunciation of "loch"
q	a "k" sound from the back of the mouth as in "caramel"
S,T	heavily pronounced "s", "t"
th	as in "thin"
Z	heavily pronounced "z"
'	this sounds like a small catch in the breath

When two different vowels occur together, for example Ae- and aA- each is pronounced separately.

IN EMERGENCY

Help!	an-najdah!
Stop!	qeff!
I want to go	oreed arooH
to a doctor	al-Ayaadah
I want to go to a	oreed arooH le saydaleeyah
pharmacist	
Where is the nearest	wayn aqrab telefoon
telephone?	
Where is the hospital?	wayn al mostashfa
I'm allergic to…	Andee Hasaaseeyah men…
…penicillin/aspirin	penicillin/aspirin

COMMUNICATION ESSENTIALS

Yes/No	naAm/laa
Thank you	shokran
No, thank you	laa shokran
Please (asking for something)	min faDlak
Please (offering)	tafaDal
Good morning	sabaaH al-khayr
Good afternoon	as-salaam Alaykum
Good evening	masa' al-khayr
Good night	teSbaH Ala khayr
(when going to bed)	
Good night	maA as-salaamah or
(leaving group early)	as-salaam Alaykum
Goodbye	maA as-salaamah
Excuse me, please	min faDlak, law samaHt
today	al-yawm
yesterday	ams
tomorrow	bokrah
this morning	haza aS-sabaaH
this afternoon	al-yawm baAd az-Zohr
this evening	haza al-masa'
here	hona
there	honaak
what?	shoo?
which?	ay?
when?	mata?
who?	man?
where?	ayn?

USEFUL PHRASES

I don't understand	ma afham
Do you speak	hal tatakalam
English/French?	engleezee/faransee?
I can't speak Arabic	ma aqdar atakalam Arabee
I don't know	ma aAref
Please speak more slowly	law samaHt takalam sheway sheway
Please write it down for me	law samaHt, ektobah Ala hazeh al-waraqah
My name is…	esmee…
How do you do,	kayf Haalak,
pleased to meet you	tasharafna be-meArefatak
How are you?	kayf Haalak?
Sorry!	aasef
I'm really sorry	aasef jeddan
Can you help me, please?	min faDlak, momken tosaAednee?
Can you tell me…?	min faDlak, momken aakhoz…?
I would like….?	oreed…
Is there…here?	fee…hona?
Where can I get…?	min wayn ajeeb…?
How much is it?	bekam?
What time is it?	as-saAh kam
I must go now	laazem arooH fawran
Do you take credit cards?	hal taqbal Visa, Access?
Where is the toilet?	wayn at-towaaleet?
Go away!	emshee!
(for children only)	
Excellent!	momtaaz!
left	yasaar
right	yameen
up	fawq
down	asfal

TRAVEL

I want to go to…	oreed arooH le…
How do you get to…	kayf farooh le…?
I'd like to rent a car	oreed asta'jer sayaarah
driver's licence	rokhSat qiyaadah
I've lost my way	ana Dalayt aT-Tareeq

Where is the nearest garage?	wayn aqrab garaaj?
garage (for repairs)	garaaj meekaaneekee
petrol/gas	banzeen
petrol/gas station	maHaTTat banzeen
When is there a flight to..?	emta be-yakoon fee reHlat Tayaraan le...?
What is the fare to...?	be-kam at-tazkarah le...?
A ticket to...please	law samaHt, tazkarat zehaab le...
airport	maTaar
ticket	tazkarah
passport	jawaaz safar
visa	veeza
airport shuttle	baaS al-maTaar
When do we arrive in...?	emta naSel le...?
When is the next train to..?	emta yaqoom al-qeTaar ellee raayeH le...?
What station is this?	hazehe ay maHaTTah?
train	qeTaar
first-class *(train)*	darajah oolah
second-class	darajah thaaneeyah
sleeping car	Arabat nawm
bus	baaS
bus station	maHaTTat al-baaSaat
boat	markeb
cruise	jawlah baHareeyah
ferry	Abaarah
taxi	taaksee

MAKING A TELEPHONE CALL

may I use your telephone?	momken astaAmel teleefoonak
How much is a call to...?	be-kam al-mokaalamah le...?
Can I call abroad from here?	momken ataSel bel-khaarej men hona?
Hello, this is...speaking	alloo, ...yatakalam
I would like to speak to...	oreed atakalam maA...
Could you leave him a message?	momken tatrok laho resaalah?
My number is...	raqamee...
telephone call	mokaalamah
emergency	Tawaare'
operator	sentraal

POST OFFICES AND BANKS

How much is a letter to...?	be-kam ersaal al-kheTaab ela...
This is to go airmail	erselha bel-bareed al-jawee
I'd like to change this into...	oreed oghayyer haza ela
bank	bank
dollar (US)	dollar
exchange rate	seAr at-taghyeer
letter	kheTaab
postbox	sondooq booSTah
package	tard
post	booSTah
postcard	beTaaqah bareedeeyah
post office	maktab al-bareed
stamp	TaabeA bareed
traveller's cheque	sheek siyaaHee

STAYING IN A HOTEL

Have you got any vacancies?	fee Andak ghoraf khaaleeyah?
I have a reservation	Andee Hajz
I'd like a room with a bathroom	oreed ghorfah be-Hammam
May I have the bill please?	momken al-faatoorah law samaHt
I'll pay by credit card	sa-asfaA al-fatoorah law Visa, Access
I'll pay by cash	sa-asfaA naqdan
hotel	fondoq
air-conditioning	mokayyef
double room	ghorfa mozdawajah

single room	ghorfa be-sareer waaHed
shower	dosh
toilet	towaaleet
toilet paper	waraq towaleet
key	meftaaH
lift/elevator	mesAd
breakfast	foToor
restaurant	maTAm
bill	faatoorah

SHOPPING

I'd like...	oreed...
Do you have...?	hal Andak...?
How much is this?	be-kam haza?
I'll give you...	be-aAteek...
Two for...	ethnayn be...
Where do I pay?	wayn adfaA?
to buy	yashtaree
to go shopping	yatasawwaq

SIGHTSEEING

mosque	jaamea
street, road	shaareA
house	bayt
square	midan
beach	shaaTee'
museum	matHaf
church	kaneesah
castle, palace	qasr

EATING OUT *(see also pp280–81)*

A table for...one/two, please	Taawlah...le-shakhS waaHed/le-shakhSayn, law samaHt
I'd like...	oreed...
May we have the bill, please?	momken al-Hesaab, law samaHt?
May we have some more...?	momken shewayah kaman ... law samaHt?
My compliments to the chef!	teslam eed at-Tabaakh!
beer	beerah
bottle	zojaajah
cake	kayk
coffee	qahwah
– no sugar	- saadah
– medium	- maZbooT
– sweet	- sukkar zeyaadah
– with milk	- bel-Haleeb
cup	fenjaan
glass	koob
plate	Tabaq
sandwich	sandwetsh
snack	wajbah khafeefah
sugar	sukkar
table	Taawlah
tea	shaay
mint	neAnaA
(mineral) water	miyaah (maAdaneeyah)
wine	nabeez

FOOD AND DRINK

soup	shorbah
fish	samak
aubergine salad	salaaTat baazenjaan
melon	shammaam
pickles	mekhallalaat
hummus	Hommos
falafel - fried balls of ground fava beans or chickpeas	falaafel
fried balls of ground fava beans with herbs	taAmeeyah
olives	zaytoon
stuffed vine leaves	waraq Aenab maHsee

aubergine and tahina paté	baaba ghanooj
cheese	jebnah
curd cheese	labnah
egg	bayDah
macaroni	makaroonah
noodles	sheAreeyat

FISH

grilled fish	samak mashwee
fried fish	samak maqlee
fish with rice	samak sayaadeeyah
smoked fish	samak medakhan
shrimp	jambaree
squid	Habaar
tuna	toonah

MEAT AND POULTRY

beef	laHm baqaree
chicken	firaakh
chicken pieces	koftat dajaaj
duck	baTT
grilled lamb kebab	kebaab
lamb	laHm Daanee
meat	laHm
meatballs	koftah
mixed grilled meats	luHoom mashweeyah
pigeon	Hamaam
roast beef	roosbeef
sliced spit-roast lamb	shaawerma
steak	boftayk

VEGETABLES

aubergine	baazenjaan
avocado	abookaado
cabbage	koronb
celery	karafs
chillies	felfel Haamee
cucumber	khiyaar
lentils	Adas
lettuce	khass
okra	baamyah
onions	baSal
potatoes	baTaaTes
rice	rozz
tomatoes	TamaaTem
vegetables	khoDaar

FRUIT AND NUTS

almonds	looz
apricots	meshmesh
bananas	mooz
dried fruits	fawaakeh mojaffafah
figs	teen
fruits	fawaakeh
lemon	laymoon HaameD
pistachio nuts	fostoq
watermelon	baTeekh

DESSERTS

cake	kayk
baclava	baqlaawah
biscuits	baskooweet
dessert	Halawiyaat
fritters in syrup	zalaabeeyah
fruit salad	salaatet fawaakeh
ice cream	aays kreem
"Mother of Ali"	omm Alee
milk pudding with raisins	
pastry with nuts and syrup	konaafah
yoghurt	zabaadee

METHODS OF COOKING

baked	feel-forn
barbecued	mashwee Ala al-faHm
boiled	maslooq
fried	maqlee
grilled	mashwee
pickled	mekhaalil
spiced	metabbel
stewed	mesabbek
stuffed	maHshee

NUMBERS

0	sefr	30	thalaatheen
1	waaHed	31	waaHed wa thalaatheen
2	ethnayn	32	ethnayn wa thalaatheen
3	thalaathah	40	arbaAeen
4	arbaAh	50	khamseen
5	khamsah	60	setteen
6	settah	70	sabAeen
7	sabAh	80	thamaaneen
8	thamaaneeyah	90	tesAeen
9	tesAh	100	me'ah
10	Asharah	110	me'ah wa Asharah
11	Hedaash	200	me'tayn
12	etnaash	300	thalaathme'ah
13	thalaathaash	400	arbaAme'ah
14	arbaAtaash	500	khamsme'ah
15	khamastaash	600	setme'ah
16	settaash	700	sabAme'ah
17	sabaAtaash	800	thamaanme'ah
18	thamaantaash	900	tesAme'ah
19	tesAtaash	1,000	alf
20	Aeshreen	2,000	alfayn
21	waaHed wa Aeshreen	10,000	Asharat aalaaf
22	ethnayn wa Aeshreen	1,000,000	malyoon

DAYS, MONTHS AND SEASONS

Sunday	yawm al-aHad
Monday	yawm al-ethnayn
Tuesday	yawm ath-tholatha'
Wednesday	yawm al-arbeAa'
Thursday	yawm al-khamees
Friday	yawm al-jomAh
Saturday	yawm as-sabt
January	yanaayer
February	febraayer
March	Maars
April	ebreel
May	maayo
June	yoonyo
July	yoolyo
August	aghosTos
September	sebtember
October	oktoober
November	noofember
December	deesember
spring	al-ar-rabeeA
summer	aS-Sayf
autumn	al-khareef
winter	ash-sheta'

THINGS YOU'LL HEAR

enshaallah	God (Allah) willing
tasharafna	you're welcome
shoo esmak?	What is your name?
bel-hanaa' wash-shefaa'	Enjoy your meal